Improving the Global Economy

Improving the Global Economy

Keynesianism and the Growth in Output and Employment

Edited by

Paul Davidson

*J. Fred Holly Chair of Excellence in Political Economy,
University of Tennessee, US*

Jan A. Kregel

Professor of Political Economy, University of Bologna, Italy

Edward Elgar

Cheltenham, UK • Lyme, US

Published by
Edward Elgar Publishing Limited
8 Lansdown Place
Cheltenham
Glos GL50 2HU
UK

Edward Elgar Publishing Company
1 Pinnacle Hill Road
Lyme
NH 03768
US

A catalogue record for this book
is available from the British Library

Library of Congress Cataloguing in Publication Data
Improving the global economy: Keynesianism and the growth in output
   and employment/edited by Paul Davidson, Jan A. Kregel.
      Includes bibliographical references.
         1. Keynesian economics. 2. Industrial productivity.
      3. Employment (Economic theory) 4. Economic policy.
      5. Competition, International. I. Davidson, Paul. II. Kregel, J.A.
      HB99.7.I57   1997
      330.15'6—dc21   97–25021
                                                                      CIP

ISBN 1 85898 541 2

Printed in Great Britain by Bookcraft (Bath) Ltd, Somerset

Contents

PART I   CONSUMPTION, INVESTMENT AND GOVERNMENT
          SPENDING

A   Consumption

B   Investment

C   Government Spending

Contributors

Michael A. Anderson, Department of Economics, Washington and Lee University, Lexington, Va, US

Kenneth J. Borghese is Senior Economist, Office of the Chief Economist, Economics and Statistics Administration, United States Department of Commerce, US

Neil H. Buchanan, Department of Economics, Barnard College of Columbia University, US

David Bunting, Department of Economics, Eastern Washington University, Cheney, Washington, US

Jerry Courvisanos, Senior Lecturer, Department of Economics, University of Tasmania, Launceston, Tasmania, Australia

William Darity Jr, Gary C. Boshamer Professor of Economics, University of North Carolina, Chapel Hill, US

Fernanda Lopes de Carvalho, Researcher at the Brazilian Institute of Social and Economic Analyses (IBASE), co-chair of the Rio de Janeiro State Committee of the Citizens' Action, Rio de Janeiro, Brazil

David Dequech, Faculty of Economics and Politics, University of Cambridge, UK

Robert Eisner, William R. Kenan Professor Emeritus of Economics, Northwestern University, US

Hartmut Elsenhans, Institut für Politikwissenschaft, University of Leipzig, Leipzig, Germany

James K. Galbraith, Lyndon B. Johnson School of Public Affairs, University of Texas, Austin, Texas, US. He is the author, with William Darity Jr, of the textbook *Macroeconomics*, Houghton-Mifflin

Arthur H. Goldsmith, Department of Economics, Washington and Lee University, Lexington, VA, US

Penny Hawkins, Economist, South African Chamber of Commerce, South Africa

David C. Lund is Senior Economist, Office of Policy Development, Economics and Statistics Administration, United States Department of Commerce, US

William Milberg, Department of Economics, New School for Social Research, New York, US

Etelberto Ortíz C., Department of Economics, Universidad Autónoma Metropolitana-Xochimilco, Iztapalapa, Mexico

Dimitri B. Papadimitriou, Jerome Levy Economics Institute, Bard College, Annandale-on-Hudson, New York, US

Christopher J. Niggle, Department of Economics, University of Redlands, Redlands, CA

Figures

Tables

Introduction

John Maynard Keynes is the most important economist of the twentieth century. The year 1996 represented both the fiftieth anniversary of the death of Keynes as well as the sixtieth anniversary of the publication of his most famous book *The General Theory of Employment, Interest and Money*.

The difference of only ten years between these two anniversaries highlights the fact that Keynes had very little time to revise and develop the revolutionary ideas put forward in the book. The time available was made even shorter because during most of the ten-year period between the publication of *The General Theory* and his death, Keynes was fully occupied – initially with planning for the war effort, and then with formulating plans for the postwar reconstruction of the international payments system.

Somewhat paradoxically, his primary concerns during the period 1936 to 1946 were with implementing the ideas of his *General Theory* in economic conditions that were far different from those in which the book had been conceived and written. Although this decade-long effort of Keynes to apply his framework to the war and postwar worlds puts to rest the idea that *The General Theory* was only applicable to conditions of deep depression, the required effort to develop practical policies left little time for Keynes to refine theoretical points that he might have made to clarify his theory. Indeed, aside from an extremely short period in 1936–37 when he dealt with the comments of reviewers and initial reactions of his readers, Keynes spent hardly any time in working out the exposition of the ideas contained in his *General Theory*. The discussion of theoretical issues was cut short by international events, and was only fully resumed in the postwar period, after Keynes's death.

As a result, a number of commonplace interpretations of the theory came to be taken as definitive, without further analysis or discussion. Unfortunately, many of these involved a misunderstanding of the most basic aspects of Keynes's approach. Most first-year economics students are taught Keynes's theory of 'effective demand' in the form of the accounting identity of income and expenditure: $Y = C + I + G$. In fact, Keynes proposed innovative explanations, in terms of what he referred to as 'psychological' factors, of current period expenditures on both C (consumption) and I (investment). For example, decisions over consumption expenditures were determined by the propensity (or tendency) to consume which relied on both objective and psychological factors rather than on an iron-clad mathematical relationship between consumption and income. This latter view was formalized in the presumed stable consumption function. For Keynes, investment decisions were explained by means of a relation between the marginal efficiency of capital, representing the (exogenous) psychological expected stream of future money returns to be earned from an investment in new productive capacity, the cost of this capacity, and the rate of interest as determined by liquidity preference.

There was no market mechanism to ensure that these psychological factors could attain values that produced a level of spending equivalent to full-employment income. This meant that the third independent variable, government expenditure, would have to be manipulated to ensure that full-employment income was attained.

The explanations of these psychological factors underlying private sector spending on C and I created difficulties for interpreters and therefore came under attack during what John Hicks described as the 'crisis in Keynesian economics' in the late 1960s. The result was a number of generally accepted interpretations of the main components of the theory even if these might conflict with Keynes's words. For example, Keynes's original formulation of the propensity to consume came to be considered as mis-specified because statistical estimates for its long- and short-term values were incompatible.

On the other hand, Keynes's explanation of investment decision was criticized because its emphasis on the volatility of entrepreneurial expectations precludes any direct statistical verification as was applied to the consumption function. The difficulties in formulating theoretical generalizations about the impact of uncertainty and expectations have led to accusations of theoretical nihilism. Indeed, when rigorous assumptions about expectations were introduced in the form of rational expectations, statistically reliable probabilistic risk was substituted for Keynes's concept of uncertainty. Assuming rational expectations implies that so-called Keynesian demand-management expenditure policies could influence real aggregate income and employment only by 'fooling' or misleading agents in the marketplace.

Keynes's *General Theory* argument that current expenditures relied on (unstable) psychological factors, produced the reformulation of the theory of consumption in terms of a statistically unmeasurable 'permanent' income or by means of a life-cycle pattern of optimal consumption which implicitly required perfect foresight. The investment function was re-specified in terms of an unmeasurable marginal productivity theory of capital producing an optimal investment structure. The introduction of rational expectations was just a logical extension of the assumptions already made in consumption and investment theory that economic agents always 'knew' the future outcome of current expenditure decisions. This voided any practical policy content from the theory since it was no longer possible for the theory to produce a less than full employment solution.

These interpretations of the errors in Keynes's theory are indeed mythical since they do not pertain to the theory that Keynes advanced. The proposed remedies presented by the mainstream interpreters of Keynes were thus unnecessary as the chapters in Part I of this book demonstrate.

The first aspect of Keynes's theory to come under scrutiny was the consumption function. One of the reasons was that it provided easy application to the newly emerging discipline of applied statistical analysis, called econometrics. Estimates of the propensity to consume were made on cross-section panel data and on yearly time-series data. Since the long-period data had an intercept approximately at the origin, while the cross-section panel data showed a large positive intercept, this was thought to imply that Keynes's theory was inconsistent, or at least required some essential amendment to preserve theoretical coherence. If the short-period function was stable and linear over time this would produce the nonsensical result that consumption would have been larger than total output. Had this problem developed in the last decade, the response would have been to introduce hysteresis. Since these statistical anomalies appeared in the first two decades after the writing of *The General Theory*, the remedies proposed by Smithies, Duesenberry and others provided for a ratcheting up of the short-period function as income increased through time. These earlier addendums were followed by both Friedman's more sophisticated suggestion that the independent income variable was something he called permanent income, and Modigliani and Brumberg's suggestion that consumption was adjusted to maximize lifetime consumption. As a result, the psychological propensity to consume was transformed into the theory of the optimal intertemporal allocation of saving over time. These theoretical remedies suggested for the apparent statistical inconsistency between the measured values for the short- and long-term consumption function, however, introduced factors which Keynes had expressly excluded in his analysis. These so-called corrections to consumption theory served to radically change the intent of Keynes's analytical framework. The natural attempt of economists to recast Keynes's approach in traditional terms was thus started by those who claimed that they only sought to improve on the consumption function. Indeed, Milton Friedman then extended his work on the consumption function to the demand for money function and resurrected the quantity theory of money – a theory that Keynes had discredited in his analysis.

Discussion at prior Post Keynesian International Workshops has dealt with the reasons for the existence of the short-run versus long-run consumption function paradox that has now come to be seen as the result of a purely statistical anomaly (compare Bunting 1994). At this Post Keynesian Workshop, the consumption question was again the subject of discussion, but from a slightly different standpoint. Borghese and Lund survey the economic discussions of the period in which Keynes was working out his approach to consumption and demonstrate that not only were all the 'improvements' that have been introduced already available at that time, but that all had been suggested to Keynes either before or after publication of *The General Theory*. Yet, Keynes rejected these alternatives in favour of his own original formulation. This not only suggests the existence of fundamental conflicts between the basic insights Keynes was attempting to convey and the modern reinterpretation of the consumption function, but Borghese and Lund also show why these alternatives are inappropriate extensions of Keynes's theory.

Bunting extends his earlier analysis of the statistical anomalies associated with the early estimation studies of the consumption function to consideration of the reasons why economists failed to recognize the inappropriate aggregation procedures upon which the original statistical anomaly estimates were based. Bunting suggests that the explanation may be found in the ubiquitous presence of the simplifying assumption of the 'representative agent' in modern theorizing. This representative agent approach allows the analysis to pass from the micro motivations to the macroeconomic results that preclude the analysis of the aggregation problem. Analysis of the aggregation problem might have alerted theorists to the differences between cross-section and time-series estimates of the consumption function. This might have avoided the introduction of the permanent income hypothesis and allowed greater attention to be paid to the cross-section studies and their implications for income distribution.

The explanation of the investment decision offered in *The General Theory* caused even more difficulty for orthodox theorists. Criticism developed based on attempts to provide a statistical estimate of the investment function Keynes had proposed. Failure to discover a sufficient empirical interest elasticity of investment spending led many economists to utilize an alternative formulation involving stock adjustment models. These models restored much of the traditional approach and eliminated the importance that Keynes placed on expectations in his theory of investment expenditures. Indeed, these stock adjustment models eventually converged on the same intertemporal allocation of savings concept that orthodox economists resurrected to replace Keynes's concept of a propensity to consume function.

Those few economists who recognized Keynes's emphasis on the importance of the long-term 'state of expectations' on investment expenditures expressed dissatisfaction with orthodox attempts to make investment spending relations 'rigorous' in a form which could be subject to statistical estimation. The orthodox theorists responded with the argument that Keynes's investment relation was without testable content and therefore it could not be a 'scientific' theory.

As a consequence of these developments, most economists spent little time attempting to measure expectations and their importance on spending decisions.

Moreover, the subsequent introduction of the concept of endogenous rational expectations made it largely unnecessary to do so. Anderson and Goldsmith, however, counter this orthodox cursory treatment of expectations. Instead, they suggest a way that expectations might be measured on the basis of existing survey data and then apply statistical estimation techniques to this data to provide a measurement of the expectations component of real-world investment decisions.

Courvisanos, in turn, extends the idea of empirical content to the volatility of investment decisions in Keynes's theory by means of the concept of the 'susceptibility' of long-term expectations. Courvisanos's approach provides an explanation of the cyclical behaviour of expectations based on corporate case studies that take into account macro-level institutional factors and micro-level, industry-specific technological changes.

Economists who read Keynes's book when it was published in 1936 may have been aware that he had already published a book on probability theory that served, in part, as background for his discussion of expectations and uncertainty. This was less true of those who participated in the discussions of expectations on spending propensities in the 1950s and 1960s. Those who introduced the rational expectations hypothesis into the literature apparently had no knowledge of Keynes's earlier analysis of probability. Recent dissatisfaction with this relatively simplistic endogenous rational expectations approach, however, has rekindled interest in Keynes's original work on probability which is now recognized as a prerequisite to an understanding of Keynes's approach to investment decisions. Dequech provides an assessment of the way in which Keynes's ideas concerning the concept and measurement of uncertainty differ from the interpretations that have come from orthodox economists in the last half century. Dequech indicates how Post Keynesian economists have relied on Keynes's earlier probability discussion. He shows how Keynes's interpretation of an uncertain future has influenced not only the specification of the investment decision, but the broader question of the specification of economic policy, to ensure that investment is sufficient to produce full-employment savings.

The discussion of the appropriate interpretation of Keynes's theory of investment has been central to the ongoing dialogue between Post Keynesian and neo-Ricardian economists who seek an alternative approach to traditional economic theory on the basis of Sraffa's theory of prices of production. Ortíz integrates an analysis of the competitive process which produces a uniform rate of profit by the allocation of investment to those sectors offering the highest rates of return with an investment function based on Keynes's theory of expectations. Ortíz indicates how such a model may produce an equilibrium over time, at less than full employment, based on the efficient allocation of resources by means of capitalist competition, rather than price imperfections or mistaken expectations.

The basic implication of Keynes's theory of effective demand was that a *laissez-faire* entrepreneurial economy does not possess any endogenous automatic mechanism to ensure that the combination of $C + I$ expenditures would produce a level of income, Y, that provided jobs for all those willing, able and capable of working at prevailing wage rates. The fundamental policy implication that emerges from this result is that the shortfall in effective demand could be made up by suitable government policies to increase aggregate spending. Many economists objected to this proposition because of Keynes's shocking assertion that any government expenditure, even wasteful ones (for example, the building of pyramids and hiding bank notes in jars in the ground for workers to dig up) would be as acceptable as consumption subsidies or productive investments for creating a prosperous fully employed entrepreneurial economy. Although his observations following the publication of *The General Theory* clearly show that Keynes preferred productive investments to wasteful projects, it still remains true that any expenditure creates income. Keynes recognized a fundamental truth, namely that, although additional capital accumulation (investment) in the presence of excess capacity could not be profitable for entrepreneurs, nevertheless the building of additional capital, such as hospitals and schools, is socially preferable to pyramid building.

There is, however, another aspect of the increase in government expenditure on available capacity that economists have spent little time investigating. This involves the question of the components of private expenditure that are induced to increase by some increase in exogenous government spending. Buchanan investigates the question of whether consumption or investment expenditures are more likely to respond to an increase in government spending. He concludes that in general it is the former.

Keynes was primarily concerned with providing jobs for those who had previously been employed, but had lost their jobs in the slump of the 1920s and 1930s. In the modern economic society of the late twentieth century, however, the problem of unemployment has become increasingly one of involving an underclass of apparently permanently unemployed persons. This underclass comprises both those who have never been employed and those who, after losing a job, appear to be unable to return to employment for an indefinitely long period. Not only are these workers unemployed, but increasingly they appear to be unemployable. Ironically, this may tend to provide a 'quantitative' solution to the problem of measured unemployment as, after some time period, these workers leave the active labour force searching for jobs. The result is a situation where a large proportion of the working-age population form a permanent 'underclass' that does not even aspire to join the official labour force or actively seek employment. This raises the question of whether Keynesian policies to increase effective demand are capable of (or suitable for) creating market conditions that will draw this underclass into productive employment. The contributions by Fernanda Carvalho, Darity, Eisner, Galbraith and Papadimitriou give a number of insights and different views of how the problem of employment and the underclass has changed in the fifty years since the publication of *The General Theory*.

Although it is generally thought that Keynes assumed a closed economy in *The General Theory*, Hicks has suggested that the theory can be considered as applicable at both the level of the individual economy and for the world economy as a whole. Keynes's book, however, left open a number of questions concerning the analysis of employment equilibrium in an open economy that engages in international trade and foreign investment. Unlike classical analysis, Keynes's framework emphasizes aggregate demand conditions rather than supply analysis in discussing trade and foreign investment. This has been particularly true of those who have argued in favour of generating domestic demand for labour by means of encouraging exports. Such an analysis, however, is usually applied to an economy attempting to increase exports to lift itself from a significant recession.

This recovery process, however, is not the applicable case for developing countries that are trying to permanently raise their growth rates. These developing countries usually specialize in primary product production and exports which normally do little *per se* to improve the productivity of the community. (Expansion of manufactured goods imports, on the other hand, usually require productivity-enhancing accumulation of capital.) Consequently, demand expansion policies in developing countries can take on a different dimension. For example, any emphasis on development through building a manufacturing goods export base will require creating a stock of industrial capital. If the developing country does not have a domestic capital goods industry then this approach may simply lead to a rise in imports that can create balance of payments problems. This question of the composition of domestic capacity in relation to demand management is therefore essential to developing nations. This problem is analysed by Hawkins in her study of the economic development of South Africa.

Elsenhans investigates another aspect of the application of Keynesian policies to developing countries, outlining the appropriate role for government expenditure policy in the development process. Traditional theories grant a dominant role to the state in developing countries, either in supporting demand through expenditure policy, or in building productive capacity by directing investment on the supply side. Elsenhans suggests that, from a Keynesian perspective, the basic problem limiting development is the surplus over domestic expenditure in the consumption sector directed to capacity expanding investment. This may also be expressed as the necessity of raising domestic productivity in this sector above the subsistence wage. Policies which aim at this result, however, may be in conflict with proposals for increased openness currently prescribed for the least-developed economies in the context of the globalization of the world economy.

Recently, the increasing interdependence of world trade and the integration of capital markets has led to the idea that this 'globalization' of the international economy will be sufficient to provide the required impetus to the growth of developing countries. Milberg surveys these issues as they relate to the way traditional theories of comparative advantage have analysed trade and development patterns. Milberg demonstrates that the more global the economy, the less relevant the theory of comparative advantage appears to be.

The last chapter in the book also deals with an aspect of development in the emerging market economies of Central and Eastern Europe. Niggle presents a survey of the available evidence on the impact of the transformation process of planned economies to market systems on the distribution of income. This is a subject that Keynes identified as being of crucial importance in the analysis of effective demand and employment, but which has thus far drawn little attention in the discussion of the transition from command to market-based systems.

The chapters published in this book are but a small sampling from more than forty stimulating presentations which composed the programme of the Fourth International Post Keynesian Workshop.[1] Organized by the J. Fred Holly Chair of Excellence in Political Economy and the *Journal of Post Keynesian Economics*, this 1996 Workshop brought more than eighty participants from twenty countries to Knoxville, Tennessee for six days of sessions and discussions.

This fourth Workshop also benefited from the technical and logistical support of the College of Business Administration of the University of Tennessee. As in the case of the previous Workshops, the successful organization and supervision of the proceedings, as well as for the editorial supervision of this book, are the responsibility of Louise Davidson, Editorial Office Manager of the *Journal of Post Keynesian Economics*. The editors of this book would like to offer their thanks to her and to all the participants in the Workshop for making it the largest and most successful yet undertaken.

Paul Davidson
Jan A. Kregel

NOTE

1. A selection of papers from the first Workshop, held in 1988, has been published as *Macroeconomic Problems and Policies of Income Distribution* (Aldershot, Hants: Edward Elgar, 1989). The publication of a selection of papers from the second (1990) Workshop has been published as *Economic Problems of the 1990s* (Aldershot, Hants: Edward Elgar, 1990).

A collection of papers from the third (1993) Workshop appeared as *Employment, Growth and Finance: Economic Reality and Economic Growth* (Aldershot, Hants: Edward Elgar, 1994).

REFERENCE

Bunting, David (1994), 'Aggregate and Household Behavior; Poverty and Savings', in P. Davidson and J.A. Kregel (eds), *Employment Growth and Finance*, Aldershot: Elgar.

PART I

Consumption, Investment and Government
Spending

A. Consumption

1. Aggregate consumption and the economics of Keynes

Kenneth J. Borghese and David C. Lund*

1 INTRODUCTION AND PLOT

Notwithstanding the criticisms and the efforts to label and to partition Keynes into ever smaller boxes, his work remains difficult if not impossible either to classify along conventional lines or to ignore. Interdisciplinary scholarship on Keynes continues to grow, and powerful cross-currents remain evident in the economics literature. Luminaries are rethinking and reinterpreting their previous assessments, acknowledging that they ignored various elements of Keynes's thinking (Hahn 1990; Patinkin 1991).

The dismissal of Keynes's treatments of probability and uncertainty, for example, has been found to be clearly at odds with the evidence. New research has reinforced the earlier fundamentalist view that Keynes's thinking on these matters was extensive, well grounded in its philosophical positions in probability theory, and represented an unanswered, revolutionary challenge to equilibrium theorizing (for example, Carabelli 1988).

Keynes advanced a concept of 'organic unity moving forward through time', as an alternative to equilibrium theory, in which the nature and behaviour of the parts are context dependent, or holistic (Hillard 1992: 67–70). His shift to an organicist position (output as a whole) had the effect of altering the language and meaning of basic economic concepts (such as labour, capital and income), rooting them in the social institution of money. Consequently, the starting point for macroeconomic analysis was no longer real but rather money values, and the 'language' or economic communication between agents was stipulated in money contracts, not real contracts (Carabelli 1992: 23–7; 1988: 167–72).

Although Keynesian economics no longer occupies pride of place among the various competing schools of thought, Keynes himself is generally acknowledged as being very and diversely learned, a polymathist, as well as being the most influential economic theorist of the twentieth century (Caravale 1987). Keynes's revolution in economic thought recast the classical dichotomy between monetary theory and value theory, changing the terms of economic discourse to one of microeconomics and (the newly born) macroeconomics.

Much of the history of mainstream twentieth-century macroeconomics may be seen as a reaction to Keynes's dichotomy between microeconomics and the theory of 'output as a whole'. The neoclassical synthesis, monetarist counterrevolution, disequilibrium theorists, new Keynesian and new classical schools of thought, variously sought, *inter alia*, to: (1) blend classical and Keynesian ideas in a schizophrenic approach, (2) preserve and extend classical ideas repudiated by the Keynesian revolution (for example, the quantity theory of money), (3) model economic processes as out-of-equilibrium states, (4) tease Keynesian notions out of microeconomic models, and (5) consciously seek to restore the classical dichotomy by dispensing with '*ad hoc*' Keynesian theoretical interpretations of reality and by embracing market-clearing microeconomics (Hoover 1988: 4). Our interpretation of Keynes will not address the complex interactions between these various schools of thought.

Instead we shall focus on the original treatment of aggregate consumption by Keynes and contrast it with the classical analysis. Implicit in our interpretation is the idea of two ruptures or sharp discontinuities in the history of economic thought. The first corresponds to the penetration of mathematics into economic discourse, with the marginalist revolution and the consequent upheaval in value theory; the second is the *General Theory*. Our aim is to flesh out some of the differences between Keynes and the classics concerning aggregate consumption and the concept of rationality. We note at the outset that we are going to follow a different route, largely bypassing mathematical formalisms and directly revisiting the original literature. Sixty years later the lessons we learned are surprisingly modern in substance and accessible as well.

1.1   Keynes's Divergence from General Equilibrium Theory

Our investigation pursues an interpretative line of inquiry initially focusing on Keynes's attitude towards probability theory and his treatment of consumption in the *General Theory*. Then we branch out to some of the controversies in economic theory endemic to the historical period. Before we begin, several prefatory remarks are needed to help frame our discussion for the reader.

We locate the demarcation of Keynes from general equilibrium theory in what Keynes calls 'a pseudo-analogy from the physical sciences', a thermodynamic metaphor which became the mathematical wellspring for the neoclassical preference function and the budget constraint (Mirowski 1989b). By applying the Mirowski thesis on the physics origins of neoclassical value theory, we find that the otherwise difficult search for the 'tacit assumptions' of the classical theory (compare Carabelli 1991; 1992) can be read directly out of the journal literature of the relevant historical period and out of a table of concordance in Irving Fisher's doctoral dissertation, written in 1892 but not published until 1926.

The nexus between Keynes, Ramsey and probability theory motivates our discussion, if only because Ramsey sits at many of the 'noisy tables in the din of conversations' on Keynes. For example, in the new Keynesian fundamentalist literature, Ramsey plays a pivotal role in the debate on whether Keynes changed his views of probability and uncertainty later in life (Gerrard 1992: 86–90; Bateman 1987). (We find that Keynes did change his views.) From the Mirowski perspective, moreover, Ramsey (1928) made a conscious attempt to find economic analogues for potential and kinetic energy and to apply to economics mathematical techniques taken from energy physics (Mirowski 1992). Indeed, Ramsey (1928) provides a more formal treatment of many of the same issues pertaining to consumption, saving and production, that we find in Fisher (1926). Lastly, Ramsey (1928) is the seminal work on aggregate consumption in the microfoundations literature and new classical economics, where theory is 'as if' Keynes had never happened.

We argue, moreover, that the divergence of Keynes from general equilibrium theory is not simply an analogical disagreement with a metaphor taken from nineteenth-century physics. The divergence from general equilibrium theory resides as well in the meaning and context of income as a 'complex magnitude' (compare Carabelli 1992: 3–7). 'Income' in the *General Theory* is an important but neglected element of the Keynesian discourse, despite Keynes's explicit statement that income, the stock of real capital and the general price level, were 'the three perplexities' which most impeded his progress in writing the *General Theory*. We examine the distinctive character of Keynes's income concept (against the backdrop of the development of national income accounting) and highlight its differences from Fisher's treatment of income and consumption.

2   PROBABILITY THEORY – KEYNES AND RAMSEY

In this section, we first note the variety of competing views on Keynes's attitude towards probability theory, point out the peculiar relationship between statistical theorizing and economic theory prior to the *General Theory*, and then focus our discussion on Ramsey's influence on Keynes's thinking.

2.1   Early Economist's Attitudes

Although there is ample precedent in the history of economics for the view that human behaviour must be intentionally 'rational', otherwise it is 'unintelligible', this prejudice did not preclude an iconoclastic attitude towards probabilistic formulations of uncertainty by (most) early twentieth-century economists (for example, Knight 1921). Furthermore, during the period 1870–1925, none of the economists who made independent contributions to probability and statistical theory (Jevons, Edgeworth, Bowley, Keynes, Slutsky, Wald, et al.) were willing to incorporate these ideas into mainstream neoclassical price theory (Menard 1987). For the period 1920–39, moreover, economists actively rejected probability theory as applied to econometric demand analysis (Morgan 1987: 176). The 1930s witnessed some progress by Frisch and Tinbergen in incorporating probability into certain types of business cycle and (micro) planning models, respectively, but overall, economic theories were still largely formulated as exact deterministic models (Morgan 1987: 181).

The irony of the roughly six decades between Walras's *Elements of Pure Economics* and the onset of the Great Depression was that while economists contributed to the development of probability theory, they nevertheless remained pugnacious in defending their discipline from its influence. It is a curious fact that not until the triumph of probability theory in physics (quantum mechanics) were mathematical economists willing to entertain probabilistic concepts (Mirowski 1989a).

Against this backdrop, it is hardly surprising that one finds little if any statistical theorizing concerning the theory of aggregate consumption in the *General Theory*. Many younger economists were persuaded by Keynes's arguments in the *General Theory*, years before the absolute income hypothesis was estimated using least squares. For the most part, Keynes's insights into the working of the macro economy took the economics profession by storm *before* these insights were formulated as statistical propositions in the 1940s and 1950s.

That is not to say that statistical and empirical work on aggregate consumption was absent during this period. Quite the contrary, there was a rich and varied empirical literature on aggregate consumption (Thomas 1989). However, lacking strong microfoundations and not being consistently derived from 'first principles', this literature is nowadays seen as crude and theoretically irrelevant and is. ignored in modern textbook treatments of aggregate consumption (for example, Blanchard and Fischer 1989).

2.2   Keynes and Ramsey – Background

Ramsey's stature as a progenitor of modern macrotheory is an acknowledgement that he was in the mathematical vanguard, along with Evans, Roos and Hotelling, of early applications of the calculus of variations to economic theory. Ramsey may have been decades ahead of his time in so far as optimal control theory did not become commonplace in economics until the 1960s (Kamien and Swartz 1988). Still, the Ramsey model tells us little about Keynes's views on aggregate consumption and even less about empirical work on consumption during the period 1930 to 1950.

That Ramsey influenced Keynes's thinking directly is clear, and his historical influence on Keynesian macroeconomics proceeds by way of the probability calculus (Bateman 1987). In a short essay published in 1931, Ramsey reviewed Keynes's *Treatise on Probability* and he appears to have induced a major revision in Keynes's thinking (Bateman 1987: 105–9). A brief look at the nuances of Keynes's views on probability follows.

The notion of probability following Hacking (1975), takes two forms: (1) aleatory probability (from the Latin *alea* or dice game) which refers to the frequency of occurrences over repeated trials, and (2) epistemic probability (from the Greek *episteme* or knowledge) meaning the degree of belief one holds given some evidence.

A further distinction is between objective and subjective conceptions of probability. Objective theories of probability imply that probabilities are unique and that different individuals will reach the same unique value when confronted by identical information. Subjectivist probability theory allows for the non uniqueness of probability values, even when individuals are confronted by identical information. In this view, probabilities are individually determined and two individuals may assign different probabilities to the same proposition without either person being mistaken.

The key to Bateman's (1987) treatment of Keynes's attitude towards probability pivots on the conception that epistemic probability theory is not solely subjective, but may be either subjective or objective as the term 'probability' is used by Hacking (1975).[1]

Although his views changed in later years, Keynes's early work in probability theory exemplified an objective epistemic outlook, 'while it is often convenient to speak of propositions as certain or probable, this expresses strictly a relationship in which they stand to a *corpus* of knowledge, actual or hypothetical, and not a characteristic of the propositions in themselves' (Keynes 1921: 3–4). Though individuals may have varying degrees of knowledge regarding certain propositions, and come to different conclusions on the probability of future events, it is the 'corpus of knowledge, actual or hypothetical' which forms the benchmark for evaluating these epistemic probabilities.

2.3 Ramsey's Influence on Keynes

Keynes's theory of induction and its attendant problems are outside the purview of the present chapter. However, by focusing on Keynes's early conception of objective epistemic probability, it is possible to isolate the influence of Frank Ramsey in changing Keynes's later thinking on probability. Ramsey's essay 'Truth and Probability' represented a constructive criticism of Keynes's *A*

Treatise on Probability, published posthumously in 1931, as part of a collection of his works entitled *Foundations* (compare Ramsey 1931; Ramsey 1978).

Ramsey denied the existence of any underlying 'objective' logical relationships, preferring instead a 'subjective' degree of belief among individuals, with no tendency for identical information to inexorably lead to identical beliefs. Furthermore, anticipating the axioms of revealed preference, Ramsey argued that 'consistency' of subjective belief was synonymous with 'rationality'; otherwise a cunning bettor could 'make book' against an individual with inconsistent subjective beliefs (Ramsey 1978: 84).

By 1931 Keynes appears to have abandoned his objective epistemic theory in favour of a subjective epistemic theory. Yet, despite Ramsey's influence, Keynes was not willing to concede that 'consistent' subjective degrees of belief were 'rational' in any substantive sense. A 'consistent' set of beliefs might be a 'useful mental habit', but it leaves open the more difficult question of how to inductively justify that such beliefs are 'rational' (Keynes 1972: 339).

Bateman summarizes Keynes's view as follows:

In *A Treatise on Probability*, Keynes's argument that probabilities were rational was based on his idea that they had been inferred correctly from the available information; in Ramsey's argument the rationality of probabilities is strictly a function of their consistency. Keynes was willing to accept that people form subjective probabilities in the course of their everyday decision making, but he was not willing to accept that such probabilities were rational. That is, he was willing to give up the idea that probabilities as he conceived them were objective, but since the rationality of probabilities was synonymous with their objectivity he insisted that these subjective probabilities were not rational. (Bateman 1987: 107–8)

In the closing chapters of *A Treatise on Probability*, Keynes was partly disposed to accept an aleatory theory, but only applied to natural science phenomena. Keynes spoke of physics and biology where aleatory theories were making headway (Keynes 1921: 427–8), but he tended to cordon off social phenomena as the realm where epistemic probabilities held sway.

Despite Keynes's willingness to switch from an objective epistemic theory to a subjective one (under prodding from Ramsey), and his later acceptance of aleatory theories in the natural sciences as justified inductively, he nevertheless maintained that the inductive groundwork for using aleatory probabilities in economics was still lacking (Keynes 1937, 1939). For example, Keynes's primary objection to the work of (former physicist) Tinbergen concerned the lack of inductive justification for the *assumption* that economic variables were stochastically distributed and that their probability distributions were stable over time. Keynes (1939) felt that Tinbergen's methods could not provide an inductive inference from which one could obtain valid predictions of the future.[2]

2.4   Moral Versus Natural Science

In a series of letters to Harrod in 1938, Keynes focuses on the requirements for an aleatory theory and contrasts them with the 'moral science' of economics.

> Economics is a science of thinking in terms of models joined to the art of choosing models which are relevant to the contemporary world. It is compelled to be this, because, unlike the typical natural science, the material to which it is applied is, in too many respects, not homogeneous through time. ... [T]he art of thinking in terms of models is a difficult – largely because it is an unaccustomed – practice. The pseudo-analogy with the physical sciences leads directly counter to the habit of mind which is most important for an economist proper to acquire. (Keynes 1973: 300; compare Keynes 1930)

Keynes was clearly unwilling to make the 'classical' assumptions that individuals had stable and rational preferences through time, but it was not an arbitrary judgement based on anecdotal information which led him to conclude that human behaviour was not 'homogeneous'. Keynes's position was intimately bound up with a complex view of probability, the influence of Ramsey's constructive criticism, and the triumph of aleatory theories in some of the natural sciences (for example, quantum physics and biology).

In Bateman's interpretation, even if 'economic agents employ subjective epistemic probabilities in their decision making, their behavior does *not* result in the stable distributions of variables necessary to employing an aleatory conception of probability in economics'(Bateman 1987: 113).

Since Keynes was intimately familiar with the expected utility model (Keynes 1921: Ch. 26), we note that with just a few assumptions facilitating aggregation, a 'classical' theory of consumption was within his reach. But Keynes did not do so. He consciously refrained from using rational, utility-maximizing individuals to ground his theory of aggregate consumption. Why? Apparently Keynes had strong theoretical priors regarding probability and economics. Perhaps he thought utility maximization was a 'pseudo-analogy from the physical sciences', dependent on an aleatory theory of probability and inductively unjustified. In the following section we argue for a sharp demarcation between Keynes and Ramsey on the theory of aggregate consumption. Indeed, when one actually reads the relevant passages in the *General Theory*, it seems hard to conclude otherwise.

3   THE TREATMENT OF INCOME AND CAPITAL – KEYNES VERSUS RAMSEY

In an effort to finesse many of the attendant problems in production and capital theory (problems which became prominent in the capital theory debates of the 1950s and 1960s) Keynes chose to redefine 'income' and 'capital', without immediate recourse to marginal productivity theory. 'Income' for the entrepreneur was simply an excess of the value of finished output sold during the period over his or her 'prime cost' (a mixture of factor costs, *excluding capital*, and 'user costs' on equipment). This conceptualization had the effect of driving a wedge between supply price and marginal factor cost as it applied to a 'quantity of capital', however defined, and served to set off Keynes's views from the earlier classical economists and their method of determining the rate of interest (Keynes 1936: 55). Prima facie, this contradicts the approach taken in the Ramsey model in which 'the rate of interest functions as a demand price for a whole quantity of capital, but as a supply price, not for a quantity of capital, but for a rate of savings' (Ramsey 1928: 556). The classical theoretical linkage between the quantity of capital, the rate of interest, the saving rate and time preference is simply not present in the *General Theory* and Keynes shows no concern for the logically necessary conditions underpinning capital in the Ramsey model, that is, the Inada conditions (Blanchard and Fischer 1989: 38).

Ramsey (1928) glides effortlessly over the arbitrary equating of factor inputs and factor income shares, in a manner similar to J.B. Clark's capital theory. Yet Keynes devotes separate chapters (Chapters 4–7) to generating alternate concepts of income, saving, investment and capital, seeing these conceptual issues as 'perplexities which most impeded my progress until I had found some solution to them' (Keynes 1936: 37).

The modern 'Keynes–Ramsey rule' is a continuous time analogue of the standard efficiency condition that the marginal rate of substitution in consumption be set equal to the marginal rate of transformation in production. This rule, however, is a purely mathematical property of differential equations, describing only *some* of the necessary conditions that have to be satisfied along any optimal growth path. That is, the Keynes–Ramsey rule is simply the Euler equation, with a designer label attached to change its pedigree.

None the less, Chapter 6 of the *General Theory* belies Ramsey's approach, as Keynes clearly sought to shift the ground of this issue (from one of capital valuation in a one-commodity world) on to the concept of income (ibid.: 52). If Keynes had followed Ramsey's formulation, simply writing down the Euler equation, in lieu of Chapter 6 of the *General Theory*, would have sufficed. Similarly, if Keynes believed that the marginal efficiency of investment was a highly unstable behavioural function (animal spirits), what purpose is served by transmuting this model into a Walrasian framework which requires well-behaved production functions in order to calculate an equilibrium?

3.1 Ramsey – Precursor to Modern Theorizing

Where Ramsey's theorizing differed from his contemporaries (such as Irving Fisher) was in his willingness to impose an assumed uniformity on individuals, goods, labour, capital, consumption, saving and utility, in order to make the mathematics tractable. In this sense he was decidedly modernistic in his model building; it was a logical exercise about a hypothetical economy, a blackboard economy.

The relation of consumption to the interest rate is the core of the Ramsey model and modern Euler equation type consumption models. These models rely heavily on the relationship between these two variables. Keynes, however, does not see a tradeoff between present and future consumption mediated by the interest rate (Leijonhufvud 1968: iv). He insists that the decision not to consume 'now'

> *does not* necessitate a decision to have dinner or to buy a pair of boots a week hence or a year hence or to consume any specific thing at a specific date. ... It is not substitution of future consumption [for current consumption] – it is a net diminution of such demand. (Keynes 1936: 210)

Indeed, the decision not to consume now may not have any implications for saving, in a world of real time instead of logical time:

> Between one economic decision and another, there has been a real passage of time, circumstances have changed, and the new decision takes place in a new environment. Long-run optimization would be impractical, even if it were emotionally acceptable, because of barriers of complexity. (Smale 1976: 289)

But real time, instead of logical time, is not the key consideration for Keynes. As Kregel puts it, there is a

> crucial feature [in] a monetary economy that allow[s] consumers not to spend all their money, not to know what they would consume in the future, and to forestall decisions over the expenditure of their income – a store of value that preserves the purchasing power of current income [that is, money]. (Kregel 1980: 39)

3.2   Keynes and Aggregate Consumption Theory

Keynes's views on aggregate consumption are contained in Chapters 8–10 of the *General Theory*. Chapters 8 and 9 address the objective and subjective factors influencing consumption, while Chapter 10 concerns consumption and the 'multiplier'. When discussing the 'community', Keynes is wont to deal with an undifferentiated aggregate rather than a simple sum of (*N*) individuals. Also present in the *General Theory* is a tendency for the analysis to devolve on to the 'physical conditions of production in the investment and consumption goods industries'(Keynes 1936: 117, fn.), further removing it from the calculus of individual decision making.

In Chapter 8 of the *General Theory*, Keynes frames the consumption of the community by reference to three broad categories: (1) income, (2) objective attendant circumstances, and (3) subjective needs, psychological propensities and distributional principles. To the extent that the absolute income hypothesis is a fair representation of Keynes's views, both the objective and subjective factors should simply be ignored, implying that Chapters 8 and 9 are superfluous. Keynes himself takes the subjective factors as given, assuming that 'the propensity to consume depends only on changes in the objective factors' (ibid.: 91).

It is interesting to note how Keynes's argument in Chapters 8–10 becomes increasingly embroiled in a struggle with 'classical ideas', thereby impeding the unfolding of the analysis. Keynes engages in the rhetorical device of legitimizing his income concept (from Chapter 6) via long digressions on national income accounting. Both objective and subjective factors grow more important for his argument, despite Keynes's explicit desire in Chapter 10 to subordinate them to the multiplier. Finally, Keynes lays the blame for this complicated state of affairs on the economists' concept of capital (ibid.: 106).

3.3   Factors That Influence Consumption

A brief summary of Keynes's 'objective factors' influencing consumption strongly suggests that he viewed the subject as being more complex than simplistic characterizations of his views often suggest. These factors are grouped under the following categories (compare ibid. 1936: 91–6):

1. *A change in the 'wage unit'*. This is more than a shift in real wages, since it includes diminishing returns to increases in physical output, as well as distributional shifts between entrepreneurs and *rentiers*.
2. *A change in the difference between (gross) income and net income*. Keynes doubts the practical importance of this issue and defers discussion until later in Chapter 8.
3. *Windfall changes in capital values* are seen as a major factor in short-period changes in the community's propensity to consume as 'the consumption of the wealth owning classes may be extremely susceptible to unforeseen changes in the money value of wealth'.
4. *A change in the rate of time discounting*. This factor also includes unforeseen shifts in the purchasing power of money (through unanticipated inflation) as well as unforeseen risks and contingencies. While Keynes identifies the rate of time discount with the interest rate (approximately), he nevertheless goes out of his way to criticize the 'classical' theory of interest as an equilibrium price for the supply and demand for saving. Here would have been a perfect place for inserting the rigorous and unambiguous statement of the Keynes–Ramsey rule from eight years earlier. Instead Keynes backs away from the implications of the Ramsey model and states:

It has long been recognized, however, that the total effect of changes in the rate of interest on the readiness to spend on present consumption is complex and uncertain, being dependent on conflicting tendencies. ... Over a long period substantial changes in the rate of interest probably tend to modify social habits considerably, thus affecting the subjective propensity to spend – though in which direction it would be hard to say, except in the light of actual experience. (ibid. 1936: 93)

5. *Changes in fiscal policy*. This effect works through income and capital taxes, redistribution issues and policies towards sinking funds in the retirement of debt. Here again, Keynes argues (against the classics) 'that the effect of fiscal policy on the growth of wealth has been the subject of an important misunderstanding' (ibid.: 95, fn. 1) and he urges the reader to wait for his theory of interest in Book IV of the *General Theory*.

6. *Changes in expectations* of the relationship between the present and future levels of income. Keynes includes expectations for the sake of 'formal completeness' and admits that expectations may have considerable effects at the level of a single individual. But in the aggregate these effects wash or 'average out for the community as a whole'. Perfectly capable of applying a mathematical expectation operator to a given time series, Keynes instead chose to dismiss future income expectations because 'as a rule .[there is] too much uncertainty for it to exert much influence'. Keynes admits of expectations at the individual epistemic level but disavows any 'consistency' or rationality at both the individual and aggregate levels, a position he took *vis-à-vis* Ramsey in 1931 and Tinbergen in 1939. Moreover, Keynes (1937) argues, in effect, that any theory that takes the existence of uncertainty and expectations seriously, would have to formulate decision-making processes, indeed human behaviour, differently from the classical theory.

3.4 The Fundamental Psychological Law Revisited

The six objective factors listed above do not meld with the traditional view of the absolute income hypothesis (AIH). The AIH relates current consumption to current income. But according to Keynes (even after dismissing the less important objective factors) we have consumption related to changes in 'wage units', capital values, the interest rate and fiscal policy, with *no presumption* that only current rather than lagged values are important.

Yet Keynes appears to accommodate the traditional AIH by collapsing the objective factors into the 'propensity to consume', thereby rendering income the principal variable upon which consumption depends (ibid.: 96). Granted that the propensity to consume is a fairly stable function, Keynes asks, 'what is the normal shape of this function?'. He then goes on to describe a 'fundamental psychological law', that the marginal propensity to consume is positive and less than one. Typically, modern interpretations of the AIH end abruptly and without comment at this point.

Fundamental psychological laws resonate with the concept of invariant individual preferences, exogenous data given to the analysis from the outside. This interpretation dovetails nicely with the 'classical' and modern notion of individual behaviour as fixed and given. But this is hardly how Keynes viewed his fundamental psychological law. On the following page of the *General Theory*, Keynes indicates that his 'fundamental psychological law' is really a kind of global stability condition for prices, having more to do with the 'community's' behaviour as a whole, than with individual propensities. Because, without this fundamental psychological rule, 'prices would rise without limit' (compare ibid. 1936: 117, 251).

In the *General Theory*, Keynes appears to be searching for an alternate expression for his 'fundamental psychological law' – the reader is referred to earlier and later chapters of the *General Theory* for explanation – and eventually investment comes to the fore of the argument (ibid.: 98). At this point in the *General Theory* it appears that the importance of 'consumption' is being subordinated to 'investment'. At the level of output as a whole, consumption then appears as a function of 'net investment' and 'expectations' (ibid.: 98–9).

Keynes follows up with a long digression on financial provisioning, sinking funds (as related to his 'user costs' idea), stationary economies, housing prices, national income accounting and a dash of economic history from the United States and the United Kingdom during the Great Depression (ibid.: 99–104). He brings his 'digression' abruptly to an end by asserting the primacy of consumption and disavowing 'saving' as a source of future output (ibid.: 104).

Subsequently, Keynes's argument becomes a digression on the 'riddles' of saving and investment, the 'popular mind's perception of public investment' and Mandeville's Fable of the Bees. In a revealing admission, Keynes ends the chapter by blaming the complexity of his argument on the 'academic' notion of capital (ibid.: 106).[3]

3.5   Keynes's Ambivalence Towards Utility Maximization

Time and again in the *General Theory* Keynes backs away from utility maximization when dealing with aggregate consumption and 'output as a whole'. He prefers to alter the language on 'capital', avoiding the standard marginal product theory and preferring (at times) to deal with capital via Marshallian quasi-rents. There are many aphorisms in the *General Theory* which Keynes does not clarify. For example, psychological laws are connected to a stability condition which keeps prices from rising without limit. In Chapter

10, Keynes speaks of having established a 'law' of the economic system via 'the logical theory of the multiplier, which holds good continuously, without time-lag, at all moments of time' (ibid.: 122). Unfortunately (for all of us), Keynes seems unwilling to explicitly differentiate his views from classical ideas. What, for example, distinguishes the marginal efficiency of investment from the classical theory?[4]

Keynes, in effect, shifted the weight of his argument from 'capital' on to 'income'; he disdained the academic discussion of capital, and sought to connect his analysis to the (allegedly) common sense notions of national income accounting. Without an explicit break from the classical theory, however, Keynesian economics came to be taught as if it were consistent with both Marshallian theory and Walrasian microeconomics (protestations by Joan Robinson notwithstanding). And more than fifty years hence, the microfoundations debate still drags on.[5]

In view of Keynes's complex views on factors influencing consumption, noted above, the absolute income hypothesis seems little more than stylized intellectual history, a poor substitute for the argument as it appears in Chapters 8–10 of the *General Theory* and an unconvincing characterization of early empirical work (compare Thomas 1989). Regressing current consumption on current income via least squares is too narrow a focus. Both the stylized history and stylized experimental facts are found wanting (Spanos 1989; Bunting 1989). Keynes points out that the best available data *at that time* were fifteen years of annual US data (1919–33). As a practical matter, given his numerous objective and subjective independent variables, as well as possible lags, the degrees of freedom would be exhausted before estimation could even begin. Only by ignoring Keynes's antipathy towards *aleatory* probability is it possible to imagine he sought a least-squares estimator of consumption, as in the AIH. A more fruitful approach to understanding Keynes is to examine 'Keynesian income' and to ask how it is different from 'classical income' or the 'social accounting income' of Kuznets et al.

4   INCOME – THREE DIFFERENT TREATMENTS

As we shall see in this section, Keynes's treatment of income is somewhat less than transparent. It is intimately bound up with academic debates on production and capital theory at the time of his writing. And, implicitly, it presages later heated debates in the theory of capital. After a brief digression, we again focus on a critical textual assessment of the *General Theory*.

Numerous and explicit references to the muddled state of production theory and capital theory are scattered throughout the *General Theory*. Keynes prefers to work with the 'marginal efficiency of investment' but a clear distinction between his views and the 'classics' is lacking, and no generally accepted theory of capital and interest existed in the 1930s (Leijonhufvud 1968: 207). The same conceptual problems between the physical productivity of capital versus the value productivity of capital, which emerged during the Cambridge debates of the 1950s and 1960s, might inhabit the intersects of Keynes's marginal efficiency of investment (compare Caravale 1987). Nevertheless, by shifting the onus of the argument on to 'income', Keynes redefined these questions outside classical equilibrium theory, with its dependence on the quantity theory of money.

> The archetypal quantity theory formula, $MV = PT$, like any identity, has to have its terms defined in such a way as to make it hold. Keynes's identities, $Y = C + I = C + S$; $S = I$, have the great advantage that they correspond to columns in the national income and product accounts, income, consumption, investment, and savings. (The formula balances because Y, I, and S are all net of depreciation and the budget and the foreign balance are either boiled in appropriately with S and I or set out separately.) Keynes, in fact, embraced the modern system of national income accounts in order to be able to convince his critics that $I = S$, not $I = S + \Delta M$. The elements in the quantity equation are not so transparent. (Robinson 1973: 77)

Robinson's assertion of the 'transparent' character of the income identity compared to the opaqueness of the quantity equation or the Cambridge equation is characteristic of the attack on the quantity theory of money launched by a number of Keynes's disciples (Aschheim and Tavalas 1990: 3–5). However, Keynes's treatment of income in the *General Theory* is not so transparent as Robinson would have us believe. Initially, Keynes simply asserts that he does not need an aggregate definition when speaking about total output.[6] Then, less than a dozen pages later, he produces a definition of total income which is allegedly identical to aggregate output. Income equals total sales minus 'user costs' (Keynes 1936: 52). Perhaps in an effort to finesse this issue, Keynes devotes the entire appendix in Chapter 6 to 'user costs', replete with various digs at the classics.

But the historical fact is that 'user costs' (the reduction in the value of equipment due to using it as compared to not using it) left everyone baffled. Opaque and counterintuitive, it made no sense to economists, business accountants or social accountants. It did not coincide with any known accounting conventions (compare Tew 1953). Keynes gave no guidance on how to construct it and it proved impossible to flesh out quantitatively. The idea was stillborn.[7]

4.1   Keynes's Definition of Consumption

This same ambiguity with respect to his chosen analytical tools also characterizes Keynes's approach to the definition of consumption. After apologizing for the prior confusion caused by his special definition of income in *Treatise on Money*, Keynes somewhat breezily defines consumption.

> Expenditure on consumption during any period must mean the value of goods sold to consumers during that period, which throws us back to the question of what is meant by a consumer–purchaser. Any reasonable definition of the line between consumer–purchaser and investor–purchaser will serve us equally well, provided that it is consistently applied. (Keynes 1936: 61)

Despite that fact that Keynes's definition of consumption does not directly depend on 'user costs', it cannot be viewed independently of the other components of the income identity since income, saving and investment all depend on 'user costs' (ibid.: 62–3). Referring to the saving equals investment identity, Keynes asserts '*any* set of definitions which satisfy the above conditions leads to the same conclusion. It is only by denying the validity of one or other of them that the conclusion can be avoided' (ibid. 1936: 63).

Thus for Keynes, the saving equals investment condition became simply a mechanical identity. Unfortunately, Keynes's attitude towards establishing the definitions, then getting on with the real business at hand (economic analysis), displays a misunderstanding of the difference between simple identities, behaviour and causation that has repeatedly bedevilled economic analysis. However, Keynes's attitude towards the 'untheoretical' issues of social and business accounting is very muted compared to his contemporaries, with whom excoriating the accounting profession is an automatic reaction.[8]

Indeed, Hicks argues in *Value and Capital* that a whole general theory of economic dynamics can be worked out without using the 'social income' concept. For Hicks, any statistical calculation of social income is fraught with error. He counsels economists to eschew this issue and the people associated with its calculation.

> The income he can calculate is not the true income he seeks; the income he seeks cannot be calculated. From this dilemma there is only one way out; it is of course the way that has to be taken in practice ... take ... social income *ex post*, and proceed to adjust it, in some way that seems plausible ... for [windfall changes in capital values]. ... The best thing the ['positive theoretical economist'] can do is to follow the practices of the Income Tax authorities. But it is the business of the theoretical economist to be able to criticize the practice of such authorities; he has no right to be found in their company himself! (Hicks 1946, in Parker et al. (eds) 1986: 109–10 and 110 fn. 1)[9]

Prior to the *General Theory*, there was no theory of aggregate 'output as a whole' and no pressing need for a national income concept in economic theory. Marshall, Pigou et al. simply accepted the Inland Revenue definition. They had no aggregate theory and no basis for reformulating the concept promulgated by the tax authorities.

4.2   Fisher's Treatment of Income and Consumption

Early in the twentieth century, Irving Fisher (1906) attempted to reconcile neoclassical value theory with the business, social accounting and popular conceptions of income. For Fisher the only income of theoretical importance is 'psychic income, based on the enjoyment derived from the consumption of goods and services'. Unfortunately, this quicksilver concept was impossible to measure (Fisher, in Parker et al. (eds) 1986: 46–7).

Indeed, Fisher goes on to equate 'income' with the 'consumption' of goods and services. All the various forms of 'income' become manifestations of a single analytic thing, time-phased receipts of various forms of postponed consumption. Investment becomes only postponed consumption, and wages, rents and profits are effectively collapsed into 'consumption'. In Fisherian income accounting, $(Y = C)$, not $(Y = C + I)$, as with Keynes and the National Income Accounts.[10]

In a nutshell, Fisher contends that net income is the net benefit obtained from capital goods over a given period, after all double counting has been eliminated. 'Investment' is not part of 'income' since it is not part of the net yield of *all* capital goods taken together, it is merely a reflection of an increase in future yields. Fisher's main contention is 'that any notion of income which is *not* consumption implies adding together undiscounted and discounted value' (Kaldor, in Parker et al. (eds) 1986: 113). For Fisher, all income ultimately depends on consumption, yet consumption is undefined, purely subjective and incapable of aggregation.

4.3   Whiggish History

It was recognized early on that Fisher's attempts to reconcile his rigorous income definition with business and social accounting conventions were a failure (Kaldor, in Parker et al. (eds) 1986: 113–18). In Fisher's view, we apply an interest rate to 'income values' and derive a 'capital value', implying that equity is the residual calculation (Fisher, in Parker et al. (eds) 1986: 52). But from the businessman's point of view, income itself is the residual calculation, after deduction for depreciation, wages, salaries, and so on. Similarly, Fisher's micro-based notion of income $(Y = C)$, contradicts the mainstream macro notion $(Y = C + I)$. Abetting the confusing state of affairs, Fisher's theory of capital and interest is taught as consistent with and complementary to Keynesian macro theory and as a theoretical justification for national income accounting. Historically, Fisher's concrete influence on national income accounting or the *General Theory* was slight, but our present understanding is gripped by a powerful, worshipful and idealizing biography.[11]

Keynes gave the impression in the *General Theory* that income, consumption, saving, and so on were simply commonsense notions rather than difficult concepts (compare Parker et al. (eds) 1986). Without an inquiry into the historical and conceptual issues surrounding the national income concept, the component parts of the income identity were simply 'numbers'. One might quibble with various plausible 'adjustments' to the numbers in Hicks's sense above, but there was no conceptual reason why purely quantitative items might not be amenable to models built around constrained maximization. Within a few years of the publication of the *General Theory*, 'user costs' disappeared, the 'marginal efficiency of investment' was transmuted into constrained maximization models of the Cobb–Douglas type, and 'animal spirits' were reduced to a second-order difference equation linking investment to changes in the level of aggregate output, Samuelson's famous multiplier–accelerator model.

Macroeconomic discourse quickly shifted to an elaboration of the various components of the 'Keynesian model' along the lines of Walrasian general equilibrium theory, with the National Income Accounts providing grist for the mills of the newly formed Cowles Commission.[12]

4.4 Income? Ask Inland Revenue

If we briefly consider a historical perspective on the income concept, it displays a varied and colourful patchwork of ideas. Income statements do not appear in business accounting prior to the eighteenth century, though there is a record of asset transactions in balance sheet form (Winjum 1972: 80). While the theoretical notion of income can be traced back to Adam Smith and the Physiocrats, the 'material product approach', which leaves out services, caused much confusion for about 100 years from the publication of the *Wealth of Nations* in 1776 (Kendrick 1970: 286–9).

Income accounting received its initial impetus from the British government's desire for taxation. William Pitt's War Tax in 1799 instituted five schedules for taxing the 'income' of specific classes: (1) rentiers, (2) farmers, (3) holders of government bonds, (4) entrepreneurs in trade and commerce, and (5) government salaries. Reverend Henry Beeke and Dr Benjamin Bell were notable in their contributions towards strengthening the coverage of Pitt's War Tax schedule and they essentially ignored the Smithian material balance approach (ibid.: 291).

Whether Smithian or not, however, it was a short intuitive leap to simply aggregate these diverse functional classes to arrive at a concept of 'national income'. The historical fact is that economic theory had little or no influence on the process of constructing these accounts. As late as 1938 it was pointed out that 'no evidence has been discussed which would lead one to suspect that the Inland Revenue definition of income has ever been seriously questioned by British students' (Weuller, in Parker et al. (eds) 1986: 142).

When considering the views of Hicks and Morgenstern (above), the impression is gleaned that business and government somehow generated these ideas *de novo*. But the historical fact is that income accounting was imposed upon economic theory via institutional constraints and historical events. Even during the heyday of Classical Political Economy (Ricardo, J.S. Mill, Malthus, et al.) income accounting had a life of its own outside the Smithian adding-up theory, with its distinction between productive and unproductive activities (Kendrick 1970: 286–92).

That Fisher's concept of income appears distinct from national income accounting is hardly surprising, since the Walrasian theory is directly concerned with the *pricing* of goods and services, while its relationship to *income* 'is tenuous, implicit and largely accidental' (Simons, in Parker et al. (eds) 1986: 95).

Fisher applied an externally given interest rate to an assumed income stream in order to recoup the 'capital value', which 'produced' the income stream in the first place. In Fisher's rather tortured prose: 'Income *is* derived from capital *goods*. But the *value* of the income is not derived from the *value* of the capital goods. On the contrary, the value of the capital is derived from the value of the income' (Fisher, in Parker et al. (eds) 1986: 52).

Fisher's argument about capital values is not comprehensible (compare Robinson 1973: 13). A more succinct and intellectually honest explanation is simply that incomes are *assumed* by, not *explained* in, the 'classical' system. The presumed identity between marginal factor products and marginal factor rewards would again become a contentious issue in the 1960s' Cambridge Debates in the Theory of Capital.

4.5   The Institutionalist Connection

Income accounting in the United States developed at the National Bureau of Economic Research (NBER) under the tutelage of Wesley Mitchell, an institutionalist economist and former student of Thorstein Veblen. Harbouring a strong ambivalence to the neoclassical constrained maximization framework, Mitchell, Colin Clark and Simon Kuznets were prompted to define the income concept based on the accounting practices and everyday parlance of commercial enterprise. As early as 1924, in his Presidential Address to the American Economic Association Meeting, Mitchell called for a new direction in economic theorizing, away from the mechanical and deterministic predilections of constrained maximization.[13]

By the 1960s, however, institutionalist influence at the NBER had been eclipsed and discussions of the 'mechanical' economic model taken from classical mechanics had waned (Pribram 1953; Sebba 1953, and discussants; Strotz 1953). The newly developed mathematical formalism had apparently rendered these issues 'old hat'.[14]

From the perspective of 'income', there were three different treatments. Keynes sought to forge his own chosen analytic tools by hybridizing 'income' from the National Income Accounts with his elusive 'user costs'. This effort was halfhearted and incomprehensible to most practitioners, so it was quickly dropped. Fisher promulgated a 'rigorous' (though unworkable and unmeasurable) concept of 'felicific income' based on utility maximization and time discounting, but he failed in his attempt to reconcile his income concept with common business usage. Finally, the government imposed a concept of income as related specific, functional 'social classes', associating particular income types with specific social classes.[15] Today the textbook treatment of income flips back and forth between these conceptions, treating 'felicific income' and 'social income' synonymously.

In the following sections we combine the various strands of our discussion, and argue that Keynes's struggle to overcome the classics entails a reasoned reluctance to use the 'first principles' of a particular theoretic model at the heart of the neoclassical synthesis. Taking our cue from modern authors, we go back to the choice theory of Irving Fisher, using his paradigm (Fisher 1926: 85–6) to differentiate various currents in the economics of the period. The methodology of choice theory is quite topical in the narrative of journal literature during this historical period and our interpretative task will be made easier by economists' candour in relation to Fisher's version of the choice-theoretic model (Viner 1925; Schultz 1931; 1938; Northrop 1941).

5 AMBIVALENCE TOWARDS CONSTRAINED MAXIMIZATION

Any attempt to frame Keynes's absolute income hypothesis in the context of twentieth-century economics must take into account the sea change in discursive practices between the time of the *General Theory*, and the life-cycle hypothesis (LCH), roughly two decades later.

Early twentieth-century theorists typically saw themselves as discoverers of natural laws, much like physical scientists (Tobin 1985: 32). As we shall see, this was hardly surprising given the nature of the choice-theoretic model. By the time of the life cycle hypothesis (LCH), however, a 'model' came to be seen as an abstract heuristic device, a thought experiment, useful for telling a story or spinning a parable. The assumptions underlying such a model were arbitrary, yet eminently fungible. For all practical purposes, the initial conditions of the model were divorced from the constraints of realism or plausibility and were limited only by the ingenuity and imagination of the model builder. As long as the initial assumptions were consistent with utility maximization (a concept itself undergoing rapid transformation during 1940–60) the only logical requirement appears to be mathematical tractability. That one model's assumptions might 'contradict' another invoked hardly a moment's discomfort. Set loose from their moorings in realism or plausibility, one assumption was as good as any other, and theorizing had become mostly instrumentalist.

5.1   Protagonists of Utility Theory

At the time of the *General Theory*, utility generally came in three flavours – cardinal, ordinal and, to a lesser degree, expected utility. Today there are endless permutations and classes of utility functions such as hyperbolic absolute risk aversion (HARA class), including constant relative and constant absolute risk aversion variants, and quadratic utility functions.

Lacking a guiding heuristic on what can or cannot be legitimately included in the utility function opened the door to any number of anomalous additions, such as money, time or further subdivisions of utility into a vector of physical qualities (the Lancaster programme). Utility could not be discussed cogently, if at all, except through its mathematical form. Mathematical tractability and analytical convenience became the only logical requirements (Blanchard and Fischer 1989: 283, 343).

Paradoxically, the modern theory of consumer behaviour is characterized by the persistent use of an unobservable and unmeasurable utility, coupled with the *assertion* that utility is simply not needed for the standard results. The origins of this curious state of affairs can be traced to the ambivalent attitude towards utility displayed by the economics profession in the period 1920 to 1940.

Though quite useful for organizing abstract theorizing, utility was not the philosophers' stone for discovering economic laws that would be on a par with the physical sciences.[16] The correspondence of the total utility function with 'potential energy' in the previous footnote is not mere coincidence. The writings of the early protagonists of the marginalist revolution are full of references to a particular mechanical model whose formal mathematical structure serves as a foundation for utility or Walras's *rareté* (Mirowski 1988: Ch. 1; 1989b: Ch. 5).

Yet, ironically, Walras's model made little headway in France because of the criticism from the natural scientists and luminaries in rational mechanics (Ingrao and Israel 1990: Ch. 4; Mirowski 1988: Ch. 2; 1991: 146–55), and had only limited influence in England because of Alfred Marshall's soft pedalling of the mathematical method (Maloney 1985). Keynes appears to have imbibed Marshall's scepticism concerning 'the pseudo-analogy with the physical sciences', and was quick to demarcate the physical sciences from the moral sciences such as economics (Keynes 1973: 300; Keynes 1930: 153).

5.2   The Potential Energy Origins of Utility Theory

The historical and intellectual relationship of mathematical economics to nineteenth-century physical theory is explored in great detail elsewhere (compare

Mirowski 1989b; Ingrao and Israel 1990). Our present aim is a modest one, to connect our earlier discussion of Keynes's views on probability and income to his conscious refusal to employ this same physics model. Furthermore, as we shall see, economists during the historical period in question were more aware of the potential energy origins of utility theory than are modern practitioners.

The clearest and most straightforward statements of the physics inspiration of utility theory can be found in the works of Pareto and Irving Fisher.

> Let us go back to the equations which determine equilibrium. In seeing them somebody – and it might be the writer – made an observation ... 'These equations do not seem new to me, I know them well, they are old friends. They are the equations of rational mechanics'. That is why pure economics is a sort of mechanics or akin to mechanics ... mechanics can be studied leaving aside the concept of forces. In reality this does not all matter much. If there is anyone who does not care to have mechanics mentioned, very well, let us disregard the similarity and let us talk directly about our equations. (Pareto 1953: 185)

In a letter to Irving Fisher, dated 1897, Pareto wrote:

> People who know neither mathematics nor rational mechanics cannot understand the principal conception of my book. ... The discussions concerning the terms ophelimity, entrepreneurs, capital, etc., are of exactly the same type as found in the last century surrounding the *force vive* in mechanics. Eh! Call what you will the quantity one half mv^2, won't the results always be the same? (Pareto, translated in Mirowski 1989b: 222)

Irving Fisher was the first economist to implement a vector characterization of utility, which he culled from the vector formalisms of his preeminent thesis advisor, Josiah Willard Gibbs, America's foremost thermodynamicist, whom many have called America's greatest indigenous scientist (compare Ingrao and Israel 1990: 245–9). In his doctoral dissertation (1892), later published in 1926, Fisher presents a table of precise analogies between classical mechanics and economics, equating 'energy' with 'utility' and 'equilibrium' in a mechanical system with 'economic equilibrium' (Fisher 1926: 85–6). Most of Fisher's analogies were culled from hydrostatics rather than electrical field theory and his book is stuffed with pictorials of vats, cisterns and other mechanical models. Fisher's vision of what constitutes 'science' was decidedly mechanistic and deterministic. His major innovation in utility theory (indifference curves) was the perfect expression of determinism, the differential equation. All time is telescoped into the present in a deterministic system and its state at any point in time completely determines all subsequent and preceding states. Integrating or solving a differential equation means to deduce from this relation the 'law of motion' for a deterministic system.[17]

The emphasis by Pareto and Fisher on the 'work' accomplished in a mechanical system and its relation to kinetic energy ($\frac{1}{2} mv^2$) has a direct interpretation: 'A utility function of a consumer looks quite similar to a potential function in the theory of gravitational or electrical fields' (Koopmans 1957: 176). Koopmans's claim is understated and coy and he quickly sought to distance economics from physics by invoking the dissimilarity between physics and revealed preference theory.[18]

Yet a closer look at the utility function reveals striking similarities *vis à vis* the nineteenth-century model of energy. Begging the reader's pardon, we need a bit of mathematical characterization ourselves to make this point. Suppose we describe a mass point moving in three-dimensional Euclidean space from point A to point B.[19] A description of this motion, developed between the years 1800 and 1860, postulates a 'force' decomposed into its perpendicular (orthogonal) components, multiplied through by the spatial displacement of the mass point. Movement was conceptualized as the following: the change in kinetic energy (T, the work integral) in the course of the motion from A to B was defined as the summation of the orthogonal infinitesimal forces multiplied by their displacements:

$$T = \int\limits_A^B (F_x dx + F_y dy + F_z dz) = \frac{1}{2} mv^2 \bigg|_A^B = T_B - T_A$$

The writings of Euler, Lagrange and especially Hamilton, argued that the total energy of this system also depends on the 'position' of the mass point. If the expression ($F_x dx + F_y dy + F_z dz$) was an exact or pure differential, this implies the existence of a function $U(x, y, z)$, such that $F_x = (\partial U/\partial x)$, $F_y = (\partial U/\partial y)$, $F_z = (\partial U/\partial z)$. The function $U(x, y, z)$ defines a gravitational field identified as 'potential energy'.

The summation of kinetic energy plus potential energy ($T + U$) was understood as being conserved within the confines of a 'closed' system. This conservation law encouraged the employment of constrained maximization techniques (such as the principle of least action, Lagrangean multipliers and the Hamiltonian calculus of variations) for describing the path of the mass point under the influence of gravity or other impressed forces.

The relationship between the nineteenth-century model of potential energy and utility-based price theory is simply a matter of relabelling the variables. If we redefine 'forces' to be prices, the 'displacements' to be infinitesimal changes in the quantities of goods (x, y, z), 'kinetic energy' to be expenditure, and relabel the 'potential energy field' to be a field of utility, then, *mirabile dictu*, we have the standard utility model.

Constrained maximization of utility leads directly to a vector field which fixes the permissible configuration of forces/prices in equilibrium. Since the potential function is *defined* by the condition that its partial derivatives with respect to the variables are equal to the forces along the associated axes, $F_n = (\partial U/\partial n)$, relative prices are (by construction and definition) equal to the ratios of the marginal utilities of the goods. As we will argue, the easiest way to grasp this model is by reference to Irving Fisher's concept of 'force'.

In pre-entropic physics (before it was realized that energy would dissipate) all physical phenomena are simple variations of a protean 'energy' which is fully and reversibly transformed from one state to another. Transporting this idea into economic theory meant that all economic goods were fully and reversibly transformed into utility and thus all other goods through the intermediary of the act of trade. Utility was suffused throughout the abstract commodity space and was seen as the primary motive force behind all economic activity; it constituted a 'force field'. In effect, utility is an individually articulated psychological field which behaves, for all intents and purposes, just like potential energy.

5.3 Wrestling With Utility

Despite the elegant mathematical formalism, early forms of utility theory (whether cardinal or ordinal) proved incapable of empirical implementation. There simply was no effective theoretical or empirical standard with which to gauge utility. As seen earlier, even the protagonists of the utility concept such as Schultz and Samuelson were hard-pressed to maintain their enthusiasm in the face of widespread professional scepticism.

The numerous permutations on the utility theme, beginning with Samuelson's revealed preference theory, have effectively served to bury the physics origins of utility theory under a surfeit of new mathematical formalisms, each intuitively less accessible than the previous one (Mirowski 1989b: 358–69). Another factor (viewed historically) is that the *early protagonists* of the utility field most familiar with the analytical imperatives of the construct, Pareto and Antonelli, *left economics for other fields* (compare Chipman et al. 1971).

Twentieth-century economics has witnessed a subtle but profound shift in the meaning attached to 'equilibrium' at both the individual and macro levels (compare Mirowski 1989c). Economic theory, originally thought to have the force of physical law, has become a purely formal mathematical proposition, with both utility and equilibrium possessing little substantive meaning outside their mathematical formulations. Viewed historically, much of the economics profession imbibed their mathematics from the vector formalisms of Fisher's choice-theoretic model.

6 INTERPRETING THE FISHERIAN MODEL

The metaphorical implications of Fisher's model are straightforward – prices are the forces and the market is the mechanism whereby the maximum of utility is realized. But 'equilibrium' is reached only because an additional linear constraint was added to the model. The 'work integral' or kinetic energy (Pareto's $\frac{1}{2}\ mv^2$) does not explicitly appear in Fisher's table of translations between mechanics and economics, because he imposed an extra independent condition on the physical model of energy – that is, the linear budget constraint.

In Fisher's model, if we simply relabel the force function (F) to be a price vector for traded goods and (dq) as a quantity vector, then the integral, $\int (F \cdot dq)$ $= T$, represents total expenditure. If $(F \cdot dq)$ is an exact or pure differential, then a scalar function $U = U(x, y, z)$ exists and can be interpreted as the 'utilities' of those goods. If we further assume, as Fisher does, that the price of each incremental quantity of a generic good is constant throughout the market (by assuming the law of one price), then the total expenditure integral T is a simple summation of prices times quantities set equal to a constant (that is, the linear budget constraint we find in economics textbooks).

Relative prices are equal to the ratio of marginal utilities *by construction* (the partial derivatives of the potential function are equal to the forces with respect to the associated axes). In 'equilibrium', the ratio of marginal utilities is identical with the ratio of prices for generic goods (given a two-good economy).

When there are more than two goods in the economy, the differential $(F \cdot dq)$ will not necessarily be 'integrable' and the mathematics rapidly becomes nasty (compare Chipman et al. 1971; Hurwicz and Richter 1979: 7). The famous 'integrability conditions' and their association with the symmetry and negative definiteness of the Slutsky or Antonelli matrix are outside the purview of the present discussion. But a reconsideration of how Fisher approached these problems is illuminating.

Fisher banishes the phenomenon of regret in the psychology of choice (Fisher 1926: 21). Thus in his model, people do not make mistakes and false trading is not possible. For Fisher there can be no divergence between the anticipation and the realization of utility; therefore no 'buyer's remorse' is allowed. The reason why he does not need integrability is surprisingly simple; he is willing to push the content of the law to be demonstrated (that is, the law of one price) back on to the initial definitions of individual exchange. Knowing in advance the 'result' he sought, the equivalence of price ratios with ratios of marginal utilities, he effectively imposed it via the law of one price, an example of *petitio principii*, begging the question.

Typically the law of one price is treated as if it were the very definition of pure competition. But the so-called 'law of one price' is neither a 'law' nor 'of one price'. Rather it is an assumption necessary to close the neoclassical model. It should go without saying that the common practice of tracing the origins of this assumption to Adam Smith is disingenuous at best.[20]

Without the law of one price (and the banishment of regret), there is nothing to prohibit trading at non-equilibrium prices (false trading) and Fisher's idea of time-independent equilibrium is compromised. Were equilibrium to be a time-dependent or path-dependent process, the Walrasian notion of *tâtonnement* comes unglued. Of course, trade *can* be time- or path-dependent; it can occur out of equilibrium and it can affect the equilibrium reached. Thus hysteresis (that is, the failure of a system to return to its original state when the cause of a change is removed) is introduced into the foundations of Fisher's model and the uniqueness of equilibrium is compromised. These problems will become more evident if we hold the law of one price in abeyance and consider the physics model directly.

The key to Fisher's choice-theoretic treatment is the one-to-one relationship or isomorphism between forces and prices – Fisher alludes to the importance of 'force' in the introduction to his 1892 dissertation.[21] Without the arbitrary imposition of the law of one price, however, the kinetic energy or work integral does not collapse into a linear budget constraint. Only if $(F \cdot dq)$ is an exact or perfect differential, will the general conditions hold for the deduction of a uniquely identified scalar utility function (U). This fact was repeatedly pointed out by natural scientists sympathetic to the Lausanne school (compare Volterra in Chipman et al. 1971; Ingrao and Israel 1990: 152–4; Mirowski 1988: Ch. 2). But there was simply no theoretical reason to make the assumption that the differential was exact. Except, of course, that without this assumption there would be no *unique* relationship between price ratios and Walras's *raretés* and, consequently, no constrained maximization of utility.

6.1 The Marshallian Treatment

Alfred Marshall, though trained as a mathematician, was quick to soft-pedal the mathematical formalism, and simply interpreted the integrating constant of the pure differential $(F \cdot dq)$ as the 'constant marginal utility' of money or income (Marshall 1920: 842). The idea of a constant relationship between utility and money, while intuitively opaque and hardly justified, actually touches on the core of the physical analogue.[22]

In the physics model, the scalar potential field (U) is *derived* as the set of constrained extremes, while in the economics model this logic is reversed and the vector field of prices is *derived* from the scalar field of utility. Utility is the fundamental exogenous data to which prices adjust. However, the mathematics are identical in both cases. In the physics model, the sum of kinetic and potential energy $(T + U)$, total energy, is conserved through any motion of the mass point and equals a constant (that is, $T + U = k$).

Translated into economics, this implies that total expenditure (E) and utility (U) are conserved in a closed trading system (in effect, $E + U = k$). Thus, when Alfred Marshall interprets the integrating constant of the exact differential $(F \cdot dq)$ as the constant marginal utility of money, he is, in effect, imposing a kind of conservation principle, money is convertible into utility at a constant ratio (*k*).[23]

Irving Fisher, on the other hand, perhaps because of the cognitive dissonance of adding money and utility, chose to revise the physics model at precisely this point. Since Fisher's model is the wellspring for the neoclassical synthesis, we can sharply differentiate Keynes from the classics by reference to the Fisherian model. But first, some fundamental concepts of physics are needed to frame our interpretation.

In the physics model, the core notion is that total energy $(T + U)$ is conserved in a closed system. Movement in a field of potential energy is along a path of (generally) minimized potential. In the 1830s this conservation principle was given rigorous specification by William Hamilton, who described the movement of the mass point from A to B (along a path of minimized potential), where the 'action integral'

$$\int_{A_{t_1}}^{B_{t_2}} (T - U)dt$$

was stationary.

The preeminent Austrian physicist Erwin Schroedinger described Hamilton's seminal work on the 'action integral' as 'the central conception of all modern theory in physics' (Crowe 1967: 17). With hindsight, it seems hardly reasonable to assume that this crucial part of the physics model is freely disposable when translated by Irving Fisher into economic theory. Yet, as we shall see, this was precisely Fisher's chosen course.

6.2   Where's the Beef?

Earlier we asserted that the law of one price implied a linear budget constraint, clouded the relevant conservation principle, and suppressed Pareto's ($\frac{1}{2}mv^2$) or kinetic energy. Modern economic texts make non-essential reference to the physics model as the starting point for the calculus of variations, but the importance of the work integral and action integral are never explicitly brought up for discussion, despite the fact that the conservation principle is the heart of the model. An example of this can be found in the opening chapter of a well-known text in dynamic economics.[24]

Although we oversimplify a complex issue in the intellectual history of economics, there appears to be a rather straightforward reason why Fisher does not discuss either the work integral or the action integral when he translates the 'notion of force' for 'scholars of the literary and historical type'. Recalling our earlier identification of kinetic energy with total expenditure and potential energy with utility, the conservation law, $(T + U = k)$, in a closed system directly translates as: the sum of income (or money) plus utility is constant in a closed trading system. The mathematics says that money and utility are two different forms of the protean concept of 'energy'. They can be converted one into the other at a fixed ratio, can be added together and are conserved in the trading process of a pure exchange economy (Walras's *tâtonnement*). The rub is that all the spilled ink over the measurability of utility and the integrability conditions is a waste of time, if money and utility are ontologically equivalent. Money works just as well as a measure of the value of commodities as does utility and besides it is already a cardinal rather than an ordinal measure. Fisher would have none of this and insisted 'money value simply measures utility by a marginal standard which is constantly changing' (Fisher 1926: 87).

The economic analogue of the physics model is a frictionless barter economy. There is no logical requirement for a specific money commodity or financial institutions because they would be redundant.[25] Yet, money and the constant marginal utility of money have a straightforward (yet undesirable) interpretation which springs directly from the mathematics of the field equations. Following Alfred Marshall, the best we might do with money is to let it stand for the integrating constant of the (allegedly) exact differential $(F \bullet dq)$. Although Marshall's treatment sidesteps the interpretative issue, the connection to the work integral is at least implicitly recognized.[26]

The connection of modern consumer theory to the physics model of energy is only obliquely admitted by modern economists (Hurwicz and Richter 1979: 14), while physicists are not nearly so circumspect:

> When I choose that function to be the potential energy minus the kinetic energy and add a single probabilistic constraint on the particle's motion, I can derive the Schroedinger equation. By neglecting this constraint ... I can derive Hamilton's principle. ... Economic theory is similarly based on the idea that an individual's behaviour is rational and hence he acts as if he maximized the expected value of some function (called his utility function). Thus the results of this paper show that there is a common foundation underlying physics and economics. This is hardly surprising inasmuch as both are rational attempts to understand behaviour – in the case of physics, the behaviour of nature, in the case of economics, the behaviour of individuals. (Bordley 1983: 803–4)

Irving Fisher's translation of the concept of 'force' into economics uses physical theory circa 1860 as its touchstone, yet Fisher dismissed measurability and integrability almost as an afterthought. The American mathematician and pioneer in cybernetics, Norbert Wiener, has described this attitude towards 'theory building' as a kind of unreflective physics envy among social scientists.[27]

6.3 A Literary Definition of Conservation

The importance of the conservation principle, measurability and integrability is argued with verve in Mirowski (1989b), but this is beyond the scope of our discussion. One might argue that these purely technical issues, which dogged economics for at least a hundred years, can be bypassed altogether via the use of hypersurfaces (Debreu 1991: 4). Still, we believe that it is useful to note a succinct and eminently literary description of the core of the Fisherian model (integrability), if only because it dovetails nicely with the legitimate concerns expressed by Norbert Wiener.[28]

Irving Fisher backed away from considering either the principle of energy conservation or the importance of integrability. He arbitrarily imposed the law of one price on his economic model translated from classical mechanics. Then he set about revising his definitions to banish the unsavoury implications mentioned earlier.

Fisher's first imposition, the law of one price, finessed the issues of commensurability, integrability and aggregation. Fisher defined 'work' as force times displacement, but he also defined 'work' as total energy (which is incorrect), (Fisher 1926: 85–6). 'Work' in the physics model is the change in kinetic energy, the work integral (T), not $(T + U)$, which is total energy.

In Fisher's table of analogies between mechanics and economics, the simple fact is that 'work' in the physics model is mixed with the different concept of 'work' in economics (the disutility of labour). Having suppressed one component (U) of total energy, Fisher further conflated 'work' with both energy and utility; thereby generating an entirely new definition of 'labour' as negative utility or disutility. Fisher's appeal is to the idea of human labour as the expenditure of effort in the disutility of work. The concept of 'work' does double duty for Fisher, appealing to rational mechanics for its scientific grounding, and to economics for the idea of work as negative pleasure. Indeed, according to Fisher's 'translation', work is defined as utility and disutility, energy and negative energy, all at the same time! So much for the clarifying influence of the study of physics (compare Fisher 1926: v).

Fisher's conception of 'work' links the physical idea of force to the economic idea of labour and lays the basis for a 'positive science' of economics. In his own words: 'To construct a positive science, force must be defined with respect to its connection with space, time and mass. So also ... when economics attempts to be a positive science, it must seek a definition which connects it with the objective commodity' (Fisher 1926: 17).

The idea that labour (negative utility) creates commodities *de novo*, or that saving generates immediately consumable output, as in (Ramsey 1928), are legacies of Fisher's treatment of work and income.[29]

Much like the law of one price, labour as disutility enters Fisher's analysis as if dropped from a helicopter. The main casualty from these *ad hoc* changes is that the heart of the physics model – that is, the conservation of energy, described mathematically by Hamilton's stationary action integral – has been misplaced.[30]

In as much as Fisher pioneered the terminological innovation of indifference curves in economics (the locus of points with the same quantitative utility; 1926: 72–81), we might argue that he was not 'mistaken' in his mechanical analogues. He clearly sought to suppress the *cardinality* of utility and this meant suppressing the potential energy function (U) in favour of Gibbs's vector formalisms (ibid.: 88).[31]

Fisher's reasoning was metaphorical, reasoning by analogy. By mixing 'work' in physics with 'work' in economics he, thereby, extirpated cardinal utility with all its psychological overtones and undesirable trappings to the Benthamite calculus (ibid.: vii, 23).

Despite our abbreviated explanation of the theoretical motivation behind Fisher's choice-theoretic model, it seems fair to argue that the ambivalence displayed by the economics profession towards utility maximization during the 1930s (the years bracketing the *General Theory*) reflects a reticence by economists towards embracing the classic Fisherian model.

6.4 Conservation – A Missing Principle?

It is interesting to note that prior to the probability revolution in econometrics in the mid-1940s, at least one author had zeroed in on the lack of conservation principles in neoclassical economics as the Achilles heel in the construction of a viable dynamic theory.[32] Stated more explicitly, conservation principles are altogether *absent* in modern treatments of constrained maximization. If the conservation law was taken seriously, however, the experimental literature on expected utility and preference reversal (compare Shoemaker 1982; Tversky et al. 1990; Tversky and Thaler 1990), would no longer appear as 'puzzles' to be solved, *but as massive disconfirming evidence* against the Fisherian deterministic model, evidence that individuals *do not* behave as inert, invariant mechanical objects in a field of force, and that individual preferences *do not* approximate a 'field'.[33]

Unless we hold the conservation principle in abeyance, as is fashionable amongst economists, we should not be surprised by the experimental results in cognitive psychology concerning preference reversals: 'Because invariance – unlike independence or even transitivity – is normatively unassailable and descriptively incorrect, it does not seem possible to construct a theory of choice that is both normatively acceptable and descriptively adequate' (Tversky et al. 1990: 215).

As Northrop pointed out over fifty years ago, there are compelling *a priori* reasons to assume that individual preferences do not obey a conservation law.[34] Put another way, preferences are not fixed and given exogenously. Preferences may change in the process of exchange since people do change their minds. This unfortunately causes problems with the neoclassical model since changing preferences have the effect of shifting the market equilibrium. Preferences may indeed display any number of idiosyncrasies, according to the work of cognitive psychologists such as Thaler, and these results are disconfirming evidence against the utility-based neoclassical theory, where preferences are *a priori* assumed to be fixed and given exogenously. The assumption of fixed and exogenously given preferences means that the conservation principle is imbedded in the utility function. But the metaphorical, social and theoretical implications of this principle, and what it implies and requires for our concept of human behaviour, are altogether left out of the neoclassical model. It is very convenient that the mathematics work under these restrictive assumptions, but disconcerting that the issues are effectively blurred in a blizzard of technical gobbledegook.[35]

If, as Fisher assumes *a priori*, preferences are independent of context, as well as being independent of the trading process through which they are satisfied, and time symmetric as well (Fisher 1926: 19–21), then disconfirming experimental evidence either implies that people's preferences *have* changed (that is, endogenous preference shifts) or, conversely, that the evidence provides 'puzzles' to be solved by further research (Deaton and Muellbauer 1980: 78; Hausman 1989). Unfortunately, the preferred interpretation nowadays is that the experimental evidence yields non-essential puzzles that have already been superseded by developments in game theory.

Roughly speaking, conservation principles are like a filing system imposed by the theorist on both theory and data prior to empirical investigation and hypothesis testing. The idea that preferences must be consistent and rational, or else they are capricious, unintelligible and not amenable to scientific investigation, is an example of such a filing system (at the microeconomic level). Without symmetry, for example, preferences are inconsistent, and mainstream theorists are presumably left with no theory at all, as all behaviour appears equally capricious and unintelligible (compare Coddington 1982: 586).

6.5   More Conservation Principles

At the macroeconomic level, an example of a conservation principle is the strong version of Say's Law – incomes generated in the production process are exactly equal to the value of total output and provide the wherewithal (in principle) to clear all markets, regardless of the behaviour of the stock of cash and the price level. Overproduction is not possible, given a smoothly functioning financial system, and total spending and output are invariant to changes in the money market. By contrast, Keynes sought to build a macroeconomics which consciously abjured this conservation principle. Neither total spending nor output was invariant. Changes in the distribution of spending between actual purchases and virtual purchases (changes in liquidity preference and unintended inventory accumulation) induced changes in total output. Not surprisingly, variants of Say's Law meld with a Walrasian framework, but not so well with the *General Theory*.

Disagreement over the consistency and rationality of individual preferences demarcates the exchanges between Keynes and Ramsey in the 1930s and animates much of the modern debate concerning Keynes and expectations (Bateman 1987). Our argument has come full circle.

The image of science promulgated by rational mechanics and its concept of force is the prime mover behind the Fisherian choice-theoretic model, and Fisher says as much in his dissertation. There was, however, a fairly widespread and nagging resistance to the implications of the Fisherian model, evidenced in the 1930s and 1940s journal literature, and these authors appeared more self-consciously aware of what Keynes called 'the pseudo-analogy with the physical sciences'. Beginning with the work of Hicks and Samuelson, a surfeit of new mathematical formalisms effectively buried the physics origins of preference theory and today there is almost complete freedom in the functional forms of 'utility', subject only to the proviso of mathematical tractability.

It is a curious fact that in modern economics, utility is a fundamental concept only in a heuristic sense; in a formal sense it is altogether expendable and unnecessary. The extreme instrumentalism and freedom in reasoning permits some authors to argue that 'the symmetry of the Slutsky substitution matrix is *the* fundamental integrability condition of demand theory'(Deaton and Muellbauer 1980: 50), while others claim that the symmetry condition is either 'trivial or simply false'(Varian 1991: 596), and still others to assert that these issues are 'old hat' and capable of being bypassed altogether by the use of hypersurfaces (compare Debreu 1990: 4).

6.6 The Physical Metaphor – Three Literary Summaries

In lieu of the quicksilver character of modern treatments of utility, preferences and aggregate consumption, we tender the modest claim that early empirical and theoretical work on consumption was more intellectually honest and did not obfuscate the issues as is the case of modern treatments (compare Thomas 1989). The early work on aggregate consumption was defined by a reticence to arbitrarily impute ever more prodigious calculating powers to individual economic agents, and a refusal to view rationality as a logical necessity verging on *a priori* truth.

Our discussion has sought to illustrate the influence of a particular physical metaphor (the energy conservation law associated with rational mechanics and the first law of thermodynamics) on the development of consumption theory. This line of investigation seemed appropriate because the neoclassical synthesis traces itself to the classical choice theory of Irving Fisher, and because Fisher did not mince words on the source of his scientific inspiration.

The metaphor has, at the very least, heuristic value for interpreting the journal literature contemporary to the *General Theory*. In a nutshell, it implies that 'classical' economists:

> [by] appropriating an analytical technique from thermodynamics, have implicitly imported a physical metaphor and imposed it upon social phenomena without ever making it explicit what social conditions would be consistent with that metaphor. Those conditions are, roughly, that in the theory there never is any feedback in the economic system from market processes to the underlying ... utility functions or given endowments which are then portrayed as 'natural' or 'exogenous' to the analysis. ... Equilibrium can be described independently of the processes which purportedly bring it about, in the same way that the thermodynamic properties of the state of a system are independent of path. No reasons are ever given by economists for this series of analytical choices, other than perhaps the fact that that's the way it's done in physics and that what is good enough for physicists should be good enough for economists. (Mirowski 1988: 101)

And new Keynesian fundamentalists paint much the same picture:

> The assumption of independence from changes in the value of money carried with it the idea of neutral money and allowed the classical theoretician to pass, without any change in reasoning, from a real exchange economy to a money exchange economy and brought with it the false analogy between the two. ... The assumption of independence from changes in the value of output and unemployment implied that the economic system was operating to its full capacity, which meant an independence from the level of output or of employment. ... [The] logical passage from an analysis at the individual level ... to one at community ... level ... transfer[s] to the system as a whole a type of reasoning which was only valid at the individual level. ... In the actual reasoning of the classical theory, all this meant that the income of the system as a whole was taken as given. ... The introduction of the hypothesis of independence by the classical theory allowed it to deal with systems as if they were *always* isolable from *all* the levels or values of the variables considered. (Carabelli 1991: 112–18)

Or as Keynes (1936: 21) remarks a bit more succinctly: 'Granted this all the rest follows'.

7   FISHER AND KEYNES: CONTRASTS AND CONCLUSIONS

Irving Fisher was the first and last mainstream economist to explore the physics origins of constrained maximization in any detail, and his changes to the model have carried it into the twentieth century. Similarly, Fisher's choice-theoretic model provided much of the raw material for the vaunted neoclassical synthesis which held sway in economics until the early 1970s. Sharp distinctions between Keynes and the classics are evidenced by comparing Keynes's views on income and rationality with their counterparts in the Fisherian model.

Fisherian income is 'psychic income', which is immediately equated with the consumption of goods and services. All component parts of national income, such as wages, rents and profits, are collapsed into a single analytic term, time-phased receipts of 'consumption'. At the individual level there is a metaphorical distinction between income as a flow and capital as a stock, much like water running out of a bathtub; nevertheless, all distinctions are blurred. Income is consumption only, $(Y = C)$, and consumption is left undefined. Fisher is adamant that investment is not part of income, only the (later) flow of consumption from the services of investment will contribute to income (Tobin 1985: 33).

As argued previously, the mathematics of the field equations implies that total expenditure and utility are ontologically equivalent and connected via the conservation principle $(E + U = k)$. Modern treatments of utility, however, have come loose from these interpretative moorings. Income is simply a number provided by social accountants, while utility is a mathematical apparition, subject only to the proviso of tractability.[36]

In contrast, Keynes took the National Income and Product Accounts (NIPA) of Wesley Mitchell and Simon Kuznets as the backdrop for his theory of 'output as a whole'. Keynes's chosen analytical tools did not exhibit a one-to-one correspondence to the NIPA, but he devoted a fair amount of the *General Theory* to explaining how his theoretical system was grounded in the tangible reality of money contracts and connected with national income accounting. This is not to say that his logic was unimpeachable. For example, his 'user costs' concept proved impenetrable to social and business accountants alike.

In the *General Theory*, Keynes pilloried conventional capital theory and, by implication, the numerous production theories of his day. For Keynes, 'income' became the font for the new theory of macroeconomics. While Keynes's appeal to income was a rhetorical device, it was an eminently effective one. As a well-ensconced Cambridge don whose reputation was cemented by earlier works, classical economists were not wont to challenge him on the income concept if only because, for most economists, accounting was a lowbrow endeavour, devoid of theoretical importance.

In the *General Theory*, Keynes never 'completed' his theory of investment by attaching to it a theory of aggregate saving. Consumption and saving were not treated symmetrically as with Fisher and Ramsey. Keynes's contentious attitude towards the muddle of production and capital theory precluded the notion of saving as consumption postponed. Income for Keynes was $(Y = C + I)$, while income for Fisher was $(Y = C)$. These differences in definitions harbour points of serious contention which cannot be reconciled without a drastic revision in one or the other doctrine. Historically, Keynes's system bears the brunt of the revision.

In the context of Irving Fisher's partial translation of 'force' into economics, rationality has a misleadingly simple yet poignant definition. Rationality can be defined tautologically as the *assumption* of a drive towards the equilibrium state. It is behaviour that is consistent with the predictions of the model that is used. In the context of the field formalisms for energy, all motion is virtual, reversible and occurs instantaneously. People behave as if they are inert, invariant, mechanical objects. They choose their consumption bundles based on a rigid algorithmic rationality taken directly from the calculus of variations.

In pre-entropic physics, the particle moves along a path of generally minimized potential, the logic (though not the mathematics) is reversed in the economic model, and the individual moves along the path of maximum utility. In the Fisherian model, all the relevant notions of income are collapsed into 'psychic income', with consumption and saving treated symmetrically. Extending this paradigm to a continuous time-optimization problem gives the Ramsey model.

Keynes's changing notion of rationality does not fit well into the Ramsey model, attribution of the Keynes–Ramsey rule notwithstanding. Keynes originally held to an objective epistemic theory of probability. But partly under influence from Ramsey and partly given advances in the physical sciences of his day, Keynes shifted to a subjective epistemic theory.

It is Keynes's implicit and sometimes explicit rejection of the 'equilibrium method', as embodied in the Fisherian choice-theoretic model, which has crystallized opposition to the central themes of the *General Theory*. Keynes insisted *vis à vis* Ramsey that subjective preferences and expectations are not consistent and aleatory, but epistemic and subject to unexpected and violent shifts. He does not object to the art of thinking in models, but: 'the pseudo-analogy with the physical sciences leads directly counter to the habit of mind which is most important for an economist to acquire. ... One has to be constantly on guard against treating the material as constant and homogenous' (Keynes 1973: 300).

The 'economics of Keynes' does not conform to the hard-core research strategy embedded in the Fisherian model of constrained optimization (Leijonhufvud 1968). By modern standards, this makes the *General Theory* somehow illegitimate and in need of microfoundations. That Keynes's offending doctrine has been pruned away is a matter of historical record, the *General Theory* fell from the standard reading list in macroeconomics more than a generation ago.

Taken at face value, Keynes's treatment of aggregate consumption in the *General Theory* is primarily discursive rather than statistical. It is characterized by the refusal to employ the 'equilibrium method' and a refusal to view rationality as a logical necessity verging on *a priori* truth. The 'community' for

Keynes is explicitly 'organic' not atomic, not a simple summation of autarchic or independent elements as in classical analysis. Individual expectations are subjective and epistemic, implying, at minimum, that Theil's necessary and sufficient conditions for linear aggregation are not satisfied (compare Ando and Modigliani 1963: 58).

Preferences, for Keynes, appear to be context dependent and subject to a herd instinct, as in the so-called 'animal spirits'. Thus, implicitly, preferences are non integrable and Keynes's treatment of aggregate consumption appears nearly immiscible with modern views based on the Ramsey model, or the 'proportionality approach' seen in the life-cycle or permanent income hypotheses.

Keynes altered the language and meaning of basic economic concepts by rooting them in the social institution of money. To the extent there was a Keynesian revolution in macroeconomics, we can locate its effects in the double-faced or Janus-faced character of the language and its analytical constructs. Only by altering the language with which the economy is described was such a revolutionary change effected (compare Kuhn in Krueger et al. (eds) 1987: 20–21). Our discussion focused primarily on the concepts of income and, to a lesser degree, probability and rationality; highlighting the revolutionary tension in the language and writing of Keynes, a tension poorly captured by modern mathematical interpretations in which the literary and interpretative dimensions are, for the most part, absent.

Today, the continual resurrection of the worries expressed by Keynes concerning the alleged time invariance of economic events seems unlikely ever to be allayed (Lawson 1989a: 258). After more than fifty years of ongoing empirical research, the absence of a generally agreed upon empirical test for aggregate consumption, capable of producing clear results and a professional consensus, may be reason enough to widen the discourse beyond formalist and positivist conventions. On revisitation, Keynes's original arguments and the journal literature of his time appear more compelling than most modern interpretations in describing the world in which we live.

NOTES

*   This chapter is based on Borghese (1993). The authors wish to thank Paul Davidson and Jan Kregel for their encouragement, Albert J. Eckstein for his careful review and suggested changes, and workshop participants for their comments and stimulating discussions, especially William Vickery, David Bunting, Gary Dymski, Basil Moore, James K. Galbraith and Cecile Dangel. The views expressed are those of the authors and not necessarily those of the US Department of Commerce. The usual error disclaimer applies.

1.   'It is especially important to realize that the two types of distinctions being made are not the same. An epistemic theory of probability, for instance, may be an objective or a subjective theory. Epistemic is not synonymous with subjective, or aleatory with objective, in this lexicon. The importance of maintaining the distinction is that while many people have

assumed that all epistemic theories are subjective, the theory which Keynes espoused in *A Treatise on Probability* was an *objective epistemic* theory. Aside from the purely technical aspect of correct attribution, however, the *objective* nature of Keynes's original conception is crucial to understanding the later changes and so must be emphasized.

Today, many philosophers of science accept that there may be both epistemic and aleatory probabilities, but at the time that Keynes was writing many probability theorists felt that one theory must preclude the other [for example, Venn, von Mises]. Keynes's principal argument in *A Treatise on Probability* was that probabilities are epistemic and not aleatory. He was adamant, though, that epistemic probabilities were not subjective' (Bateman 1987: 100).

2. See Kregel (1976) for discussion of uncertainty and expectations and Kregel (1977) for the historical context thereof.
3. Leijonhufvud (1968: 44) notes the furious controversies surrounding capital theory at this time between Fisher, Knight, Kaldor, Hayek and Cassel.
4. Proposed answers to this issue vary widely, even within the Cambridge and Anglo-Italian versions of the neo-Keynesian school (Caravale 1987: 9–14).
5. '(*The General Theory*'s) effectiveness is diminished if you try to eradicate very deep-rooted habits of thought *unnecessarily*. One of these is supply and demand analysis. I am not merely thinking of the aged and fossilized, but of the younger generation who have been thinking perhaps only for a few years but very hard about these topics. It is doing a great violence to their fundamental groundwork of thought, if you tell them that two independent demand and supply functions won't jointly determine price and quantity. Tell them that there may be more than one solution. Tell them that the *ceteris paribus* clause is inadmissable and that we can discover more important functional relationships governing price and quantity in this case which render the supply and demand analysis nugatory. But don't impugn that analysis itself' (Letter from Harrod, Keynes 1973, Vol. 8: 531, 533–4).
6. 'The concepts of output as a whole and its price-level are not required in this context, since we have no need of an absolute measure of current aggregate output, such as would enable us to compare its amount with the amount which would result from the association of a different capital equipment with a different quantity of employment' (Keynes 1936: 40).
7. Sympathetic commentators on the *General Theory* sometimes employ the user cost idea as a heuristic device (compare Minsky 1975).
8. For example, Hicks on social accounting: 'My decision to abstain from using these concepts in the last five chapters was, of course, quite deliberate. In spite of their familiarity, I do not believe that they [Income, Savings, Investment *inter alia*] are suitable tools for any analysis which aims at logical precision. There is far too much equivocation in their meaning, equivocation which cannot be removed by the most painstaking effort. At bottom, they are not logical categories at all; they are rough approximations, used by the business man to steer himself through the bewildering changes of situations which confront him. For this purpose, strict logical categories are not what is needed; something rougher is actually better. But if we try to work with terms of this sort in the investigations we are here concerned with, we are putting upon them a weight of refinement they cannot bear' (Hicks, in Parker et al. (eds) 1986: 102).

    Also, Morgenstern on business accounts: 'Both balance sheets and ... profit and loss accounts represent a mixture of figures that belong in widely separate categories. Yet these figures are treated conceptually and arithmetically as if they were completely homogeneous. ... There simply cannot be a financial statement which is not ultimately the report of some physical event; money passing from one hand to another ... or a record made of some physical entities allegedly in the possession of the business. The record, however, may contain an additional element, namely that of *evaluation* of the physical activity' (Morgenstern 1963: 72).
9. Towards the end of his career, Hicks appears to recant his earlier views on social accounting (compare Klamer 1989).
10. 'Perhaps the most remarkable feature is Fisher's insistence that "income" is consumption, including of course consumption of the services of durable goods. In principle, he says, income is psychic, the subjective utility yielded by goods and services consumed. More practically, income could be measured as the money value, or value in some other *numeraire*, of the goods and services directly yielding utility, but only of those. Receipts saved and invested,

for example in the purchase of new durable goods, are not "income" for Fisher; they will yield consumption and utility later and those yields will be income. To include both the initial investment and the later yields as income is, according to Fisher, as absurd as to count both flour and bread in reckoning net output' (Tobin 1985: 33).

11. 'These insights contain the makings of a theory of determination of economic activity, prices, and interest rates in short and medium runs. Moreover, in his classical writings on capital and interest Fisher had laid the basis for the investment and saving equations central to modern macroeconomic models. Had Fisher pulled these strands together into a coherent theory, he could have been an American Keynes. Indeed the "neoclassical synthesis" would not have had to wait until after the second world war. Fisher would have done it all himself' (Tobin 1985: 36–7).

12. This work began in earnest only after the Second World War. The national income estimates were only transformed into *systems* of national accounts during the period 1939 to 1944 (Kendrick 1970: 306–11).

13. 'Indeed any theorist who works by ascribing motives to men and arguing what they will do under guidance of these forces will produce a mechanical type of explanation' (Mitchell 1925: 10).

14. A sophisticated discussion of the rise of the new mathematical formalisms in general equilibrium theory, under the influence of the 'Vienna Circle' and the Mathematical Symposium moderated by Karl Menger's son, is detailed in a recent work by Ingrao and Israel (1990). This also appears to be the (formalist) tack taken by the Cowles Foundation soon after the measurement without theory controversy of the late 1940s.

15. The institutionalist treatment of income as entitlements or claims on existing cash flows sought to clarify the 'juridical dimension' of property claims within the business enterprise, under the government-imposed tax structure. To paraphrase an aphorism of J.R. Commons, 'income' for the institutionalist economist was 'whatever the Supreme Court declared it to be'.

16. 'But what equations of motion and what laws of conservation of comparable scope do we have in economics? To ask the question is to answer it. There are none that have the definiteness and universal demonstrability of the corresponding physical law ... we can think of the total utility function – if it exists – as corresponding to the energy potential whose partial derivatives measure the forces which guide the movements of the individual. But unfortunately, we know neither the values nor the forms of the required functions' (Schultz 1938: 57).

17. Differential equations were created by Newton to derive Kepler's laws of planetary motion from the sun's gravitational pull (Ekeland 1988: 20).

18. Though two decades later this isomorphism between physics and economics would again become apparent (Hurwicz and Richter 1979: 14; Bordley 1983: 803–4).

19. The immediately following discussion is culled from Mirowski (1989b, Ch. 5; 1988: Ch. 1). See also (Mirowski (ed.) (1994) for further interdisciplinary work on this theme.

20. It is commonly asserted that pure competition can be traced back to Adam Smith, although this misrepresents Classical Political Economy (Dennis 1977). Within Classical Political Economy, in fact, there are two prices – the 'natural price' and 'market price'. This presents the horns of a dilemma for the neoclassical idea of a single, market-clearing price for generic commodities.

21. 'The truth is, most persons, not excepting professional economists, are satisfied with very hazy notions. How few scholars of the literary and historical type retain from their study of mechanics an adequate notion of force!' (Fisher 1926: v).

22. In the modern literature, money is sometimes 'inside' the utility function, just like any other commodity or service, yet inexplicably it is not subject to diminishing returns. Though much ink has been spilled on this issue, rarely is the discussion mooted along the lines of the energy field equations.

23. See Mirowski (1989b: Appendix) for a brief demonstration of the mathematics of energy conservation as expressed in the Hamiltonian and Lagrangean formalisms.

24. 'The calculus of variations began with the solution to a particular physical planning problem obtained by the Bernoulli brothers in the very late 1600s. (If a small object moves under the influence of gravity, what shape of path between two fixed points [A and B] enables the object to make the trip most quickly?) Other specific problems were solved and a general mathematical

theory developed over the years. Early applications to economics appeared in the late 1920s and early 1930s by Roos, Evans, Hotelling and Ramsey, with further applications published occasionally thereafter' (Kamien and Schwartz 1988: 3).

25. The fact that modern economics strains mightily to 'neutralize' money is an analytical imperative of Fisher's choice-theoretic model. In Keynes's system, however, liquidity matters and money can no more be neutral than feathers can fall at the same rate as rocks from the Leaning Tower of Pisa. The doctrinal historical record of neutral money and money illusion is discussed in Aschheim and Tavlas (1990) and Aschheim (1973; 1977). Given the above, it should come as no surprise that 'The most serious challenge that the existence of money poses to the theorist is this: the best developed model of the economy cannot find room for it' (Hahn 1983: 1).

26. Modern treatments usually bring money and the constant marginal utility of money into the analysis via arbitrary fiat.

27. Wiener states without reservation that: 'The success of mathematical physics led the social scientist to be jealous of its power without quite understanding the intellectual attitudes that had contributed to the power. The use of mathematical formulae had accompanied the development of the natural sciences and become the mode of the social sciences. ... The mathematics that the social scientists employ and the mathematical physics that they use as their model are the mathematics and the mathematical physics of 1850. ... Their quantitative theories are treated with the unquestioning respect with which the physicists of a less sophisticated age treated the concepts of Newtonian physics. Very few econometricians are aware that if they are to imitate the procedure of modern physics and not its mere appearances, [then] a mathematical economics must begin with a critical account of these quantitative notions and the means adopted for collecting and measuring them' (Wiener 1964: 89–90).

28. 'Now what *is* the economic meaning of the obscure, abstruse, deep, complex, opaque principle of integrability. It is simply this: The utility gradient must be a conservative vector field if it is subject to deterministic constrained maximization. This in turn dictates that utility must be path-independent – that is, by whatever sequence of events one arrives at a particular commodity bundle, one must always experience the identical level of utility ... this is the principle that guarantees that there is something more than a mere preference ordering being represented by a utility function ... this is the one principle that guarantees that, in principle, energy (and therefore) utility should be measurable. Why? Because conservation principles dictate that phenomenon *W* remains the "same" under transformations *A*, *B*, ..., *N* and therefore will report the same measurement under repeated examination. Precisely because it is constant under specific controlled conditions, a scale may be constructed that numerically relates changes in phenomenon *W* to changes in external conditions *X*, *Y*, *Z* such that every alteration of {*X*, *Y*, *Z*} will map into an alteration of *W*. In other words, it states that the conditions for an algebra are met by the phenomenon'(Mirowski 1989b: 370).

29. Prior to the neoclassical synthesis there were a host of production theories. Fisher had labour as negative utility, then later in life he switched to a backward imputation of the utility of final goods to their intermediate inputs. J.B. Clark had his own parable in production theory. Walras pushed the utility of final goods on to unexplained scarce endowments. Marshall's quasi-rents and Pareto's *ophelimity* were further permutations on the production theme. Keynes sought to bypass all previous theory by reconstituting the income concept. Finally, the neoclassical synthesis asserted that the field metaphor of energy applied equally well to engineering blueprints or 'production functions' and treated consumption and production symmetrically via duality theory (compare Deaton and Muellbauer 1980).

30. The conservation principle is repeatedly 'reinvented' during the twentieth century under various rubrics – the Antonelli conditions, Slutsky conditions, integrability, or the strong axiom of revealed preference – but its march to obscurity continued unabated (Mirowski 1989b: Ch. 7).

31. Only a small number of economists with training in engineering and physics could grasp Fisher's use of Gibbs's vector formalisms.

32. 'This brings us to the other requirement for such a theoretical science: the relation of a necessary connection joining the specific state of a system at one time to a unique specific state at any later time. This relation was present in Newtonian mechanics only because the

law of conservation of momentum was empirically valid in that science. Even though its concepts of momentum and position define the specificity of the present state of the system, Newtonian mechanics would be quite unable to deduce a future state, and thereby obtain a theoretical dynamics, if the total momentum of a physical system changed with time.

This conclusion can be generalized for any dynamical theory whatever. To assert that a science has a theoretical dynamics is to maintain that the principle of mechanical causation holds for it. This principle asserts that a knowledge of the present specific properties of the state of a given system enables one to deduce all future states. This presupposes that all future effects are the result of causes or properties of the elementary subject matter which are present now. Such can be the case only if the properties of the subject matter obey conservation laws.

It is to be noted that every concept entering into the definition of a state of a system in Newtonian mechanics meets this requirement. These concepts are momentum and position. The law of the conservation of the momentum guarantees this for the former; the fact that space in Newtonian mechanics has Euclidian metrical properties which are constant through time insures it for the latter. ... [A] theoretical dynamics is possible only for a subject matter which obeys conservation laws. As logicians, we must add that there is no *a priori* reason why every subject should do this. Thus it must be seriously asked whether the quest for an economic dynamics may not have its basis in a dogmatic assumption, with respect to which our empirical knowledge already gives the lie [that economic wants are not constant through time but in continual flux]' (Northrop 1941: 9,13).

33. Field is defined as a region of space characterized by a physical property (for example, gravity) having a determinable value at every point of the region.
34. The exchanges between Keynes and Ramsey concerning the consistency and rationality of individual preferences are prescient in this regard and intimate at the division between the physical and 'moral' sciences (Keynes 1972: 338–339; compare Keynes 1930).
35. The definition of 'economic rationality' is part and parcel of the image of economic man. Moreover, the paradoxes of 'rationality' run much deeper when we extend rationality to include forward-looking expectations (compare Ingrao 1989b).
36. Invariably these models are cast in instantaneous, time reversible worlds having only one commodity (Blanchard and Fischer 1989: 38–48). Deployment of the present value Hamiltonian function in these instances is mathematical overkill and somewhat disingenuous. Hamiltonians are used for integrable systems, a problem which only arises when there are three or more commodities (compare Volterra in Chipman et al. 1971). In a one-commodity world this problem is solved because it is neutralized *a priori*. Ramsey (1928: 543) did not need a Hamiltonian function because he assumed at the start of his model that 'enjoyments and sacrifices at different times can be calculated independently and added', that is, a one-commodity world.

REFERENCES

Ahonen, G. (1989), 'On the Empirical Content of Keynes's General Theory', *Ricerche Economiche*, **XLIII** (1–2): 256–68.

Alogoskoufis, G. and R. Smith (1991), 'On Error Correction Models: Specification, Interpretation, Estimation', *Journal of Economic Surveys*, **5** (1): 97–128.

Ando, A. and F. Modigliani (1963), 'The "Life Cycle" Hypothesis of Saving: Aggregate Implications and Tests', *American Economic Review*, **LIII** (1), Part 1, March: 55–84.

Arrow, K. and F. Hahn (1971), *General Competitive Analysis*, San Francisco: Holden Day.

Aschheim, J. (1973), 'Neutral Money Reconsidered', *Banca Nazionale Del Lavoro*, No. 105, June: 75–83.

Aschheim, J. (1977), 'From Money Illusion to Money Disillusion', *Banca Nazionale Del Lavoro*, No. 123, December: 319–33.

Aschheim, J. and G. Tavalas (1990), 'Revolutions and Counterrevolutions in Monetary Economics: Keynes, Keynesians, and New Classicists', *Atlantic Economic Journal*, **XVIII** (4), December: 1–13.

Bateman, B.W. (1987), 'Keynes's Changing Conception of Probability', *Economics and Philosophy*, **3**: 97–120.

Bateman, B. and J. Davis (eds) (1991), *Keynes and Philosophy*, Vermont: Elgar Publishing.

Bausor, R. (1982), 'Time and Economic Analysis', *Journal of Post Keynesian Economics*, **V** (2), Winter: 163–79.

Bausor, R. (1983), 'The Rational Expectations Hypothesis and the Epistemics of Time', *Cambridge Journal of Economics*, **7**: 1–10.

Bausor, R. (1984), 'Toward a Historically Dynamic Economics: Examples and Illustrations', *Journal of Post Keynesian Economics*, **VI** (3) Spring: 360–76.

Blanchard, O.J. and S. Fischer (1989), *Lectures on Macroeconomics*, Cambridge, MA.: MIT Press.

Bordley, R. (1983), 'Reformulating Classical and Quantum Mechanics in Terms of a Unified Set of Consistency Conditions', *International Journal of Theoretical Physics*, **22**: 803–20.

Borghese, K.J. (1993), 'Aggregate Consumption and the Economics of Keynes', Unpublished dissertation, George Washington University.

Boulding, K. and G. Stigler (eds) (1952), *AEA Readings in Price Theory*, Homewood, IL: Irwin.

Breeden, D. (1979), 'An Intertemporal Asset-Pricing Model with Stochastic Consumption and Investment Opportunities', *Journal of Financial Economics*, **7**: 265–96.

Bunting, D. (1989), 'The Consumption Function Paradox', *Journal of Post Keynesian Economics*, **XI** (3), Spring: 347–59.

Bye, R. (1940), 'An Appraisal of F.C. Mills's Behavior of Prices', New York: Social Science Research Council.

Caldwell, B. (1989), 'The Trend of Methodological Thinking', *Ricerche Economiche*, **XLIII** (1–2): 8–20.

Carabelli, A. (1988), *On Keynes's Method*, New York: St. Martin's Press.

Carabelli, A. (1991), 'The Methodology of the Critique of the Classical Theory: Keynes on Organic Interdependence', in Bateman and Davis (eds) (1991): pp. 104–25.

Carabelli, A. (1992), 'Organic Interdependence and Keynes's Choice of Units in the *General Theory*', in Bill Gerrard and John Hillard (eds), *The Philosophy and Economics of John Maynard Keynes*, Vermont: Elgar Publishing, pp. 3–31.

Caravale, G. (1987), 'The Neo-Keynesian School: Some Internal Controversies', *Atlantic Economic Journal*, **XV**, December: 1–15.

Chipman, J.S., L. Hurwicz, M.K. Richter, and H.F. Sonnenschein (1971), *Preferences, Utility, and Demand*, New York: Harcourt Brace Jovanovich.

Christensen, L., D. Jorgenson and L. Lau (1975), 'Transcendental Logarithmic Utility Functions', *American Economic Review*, **65**: 367–83.

Coddington, A. (1976), 'Keynesian Economics: The Search for First Principles', *Economic Journal*, **XIV** (4): 1258–73.

Coddington, A. (1982), 'Deficient Foresight: A Troublesome Theme in Keynesian Economics', *American Economic Review*, **72**: 480–87.

Cross, R. (1982), 'The Duhem–Quine Thesis, Lakatos and the Appraisal of Theories in Macroeconomics', *Economic Journal*, **92**: 320–40.

Crowe, M. (1967), *A History of Vector Analysis*. Notre Dame: Notre Dame Press.

Davidson, P. (1982), 'Expectations: A Fallacious Foundation for Studying Crucial Decision Making Processes', *Journal of Post Keynesian Economics*, **V** (2): 182–97.

Davidson, P. (1991), 'Is Probability Theory Relevant for Uncertainty? A Post Keynesian Perspective', *Journal of Economic Perspectives*, **5** (1), Winter: 129–44.

Deaton, A. and J. Muellbauer (1980), *Economics and Consumer Behavior*, Cambridge: Cambridge University Press.

Debreu, G. (1984), 'Economic Theory in the Mathematical Mode', *American Economic Review*, **74**: 267–78.

Debreu, G. (1991), 'The Mathematization of Economic Theory', *American Economic Review*, **81** (1): 1–7.

de Carvalho, F. (1988), 'Keynes on Probability, Uncertainty, and Decision Making', *Journal of Post Keynesian Economics*, **XI** (1), Fall: 66–81.

Dennis, K. (1977), *Competition in the History of Economic Thought*, New York: Arno.

Duesenberry, J. (1949), *Income, Saving and the Theory of Consumer Behavior*, Cambridge, MA: Harvard University Press.

Ekeland, I. (1988), *Mathematics and the Unexpected*, Chicago: University of Chicago Press.

Engle, R.F. and C.W.J. Granger (1987), 'Co-integration and Error Correction: Representation, Estimation, and Testing', *Econometrica*, **55** (2), March: 251–76.

Favero, C. and D.F. Hendry (1989), 'Testing the Lucas Critique: A Review', A.W. Philip Lecture, Australian Meeting of the Econometrics Society, December.

Fisher, I. (1906), *The Nature of Capital and Income*, New York: Macmillan.

Fisher, I. (1926), *Mathematical Investigations into the Theory of Value and Prices*, New Haven: Yale University Press.

Fisher, I. (1930), *The Theory of Interest*, New Haven: Yale University Press.

Friedman, M. (1957), *A Theory of the Consumption Function*, Princeton: NBER.

Georgescu-Roegen, N. (1971), *The Entropy Law and the Economic Process*, Cambridge, MA: Harvard University Press.

Georgescu-Roegen, N. (1976), *Energy and Economic Myths*, Elmsford, NY: Pergamon Press.

Gerrard, B. (1992), 'From *a Treatise on Probability* to the *General Theory*: Continuity or Change in Keynes's Thought?', in Bill Gerrard and John Hillard (eds), *The Philosophy and Economics of John Maynard Keynes*, Vermont: Elgar Publishing, pp. 80–95.

Gilbert, C.L. (1986a), 'The Development of British Econometrics 1945–85', Oxford Applied Economics Discussion Paper 8, Institute of Economics and Statistics.

Gilbert, C.L. (1986b), 'Professor Hendry's Econometric Methodology', *Oxford Bulletin of Economics and Statistics*, **48** (3): 283–307.

Granger, C.W.J. (1986), 'Developments in the Study of Cointegrated Variables', *Oxford Bulletin of Economics and Statistics*, **48** (3): 213–28.

Haavelmo, T. (1944), 'The Probability Approach in Economics', *Econometrica*, Supplement, **12**, July: 1–118.

Haavelmo, T. (1947), 'Methods of Measuring the Marginal Propensity to Consume', *Journal of the American Statistical Association*, **42**: 105–22.

Hacking, I. (1975), *The Emergence of Probability Theory*, New York: Cambridge University Press.

Hadjimatheou, G. (1987), *Consumer Economics after Keynes, Theory and Evidence of the Consumption Function*, Brighton, UK: Wheatsheaf Books.

Hahn, F. (1990), 'Expectations', in J.D. Hey and D. Winch (eds), *A Century of Economics*, Oxford: Basil Blackwell, pp. 232–60.

Hall, R.E. (1978), 'Stochastic Implications of the Life Cycle–Permanent Income Hypothesis: Theory and Evidence', *Journal of Political Economy*, **86** (6), December: 971–87.

Hall, R.E. (1987), 'Consumption', Working Paper 2265, NBER, May.

Hausman, D. (1989), 'Decision Theory and the Deductive Method', *Ricerche Economiche*, **XLIII** (1–2): 199–217.

Hillard, J. (1992), 'Keynes, Orthodoxy and Uncertainty', in Bill Gerrard and John Hillard (eds), *The Philosophy and Economics of John Maynard Keynes*, Vermont: Elgar Publishing, pp. 55–79.

Hoover, K. (1988), *The New Classical Macroeconomics, A Skeptical Inquiry*, Oxford: Basil Blackwell.

Hotelling, H. (1932), 'Edgeworth's Taxation Paradox and the Nature of Demand and Supply Function', *Journal of Political Economy*, **XL**, October: 577–616.

Hurwicz, L. and M. Richter (1979), 'An Integrability Condition with Applications to Utility Theory and Thermodynamics', *Journal of Mathematical Economics*, **6**: 1–14.

Ingrao, B. (1989a), 'From Walras's General Equilibrium to Hicks's Temporary Equilibrium', *Recherches Economiques de Louvain*, **55** (4): 365–98.

Ingrao, B. (1989b), 'The Hidden Epistemology of Rational Expectations and the Paradoxes of Rationality', *Ricerche Economiche*, **XLIII** (1–2): 100–28.

Ingrao, B. and G. Israel (1990), *The Invisible Hand*, Cambridge, MA: MIT Press.

Kamien, M.I. and N.L. Schwartz (1988), *Dynamic Optimization*, New York: North-Holland.

Kendrick, J. (1970), 'The Historical Development of National Income Accounts', *History of Political Economy*, **2** (2), Fall: 284–315.

Keynes, J.M. (1921), *A Treatise on Probability*, New York: Harper & Row (reprinted 1962).

Keynes, J.M. (1930), 'Obituary: F.P. Ramsey', *Economic Journal*, **XL** (157): 153–4.

Keynes, J.M. (1936), *The General Theory of Employment, Interest and Money*, New York: Harcourt, Brace & Company.

Keynes, J.M. (1937), 'The General Theory of Employment', *Quarterly Journal of Economics*, **LI** (2), February: 209–23.

Keynes, J.M. (1939), 'Professor Tinbergen's Method'. *Economic Journal*, **XLIX** (195), September: 558–68.

Keynes, J.M. (1953), *A Treatise On Money*, Vol. I, London: Macmillan & Co.

Keynes, J.M. (1972), *Essays in Biography*, Vol. X, *Collected Writings of John Maynard Keynes*, ed. by D. Moggridge, New York: St. Martin's Press.

Keynes, J.M. (1973), *The General Theory and After. Part II: Defense and Development*, Vol. XIV, *Collected Writings of John Maynard Keynes*, ed. by D. Moggridge, New York: St. Martin's Press.

Kirman, A.P. (1992), 'Whom or What Does the Representative Individual Represent?', *Journal of Economic Perspectives*, **6** (2), Spring: 117–36.

Klamer, A. (1984), *Conversations with Economists*, Totowa, NJ: Rowman & Allanheld.

Klamer, A. (1989), 'An Accountant Among Economists: Conversations With Sir John R. Hicks', *Journal of Economic Perspectives*, **3** (4), Fall: 99–118.

Klamer, A., D. McCloskey and R. Solow (1988), *The Consequences of Economic Rhetoric*, New York: Cambridge University Press.

Kmenta, J. (1971), *Elements of Econometrics*, New York: Macmillan.

Knight, F. (1965) (1921), *Risk, Uncertainty and Profit*, New York: Harper & Row.

Kotlikoff, L. (1984), 'Taxation and Saving: A Neoclassical Perspective', *Journal of Economic Literature*, **XXII** (4): 1576–629.

Kregel, J. (1980), 'On the Existence of Expectations in English Neoclassical Economics', *Journal of Economic Literature*, **15** (2), June: 495–500.

Krueger, Lorentz, Lorraine Daston and Michael Heidelberger (eds) (1987), *The Probabilistic Revolution* (Vols I & II), Cambridge, MA: MIT Press.

Kuznets, S. (1946), *National Product Since 1869*, New York: NBER.

Lawson, T. (1981), 'Keynesian Model Building and the Rational Expectations Critique', *Cambridge Journal of Economics*, **5**: 1–10.

Lawson, T. (1983), 'Different Approaches to Economic Modeling', *Cambridge Journal of Economics*, **7**: 77–84.

Lawson, T. (1988), 'Probability And Uncertainty in Economic Analysis', *Journal of Post Keynesian Economics*, **XI** (1): 38–65.

Lawson, T. (1989a), 'Realism and Instrumentalism in the Development of Econometrics', *Oxford Economic Papers*, **41** (1), January: 236–58.

Lawson, T. (1989b), 'Abstraction, Tendencies and Stylized Facts: A Realist Approach to Economic Analysis', *Cambridge Journal of Economics*, **13**: 59–78.

Lawson, T. and H. Pesaran (eds) (1985), *Keynes's Economics*, New York: M.E. Sharp.

Leijonhufvud, A. (1968), *On Keynesian Economics and the Economics of Keynes: A Study in Monetary Theory*, New York: Oxford University Press.

Maloney, J. (1985), *Marshall, Orthodoxy and the Professionalization of Economics*, Cambridge: Cambridge University Press.

Marshall, A. (1920), *Principles of Economics*, 8th edn, London: Macmillan.

McCloskey, D. (1983), 'The Rhetoric of Economics', *Journal of Economic Literature*, **XXI** (2), June: 481–517.

McCloskey, D. (1987), *The Writing of Economics*, New York: Macmillan.

McCloskey, D. (1989), 'Formalism in Economics, Rhetorically Speaking', *Ricerche Economiche*, **XLIII** (2): 57–75.

Meltzer, A.H. (1981), 'Keynes's General Theory: A Different Perspective', *Journal of Economic Literature*, **19**: 36–64.

Menard, C. (1987), 'Why Was There No Probabilistic Revolution in Economic Thought?', in Krueger et al. (eds) (1987): 139–49.

Minsky, H. (1975), *John Maynard Keynes*, New York: Columbia University Press.

Mirowski, P. (1988), *Against Mechanism*, Totowa, NJ: Rowman & Littlefield.

Mirowski, P. (1989a), 'The Probabilistic Counter-Revolution, or How Stochastic Concepts Came To Neoclassical Economic Theory', *Oxford Economic Papers*, **41** (1), January: 217–35.

Mirowski, P. (1989b), *More Heat than Light*, New York: Cambridge University Press.

Mirowski, P. (1989c), 'The Rise and Fall of the Concept of Equilibrium in Economic Analysis', *Recherches Economiques de Louvain*, **55** (4): 447–68.

Mirowski, P. (1991),'The When, the How and the Why of Mathematical Expression in Economic Analysis', *Journal of Economic Perspectives*, **5** (1), Winter: 145–58.

Mirowski, P. (1992), Book Review: 'Conservation Laws and Symmetry: Applications to Economics and Finance, Edited by Ryuzo Sato and Rama Ramachandran', *Journal of Economic Literature*, **XXX**, March: 193–4.

Mirowski, P. (ed.) (1994), *Natural Images in Economic Thought*, New York: Cambridge University Press.

Mitchell, W. (1925), 'Presidential Address', *American Economic Review*, **XV** (1), March: 1–12.

Morgan, M. (1987), 'Statistics without Probability and Haavelmo's Revolution in Econometrics', in Krueger et al. (eds) (1987): 171–200.

Morgenstern, O. (1963), *On the Accuracy of Economic Observations*, 2nd edn, Princeton, NJ: Princeton University Press.

Nickell, S. (1985), 'Error Correction, Partial Adjustment And All That: An Expository Note', *Oxford Bulletin of Economics and Statistics*, **47** (2): 119–29.

Northrop, F.S.C. (1941), 'The Impossibility of a Theoretical Science of Economic Dynamics', *Quarterly Journal of Economics*, **LVI** (1), May: 1–17.

Pagan, A.R. (1987), 'Three Econometric Methodologies: A Critical Appraisal', *Journal of Economic Surveys*, **1**: 3–24.

Pagan, A.R. and M.R. Wickens (1989), 'A Survey of Some Recent Econometric Methods', *Economic Journal*, **99**, December: 962–1025.

Pareto, V. (1953), 'On the Economic Phenomenon', *International Economic Papers*, No. 3.

Parker, R.H., G.C. Harcourt and G. Whittington (eds) (1986), *Readings in the Concept and Measurement of Income*, 2nd edn, Oxford: Philip Allan.

Patinkin, D. (1991), 'On Different Interpretations of the *General Theory*', *Journal of Monetary Economics*, **26**: 205–43.

Pribram, K. (1953), 'Patterns of Economic Reasoning', *American Economic Review, Papers and Proceedings*, **XLIII** (2): 243–58.

Ramsey, F.P. (1928), 'A Mathematical Theory of Savings', *Economic Journal*, **XXXVIII** (152): 543–59.

Ramsey, F.P. (1931), 'Truth and Probability', in *The Foundations of Mathematics and Other Logical Essays*, London: Paul, Trench & Trubner.

Ramsey, F.P. (1978), *Foundations: Essays in Philosophy, Logic, Mathematics, and Economics*, ed. by D.H. Mellor, London: Routledge & Kegan Paul.

Robinson, J. (1973), *Economic Heresies*, New York: Basic Books.

Roth, T.P. (1989), *The Present State of Consumer Theory*, Lanham, MD: University Press of America.

Rotheim, R. (1988), 'Keynes and the Language of Probability and Uncertainty', *Journal of Post Keynesian Economics*, **XI** (1), Fall: 82–99.

Rotheim, R. (1992), 'Interdependence and the Cambridge Economic Tradition', in Bill Gerrard and John Hillard (eds), *The Philosophy and Economics of John Maynard Keynes*, Vermont: Elgar Publishing, pp. 32–58.

Samuelson, P. (1972), 'Maximum Principles in Analytical Economics', *American Economic Review,* **62**: 249–62.

Schoemaker, P.J.H. (1982), 'The Expected Utility Model: Its Variants, Purposes, Evidence and Limitations', *Journal of Economic Literature*, **XX**, June: 529–63.

Schultz, H. (1931), 'Review of G.C. Evans' Mathematical Introduction to Economics', *Journal of the American Statistical Association*, **26**: 484–91.

Schultz, H. (1938), *The Theory and Measurement of Demand*, Chicago: University of Chicago Press.

Sebba, G. (1953), 'The Development of the Concepts of Mechanism and Model in Physical Science and Economic Thought', *American Economic Review, Papers and Proceedings*, **XLIII** (2), May: 259–68.

Sen, A. (1973), 'Behavior and the Concept of Preferences', *Economica*, **40**: 241–59.

Smale, S. (1976), 'Dynamics in General Equilibrium Theory', *American Economic Review,* **66**: 288–94.

Solow, R. (1985), 'Economic History and Economics', *American Economic Review, Papers and Proceedings*, **75**: 328–31.

Spanos, A. (1986), *Statistical Foundations of Econometric Modeling*, Cambridge: Cambridge University Press.

Spanos, A. (1989), 'Early Empirical Findings on the Consumption Function, Stylized Facts or Fiction: A Retrospective View', *Oxford Economic Papers*, **41** (1), January: 150–69.

Stigler, S. (1986), *The History of Statistics*, Cambridge, MA: Harvard University Press.

Stone, R. (1954), 'Linear Expenditure Systems and Demand Analysis: An Application to the Pattern of British Demand', *Economic Journal*, September: 511–27.

Strotz, R.H. (1953), 'Cardinal Utility', *American Economic Review, Papers and Proceedings*, **XLII** (2), May: 284–97.

Swamy, P.A.V.P., P. von zur Muehlen and J.S. Mehta (1989), 'Co-integration: Is It a Property of the Real World?', *Federal Reserve Board, Finance and Economics Discussion Series*, No. 96, November.

Tew, B. (1953), 'Keynesian Accountancy', *Yorkshire Bulletin of Economic and Social Research*, **5** (2), August: 147–54.

Theil, H. (1954), *Linear Aggregation of Economic Relations*, Amsterdam: North-Holland.

Thomas, J. (1989), 'The Early Econometric History of the Consumption Function', *Oxford Economic Papers*, **41** (1), January: 131–49.

Tobin, J. (1951), 'Relative Income, Absolute Income and Saving', in *Money, Trade, and Economic Growth: Essays in Honor of John H. Williams*, New York: Macmillan, pp. 135–56.

Tobin, J. (1985), 'Neoclassical Theory in America: J.B. Clark and Fisher', *American Economic Review*, December: 28–38.

Tversky, A., P. Slovic and D. Kahneman (1990), 'The Causes of Preference Reversal', *American Economic Review*, March: 204–17.

Tversky, A. and R.H. Thaler (1990), 'Anomalies: Preference Reversals', *Journal of Economic Perspectives*, **4** (2), Spring: 201–12.

Varian, H. (1991), Book Review: '*More Heat than Light* by Phillip Mirowski', *Journal of Economic Literature*, **XXIX** (2), June: 595–6.

Viner, J. (1925), 'The Utility Concept and Its Critics', *Journal of Political Economy*, **33** (4), August: 638–59.

Walker, D.A. (1987), 'Walras's Theory of Tâtonnement', *Journal of Political Economy*, **95** (4): 758–74.

Weintraub, E.R. (1979), *Microfoundations: The Compatibility of Microeconomics and Macroeconomics*, Cambridge Surveys of Economic Literature, Cambridge: Cambridge University Press.

Weintraub, E.R. (1983), 'On the Existence of a Competitive Equilibrium: 1930–1954', *Journal of Economic Literature*, **XXI**, March: 1–39.

Wiener, N. (1964), *God and Golem Inc.*, Cambridge, MA: MIT Press.

Winjum, J. (1972), 'The Role of Accounting in the Economic Development of England 1500–1750', Champaign, IL: CIERA.

Wong, S. (1973), 'The F-Twist and the Methodology of Paul Samuelson', *American Economic Review*, June: 312–25.

Wong, S. (1978), *The Foundations of Paul Samuelson's Revealed Preference Theory*, Boston: Routledge & Kegan Paul.

2. Fictional basis of modern macroeconomics

David Bunting

1 INTRODUCTION

Consumption accounts for about 70 per cent of national income while its symmetrical opposite, personal savings, largely determines income growth. Because of this importance, theories of aggregate consumption are a fundamental component of macroeconomic theory. Modern consumption theories can be traced from early efforts to verify Keynes's (1936) conjectures regarding the determinants of aggregate consumption which found that time-series and cross-sectional data produced different estimates of spending behaviour. Perceived as a flaw in the Keynesian formulation, this inconsistency quickly became known as the consumption function 'paradox' or 'puzzle' (Thomas 1989). In the late 1940s and early 1950s, Modigliani and Brumberg (1954) and Friedman (1957) developed two fictions which seemed to resolve the problem. First, the conflicting studies were treated as if they represented the behaviour of a single person rather than cross-sections of households and aggregations of economies, all of which might have differing behavioural and demographic characteristics. This 'representative person' fiction clearly established the consumption function puzzle because obviously the same person could not have different marginal propensities at the same time. Second, a fictional lifetime or permanent income was developed to explain spending behaviour. This 'permanent income' fiction allowed easy dismissal of the cross-sectional studies as defective. Since consumption depends on permanent income, cross-sectional studies, all of which utilized current income, simply used the wrong income to measure the consumption relationship. Together the fictions of representative behaviour and permanent income provided a neat, clear resolution of the consumption function puzzle.

The fictions also appealed to researchers indoctrinated in neoclassical rather than Keynesian economics because they directly linked macroeconomic spending behaviour to the microeconomic theory of consumer choice. This fundamentally altered the idea of aggregate consumption by shifting it from an intratemporal to an intertemporal activity. Keynes (1936: 96) initially observed that the pattern of aggregate consumption suggested the marginal utility of consumption declined as income increased:

> The fundamental psychological law, upon which we are entitled to depend with great confidence both *a priori* from our knowledge of human nature and from the detailed facts of experience, is that men are disposed, as a rule and on average, to increase their consumption as their income increases, but not by as much as the increase in their income.

While unbounded in time, the Keynes view essentially focused on a point where aggregate consumption simply summarized many different consumption decisions produced by many different incomes. On the other hand, the neoclassical view (Scarth 1988) involved an important shift in time perspective. Rather than maximizing current utility, consumption was an intertemporal activity in which households sought to maximize lifetime utility, subject to the constraint that the present value of lifetime consumption equalled the present value of lifetime income.

By shifting the time perspective, the neoclassical view never actually resolved the consumption function puzzle. Instead, it took the problem 'Why does the marginal propensity to consume estimated with time-series data differ from that estimated with cross-sectional data?' and substituted another, 'How can the marginal propensity to consume differ between the short and long run?'. This was accomplished through two fictions. Representative behaviour reduced the problem from an aggregate to an individual basis while the concept of permanent income redirected attention from short-run to long-run spending behaviour.

2   DIFFERENT MARGINAL PROPENSITIES

Instead of utilizing a representative household to describe aggregate spending behaviour, consider the behaviour of all m households. In any year t, the spending and income of these households can be used to estimate a cross-sectional consumption function,

$$c_{ti} = a + by_{ti},\qquad(2.1)$$

while total household spending and income constitutes aggregate consumption and aggregate income,

$$\Sigma c_{ti} = C_t \text{ and } \Sigma y_{ti} = Y_t.\qquad(2.2)$$

These same sort of calculations and definitions can be repeated all the n years that constitute the long run to produce Table 2.1. In any year, the aggregate measures simply summarize household consumption and income. These measures are not influenced by any sort of cross-sectional spending behaviour because the marginal propensity (b) indicates functional dependency rather than the size. For example, the coefficient could be zero or negative but this will not affect the size of either aggregate consumption or income.

Table 2.1   Cross-sectional and times-series relationships

Year	Cross-sectional consumption function	Aggregate consumption	Aggregate income
1	$c_{1i} = a_1 + b_1 y_{1i}$	$\sum c_{1i} = C_1$	$\sum y_{1i} = Y_1$
2	$c_{2i} = a_2 + b_2 y_{2i}$	$\sum c_{2i} = C_2$	$\sum y_{2i} = Y_2$
.	.	.	.
.	.	.	.
.		.	.
n	$c_{ni} = a_n + b_n y_{ni}$	$\sum c_{ni} = C_n$	$\sum y_{ni} = Y_n$

The time-series marginal propensity is found by regressing aggregate consumption (C_t) on aggregate income (Y_t), using n years of cross-sectional spending. This produces the familiar aggregate consumption function without a significant intercept:

$$C_t = \beta Y_t. \tag{2.3}$$

While the time-series marginal propensity is consistent with any cross-sectional value, the consumption function puzzle involved determining why the propensities differed. This can be answered by finding the conditions when they are equal, that is when

$$b = \beta. \tag{2.4}$$

The cross-sectional marginal propensity is a regression coefficient while the time-series one equals the aggregate average propensity to consume:

$$\frac{\operatorname{cov}(c_{ti}, y_{ti})}{\operatorname{var}(y_{ti})} = \frac{C_t}{Y_t}. \tag{2.5}$$

It is important to note that household consumption or income is also a weighted average of aggregate consumption or income. That is, with $c_{ti} = w_i C_t$ and $\Sigma w_i = 1$,

$$C_t = \Sigma c_{ti} = c_{t1} + \dots + c_{tm} = w_1 C_t + \dots + w_m C_t. \tag{2.6}$$

By similar substitution for income with $y_{ti} = v_i Y_t$ and $\Sigma v_i = 1$,

$$Y_t = \Sigma y_{ti} = y_{t1} + \dots + y_{tm} = v_1 Y_t + \dots + v_m Y_t. \tag{2.7}$$

The weights w_i and v_i represent the relative household shares of consumption and income, respectively.

Substituting for c_{ti} and y_{ti}, the regression equation for the cross-sectional marginal propensity becomes:

$$\frac{C_t}{Y_t} \frac{\text{cov}(w_i, v_i)}{\text{var}(v_i)} = \frac{C_t}{Y_t}. \tag{2.8}$$

The cross-sectional and time-series marginal propensities to consume will be equal when the regression coefficient of relative household consumption on relative household income equals one,

$$\frac{\text{cov}(w_i, v_i)}{\text{var}(v_i)} = 1. \tag{2.9}$$

This condition implies $v_i = w_i$, that the relative share of consumption for every household equals its relative share of income. This is equivalent to assuming the time-series condition, that the aggregate average propensity to consume is constant. This behaviour has never been found in studies of household spending (Friedman 1957; Bunting 1991). Instead, a pattern consistent with the original speculations of Keynes (1936: 97) has always been found: low-income households spend more than they earn, middle-income ones spend about what they earn and high-income ones spend less than they earn.

The difference between the time-series marginal propensity to consume and the cross-sectional propensity is exactly explained by relative distribution of income and consumption. This resolution was not encountered by researchers who adopted the fiction of representative spending behaviour. Since representative models focused only on the behaviour of a single household, questions concerning distributional influences and relative shares were meaningless and were never considered.

3   INCOME SHARE ELASTICITY

With ungrouped data, the coefficient from regressing the share of consumption on the share of income is also an elasticity showing the relative change in consumption share from a relative change in income share. This share elasticity, in this case, an income share elasticity, equal to

$$e_s = \frac{\text{cov}(w_i, v_i)}{\text{var}(v_i)},\qquad(2.10)$$

simplifies the relationship between the cross-sectional and time-series marginal propensities to

$$b = \beta e_s \qquad(2.11)$$

The share elasticity has a number of important implications. Because it is generally not unity, it indicates that cross-sectional and times-series estimates of the same behaviour will always produce different coefficients. This not only provides a complete explanation for some puzzling empirical results but also identifies distributional rather than behavioural influences as the cause of the differences. The share elasticity shows that cross-sectional and time-series coefficients are related in an exact mathematical sense rather than in some vague conjectural way. Cross-sectional data can be used to exactly calculate time-series coefficients but the reverse is not possible because the time-series data does not permit separation of behavioural and distributional influences.

These conclusions can be illustrated using cross-sectional income and expenditure data from the 1992 *Consumer Expenditure Survey* (BLS 1995), organized by income quintile. The statistics of interest are the marginal propensity, average propensity (*apc*) and share elasticity, respectively, $b = 0.54272$, $apc = 0.89178$, and $e_s = 0.60858$. As expected, the cross-sectional average and marginal propensities are not equal but the difference is explained by the tendency of households with different shares of income to have different shares of consumption. This explanation is exact, $0.89178 \times 0.60858 = 0.54272$, as well as complete since it is derived from data itself rather than from other sources or hypothesized. The cross-sectional average propensity is also equal to both the time-series average and marginal propensities, $apc = APC = \beta$. These time-series values can be directly calculated from the cross-sectional statistics because $apc = b/e_s$. However, the cross-sectional marginal propensity cannot be derived from the time-series statistics without knowledge of the cross-sectional share elasticity. In effect, this exact correspondence of different marginal propensities indicates that cross-sectional and time-series data simply provide different perspectives on the same macroeconomic behaviour.

4 REPRESENTATIVE BEHAVIOUR

The idea of representative behaviour can be traced back to Marshall (1920, 1959: 265) who devised a representative firm to show the determination of the supply price for a commodity. What the representative firm actually represented caused Marshall some problems. It 'is in a sense an average firm. But there are many ways in which the term "average" might be interpreted. ... a Representative firm is that particular sort of average firm. ... We cannot see this by looking at one or two firms taken at random: but we can see it fairly well by selecting, after a broad survey, a firm ... that represents, to the best of our judgment, this particular average'.

This imprecision provoked a caustic review by Robbins (1928: 387) who concluded that the representative firm is a 'pale vistant from the world of the unborn waiting in vain for the comforts of complete tangibility'. It is superfluous, a 'clumsy and unnecessary expedient, and one which may give rise to false ideas of the ultimate processes of causation involved' (396). 'There is no more need for us to assume a representative firm or representative producer, than there is for us to assume a representative piece of land, a representative machine, or a representative worker' (393). Later, in response to efforts to revive the concept, Davis (1955: 711) wondered if the firm represented a business organization or plant. What does it represent in oligopoly? Does it have a representative entrepreneur? 'Are we to imagine a representative Board of Directors? a Representative Financier? a Representative Sales Manager? a Representative Engineer, etc.? ... It is equally useless under modern conditions'. Despite these comments, Carter (1963) later proposed a 'representative farm' but the notion failed to attract a following.

In a broad, interesting review with detailed references to both economic and econometric thought, van Daal and Merkies (1988) trace the use of 'representativity' (as does one so do all) in macroeconomics back to Hicks (1939: 245) who sought to reduce complexity: 'the behaviour of a group of individuals, or group of firms, obeys the same laws as the behaviour of a single unit'. They ask 'how came economists to reasoning by analogy?' (van Daal and Merkies 1988: 626). While convenience, tastes, necessity and similarity seem to be major reasons, the tactic has inherent limitations. If 'the macro model can be considered as the result of consistent aggregation of micro models over individuals then ... the additional requirement of some kind of representativity is superfluous. It can even be argued that ... representativity is harmful in the sense that a false impression is raised about the individuals' behavior from macro data only' (ibid.: 631). On the other hand, if representative behaviour is introduced at the aggregate level as typical behaviour, then 'there remains a need for showing that this "representative behavior" is consistent with actual individual behavior. To charge simply the "representative" with some particular behavior, only helps in the sense that it shows that there is at least one possibility, viz. that where there is only one individual, with the indicated behavior' (ibid: 632).

Coefficients estimated as representative coefficients present similar problems in explication. Macroeconomic coefficients are weighted averages, reflecting household behaviour weighted by a relative share of the explanatory variable. For example, under the permanent income hypothesis, Friedman (1957: 119–24) argued that permanent consumption was a constant fraction of permanent income:

$$C_p = kY_p. \tag{2.12}$$

As an aggregate relationship, aggregate permanent consumption and income simply summarize household permanent consumption and income:

$$C_p = \sum c_{pi} = c_{p1} + \ldots + c_{pm}$$

and

$$Y_p = \sum y_{pi} = y_{p1} + \ldots + y_{pm}.$$

Each household has its own consumption function

$$c_{pi} = k_i y_{pi}.$$

After substitution, noting that a household's relative share of aggregate permanent income is $y_{pi} = z_i Y_p$ with $\sum z_i = 1$, aggregate permanent consumption becomes a weighted average of household permanent income:

$$
\begin{aligned}
C_p &= c_{p1} + \ldots + c_{pm} \\
&= k_1 y_{p1} + \ldots + k_m y_{pm} \\
&= [\sum(k_i z_i)] Y_p. \tag{2.13}
\end{aligned}
$$

Since there are no restrictions on the household constants (k_i), Friedman's measure of permanent consumption is a weighted average, for example, $k = \sum(k_i z_i)$, whose value does not depend on any particular type of household behaviour. That is, some households could permanently spend more than their incomes, others permanently spend about their incomes and still others permanently spend less than their incomes. The extent these types of permanent behaviour are represented by the representative coefficient depends entirely on their relative share of permanent income.

Table 2.2   Average consumption and income, quintile shares

Quintile	c ($)	y($)	w	v
1	12,354	5,841	0.09008	0.03798
2	18,421	14,115	0.13432	0.09178
3	24,509	23,399	0.17871	0.15215
4	32,157	36,957	0.23447	0.24031
5	49,706	73,479	0.36243	0.47778
Average/total	27,429	30,758	1.00000	1.00000

Source: 1992 Consumer Expenditure Survey (BLS 1995).

Table 2.2 shows that households spending less than their income account for 72 per cent of total income, those spending about their income account for 15 per cent, and those spending more account for 13 per cent, a distribution consistent with cross-sectional tabulations for other years (Bunting 1994). The aggregate measure of permanent consumption, which Friedman approximates as the long-run marginal propensity, will reflect this weighting. However, the permanent coefficient does not represent 'average' household behaviour because the spending of 40 per cent of the households receives a weight of only 13 per cent while the spending of another 40 per cent of households receives a weight of 72 per cent. In effect, Friedman's measure of permanent consumption (as well as Keynes's measure of aggregate consumption) represents the spending behaviour of the rich rather than the common.

A second example illustrating the difficulty of interpreting aggregate coefficients as representative behaviour involves efforts to explain the recent decline in the aggregate saving rate. Bernheim (1991) reviews many explanations, ultimately laying blame with psychological/attitudinal rather than economic factors. Like all other aggregate coefficients, the aggregate saving rate is a weighted average, $S_t = sY_t = [\Sigma s_i v_i]Y_t$, where s_i and v_i represent household saving rates and income shares, respectively. Table 2.3 shows quintile saving and income shares from the 1992 Consumer Expenditure Survey (BLS 1995). Since the lowest three income quintiles have negative savings, their share of savings is negative; however, this is more than offset by the positive savings of the highest quintile. These differences in quintile savings behaviour, perhaps best indicated by the income share elasticity of savings of 4.23, strongly suggest that economic circumstances rather than psychological/attitudinal factors have caused the decline in the aggregate saving rate. However, these differences are meaningless when aggregate trends are explained by the behaviour of a single representative saver.

Table 2.3   Average savings and income, quintile shares

Quintile	$s(\$)$	$y(\$)$	u	v
1	–6,513	5,841	–0.39131	0.03798
2	–4,306	14,115	–0.25871	0.09178
3	–1,110	23,399	–0.06669	0.15215
4	4,800	36,957	0.28839	0.24031
5	23,773	73,479	1.42832	0.47778
Average/total	3,329	30,758	1.00000	1.00000

Source: 1992 Consumer Expenditure Survey (BLS 1995).

These two examples clearly indicate that aggregate coefficients are consistent with nearly any type of household behaviour. Neither the consumption coefficient of permanent income nor the aggregate saving rate approximate the behaviour of most households. Instead, these coefficients are income weighted averages, disproportionately representing the behaviour of high-income households. This conclusion has an important implication for macroeconomic policy in that aggregate coefficients will be poor predictors of potential economic effects unless the proceeds from particular policies follow the prevailing pattern of distribution. For example, tax reductions and saving incentives might increase the saving rate of high-income households, but they will have little effect on the saving behaviour of low-income households. Conversely, income changes will effect first quintile spending much more than fifth quintile spending. Overall, the effects of macroeconomic policies are determined by the relative influence of the weights constituting the aggregate coefficients rather than by the coefficients themselves. For this reason, the representative model offers little guidance into designing successful macroeconomic policies.

5   MODERN MACROECONOMICS

Researchers oriented towards neoclassical economics commonly allege that the fundamental difference between modern macroeconomics and its main alternative, Keynesian economics, is that the modern variant is derived from 'the rigorous implications of microeconomics' (Kotlikoff 1992: viii). In particular, this approach assumes 'that people make consumption and saving decisions rationally, which means, among other things, that they fully consider their future incomes as well as their current incomes in making these decisions' (ibid. 31–3). On the other hand, as the argument goes, the Keynesian view simply ignores the future and assumes 'that households partly or fully ignore their future incomes in making their current consumption decisions'. These households 'are either so extremely myopic or so highly cash-constrained that their consumption decisions are based only on their immediate cash-flow, namely, their immediate disposable incomes'. While theoretical rigour and intellectual origins might have some academic importance, the actual difference between the protagonists depends on the acceptance of representative behaviour and, to a lesser degree, permanent income.

In macroeconomics, distinctions between types of household spending behaviour are irrelevant. Since macroeconomic variables simply summarize individual activity, they are consistent with any kind of microeconomic behaviour. Households could be forward looking, myopic or backward looking; their spending coefficients could be positive or negative, large or small. Any or all of this behaviour, alleged or actual, does not matter because it has no effect on the magnitude of the aggregate variables.

On the other hand, the fiction of representative behaviour, by effectively eliminating any distinction between microeconomic and macroeconomic behaviour, permits neoclassical techniques to be applied to aggregative problems. Unfortunately, this fiction along with that of permanent income which has more motivational than practical consequences, has caused great confusion and misdirected research. Whenever the appropriate share elasticities are not unity, coefficients of relationships estimated with cross-sectional or microeconomic data will differ from those estimated with macroeconomic data. These differences have caused researchers using representative models but unaware of the possibility of distributional effects to search for explanations, usually by developing more elaborate models and econometric tests. As a result, modern macroeconomics evolved away from its Keynesian origins and towards a highly stylized, essentially neoclassical microeconomic description of aggregate activity.

Calculation of appropriate share elasticities provides an alternative explanation for differences in microeconomic and macroeconomic behaviour which is both simple and exact. These elasticities provide a means to directly calculate macroeconomic coefficients from microeconomic data. Representative behaviour and permanent income were fictions developed so that microeconomic techniques could be used to analyse macroeconomic behaviour. Because coefficients describing macroeconomic behaviour now can be directly derived from microeconomic coefficients and appropriate share elasticities, these fictions can be discarded, thereby permitting modern macroeconomic to be reconstituted on a factual basis.

REFERENCES

Bernheim, B.D. (1991). *The Vanishing Nest Egg: Reflections on Saving in America*, Twentieth Century Fund Paper. New York, NY: Priority Press Publications.

Bunting, D. (1991), 'Savings and the Distribution of Income', *Journal of Post Keynesian Economics*, **14**: 3–22.

Bunting, D. (1994). 'Aggregate and Household Behavior: Poverty and Savings', in P. Davidson and J.A. Kregel (eds), *Employment, Growth and Finance*, Aldershot, Hants, UK: Edward Elgar Publishing: pp. 34–46.

Carter, H.O. (1963), 'Representative Farms: Guides for Decision Making?', *Journal of Farm Economics*, **45**: 1448–57.

Davis, J.H. (1955), 'The Industry and the Representative Firm', *Economic Journal*, **65**: 712–14.

Friedman, M. (1957), *A Theory of the Consumption Function*, Princeton, NJ: Princeton University Press.

Hicks, J.R. (1939), *Value and Capital*, Oxford: Clarendon Press.

Keynes, J.M. (1936), *The General Theory of Employment, Interest and Money*, New York: Harcourt, Brace & World, Inc.

Kotlikoff, L.J. (1992), *Generational Accounting*, New York: The Free Press.

Marshall, A. (1920, 1959), *Principles of Economics*, 8th edn, London: Macmillan & Sons.

Modigliani, F. (1986), 'Life Cycle, Individual Thrift, and the Wealth of Nations', *American Economic Review*, **76**: 297–313.

Modigliani, F. and R.E. Brumberg (1954), 'Utility Analysis and the Consumption Function', in K.K. Kurihara (ed.), *Post Keynesian Economics*, New Brunswick, NJ: Rutgers University Press, pp. 388–436.

Robbins, L. (1928), 'The Representative Firm', *Economic Journal*, **38**: 387–404.

Scarth, W.M. (1988), *Macroeconomics: An Introduction to Advanced Methods*, Toronto: Harcourt, Brace Jovanovich.

Thomas, J. (1989), 'The Early Empirical Studies of the Consumption Function', in N. de Marchi and C. Gilbert (eds), *History and Methodology of Econometrics*, New York: Oxford University Press: 131–49.

US Bureau of Labor Statistics (BLS) (1995), *Consumer Expenditure Survey: 1992–93*, Bulletin 2462, Washington, DC.

van Daal, J. and A.H.Q.M. Merkies (1988), 'The Problem of Aggregation of Individual Economic Relations; Consistency and Representativity in a Historical Perspective', in W. Eichorn (ed.), *Measurement in Economics*, New York: Springer-Verlag: 607–37.

B.   Investment

3. A direct test of Keynes's theory of investment: assessing the role of profit expectations and weight*

**Michael A. Anderson and
Arthur H. Goldsmith**

1 INTRODUCTION

J.M. Keynes differed from economists of his era, and from many who would follow, in the emphasis he placed on the role of expectations in the determination of investment. Early views of investment saw the level of the capital stock adjusting due to a difference between the current level of capital and some target value. Modern neoclassical theories emphasize that entrepreneurs calculate an optimal capital stock that will maximize the present value of the firm. Investment, then, is simply the path to this optimal level.[1]

The conventional view of Keynes's theory of investment is that additions to the stock of plant and equipment depend on both the interest rate and the marginal efficiency of investment (MEI).[2] The firm commits resources to all projects in which the forecast return, given by the MEI, exceeds the interest rate. The key to Keynes's theory, however, is his emphasis on the problem inherent in the calculation of the MEI. Since this value requires firms to forecast returns in future time periods, the level of investment will fall or rise with the perceived profitability from future business activity. And since expectations of future profitability are volatile, we can expect investment to also follow a volatile time path.

Keynes also believed that the degree of confidence that managers place in their forecasts influences capital expenditures. If forecasts are deemed reliable by the decision maker, then they will be more inclined to base investment decisions on their forecasts. Although this determinant of investment may be quite important it has been largely neglected in the theoretical literature on Keynes's theory of investment and is yet to be subject to empirical evaluation.[3]

Researchers' attempts to test Keynes's theory have all been plagued by the absence of any direct measure of entrepreneurs' expectation of future profits. Harrod (1936), a contemporary of Keynes, used recent variations in product demand to explain the variation in investment. Later investigators used either lagged values of past demand or profits.[4] Measuring profit expectations in this manner is problematic. Demand in previous periods depends on product prices, prices of complements and substitutes, tastes and macroeconomic conditions, which may be vastly different in the future. Similarly, prior profits depend on past equilibrium outcomes in various input and product markets. Future developments may alter demand and profit outcomes significantly, and researchers should expect profit-maximizing managers to form forward-looking expectations, rather than relying solely on the values of any past parameters.[5]

Unfortunately, while economists now readily admit to the problems in these adaptive approaches to modelling expectations, lack of data has permitted few alternatives. One popular technique has been to use Granger-causality tests.[6] Another approach has been to estimate a reduced-form structural model of investment.[7] While the debate has been lively, with different models producing different explanations of investment, they all suffer from having to use the values of past performance parameters, and hence fail as a test of Keynes's proposition. Lastly, lacking any direct measure of profit expectations, researchers have been inherently unable to test Keynes's proposition that the weight assigned to a profit expectation will also influence investment. As such, there has been no empirical test of this proposition.

The purpose of this chapter is twofold. The first is to use recently available data that directly measures business managers' expectation of future profits to examine Keynes's notion that investment is influenced by profit expectations. The second is to construct a measure of the confidence decision makers assign to their profits forecasts to test whether weakly-held forecasts have a different effect on investment than do more strongly-held convictions. The unique contribution of this chapter, then, is our use of forward-looking data on profit expectations and a measure of confidence. This eliminates two shortcomings in the literature on Keynes's theory of investment.

While this chapter is valuable as an empirical test of Keynes's theory of capital formation, it is also consistent with current theories of investment that are not explicitly based upon Keynes or other specific macroeconomic schools of thought. Pindyck (1991) argues that because investment expenditures are largely irreversible, firms structure investment projects so that if managers' expectations change, the pace of investment projects may be delayed or postponed.[8] Indeed, Pindyck suggests that 'changing economic conditions that affect the perceived riskiness of future cash flows can have a large impact on investment spending, larger than, say, a change in the interest rate' (Pindyk 1991: 1112). Thus, while our chapter is of interest for its test of Keynes's theory, it can be viewed more broadly as a test of those theories that suggest that expectations matter in the determination of investment.

2   MR KEYNES AND HIS THEORY OF INVESTMENT

Keynes viewed investment as being determined by the MEI, and the rate of interest. The MEI is, in fact, a present discounted value of an expected stream of returns derived from the investment project. Thus investment is governed by the MEI and the MEI is governed by expectations. Indeed, Keynes stated explicitly that long-term expectations are 'concerned with what the entrepreneur can hope to earn in the shape of future returns if he purchases (or, perhaps, manufactures) "finished" output as an addition to his capital equipment' (Keynes 1936: 47). Thus investment is driven by perceptions of future profitability. Hart (1950), echoing Keynes, described it this way: 'the driving force of the economy lies in the future, but the future as visualized in the present' (Hart 1950: 415).

Since investment is founded on expectations of future profitability, Keynes saw the business cycle as largely the outcome of fluctuations in these expectations.

> Now, we have been accustomed in explaining the 'crisis' to lay stress on the rising tendency of the rate of interest under the influence of the increased demand for money both for trade and speculative purposes. At times this factor may certainly play an aggravating, and, occasionally perhaps an initiating part. But I suggest that a more typical, and often the predominant, explanation of the crisis is, not primarily a rise in the rate of interest, but a sudden collapse in the marginal efficiency of capital. (Keynes 1964: 315)

While Keynes focused on the role of expectations in the determination of the MEI, he was also concerned with another determinant of investment. According to Keynes, the degree of confidence decision makers hold regarding their forecasts mattered as well. The forecasters may lack the confidence to act upon their expectation of future profits if they attach little 'weight' to their predictions. To Keynes, weight captured the notion of confidence by accounting for the amount and quality of information that went into that prediction.[9] As a result, a greater weight is assigned to propositions derived with superior information. Conversely, low-quality information leads to a low weight, which could lead to a delay or cancellation of an investment project despite a favourable profits forecast.[10] Consider the following observation in *The General Theory*:

> The state of long-term expectation, upon which our decisions are based, does not solely depend, therefore, on the most probable forecast we can make. It also depends on the *confidence* with which we make this forecast – on how highly we rate the likelihood of our best forecast turning out quite wrong ... (Keynes 1936: 148, emphasis added)

Thus, *ceteris paribus*, a manager is more likely to invest when he or she expects a greater stream of returns from a contemplated capital formation project. But a manager will be less likely to invest, for any given forecast of profitability, the lower the weight assigned to that forecast.

3 THE DATA

In 1976, the Conference Board began collecting quarterly data on business executives' expectations. In this series, executives were asked two questions. First, what are your 'expectations for your own industry six months ahead?'. Second, what is your evaluation of 'current conditions in your own industry versus six months ago?'. In each case executives used a 100 point scale in which 50 means no change. Thus, if an executive answered 55 to the first question, he or she means that his or her industry will improve over the next six months.

We assume that when executives are asked about 'expectations for your own industry' that they answer given a goal of long-run profit maximization. Thus we interpret the first question to measure the expected level of profits six months from now in the industry compared to the present. We interpret the second question to measure today's profits relative to six months ago.

The survey is administered to the same 125 corporate executives in each of 25 two-digit standard industrial codes (SIC) industries. Responses are anonymous and only industry averages for those responding are reported. Thus this data provides a direct measure of business expected profitability and can be used to construct a measure of the accuracy of their forecasts. Use of this data will allow a test of Keynes's entire theory of investment, including both the role of expectations and the role of forecast weight. The principal advantage of this data base is that expectations of future profits, used to calculate the MEI, are measured directly. Past studies were forced to rely on proxy variables for profit expectations (such as changes in past output or profits). Surprisingly, these unique data have yet to be used to study investment.[11]

In addition to forcing an assumption on the interpretation of what 'expectations in own industry' means, the other principal issue is that the data are not necessarily derived from a matched sample. While the same 125 executives in each industry were polled each quarter, the subset that responded may have changed quarter to quarter.[12] As a result, the average response reported could be affected by the characteristics of the subset of executives that answered the survey in that particular time period. This selection bias problem will be small if there is little change in the subset that responded and if those executives responding are not systematically different in their views from the industry population.

Quarterly data on gross investment expenditures come from Citibase. The investment data combine plant and equipment expenditures in 1982 dollars.[13] The Citibase data, like the Conference Board data, are classified by two-digit

SIC. Because the Conference Board combined several two-digit industries, we were able to match only fourteen industries using both data series.

4 MODEL SPECIFICATION

To test Keynes's theory of investment, we specify a model in which investment is determined by expected profits in the industry and the weight (or confidence) managers assign to that forecast. A forecast in period $t - 2$ of positive profits six months hence (which using quarterly data would be in period t) will lead to investment in period t as long as there is sufficient weight associated with that forecast. In addition, for a given weight, the larger is the expected future profits the greater will be the number of profitable investment projects. The larger the number of profitable projects, the larger will be total investment expenditure.

Therefore the Keynesian model of investment, omitting for the moment any discussion of time specification, may be specified as follows:

$$I = f (\text{BEF, WEIGHT})$$

where BEF is the business executive forecast and WEIGHT is the confidence associated with that forecast.[14]

BEF is calculated using the Conference Board series on executive perceptions regarding future profitability in own industry. As reported, the series measures expected changes in profitability in six months relative to current profitability. Suppose at period $t - 2$ the reported expectation was 52. Managers are thus suggesting a slight improvement in profitability six months hence (period t) compared to period $t - 2$'s profitability. However, period $t - 2$'s profitability may be either quite low or extraordinarily high. A slight improvement in profitability may have very different implications for investment depending upon the base level of profits. If period $t - 2$'s profitability were negative, we would expect little or no investment due to an expected slight improvement. However, if period $t - 2$'s profits were positive an expected small improvement in profit would presumably generate investment spending.

Since each time period used its own current level of profits as the base, we were forced to rebase the data series to a common value. In the form entered into the model, BEF reflects a forecast relative to a uniform, or common, base period. Thus if in period t the value of BEF is 54, then managers are expecting an improvement in profitability in six months *compared to the base period*. If in period $t + 1$ the value is 55, then the data tells us that managers expect a slightly larger improvement in six months *over the same base used to calculate period t's BEF*. The appendix details the construction of BEF.

As noted earlier, Keynes argues that the weight decision makers attach to their forecast will influence their willingness to act on that forecast. To measure WEIGHT we employ a variable that measures the prior accuracy of managers' forecasts. The poorer the track record in prediction, the less will be the weight assigned to a current prediction, and the lower will be the value of investment for any given level of expected profits. The degree of forecast inaccuracy, MISS, is the inverse of WEIGHT. Thus our model has become:

$$I = f(\text{BEF, MISS})$$

where MISS = 1/WEIGHT.

The Conference Board data allows easy calculation of this MISS variable. As noted earlier two series were reported by the Board. The first series provides a forecast of profits compared to the current period. The second evaluates current profits compared to six months ago. We used these two series to allow the managers to reveal their own evaluation of their forecast accuracy. Suppose managers in period t state that their BEF equals 55. That is, they forecast a value of future profits higher than the base period. But now suppose that six months hence (which using quarterly data would be period $t + 2$) they reveal an evaluation of current profits compared to t of 50. That is, they believe that profitability has been unchanged over the six-month period. Managers thus reveal their forecast has been inaccurate ($55 - 50 = 5$). We measure MISS as the *absolute value* of the difference between the forecast and the evaluation. In this case we calculate a degree of inaccuracy, MISS, in period $t + 2$ of 5. Suppose instead that the BEF forecast in t was 45 resulting in an error of –5. MISS again would equal 5 (the absolute value) since we assume that inaccuracy retards investment independent of the direction of error.[15] The higher is MISS the lower will be WEIGHT, the confidence placed in any profit forecast (BEF) in period $t + 2$.

5 ESTIMATION

The principal issue in specifying the equation to be estimated is the lag structure on BEF and MISS. Clearly, investment in period t depends upon the profit expectation, and associated weight attached to that expectation, from some previous period. There are several reasons why the regression equation should be specified so that investment at t depends on a series of lagged BEF and MISS. Investment in some period t will be initiated during some period $t - k$ based upon the level of profit expectations and associated weight in that expectation. It is quite possible that k varies depending upon the nature of the project or the state of the economy. For example, a project of short duration will likely have a lower k value than a project that requires a longer time to complete. In addition, even if k does not vary, because investment projects take more than one quarter to complete, investment at t will represent projects begun during different time periods. Finally, as noted earlier, it is possible that managers will augment or diminish the rate of spending on projects already started as new information (captured in later BEF and MISS) becomes available. Thus investment in period t is composed of a number of projects, begun during different past time periods, and proceeding at different rates.

The exact nature of the lag structure is difficult to discern. There are two issues in specification. The first is, what is the most recent period that expectations, or weight, can still affect current investment? Since the expectations data look six months ahead, we allow expectations and weight at $t - 2$ to influence investment at period t.[16] We chose, therefore, to select six months as the most recent period in the lag structure.

The second issue is how long of a lag structure should be specified? That is, what is the latest period that should enter the regression? The literature on investment is conspicuous for its lack of evidence or discussion of the time between project approval and project spending, or on time profile of a project's investment expenditure. We report a lag length beginning six months before current investment expenditure and continuing for eight additional quarters. With this lag structure the latest period that can affect current investment spending is two years and six months back. We put no constraints on the nature of the lag distribution, preferring instead to allow the data to demonstrate the nature of the response.

The equation estimated is:

$$I_t = \beta_0 + \sum_{i=1}^{9} \beta_i BEF_{t-i-1} + \sum_{i=1}^{9} \beta_{i+9} MISS_{t-i-1}.$$

6   RESULTS

We estimated the investment equation for manufacturing, for eight separate component industries of manufacturing, and for five non-manufacturing industries. Table 3.1 presents a list of industries included in the study. Table 3.2 provides the means and standard deviations for Investment, BEF and MISS for each industry. Each equation was estimated using ordinary least squares and was purged of serial correlation using a Cochrane–Orcutt procedure.

The use of lagged regressors in time-series models produces problems with multicollinearity. Given this problem, the interpretation of any *one* lagged coefficient on a BEF or MISS variable is problematic. This would be an issue for a researcher wanting to distinguish the influence on investment of profit expectations or weight in different periods. However, we are primarily interested in testing whether expectations or weight influence investment, without distinguishing the eaffect of separate periods. To evaluate the influence of expectations the proper statistic is the *sum* of all lagged BEF coefficients.[17] Similarly, to test the effect of weight on investment, we present the *sum* of the lagged MISS coefficients. Table 3.3 reports the sum of lagged BEF and MISS coefficients and their associated *t*-statistics.[18]

Table 3.1   Industry names and abbreviations

Man.	=	Manufacturing
Pri. met.	=	Primary metals
Fab. met.	=	Fabricated metals
Elec. mach.	=	Electric machinery
Non-elec. mach.	=	Non-electric machinery
Mining		
Paper		
Trans. equip.	=	Transportation equipment
Food		
Chemicals		
Trans.	=	Transportation
Utility		
Whole/retail	=	Wholesale–retail trade
Banking/finance		

Table 3.2   Regression variables: means and standard errors

Industry	Investment		BEF		MISS	
	x	*s*	*x*	*s*	*x*	*s*
Manufacturing	138.8	25.7	40.2	16.4	33.9	15.6
Primary metals	7.5	0.99	28.2	29.6	18.7	26.5
Fabricated metals	3.7	0.4	26.5	15.2	25.5	17.6
Electric machinery	11.7	3.6	47.8	15.5	43.2	17.1
Non-electric machinery	13.5	2.6	39.5	21.9	30.8	19.5
Mining	17.6	3.6	60.5	42.5	50.2	35.2
Paper	7.7	2.7	36.3	24.1	31.2	22.4
Transportation equipment	15.6	2.9	29.1	20.4	20.5	14.7
Food	9.6	1.2	39.9	12.3	32.5	9.4
Chemicals	14.6	2.8	51.3	22.9	46.4	25.1
Transportation	17.3	2.0	34.6	22.6	25.8	19.9
Utility	43.3	2.4	69.4	42.7	67.5	44.5
Whole/retail trade	43.1	13.6	41.44	14.75	33.4	24.9
Banking/finance	36.5	20.3	44.5	26.6	38.3	26.5

Table 3.3 *Impact of the sum of lagged forward-looking expectations (BEF)*
and weight (MISS) on real investment expenditures

	Man.	Pri. met.	Fab. met.	Elec Mach.	Non-elec Mach	Mining	Paper
$\sum_{t=-2}^{-10} BEF_t$	2.08 (14.1)***	−0.42 (0.97)	0.09 (3.06)***	0.18 (6.06)***	−0.22 (5.40)***	−0.21 (1.07)	0.17 (3.15)***
$\sum_{t=-2}^{-10} MISS_t$	−4.03 (8.18)***	1.21 (1.46)*	−0.13 (3.36)***	−0.63 (5.97)***	0.46 (4.15)***	0.16 (0.32)	−0.49 (4.87)***
N	37	28	27	28	30	29	29
F	28.3***	1.19	23.8***	15.43***	8.03***	2.42**	9.00***
R^2	96.6	70.4	98.2	96.9	92.9	81.4	94.2
Adj. R^2	93.2	11.1	94.1	90.6	81.3	47.8	83.7

	Trans. equip.	Food	Chemicals	Trans.	Utility	Whole/ retail	Banking/ finance
$\sum_{t=-2}^{-10} BEF_t$	0.51 (2.99)***	0.68 4.31***	0.13 (3.61)***	0.25 (3.80)***	0.03 (1.11)	1.31 (6.38)***	0.72 (3.76)***
$\sum_{t=-2}^{-10} MISS_t$	−0.79 (2.10)**	0.32 (1.37)	−0.39 (7.23)***	−0.51 (2.08)**	−0.78 (2.60)**	−1.17 (1.52)*	−0.92 (0.55)
N	29	29	29	29	38	36	34
F	2.36*	4.01**	22.6***	3.33**	1.51	6.98***	3.99***
R^2	81.0	87.8	97.6	85.7	58.8	88.1	82.7
Adj. R^2	46.7	65.9	93.3	60.0	19.9	75.5	62.0

Notes: Absolute *t*-statistics are given in parenthesis.
*   Statistically significantly different from zero at the 0.1 confidence level.
**   Statistically significantly different from zero at the 0.05 confidence level.
*** Statistically significantly different from zero at the 0.01 confidence level.

The sum of the BEF coefficients was significant in eleven out of fourteen
regressions and of the expected positive sign in ten of the eleven cases where
significant. The values range between a low of 0.09 to a high of 2.08 for cases
where BEF was significant with the expected sign. Using the regression on
manufacturing, a one unit increase in profit expectations, over the lag period,
will lead to a predicted expansion in plant and equipment expenditures of 2.08
billion dollars. This represents a 1.5 per cent increase over the mean level of
investment in manufacturing.

The MISS variable was significant in eleven of the fourteen models estimated
and of the expected negative sign in nine of the eleven cases where significant.

Of these nine cases in five industries MISS was significant at the 0.01 level, in three industries at the 0.05 level, and in one industry at the 0.1 level. The values, when significant, range between −4.03 as the lowest value and −0.13 for the largest value. In manufacturing a one unit increase an inaccuracy will lead to a predicted decrease in investment of 4.03 billion dollars, a 2.9 per cent decrease below mean investment spending.

Table 3.3 reports R-squared, R-squared adjusted, and the 'regression F' coefficient as measures of goodness of fit. The R-squared values range between 59.8 and 98.2 per cent. The R-squared adjusted range between 11.1 and 94.1 per cent. The F-tests on the regression equations (testing whether all of the coefficients on BEF and MISS equal zero) were significant in twelve of the fourteen equations, at the 0.01 level in eight of the twelve cases. Those equations with a significant F-value had R-squared adjusted values all over 46.7 per cent.

7   INTERPRETATION AND CONCLUSIONS

What is surprising about our results is the remarkable explanatory power of this simple representation of Keynes's theory of investment. We have only two variables, expectations and weight; yet in the twelve models estimated where the F-statistic is significant we are able to explain between 81 and 98 per cent of the most volatile component of GNP. Moreover, the two variables in the model are frequently statistically significant with the correct sign.

It was Keynes's view that investment is driven by expectations of future profitability. By using data that directly measures an expectation of profits, instead of rough proxies based on past values of profits or output, we are now able to evaluate that theory. Our analysis strongly supports Keynes. In addition Keynes suggested that the weight, or degree of confidence, decision makers place on their profit forecast will influence their willingness to act on that forecast. In our model we specified that forecast inaccuracy, MISS, is inversely related to weight. We found an increase in inaccuracy, which reduces weight, to decrease investment.

The strong performance across industries as seemingly disparate as mining and wholesale–retail trade suggests a high level of generality to Keynes's theory of investment. This level of generality points to the importance of managers' perceptions. Whether ill-formed or not, whether rational or not, whether stable or not, they clearly are of fundamental importance in the determination of investment and, hence, macroeconomic stability. This suggests that policy makers would be well advised to consider the mind set of executive decision makers when formulating economic policy. Finally, it is clear from Keynes that expectations that drive investment are forward looking, despite the way later researchers have tested this theory. That view seems now to be strongly supported. Clearly, managers see an evolution in their industry's profits that forces them to rely on judgements of the future rather than observations of the past. However, it is also clear that Keynes gave little guidance to the nature of how expectations were formed, even arguing at one point for 'animal spirits'. It remains, therefore, an area in need of further research to determine how these expectations are formed.[24]

NOTES

* This chapter is drawn from a paper forthcoming in the *Journal of Economic Psychology*. The authors are indebted to Stuart Low, William Darity Jr and Kurt Schaefer for useful discussions. Bradley Bateman, Alfred Field Jr, Alan Haight, Alan Isaac, Todd Lowry, William Osterberg and Jerry Stevens provided useful comments on an earlier draft of this chapter. Matt Wherry assisted in data preparation during project initiation. We also wish to acknowledge the generous support of an R.E. Lee Research Grant from Washington and Lee University. Author names are listed alphabetically. Any remaining errors are solely ours.

1. Jorgenson (1967) developed a model where investment is a function of the price of capital relative to other inputs. In a later version, Jorgenson and Stephenson (1967b), investment depends on the level of output, which is exogenous, as well as relative input prices. For an excellent review and comparison of the classical and neoclassical theories of investment, see Bernstein (1988).

2. The marginal efficiency of investment is that rate of discount that would make the present value of the series of annuities given by the returns *expected* from the capital asset during its life just equal to its supply price.

3. Darity and Horn (1993) do address the question of the role of entrepreneurial confidence. While they do not test this theory empirically, they do a detailed historical analysis based upon an extensive review of Keynes's writing on probability and investment.

4. Kalecki (1971: 111) argued for a theory of investment based upon retained earnings, changes in profit, and changes in fixed capital. Eisner and Nadiri (1968) emphasize the role of demand fluctuations in investment decisions, in opposition to Jorgenson's (1967) emphasis on relative prices. Eisner (1978) focuses on profits as an explanation of investment. Eisner adopts what is commonly referred to as the 'profits principle' by assuming past profits can be used as a proxy for expectations of future profits.

5. See Muth (1961) for the seminal article on what has now been named 'rational expectations'.

6. See, for example, Abdullah and Tank (1989), and Lawrence and Siow (1985). Abdullah and Tank found that only the long-run interest rate matters in the determination of investment. Lawrence and Siow found both long and short rates are important.

7. See Clark (1979) for a well-known version of this type of model. Clark found that the accelerator model is a better predictor of investment than are various forms of the neoclassical model.

8. For a less analytical treatment of Pindyck and the literature on firm investment behaviour given project irreversibility and continuous information flow, see Dixit (1992).

9. In Chapter 6, page 59, of *A Treatise on Probability* (1921), which Keynes refers to in *The General Theory*, Keynes points out that as the relevant evidence at the disposal of an individual increases the *weight* of the argument must have gone up. Therefore when Keynes referred to entrepreneurs being 'very uncertain' about the evidence relevant to the formulation of long-term expectations, he was suggesting that they assign a low weight to their forecasts.

10. Keynes did not distinguish between delaying a project and cancellation due to changing weights associated with profits forecasts. However, Pindyck (1991) makes a strong case that the pace of investment may be influenced by the quality of current information available to the decision maker. If the project is delayed, additional information is obtained. If the current

stock of information is of low quality, Pindyck suggests, then managers will consider delaying investment if the expected marginal value of the additional information is greater than the marginal cost of delay. In our view, Pindyck's notion that the pace of investment varies with the value of additional information is consistent with Keynes's theory that investment is dependent upon the weight associated with a forecast.

11. The Conference Board also publishes a series on consumer confidence that has been widely used to evaluate the current position of the economy and to forecast future movements in consumption and gross national product. See, for example, Wessel (1992: 1). We find it surprising that the consumer series has received so much attention, and the executive survey so little note.

12. The Conference Board only reports that the average number of respondents in each industry was approximately 25 to 30. If those response rates could not be maintained, the Conference Board dropped that industry from the survey.

13. Separate series on plant and equipment are only available on an annual basis while the Conference Board data is collected quarterly. Consequently, we used the combined quarterly investment data.

14. While Keynes is clear that the rate of interest plays a role in determining investment, it would be improper to include the interest rate in our model. BEF, since it is a prediction of future profits, takes into consideration all sources of revenue and cost, including the interest rate.

15. We considered the possibility that a positive forecast error (forecasters were overoptimistic) may retard investment more than negative errors (underoptimistic). If managers find that they systematically err in a particular direction then those who err frequently negatively may place higher weight on a given forecast, for a specific absolute error, than those who frequently err positively.

16. While six months seems like a short time period for expectations to influence spending on structures, it is possible that equipment expenditures may respond over such a short time period. Our specification allows the data to reveal whether investment is sensitive to recently formed profit expectations and weight.

17. Gene Grossman (1982) used this technique to study the affect of lagged price terms on US import demand.

18. Individual coefficient estimates and associated *t*-statistics are available from the authors upon request.

19. Keynes (1936: 152) noted the possibility that investors would adopt conventions, a set of rules or interpretative procedures, to assist in the formation of expectations. For example, these would include a follow-the-leader rule or the reliance on 'expert' opinion.

REFERENCES

Abdullah, Dewan A. and Frederick E. Tank (1989), 'The Determinants of Fixed Investment Over the Business Cycle: Some Time Series Evidence', *Journal of Macroeconomics*, **11** (1), Winter: 49–65.

Bernstein, Sarah (1988), 'Investment, Profitability, Demand and Interest Rates: A Study of the Cross-Sectional and Time Series Determinants of Investment for U.S. Manufacturing Industries', PhD Dissertation, New York's New School for Social Research, December.

Clark, P. (1979), 'Investment in the 1970s: Theory, Performance, and Prediction', *Brookings Papers on Economic Activity*, No. 1: 73–124.

Darity, W. Jr. and B.L. Horn (1993), 'Rational Expectations, Rational Belief, and Keynes' General Theory', in Warren Samuels (ed.), *Research in the History of Economic Thought and Methodology*, Greenwich: JAI Press.

Dixit, Avinash (1992), 'Investment and Hysteresis', *Journal of Economic Perspectives*, **6** (1), Winter: 107–32.

Eisner, R. (1978), *Factors in Business Investment*, Chicago: National Bureau of Economic Research.

Eisner, R. and M. Nadiri (1968), 'Investment Behavior and the Neo-Classical Theory', *Review of Economics and Statistics*, **52**, August: 369–82.

Grossman, Gene (1982), 'Import Competition from Developed and Developing Countries', *Review of Economics and Statistics*, **64**, 271–81.

Harrod, R. (1936), *The Trade Cycle*, Oxford: Clarendon Press.

Hart, A.G. (1950), 'Keynes' Analysis of Expectations and Uncertainty', in Seymour Harris (ed.), *The New Economics: Keynes' Influence on Theory and Public Policy*, New York: Alfred Knopf: 415–24.

Jorgenson, D. (1967), 'The Theory of Investment Behavior', in R. Ferber (ed.), *Determinants of Investment Behaviour*, Universities–National Bureau Conference Series, No. 18, New York: Columbia University Press, pp. 129–55.

Jorgenson, D. and J. Stephenson (1967a), 'The Time Structure of Investment Behavior in U.S. Manufacturing, 1947–1960', *Review of Economics and Statistics*, **49**, February: 6–26.

Jorgenson, D. and J. Stephenson (1967b), 'Investment Behavior in U.S. Manufacturing, 1947–60', *Review of Economics and Statistics*, **35**, April: 169–220.

Kalecki, Michael (1971), *Selected Essays on the Dynamics of the Capitalist Economy 1933–1970*, Cambridge: Cambridge University Press.

Keynes, J.M. (1936), *The General Theory of Employment, Interest and Money*, London: Macmillan.

Keynes, J.M. (1964), *The General Theory of Employment, Interest and Money*, New York: Harbinger Press.

Keynes, J.M. (1971), *The Collected Writings of John Maynard Keynes, Vol. 8: Treatise on Probability*, New York: St. Martin's Press.

Lawrence, Colin and Aloysius Siow (1985), 'Interest Rates and Investment Spending: Some Empirical Evidence for Postwar U.S. Producer Equipment 1947–80', *Journal of Business*, **58** (4): 359–75.

Muth, John (1961), 'Rational Expectations and the Theory of Price Movements', *Econometrica*, **29**, July: 316.

Pindyck, Robert S. (1991), 'Irreversibility, Uncertainty, and Investment', *Journal of Economic Literature*, **29** (3), September: 1110–48.

Wessel, David (1991), 'Confidence Surveys May Help to Predict Shape of the Recovery', *The Wall Street Journal*, 5 March: 1.

APPENDIX

As reported by the Conference Board, the managers in each of 25 two-digit SIC industries answered two questions:

1. What are your 'expectations for your own industry six months ahead?'.
2. What is your evaluation of 'current conditions in your own industry verses six months ago?'.

This questionnaire was sent to the managers every three months. For example, for the aggregate manufacturing industry a subsample of the data are reported in Table 3A.1. Each question was answered on a 100 point scale where 50 represents no change. Numbers above 50 indicate improvement and numbers below 50 indicate decline. We interpret the answers to these questions to indicate the managers' *perception of profitability*. For example, the value of 48 in Q3 1978 for question 1 is less than 50. Thus, in the third quarter of 1978 the managers predict a slight decline in profits for quarter 1 in 1979. The managers also regard Q3 1978 as being significantly better than Q1 1978, as evidenced by a mean response of 62.

The difficulties for our study are:

a. Each period's prediction (in question 1) references its *own* time period as the base for the prediction. The predictions of 44 made in Q4 1978 and again in Q2 1979 are *not* directly comparable since each is a forecast of profitability *compared to the conditions when the forecast was made*. If the business cycle in Q4 1978 differs from Q2 1979, then each 44 predicts a different level of expected profits. Clearly, any model of investment using this data requires that the data be adjusted to a common base period. We refer to this as 'rebasing'.

b. We have quarterly data on six-month predictions. We in essence have two series, the odd quarters and the even quarters, which could each be adjusted, but do not permit an easy rebasing for the *entire* time series.

We addressed these issues as follows. The raw data for question two and the rebased data are in Table 3A.2. We created a single series that evaluates current business conditions against a common base period. That base period, given the series for manufacturing, is 31 March 1978, midway between Q1 and Q2 1978. We first averaged the values from Q3 and Q4 1978 to a 59. This gives us one series instead of two (addressing issue (b) above). Each value of 59 reflects the conditions in that quarter compared to 31 March 1978. We then took all following values and rebased them to reflect changes above or below the 31 March 1978 base. For example, Q1 1979 in the raw data is 58. This 58 says that managers regard Q1 1979 as being 16 per cent (16 per cent = $((58 - 50)/50)\cdot100$) better than Q3 1978. If Q3 1978 is a 59 then we increase the value of 59 by 16 per cent to create the new value of 68.44. The value of 68.44 is also based upon 31 March 1978 and is therefore directly comparable to the value in either Q3 or Q4 of 1978.

Table 3A.1   Conference Board data: manufacturing

Date	Question 1	Question 2
Q3 1978	48	62
Q4	44	56
Q1 1979	47	58
Q2	44	57
Q3	37	41
Q4	77	42

Table 3A.2   Evaluation of current conditions: raw data and rebased

Date	Question 2	Question 2 rebased by Anderson and Goldsmith
Q3 1978	62	59
Q4	56	59
Q1 1979	58	68.44
Q2	57	67.26
Q3	41	56.12
Q4	42	56.50

Consider finally Q3 1979 whose raw value is 41. The managers evaluate Q3 1979 as being 18 per cent worse than Q1 1979. However we want the evaluation to be relative to 31 March 1978. We therefore adjust the value to show an 18 per cent worsening from 68.44, which reflects business conditions in Q1 1979 relative to 31 March 1978. An 18 per cent decline from 68.44 is 56.12, the value we report.

Now we are able to adjust the values that managers report in their answers to question 1 to reflect a common base (see Table 3A.3). For example, note that the prediction in Q3 1978 of 48, and the prediction in Q4 1979 of 37, are not currently comparable. Each is based on whatever current conditions exist in the industry. We therefore use the rebased data from question 2 to provide a common base (31 March 1978) for question 1.

Consumption, investment and government spending

Table 3A.3   Forecasted profits: raw data and rebased

Date	Question 1	Question 2 rebased	Question 1 rebased by Anderson and Goldsmith
Q3 1978	48	59	56.64
Q4	44	59	51.92
Q1 1979	47	68.44	64.33
Q2	44	67.26	59.18
Q3	37	56.12	41.53
Q4	77	56.50	87.01

In Q3 1978 managers predict a 4 per cent decline for Q1 1979; that is, they report a value for question 1 of 48. Since Q3 1978 is evaluated as a 59, an improvement of 18 per cent over 31 March 1978, then managers are predicting a 4 per cent decline from the value of 59. Thus we calculate a rebased answer to question 1 of 56.64. As a second example, consider the prediction made in Q3 1979 of 37. Managers are predicting a 26 per cent decline for Q1 1980, relative to the conditions current in Q3 1979. To rebase this prediction to 31 March 1978 we apply the 26 per cent decline to the value of 56.12, which is the evaluation of Q3 1979 compared to 31 March 1978. Thus we calculate a value of 41.53. While the original values in Q3 1978 and Q3 1979 are not directly comparable, the rebased values may be contrasted.

4. Keynes and the susceptibility of investment

Jerry Courvisanos

1 VOLATILITY AND SUSCEPTIBILITY

Keynes, in *The General Theory*, uses Simon Kuznets's estimates of net investment in the United States to show the critical role that wide fluctuations in investment have on the pattern of business cycles (1936: 102–6). The empirical proposition that investment fluctuates widely, frequently and quickly can be defined as the *volatility* of private business fixed capital formation.

Later in Chapter 12 of the same book, Keynes goes on to develop a theoretical proposition as to the reasons for this volatility in investment. He examines the state of confidence entrepreneurs have with their investment decisions based on the long-term expectations (LTE) they form from past knowledge. Instability of investment occurs when the continuity of stable LTE become precarious. 'What Keynes is emphasizing is the *susceptibility* of LTE to change; how frequently they do change and to what degree is an important but largely empirical matter' (O'Donnell 1989: 262, original emphasis). The extent of susceptibility to investment decisions is a theoretical notion which determines whether or not there is volatility in investment activity.

Many empirical studies since Kuznets have supported the volatility of investment and its crucial role in the pattern of business cycles. What has been lacking is the development of Keynes's behavioural notion of susceptibility which links the occurrence of volatility to human action. Nearly twenty years after *The General Theory*, Goodwin (1987: 63) observes that '[i]nvestment, because current decisions depend on an unknown future, has tended to be something of a black hole in economic theory'. Attempting to develop this area further has led to analysis of investment confidence (for example, Boyd and Blatt 1988) and its impact on business cycles as 'an endogenous generator of irregularity' (Goodwin 1987: 125). This chapter aims to show how Keynes's behavioural notions of investment decision making can be used to develop an endogenous model of investment cycles. Such a model can provide an understanding of investment instability at the firm and industry level and how that instability varies in an economy over different periods of economic history.

This chapter first outlines some empirical studies that indicate the extent of investment volatility and the problems these studies have in their theoretical explanation. The concept of susceptibility is then introduced in terms of Keynes's analysis, and a behavioural model of investment cycles is developed. Empirical support for this model is briefly set out. Finally, implications of this analysis are examined in terms of the development of Keynes's economic thought, and for the role of investment in the 1990s deregulated environment.

2   STUDIES ON INVESTMENT VOLATILITY

There is no standard history (or review) of empirical studies in investment volatility, reflecting the essentially static mainstream economic analysis. Recent reviews of business cycle studies by Zarnowitz (1992) and Hillinger (1992) support Keynes's proposition of investment volatility and its central role in macroeconomic fluctuations.

The strongly empirical-based work on credit expansion by Tooke (1844) emphasizes the role of fixed investment in fluctuations, which was later developed into a real rate of profit theory of economic fluctuations by Karl Marx. Spiethoff (1953) reinforces the role of plant and equipment investment in fluctuations. The emergence of econometric studies in the 1930s, particularly by Michal Kalecki, confirms the volatility of investment and its crucial role in explaining economic cycles. Hillinger (1992: 22) summarizes the results of these econometric studies in two stylized facts:

1. Fluctuations mainly take the form of investment cycles.
2. The principal explanation of investment cycles is the complex lag structure of the investment process.

A large amount of post-Second World War empirical research by the US National Bureau of Economic Research (NBER) supports these stylized facts (see Zarnowitz 1992).

The dominant modern macroeconomic schools of thought have persistently ignored or denied the existence of the stylized facts on investment volatility (Hillinger 1992: 30). One significant mainstream study by Gordon and Veitch (1986) shows evidence of investment volatility in producer-durable equipment substantially being 'determined by its own lagged values' (Hillinger 1992: 33). The explanation of such dynamic phenomena has not been the concern of the recent dominant macroeconomic schools of monetarism, new classical and new Keynesian economics.

Over the last 15 years, Hillinger and his colleagues at the University of Munich's SEMECON (Seminar for Mathematical Economics) centre have conducted empirical work based on the above two stylized facts. Their work has shown that 'the fluctuations in investment are taken to be quasi-periodic, the period of the equipment cycle being typically in the 7–12 year range, and that of the inventory cycle in the 3.5–5 year range' (Hillinger 1992: 30). This investment volatility has been explained by these studies in terms of the dynamics of disequilibrium adjustment processes. In their investment cycle theory they use the second-order accelerator (SOA) to model fixed investment.

The SOA model underwrites the observed stylized facts with microeconomic foundations based on 'intertemporal optimisation of the firm in the presence of adjustment costs' (Hillinger, Reiter and Weser 1992: 168). This is done by taking the differential of the flexible accelerator, which means that the investment cycle derives from the rate of change (and not the level) of investment as it is affected by the difference between actual and desired fixed capital. A second-order differential equation in terms of capital stock is the terminology, while adjustment costs in the gradual movement of capital stock to the new desired level is the reasoning. Thus, growing idle capacity adds to adjustment costs, which leads to investment contraction. The SEMECON researchers refer to this as '*inertia of investment* ... [which] is central in explaining *investment overshooting* and thus cyclical behaviour' (ibid.: 170, original emphasis).

The strength of the SOA model is its ability to discriminate between investment cycles of differing amplitudes (or volatility). Investment cycles are pronounced if firms discount future adjustment costs strongly due to short foresight, whereas longer foresight by firms tends to prevent the discounting of adjustment costs with the concomitant attenuation of investment cycle behaviour. Kalecki, in his investment cycle theories, recognized that the role of both the incentive and ability to invest is signalled by the firms' profits. As profits are closely related to output levels and via optimal adjustment to desired capital stock, then the profit element of Kalecki's model resembles the accelerator.

Kalecki (1933) identified this endogenous investment cycle mechanism, yet he continued throughout his life to search for a more comprehensive theory of investment *decisions* (Laski 1987: 10). The SEMECON studies, in contrast, seem to be satisfied by the SOA investment decision model (see Hillinger, Reiter and Weser 1992). The weakness of the SOA model is its mechanistic approach within an optimizing behavioural paradigm. Investment is not a symmetrical process at the downturn and upturn of the investment cycle. The upturn is much more problematical. As excess capacity mounts in a recession there are specific reasons, related to technological innovation, for new investment commitments when there exist already adequate productive capacity. Also, once the adjustment mechanism in investment is recognized, there are many issues that a simple acceleration mechanism cannot handle (even in a second-order derivative form): ability of the capital-producing industry to meet the demand for capital goods (traverse problem); when decisions on decommissioning capital stock occur; role of modifications to already committed investment projects; and changes in expectations within the same foresight perspective.

At a deeper level, the firm-optimizing behavioural assumption is too limiting as it provides no clear role for human agency in the organization. The role of the entrepreneur in making investment decisions within a framework of cognitive limitations is completely denied in the accelerator process. It is the special case of limitation of human ability to deal with uncertainty which goes to the root of investment volatility. Bounded rationality with the need to develop (and adjust) rules of thumb to cope with cognitive limitations is a more appropriate framework to appreciate investment volatility than mechanistic optimizing rationality (Simon 1987).

3 KEYNES'S ANALYSIS OF INVESTMENT DECISION MAKING

Keynes (1936) placed the investment function at centre stage of the analysis of why a market capitalist economy does not necessarily achieve a full-employment equilibrium. In doing so, Keynes took the neoclassical (Marshallian) theory of the firm as the micro foundations for his downward-sloping marginal efficiency of capital (MEC) concept, the essential determinant for an underemployment equilibrium position (Sardoni 1987: 111). Then, through Chapter 22 of *The General Theory*, Keynes (1936) was able to link his analysis to the previous business cycle theorists who pointed to investment as the key variable in the instability of the economy.

In Chapter 12 of *The General Theory*, Keynes attempts to account for the observed instability in investment. By highlighting the role of psychological factors in the determination of investment, Keynes brought behavioural motivation to economics (Earl 1988: 13), not just in terms of assumptions, but also as central to the economy's progress over time. Keynes's analysis of uncertainty is the essence of this behavioural element in investment. Where Keynes has been open to criticism is in his approach to uncertainty.

There is a strong classical behavioural perspective in Keynes (1936) based on the role of the entrepreneur. In fact, the concept of the 'entrepreneur economy' is developed in Keynes's early draft of *The General Theory* and is applied there to an oligopolistic competitive economy (Sardoni 1987: 133). This surfaces in the published book form only in an informal description when at the beginning of the chapter Keynes refers to 'business as a way of life' (Keynes 1936: 150). Within this framework Keynes starts this enquiry into uncertainty where Kalecki had left off. Both economists agree that investment decisions are based on entrepreneurs' rationality which is guided by past and present experiences (the diachronic mechanism).[1] This mechanism constrains the imagination of entrepreneurs; in this situation, it is the only response perceived as rational. Thus, when making investment decisions, entrepreneurs ensure that 'the facts of the existing situation enter, in a sense disproportionately, into the formation of … [their] long-term expectations' (ibid.: 148).

Keynes then examines the state of confidence entrepreneurs have with regard to the long-term expectations (LTE) formed from past knowledge. Recent studies of Keynes's uncertainty concept all agree that conventions, or simple rules, are established as devices for building the degree of confidence with which investment decisions are made (Earl 1988: 13).[2] Keynes's 'chief' convention 'is to assume, contrary to all likelihood, that the future will resemble the past' (Keynes 1973: 124). This attempts to preserve stability in an uncertain world. Business practices (like mark-up pricing, discounted cash flow and pay-back rule) are established around these conventions, with different institutional frameworks giving rise to different specific motives and rules.

Keynes then introduces the concept of speculative rationality based on short-term financial gains by 'outwitting the psychology of the market' and anticipating its movements which are governed by doubt and fear (O'Donnell 1989: 258). Investors' convention is undermined by increased lack of confidence which leads to enterprise giving way to speculation (or 'animal spirits'). Uncertainty surrounding LTE makes new capital formation illogical, the implication being that entrepreneurs act to protect their liquidity position, while speculation abounds. Thus a speculative MEC emerges from the introduction of financial markets. The speculative MEC, reflecting 'a prediction of short-run majority opinion in the [financial] market place', diverges from the objective MEC 'in the latter stages of a boom and during the contraction phase of the trade cycle' (Burkett and Wohar 1987: 41). Thus, short-term expectations undermine fundamental (objective) LTE that go into investment strategies.

Lawson (1985: 921) argues that Keynes's investment instability stems from structural breaks, when 'moments of crisis' in confidence over reasonably steady LTE and existing conventions disrupt accepted business practices. This leads to a period of 'adaptive learning' or readjustment, 'before the process can settle down to one of knowledgeably reproduced social practices' (ibid.: 922). This approach received strong impetus a year later in the opening remarks of Keynes (1937) about uncertainty inherent in investment decisions which lead to variations in aggregate expenditures.

The exogenous role of uncertainty in investment volatility, as outlined by Keynes, is seen by Levine (1984) as inherently weak because it fails to carry through the classical idea of enterprise. Instead, Keynes falls back on the neoclassical notion that the financial market is populated by individual wealth-holders.[3] Under this assumption, firms end up using the same criteria as individual investors in deciding how to dispose of liquid assets. This ignores the 'fixity of investment within an irreversible flow of time, and the force of competition' (ibid.: 49), both of which constrain firms' investment decisions. Levine sees past investments affecting both the current use of funds and the difficulty of liquidating existing capital stock. Once set on a path of business development, past investments limit options for future investment. Also competition, and the threat of competition, can erode market position and constrain 'the firm to funnel financial resources into the preservation and expansion of existing capital investment in particular lines even when greater short-term profits could be made by speculation' (ibid.: 49).

Levine (1975) has a self-expansion perspective of firm development based on Schumpeter's capitalist entrepreneurial class. This investor class is affected by the uncertainties of financial markets, but its objective is the firm's survival. Capitalists have a strategic interest in their firms. A Kaleckian class-based institutional framework, with capitalists as central ('masters of their fate') to the entrepreneur economy, can provide a structure which can then be developed to account for both oligopoly behaviour in goods markets and speculative behaviour in financial markets. This endogenous approach to uncertainty is developed in the next section.

4   THE SUSCEPTIBILITY CYCLE MODEL

Increased susceptibility of LTE to change is the mirror image of decreasing confidence in existing practices. This happens when the 'weight of argument' lowers due to entrepreneurs' increased incompleteness of knowledge (or information). In this sense increased uncertainty is related to lower weight. Low weight renders beliefs, based on established conventions, sensitive to new information and induces investors to try new conventions. This is the basis of Keynes's epistemic instability of beliefs, which can be reinforced and magnified by institutional features in financial markets and in technological change (Runde 1991: 142–3).

Keynes's 'weight of argument' can be used to augment the Steindl (1941) notion of 'subjective attitude to risk'. In Steindl's analysis, the three cyclical variables in Kalecki's investment model – profits, excess capacity, increasing risk (see Laski 1987: 10–11) – inform the entrepreneurs on their 'subjective attitude'. This leads to raising or lowering the 'weight of argument', depending on how these variables are changing. For example, the 'weight' of entrepreneurs' subjective attitude to risk would be lowered by reduced profits. In this way,

Keynes's concepts of uncertainty and susceptibility can be linked to the Kaleckian framework.

Investment instability based on 'weight of argument' places the accent on uncertainty, which has a numerically immeasurable probability. Keynes, like Kalecki, accepts that uncertainty which has a measurable probability should be incorporated into investment project evaluation as a risk premium. Such risk calculation is consistent with Knight's view of probability (O'Donnell 1989: 263). Kalecki's 'increasing risk' attempts to take the 'preference for safety' element of uncertainty out of what Keynes and Knight regard as immeasurable, and give it a more institutional focus in investment instability analysis. However, Kalecki's principle is essentially a behavioural convention about constraints on financing investment which increase as the 'weight of argument' falls (and vice versa).

Keynes's epistemic instability of beliefs is developed, with Minsky's work on euphoric (Ponzi-style) behaviour followed by financial fragility and collapse (see Minsky 1982), into a cumulative process of expansion and contraction in investment decision making. Then, by introducing Simon's convention-based satisficing behaviour, a specific Shacklean kaleidic susceptibility to expectational changes in investment is conceived. This makes investment decisions highly sensitive and subject to change. Decisions are regularly revised to satisfy changing expectations, while investment orders at the implementation stage are subject to modifications and delay.

Susceptibility refers to the psychological tension felt by entrepreneurs in relation to their fragile confidence about a particular investment decision, given the level of investment orders already committed. The fragility of this confidence in convention-based investment decisions explains unstable investment behaviour. Increasing fragility arises when tension related to current investment decisions escalates as confidence is eroded. This cumulative process renders entrepreneurs' confidence increasingly fragile (or sensitive) as investment order levels rise. When investment order levels are falling, cumulative pressures are being eased on the fragile confidence of entrepreneurs. In this formulation, the level of investment orders is susceptible to change. This susceptibility is a function of the tensions generated by the degree of fragile confidence felt by entrepreneurs from exposure to risk and uncertainty.

The fragile confidence formed by entrepreneurs in their investment decisions is based on the objective evidence from the three Kaleckian elements (profits, increasing risk and capacity utilization) identified as central to investment. Growth, in terms of firm size or market share, is the wellspring that dominates optimistic confidence formation. This drive for growth, built on the three Kaleckian elements, is the *raison d'être* of investment. A firm also aims to 'avoid threats to its decision-making autonomy or its financial security' (Crotty 1992: 491). This safety objective erodes confidence when the three Kaleckian elements provide information that the push for growth has resulted in serious safety-threatening problems. At such a level of investment orders, further planned investment commitments are increasingly susceptible (or prone) to postponement and even (if the threat to safety is perceived as serious enough) modification or cancellation of current orders.

The cumulative building up and easing down of tensions ensue from the objective data of the three Kaleckian elements, giving rise to *susceptibility cycles*. These cycles map the feelings of susceptibility in relation to current investment decisions that originate in the building up of tension as businesses are exposed to more uncertainty and higher costs, and the breaking down of tension as businesses are exposed to less uncertainty and lower costs.

In all cycles, explanation of turning points is crucial. Turning points in susceptibility cycles occur when entrepreneurs' susceptibility is such that current conventions used for investment decision making are rejected, leading to structural breaks in patterns of investment behaviour. This echoes Keynes in his view that 'a *conventional* judgement ... is subject to sudden and violent changes ... [when] certainty and security, suddenly breaks down' (1937: 214–15, original emphasis). The difference is that with Keynes such breaks are exogenously induced, while in this susceptibility analysis they are endogenously based on given levels of investment orders already committed.[4]

It is important to appreciate the asymmetry between the susceptibility to changes in investment orders in the expansion and contraction phases. While increasing susceptibility provides the basis for the explanation of an endogenously generated upper turning point, it is the receptiveness of entrepreneurs at low susceptibility to take greater risks when the costs of postponing new investment projects become large that induce an increase in investment orders.

Investment behaviour is susceptible to specific factors which are based on the distinctive capitalist institutional structure of a particular economy. Susceptibility cycles vary with different economies and over different historical periods because each economy's institutional structure at a particular historical point affects the endogenous and exogenous factors differently. The analytical implication of this susceptibility view of Keynes's uncertainty is the need 'to devote more resources into [sic] learning about institutional behaviour, norms, conventions – or, more generally, rule systems – that are produced and reproduced by people' (Lawson 1985: 925). Lawson explains that such learning requires interpretative analytics to be conducted on practical primary source material derived from case studies and personal histories. Empirical patterns based on such research are outlined in the following section of the chapter.

A historically situated susceptibility cycle is best understood in terms of entrepreneurs' relative proportions between spontaneity and constraints on human action (Oakley 1993: 12–15). The former refers to the chaotic responses of free human actions (or Keynes's 'animal spirits'), while the latter refers to the 'rules of the game' in Keynes's 'entrepreneur economy' that constrain action. In periods of strong recently established technological systems with a state responsive to planning and stabilization, relative proportions lean towards 'rules'. This produces moderate amplitudes in investment cycles with relatively strong growth rates (subdued susceptibility cycles). In periods of declining relevance of older established technological systems with a state that is market forces oriented, relative proportions lean towards 'animal spirits'. This produces larger amplitudes in investment cycles with more moderate growth rates (pronounced or severe susceptibility cycles).

The susceptibility cycle model takes the basic theoretical model and incorporates the historical structural changes that accompany various stages of firm development. Endogenous-based increasing and decreasing susceptibility merges with exogenous influences which can intensify or ameliorate susceptibility. In specific historical situations, this produces subdued, pronounced or severe susceptibility cycles which determine the extent of investment volatility. In this way, historical explication enriches purely theoretical formulation. Empirical analysis enhances the theoretical propositions, developing a closer approximation to understanding behaviour which is not directly observed.

5 EMPIRICAL SUPPORT

With many studies identifying the pattern of aggregate investment volatility, as set out in Section 2 of this chapter, there is a need to provide microeconomic empirical support to susceptibility of investment behaviour in industries and firms. Such support would provide an explanatory hypothesis to the differing states of investment volatility experienced by capitalist economies in the recent period of oligopoly and monopoly market structures. Following Lawson (1985), an interpretative analysis of firm and industry histories is required to isolate the crucial elements that make up investment decision making. On their own, survey and interview techniques provide little data, given the sensitive nature of investment in relation to 'competitive advantage'. They can merely complement a more thorough investigation of primary source material through case studies of corporate and industry histories.

Courvisanos (1994) reports on such case study analysis in the postwar corporate histories of three Australian manufacturing industries: motor vehicle, steel and aluminium. The analysis concentrates on three different periods within the postwar era, recognizing pattern-matching explanations of investment decisions in terms of susceptibility behaviour. The first period (1945–70) of high investment growth with subdued susceptibility cycles was based essentially on the role of profits in an accelerator-type mechanism (leverage ratios and their limits were low, while capacity utilization was high). The second period (1970–80) of declining and low investment as a proportion of GDP had more pronounced susceptibility cycles with excess capacity becoming increasingly a major concern over the period. The third period (1980–94) of extremely large fluctuations in investment as a proportion of GDP had not only large variability in profits and excess capacity, but growing concern over the rising leverage ratios (often well above convention setting limits). The combination of all three endogenous elements, having large and variable susceptibility in this third period, led to severe susceptibility cycles.[5]

Historical patterns of capacity utilization and increasing risk (measured by leverage ratios) show that, under specific conditions, profit improvements may not be adequate to encourage investment growth. This is because susceptibility is not low (or resilient) enough to generate competition for new markets until the capacity utilization and increasing risk characteristics have reached more acceptable levels – levels that are more appropriate for another strong investment expansion. No amount of profit improvement and support from governments along this profit-based path (for example, tax concessions and accelerated investment allowances) can succeed without these two elements being at more acceptable positions in terms of susceptibility. It is for this reason that the acceleration mechanism on its own is an inadequate explanation.

Two exogenous factors that can *shift* the susceptibility cycle by exacerbating or ameliorating the investment volatility are examined in Courvisanos (1996). These are innovation and the role of the state. First, a historical investment pattern emerges of susceptibility cycles interacting with technological innovation. Low susceptibility with war-established process innovations in the early postwar period produced subdued and upward-biased investment cycles. Much higher susceptibility due to excess capacity produced a downward bias with slightly more instability in the 1970s. High gearing in the 1980s together with powerful exogenous innovations based around shifts from energy-based oil input to electronic-based information input produced very sensitive susceptibility conditions, with manufacturing industries in a transition stage and information technology service industries (for example, telecommunications, banks and finance) in a growth stage. This combination created strong booms and slumps in investment. For example, Australian manufacturing showed signs of investment growth in emerging technologically sophisticated industries during the late 1980s (Wood et al. 1991), but the early 1990s recession heightened the exogenous innovation problems, intensifying susceptibility and sending investment activity into a deep extended trough.

Susceptibility of investment is intensified by paradigm shifts in basic technologies. Leading-edge technologically sophisticated (infant) industries have an unstable demand and high leverage. At the same time, old cheap energy-based industries (including mineral non-differentiated oligopolies) are determined to hold on to their diminishing power, resulting in severe excess capacity and thus weak investment. Such investment instability is a limitation to efficient and smooth structural change. Allowing the market to resolve this limitation is long and painful. Old capital stock (for example, in the motor vehicle industry of the third period) refuse to give their dominance away, yet they are still trying to make some transition to alter process innovation. New capital stock (for example, in the biotechnology industry of the third period) find lack of market power and experience in new technology management as major stumbling blocks to strong investment growth.

The role of the state in capitalist economies is only at the margins of the investment cycle analysis. The state plays two supporting roles within this investment process. One is as a supplement to the endogenous elements through the operation of the political business cycle. The other is as an exogenous element which alters susceptibility in line with longer-term strategies of the state, whether at the micro-industry policy level or the macro-effective demand level. The state's supporting role has changed over the postwar period, while the direction of change has been roughly the same in all capitalist economies. In the immediate postwar period there was a strong strategic interventionist role for the state as part of the war reconstruction process, which ameliorated the susceptibility cycle. Slowly this altered towards a more deregulatory and market-guiding support from the state which further promoted the already highly volatile susceptibility cycle.

6   IMPLICATIONS

Two implications derive from this discussion. One is related to the history of economic thought, while the other is policy oriented. The Keynes (1936) LTE analysis in Chapter 12 is not just an interesting digression from the MEC static investment model (the neoclassical perspective), or a conflicting explanation which starts with classical enterprise ('way of life') but ends up as individual-based speculative ('animal spirits') behaviour (the Levine criticism). This chapter argues that investment volatility is central to Keynes's critique of the static investment–interest rate negative relationship. The mechanism is based on the factors lying behind the LTE in MEC calculations. Keynes's LTE relate to the cumulative instability of investment behaviour, beginning with entrepreneurial rationality in an economy with established technology and state support. This leads to strong conventions which result in moderate susceptibility to investment and relatively weak investment volatility.

Keynes goes on in the chapter to show how the development of more speculative rationality occurs in economies where new technological systems and more reliance on market forces lead to more spontaneity and less constraints on decision making. Conventions are then changed regularly and even flouted. This leads to exacerbated susceptibility to investment and relatively strong investment volatility. There is a tension between the relative proportions of convention-based constraints and speculative-based spontaneity which the susceptibility cycle model can operationalize to appreciate the extent of investment volatility in an economy at different points in its historical development.

This above historical note leads to the policy-oriented conclusion that the role of investment in a deregulated environment with quickly changing technological systems must lead inevitably to strong susceptibility and thus a high level of investment volatility. Under such conditions, the period of future-based expectations is shortened, with concomitant shorter payoff periods and larger expected returns. This exacerbates susceptibility, with very limited amelioration from any state support. Planning for large long-term investment projects is sacrificed for smaller shorter-term investments which can weaken investment growth and pull the trend of capital stock growth down. It is this concern that leads Keynes (1936: 378) in his own conclusion of the need for the state to 'exercise a guiding influence' through the 'socialisation of investment'. This is aimed at establishing stronger conventions that reduce susceptibility and increase capital stock growth rather than any notion of public ownership patterns, which he expressly rejects.

NOTES

1. Keynes's rational economic person is wider than the conventional neoclassical view of rationality which is purely based on known and measurable probability, even if that measure is less than full certainty. The bulk of Keynes's discussion on uncertainty relates to known probability relations, but which are 'numerically immeasurable' (Lawson 1985: 914).
2. See Carvalho (1988); Fitzgibbons (1988); Lawson (1985, 1990); O'Donnell (1989); Runde (1991).
3. For Carvalho (1988: 80), Keynes's 'long-term expectations are, thus, exogenous, because they cannot be definitely related to any current economic variable'.
4. For a detailed explanation of the turning points in the susceptibility cycle model, see Courvisanos (1996) – especially Chapter 5.
5. A large set of case studies which have examined investment behaviour in various western industrial economies since the Second World War have identified investment patterns that lend support to the susceptibility hypothesis and the historical analysis discussed in this section. A large number of these studies and their relevant areas of study are listed in Courvisanos (1996: Chapter 7, endnote 2: 215).

REFERENCES

Boyd, I. and J.M. Blatt (1988), *Investment Confidence and Business Cycles*, Berlin: Springer-Verlag.

Burkett, P. and M. Wohar (1987), 'Keynes on Investment and the Business Cycle', *Review of Radical Political Economics*, **19** (4): 39-54.

Carvalho, F. (1988), 'Keynes on Probability, Uncertainty, and Decision Making', *Journal of Post Keynesian Economics*, **11** (1), Fall: 66–81.

Courvisanos, J. (1994), 'A Kaleckian Behavioural Theory of Investment Cycles', PhD dissertation, Department of Economics, University of Newcastle, NSW, Australia.

Courvisanos, J. (1996), *Investment Cycles in Capitalist Economies: A Kaleckian Behavioural Contribution*, Cheltenham, UK: Edward Elgar.

Crotty, J.R. (1992), 'Neoclassical and Keynesian Approaches to the Theory of Investment', *Journal of Post Keynesian Economics*, **14** (4), Summer: 483–96.

Earl, P.E. (1988), 'Introduction', in P.E. Earl (ed.), *Behavioural Economics*, Vol. II, Aldershot: Edward Elgar: 1–16.

Fitzgibbons, A. (1988), *Keynes's Vision: A New Political Economy*, Oxford: Clarendon Press.

Goodwin, R.M. (1987), 'Macrodynamics', in R.M. Goodwin and L.F. Punzo, *The Dynamics of a Capitalist Economy: A Multi-Sectoral Approach*, Cambridge: Polity Press: 1–160.

Gordon, R.J. and J.M. Veitch (1986), 'Fixed Investment in the American Business Cycle', in R.J. Gordon (ed.), *The American Business Cycle: Continuity and Change*, Chicago: University of Chicago Press: 267–349.

Hillinger, C. (ed.) (1992), *Cyclical Growth in Market and Planned Economies*, Oxford: Clarendon Press.

Hillinger, C. (1992), 'Paradigm Change and Scientific Method in the Study of Economic Fluctuations', in Hillinger (ed.) (1992): 5–46.

Hillinger, C., M. Reiter and T. Weser (1992), 'Micro Foundations of the Second-Order Accelerator and of Cyclical Behaviour', in Hillinger (ed.) (1992): 167–80.

Kalecki, M. (1933), *Essay on the Business Cycle Theory*, Warsaw: Institute for the Study of Business Cycles and Prices, June (in Polish). Translated into English in J. Osiatyński (ed.) (1990), *Collected Works of Michal Kalecki*, Vol. I, Oxford: Clarendon Press: 65–108.

Keynes, J.M. (1936), *The General Theory of Employment, Interest and Money*, London: Macmillan.

Keynes, J.M. (1937), 'The General Theory of Employment', *Quarterly Journal of Economics*, **51** (2), February: 209–23.

Keynes, J.M. (1973), *The Collected Writings of John Maynard Keynes*, Vol. XIV, D. Moggridge (ed.), London: Macmillan.

Laski, K. (1987), 'Kalecki', in J. Eatwell, M. Milgate and P. Newman (eds), *The New Palgrave: A Dictionary of Economics*, Vol. 3, London: Macmillan: 8–14.

Lawson, T. (1985), 'Uncertainty and Economic Analysis', *The Economic Journal*, **95**, December: 909–927.

Lawson, T. (1990), 'Realism, Closed Systems and Expectations', presented at the Ninth International Summer School of Advanced Economic Studies, Centro Internazionale di Studi di Economica Politica, Trieste, Italy, 21–31 August.

Levine, D.P. (1975), 'The Theory of the Growth of the Capitalist Economy', *Economy Development and Cultural Change*, **23**, October: 47–74.

Levine, D.P. (1984), 'Long Period Expectations and Investment', *Social Concept*, **1** (3), March: 41–51.

Minsky, H.P. (1982), *Can 'It' Happen Again?*, Armonk, NY: M.E. Sharpe.

Oakley, A. (1993), *The Traverse as a Problem of Human Agency*, Department of Economics Research Reports or Occasional Paper No. 193, Newcastle NSW, University of Newcastle, September.

O'Donnell, R.M. (1989), *Keynes: Philosophy, Economics and Politics*, London: Macmillan.

Runde, J. (1991), 'Keynesian Uncertainty and the Instability of Beliefs', *Review of Political Economy*, **3** (2): 125–45.

Sardoni, C. (1987), *Marx and Keynes on Economic Recession*, Brighton: Wheatsheaf.

Simon, H.A. (1987), 'Bounded Rationality', in J. Eatwell, M. Milgate and P. Newman (eds), *The New Palgrave: A Dictionary of Economics*, Vol. 1, London: Macmillan: 266–8.

Spiethoff, A.A.K. (1953), 'Business Cycles', *International Economic Papers*, **3**: 75–171. Original published in German in 1923.

Steindl, J. (1941), 'On Risk', *Oxford Economic Papers* (5), June: 43–53.

Tooke, T. (1844), *An Inquiry into the Currency Principle*, 2nd edn, Series of Reprints of Scarce Works on Political Economy, No. 15, London: London School of Economics and Political Sciences, 1959.

Wood, G.A., P.E.T. Lewis and R. Petridis (1991), 'Has Investment in Australia's Manufacturing Sector Become More Export Oriented?', *The Australian Economic Review*, **94**, Second Quarter, April–June: 13–19.

Zarnowitz, V. (1992), *Business Cycles: Theory, History, Indicators and Forecasting*, Chicago: University of Chicago Press for NBER.

5. Different views on uncertainty and some policy implications*

David Dequech

1 INTRODUCTION

This chapter examines some post Keynesian policy suggestions in the light of different conceptions of uncertainty. Section 2 examines some of these conceptions, Section 3 turns to policy, and Section 4 concludes.

2 DIFFERENT VIEWS OF UNCERTAINTY IN A STRONG SENSE[1]

Uncertainty in a strong sense refers to a situation in which knowledge, due to the paucity of evidence, is incomplete to an extent that makes it not completely reliable as a guide to conduct. This uncertainty does not refer to a situation where the necessary information potentially exists but the agents' computational capability is not strong enough to perceive it. Uncertainty in this strong sense appears in different forms and under different names in some lines of research outside mainstream economics.

Different conceptions of probability may underlie the different ways in which uncertainty in the strong sense suggested above may in principle be expressed. One important distinction is that between the (so-called epistemic) theories of probability in which probability is a property of the way one thinks about the world, a degree of belief, and those theories (sometimes called aleatory) where probability is a property of the real world. Keynes's logical theory of *A Treatise on Probability* (TP hereafter) and the subjective probability theory are examples of the former, while the frequency theory belongs in the second category. As I argue below, if a property of the real world implies paucity of evidence, this does not necessarily prevent approaches using an epistemic theory of probability from expressing a notion of uncertainty in my strong sense. Probability may also refer to different things (such as arguments, events and states of nature) in the different approaches.

In this chapter, I concentrate on works inspired by Keynes. His notion of uncertainty has become the object of much controversy since the 1980s, especially because of the literature that explores the connection between Keynes's philosophical work (especially TP) and his economic writings. The issue of a possible continuity between the TP and Keynes's later works is part of this controversy. Another issue, emphasized here, is the connection between this literature and another attempt, by Paul Davidson, to make Keynes's later notion of uncertainty more precise.

2.1 *A Treatise on Probability* and Keynes's Strong Notion of Uncertainty

Probability in the TP is a relation between a proposition a and a proposition h, where h refers to the evidence. The probability represents the rational degree of belief one can have in the proposition a given the evidential proposition h. Thus, probability is always relative to the evidence. It lies between 0 and 1, that is, between impossibility and certainty.

Distinct from probability, and also important in the TP approach, is Keynes's notion of weight. Weight has to do with the evidence on which the probability relation is based. According to Runde (1990), Keynes uses three concepts of weight in the TP (1973a: 77, 84, 345), two of which amount to the same thing. Weight represents either the amount of relevant evidence (as opposed to probability, which depends on the balance of favourable and unfavourable evidence) or the evidence's degree of completeness[2] (the latter is equivalent to the balance of relevant knowledge and relevant ignorance).

In the TP framework, uncertainty in a strong sense is related both to non-numerical probabilities and to low weight. Contrary to O'Donnell (1989, 1991a), the TP notion of unknown probabilities does not refer to uncertainty in a strong sense.

Keynes asserted in the TP: 'The problem [of non-numerical probabilities] does not concern the case that the method of calculation prescribed by theory is beyond our powers or too laborious for actual application. *No* method of calculation, however impracticable, has been suggested' (1973a: 32, original emphasis; see also Carabelli 1988: 43; Lawson 1988: 43). This could qualify for an association with Keynes's famous quote in his 1937 QJE article, in which he states that about uncertain matters 'there is no scientific basis on which to form any calculable probability whatever. We simply do not know' (1973c: 114).

Runde (1991: 131, 133) argues that in the TP uncertainty does not mean only a complete absence of probable knowledge, referring also to a situation in which there is some sort of probable knowledge, but the argument has little weight (see Keynes 1973a: 342; Hoogduin 1987: 54n; Runde 1990: 290; Meeks 1991: 153; Gerrard 1995: 184). In Runde's (1990, 1991) view, uncertainty in this case refers to the reliability of probable knowledge as a guide to conduct in practice.

2.2 Davidson's Emphasis on Nonergodicity and Keynes's Strong Notion of Uncertainty

Davidson (1988a, 1991a) has borrowed modern terminology from the theory of stochastic processes to express Keynes's notion of uncertainty in terms of nonergodicity. In Davidson's conceptualization, probability seems to be a property of the real world (see Lawson 1988: 51 and O'Donnell 1991a: 57–8n). For those who propose that we interpret Keynes's mature economic work in terms of the TP framework, this is not a proper way of presenting Keynes's position, since Keynes defended in the TP a logical theory of probability.

In my opinion, though, the difference between Davidson's approach and one based on the TP, regarding the roots of a strong concept of uncertainty, is not as significant as it is argued or implied by some of those who have defended the thesis of continuity between TP and *The General Theory* (GT hereafter) (there is a potential difference in another respect, which I discuss below). Nonergodicity refers to an ontological characterization of uncertainty and it is compatible with different conceptions of probability. In the previous section, I referred to the absence of numerical probabilities and low weight as situations in the TP whose origins can be located in the paucity of evidence. Nonergodicity is associated with the possibility of structural changes and this possibility is a reason why the evidence available to economic decision makers is scant and knowledge not entirely reliable. It is not the only reason for this,[3] but I believe it is, directly and indirectly, the most fundamental one in the most relevant economic decisions. Some examples used by Keynes himself to clarify his notion of uncertainty in his later writings are connected with structural change (and thus with nonergodicity).[4]

The possibility of structural change is a property of the real world, but it can – and must – be dealt with in an epistemic approach such as the TP's. My suggestion in this regard is that the possibility of structural change affects weight, by implying incompleteness of evidence – the possibility of structural change may be seen as sufficient but not necessary for low weight. I am arguing thus that the reliability, as a guide to conduct, of probability as a feature of the way one thinks about the world is affected by the features of the world. Therefore, another important point to make is that, even if one uses a logical or, more generally, an epistemic theory of probability, this very important source of strong uncertainty lies in the external reality.[5] This is valid even if low weight is associated with some probable knowledge in the TP sense.

2.3 Is Uncertainty Gradable?

However, different conceptions of strong uncertainty may lead to importantly different answers to the following question: is uncertainty gradable, at least in *ordinal* even if not in cardinal terms? We can also ask: is some type of knowledge possible in a nonergodic environment? Given that uncertainty implies some ignorance, if this ignorance is not complete, then uncertainty can be gradable.

On some occasions, Shackle (for example, 1967: 228) seems to believe that uncertainty implies complete ignorance. So does Vickers (1994: 12). However, the association of uncertainty with nonergodicity does not have to lead to an association of the absence of numerical probabilities (either in the frequency-theory sense or the TP's) with complete ignorance.[6] For example, according to some interpreters (Hoogduin 1987; Runde 1991) the TP notion of weight provides a measure for uncertainty. Having weight as its measure, uncertainty would then be gradable.[7]

At any rate, in my opinion even those who argue that it is possible to have some kind of probable knowledge (in the TP sense) under uncertainty must recognize that such knowledge is incomplete and not fully reliable as a guide for conduct (Kregel (1987: 526) and Feltz and Hoogduin (1988: 107–8) do this implicitly, while Runde (1991) is more explicit). This is so because it is accepted that in this case uncertainty is marked by low weight, which implies a significant degree of ignorance. Factors such as what I call an optimistic disposition to face uncertainty (Dequech 1995b) must influence action, even if expectations are based on probable knowledge (in the TP sense). When probable knowledge is not possible, these factors affect not only the state of confidence but also expectations themselves.[8]

Furthermore, weight may not provide an incontestable measure of uncertainty, since there is disagreement among Keynes's interpreters as to the objective or otherwise character of weight.[9] If weight is to measure uncertainty (actually, a complement of uncertainty), then the notion of uncertainty becomes affected by the same problem involved in defining weight as the evidence's degree of completeness:[10] how can we, under uncertainty, know how ignorant we are? I do not conceive a completely objective answer to this question.

Followers of the TP-based or of the Davidson approaches could agree on the definition of uncertainty in a strong sense as the situation in which knowledge is incomplete and not totally reliable. The gradability or otherwise of uncertainty depends on the notion of knowledge. If knowledge is restricted to knowledge of completely reliable probability distributions, then uncertainty cannot be gradable. Knowledge would be absent, more than incomplete, and reliability would not be an issue.[11]

If knowledge is not restricted to that, then one can have some knowledge, even under uncertainty. To accept this point one does not necessarily have to adopt the TP logical theory of probability – as exemplified by Vercelli's (1991) notion of gradable '*k*-uncertainty' and by some generalizations of expected utility theory, discussed in Dequech (1996a).

For me, uncertainty does not mean complete ignorance. First of all, agents are or at least may be aware of uncertainty. In Hicks's (1977: vii) aphorism, 'people [may] know they don't know'. One of the aspects of reality about which some knowledge is possible is the existence of some institutions, to which I refer below. Furthermore, in a perhaps rockier terrain, Lawson (1985: 916–17) maintains that 'people have an extensive knowledge of social practices' such as conventions (also Darity and Horn 1993: 30). The knowledge of social practices (or institutions, in a broad sense) also appears in the institutionalist literature (Dequech 1995c).

Uncertainty can be gradable as one can have knowledge of more aspects of reality in some situations than in others. One should, however, distinguish between the knowledge of how institutions and conventions have worked so far and the knowledge of how they will work in the future. The potential for unpredictable social change must be admitted. At any rate, it seems that we do have some type of knowledge (which is not knowledge of completely reliable probability distributions) about the working of the social world that allows us to believe in the stability of at least some social practices. This belief is not totally unfounded; on the other hand, knowledge under uncertainty is incomplete and not fully reliable.

3 POLICY

3.1 Keynes and the Post Keynesians on Policy

This section briefly presents the main policy recommendations based on the post Keynesian interpretation of Keynes. These recommendations are directed against the two major problems of capitalism, in Keynes's view: unemployment and income distribution inequality (1936: 372). The distribution of income should be made more progressive essentially through fiscal policy (Carvalho 1992: 213), in two ways: (a) higher taxes on higher income and wealth and/or lower taxes on lower income and wealth; (b) government spending in social programmes (housing, hospitals, schools, and so on).[12] Given the intention of relating the policy discussion to the section on uncertainty, I concentrate here on anti-unemployment policies, for reasons that should become clear below.[13] Consumption would be stimulated by income redistribution, but the major problem is investment. Private investment may be insufficient for two reasons: firms' optimistic disposition to face uncertainty is not strong enough and/or firms are not able to obtain from the banking system the necessary financial provisions to entertain production and investment plans that they would otherwise carry out. The latter problem can be dealt with by a flexible monetary policy. The former can be attacked by the government in two ways. The first is the 'socialization of investment', which has been interpreted by post Keynesians as meaning that 'public or semi-public bodies' should be responsible for a considerable proportion of investment.[14] Keynes (CW XXVII: 322, *apud* Kregel 1985: 32) argued that 'the main task should be to prevent large fluctuations by a stable long-term programme' (see also Bateman 1994: 114). Private investment may grow directly in response to government incentives or because government expenditure creates demand for the private sector. The second way of increasing private investment, which has perhaps received less attention, is the establishment and/or reinforcement of institutional arrangements to reduce instability and foster confidence (Davidson 1991a: 142; Carvalho 1992: 210; Harcourt 1994: 36).[15] Examples of such arrangements are the legal system of contracts and market makers to reduce volatility, as Davidson emphasizes in several writings. A very important market maker is the central bank in its role of lender of last resort (Minsky 1986; Davidson 1988b: 623–4). Tax policy may also be useful in controlling speculation (Pressman 1987, 1989; Harcourt 1995).

3.2 A Brief Digression on the Determination of Employment

In Section 3.3, I relate the discussion about the concept of uncertainty with the above presentation of policy proposals based on Keynes. Before doing that, as I shall concentrate on policy measures aimed at fighting unemployment, it is useful to make explicit some points concerning the determination of employment in the private sector.[16]

Private employment is determined by the producers' state of short-term expectations. Thus, what matters most is expected results rather than realized results. The state of expectation depends on expectations themselves and on the state of confidence in them (see Keynes 1936: 148, where he refers to long-term expectations; I extend his comments to short-term expectations). These expectations involve uncertainty, especially concerning the proceeds from sales (Davidson 1978: 12–14; Kregel 1980: 37). How are these expectations formed?

In Chapter 5 of the GT, Keynes (1936: 50–51) wrote:

> the most recent results usually play a predominant part in determining what these expectations are. It would be too complicated to work out the expectations *de novo* whenever a productive process was being started; and it would, moreover, be a waste of time, since a large part of the circumstances usually continue substantially unchanged from one day to the next. Accordingly it is sensible for producers to base their expectations on the assumption that the most recently realised results will continue, except in so far as there are definite reasons for expecting a change.

This is exactly the essence of the convention that Keynes explicitly applied to the stock exchange (1936: 151–2). Keynes did apply it to product markets, but did not explicitly call it a convention. The resort to this convention may be what *usually* happens, but not necessarily. Some news may appear which breaks the producers' confidence in this convention. Only when this convention is followed do current investment and consumption determine employment in the next period. Whatever the particular pattern of short-term expectations that producers adopt, confidence in these expectations is necessary for them to actually determine employment decisions. Confidence *per se* is not sufficient for a high level of employment to be offered: optimism is also necessary. For example, if the economy is stuck in a depression, it is conceivable that producers will confidently adhere to the convention of projecting this situation into the future, with bad results in terms of employment.

3.3 The Concept of Uncertainty as a Theoretical Basis for Policy Suggestions

In this section, I discuss how some of the above policy suggestions relate to the discussion of whether uncertainty implies, or does not imply, complete ignorance.[17] Initially, though, I have a comment to make which is general in the sense that it applies to any policy measure. Uncertainty implies that factors such as animal spirits and the like influence people's behaviour, which in turn creates uncertainty about people's behaviour, therefore creating uncertainty also for policy makers.[18] A change in economic policy is a change in one of the structural parameters of the economic system and may create a negative reaction on the part of the private agents.[19] These agents may lose their confidence in the conventions they might have been adopting before the new policy. This is not necessarily a bad thing if those conventions were keeping the economy in a bad situation. Actually, policy makers may be described as trying to induce a new, better convention, but the uncertainty possibly created by the change in policy regime may lead agents to prefer liquidity instead of adopting a convention more in line with the policy objectives. None the less, if uncertainty does not imply complete ignorance, then policy makers can have some reasonable basis to decide which policy seems best. They must also try to win the public's confidence. In contrast, if uncertainty implies complete ignorance, policy makers are also completely ignorant as to people's possible reactions to their policies.

Let me now turn to two policy measures mentioned above: the creation/ reinforcement of institutions to foster stability and the programme of government expenditure, including that associated with the 'socialization of investment'.

Institutions for stability
My personal position, presented in Section 2, is that some type of knowledge is possible under uncertainty which is not knowledge of completely reliable

probability distributions. Whether we should call this knowledge probable or otherwise is not very important to me. I maintain that institutions such as contracts and market makers provide agents with a relatively reliable knowledge and thereby *reduce* uncertainty.[20] Under uncertainty, agents may resort to conventions. Factors that are at least partly subjective, such as what I call people's optimistic disposition to face uncertainty, will have to influence people's decision to use or not these conventions (Dequech 1995b). Nevertheless, these conventions can have a somewhat objective basis. Following Keynes's (1973b: 137) warning that one 'must not confuse instability with uncertainty', Davidson (1978: 385) argues that 'the economic system is *potentially* very unstable. Recognising the mercurial possibility of the economic system, man has, over time, devised certain institutions and rules of the game, which, as long as they are operational, avoid such catastrophes by providing a *foundation* for a conventionality of belief in the stability of the system and hence in the quasi-stability of the state of expectations' (emphasis added).[21] Therefore, institutions may provide a reasonable basis for the convention of projecting the current situation, a convention highlighted by Keynes in several instances. Furthermore, conventions themselves contribute for stability[22] and thus may reinforce themselves. As Davidson might repeat, institutions and conventions do that 'as long as they are operational', but the belief that they are operational does not have to be completely arbitrary. This belief tends to be more reliable in a country with more stable institutions and social practices, for example.

If uncertainty implied complete ignorance, then people would not have any objective reason to believe in the stabilizing operation of institutions. By the same token, policy makers would again have no objective reason to believe that these institutions would increase agents' confidence and stimulate private spending.[23]

Government expenditure

In part, employment can grow directly in the public sector. The impact of public expenditure on private employment is not so immediate. If public expenditure is to lead to higher employment, producers have to believe that this public expenditure will (either directly or through its multiplier effects on private spending) provide a higher demand for their products at the end of the next production period. This may happen in two ways. Producers may abandon their current convention or abandon their current preference for liquidity and adopt a new convention. Or, if they have been following a convention of projecting the current situation into the future and if the change in policy is gradual, they can continue to use this projection. In this case, a higher level of current demand (caused by government expenditure) would be projected into the future.

Likewise, if public expenditure is to have a positive effect on employment through its effects on private investment, then investors have to form confident expectations that public expenditure will directly or indirectly provide a higher demand for their products in the years to come. Higher current demand may provide an incentive for private investment through its impact on the rate of capacity utilization, but a stronger incentive would come from a long-term, stable programme of government spending. A public announcement of this programme would probably be helpful (see also CW XXVII: 413, *apud* Bateman 1994: 116; Carvalho 1992: 211).[24]

Kregel (1985: 45) observes that

> Keynes's proposed high and stable level of investment was meant to decrease our degree of distrust in our calculation of future conditions. By thus creating more stable, more certain conditions ... the degree of liquidity preference would be reduced. A reduction in liquidity preference would bring forth both reduction in interest rates and increased expectation of future return by raising the efficiency of capital.

Smithin (1989: 219–20) also maintains that 'Keynes's proposals for the social control of investment' would not only add to private investment but 'also encourage more private investment itself (crowding in rather than crowding out) by promoting a more stable environment and lowering uncertainty'. Similarly, Bateman (1994: 115) argues that Keynes 'offered his proposals for stable monetary policy and the socialization of *public* investment with the intention that they would both help to create more stable expectations among *private* investors' (original emphasis).

In my opinion, the notion that uncertainty is gradable and therefore reducible supports this. If uncertainty is gradable, government action may reduce it and thereby increase confidence. In contrast, if again uncertainty implied complete ignorance, then entrepreneurs would not have any objective reason to project a higher current level of demand into the future or to abandon their current convention or liquidity preference in favour of a more optimistic position. Again, by the same token, policy makers would have no objective reason to believe that increasing public expenditure is an adequate policy to pursue.

4   CONCLUDING REMARKS

The notion of uncertainty as something gradable and consequently reducible gives theoretical support to at least some important policy proposals based on Keynes's ideas. I am not saying that uncertainty would be eliminated, but it can be reduced by government action which: (1) introduces and/or reinforces institutional arrangements that create stability; (2) indicates to private agents a long-term programme of public spending.[25] If uncertainty implied complete ignorance (and therefore were not gradable), no objective basis would exist on which private decision makers could acquire more confidence in their expectations as a result of policy measures. Policy makers themselves would have an overwhelmingly difficult task in reasoning about the appropriate policy measures.

NOTES

*   This chapter explores ideas developed in the author's PhD dissertation and some of their policy implications. The author thanks his supervisors, Geoff Harcourt and Paul Davidson, for their advice and support. The usual caveat applies. Financial support from CNPq is also gratefully acknowledged.
1.   This section is based on Dequech (1996a, 1996b).
2.   Most authors take the first view. See, for example, Rutherford (1984: 379n), Hoogduin (1987: 57), Kregel (1987: 525–6), Carabelli (1988: 55–6), and Darity and Horn (1993: 26). O'Donnell (1991b: 71–2) sees weight as 'one of the indefinables' of Keynes's system, but argues that weight 'reflects' or increases with the amount of relevant evidence. The second interpretation is favoured by Lawson (1988: 49n) and, while recognizing that Keynes has different concepts of weight in the TP, by Runde (1990) and McCann (1994: 44). Runde convincingly argues that the second sense is the one required for connecting weight with confidence in *The General Theory*. Only in this sense may new evidence reduce weight and confidence.
3.   For example, the issue of structural change does not even appear in the analysis of the bets offered to subjects in Ellsberg's 1961 experiment and its replications and extensions (for a survey of these experiments, see Camerer and Weber 1992: Section 3.1). In these cases, reliability – and, in the TP framework, weight – is nevertheless involved.
4.   Keynes (1973c: 113–14) mentions 'the obsolescence of a new invention' as an example of uncertain matter about which 'we simply do not know'. In the GT (1936: 252; see also p. 141), Keynes refers to 'epoch-making inventions' as a factor of instability for the prospective yield of capital-assets. The connection between Keynesian uncertainty and Schumpeterian innovation is also made by Davidson (1982–83: 192–3) and Rutherford (1984: 381). Keynes also considers structural change of a more typically political or social nature. His 1937 examples of uncertain matters include 'the prospect of an European war' and 'the position of private wealth owners in the social system' some thirty years from now. In a 1938 letter regarding Tinbergen's work, Keynes (1973c: 287) again refers to the factors pointed out here: 'What place is allowed for non-numerical factors, such as inventions, politics, labour troubles, wars, earthquakes, financial crises?'. See also another comment on Tinbergen (1973c: 309).
5.   See Carvalho (1988: 78), for whom uncertainty 'is not simply a result of defective methods of reasoning. The insufficiency of premises is rooted in objective features of actual social processes'. See also Dow (1995: 118).
6.   See the exchange between Runde and Davidson in the *Critical Review*. Regarding Davidson's position, compare 1993: 431–2 with 1991a: 142; 1991b: 75.
7.   When referring to his TP chapter on weight, Keynes himself uses the expression '*very* uncertain' (emphasis added) in the GT (1936: 148n), which suggests that he treated uncertainty as gradable (also 1973c: 113).
8.   See also Carvalho (1988: 77n). The state of expectation depends on expectations themselves and on the state of confidence in them (Keynes 1936: 148). The concept of optimistic disposition is not exactly the same as that of animal spirits (Dequech 1995b).
9.   Contrast Runde (1990: 286–7) and Hoogduin (1987: 59) with Kregel (1987: 526).
10.   This is the definition that allows for a connection between weight in the TP and confidence in the GT (Runde 1990).

11. Reliability could not then be used to contradict the claim, made by defenders of strict versions of subjective expected utility theory, that the distinction between strong and weak uncertainty (or risk) is meaningless, or to address the Ellsberg paradox (Dequech 1996a). It is interesting to note that Keynes's *Treatise on Probability* is mentioned by many proposals or discussions of attempts to generalize the expected utility model in order to deal with situations where information is ambiguous or not totally reliable.

12. Both measures also contribute to reduce unemployment. A more progressive taxation does that by redirecting income towards groups with a higher propensity to consume and thus stimulating consumption.

13. Reference should also be made, even if briefly, to anti-inflation measures such as buffer stocks and incomes policy.

14. See Kregel (1985: 32–3), Chick (1987: 6), Pressman (1987: 17), Carvalho (1992: 212), Brown-Collier and Collier (1995: 342). Keynes did not specify the meaning of this expression in the GT (Davis 1992; Chick 1987: 6), even though he (1936: 378) clearly stated that it 'is not the ownership of the instruments of production which is important for the state to assume'. His budget proposals in the 1940s help to elucidate his position. See Brown-Collier and Collier (1995: 342) for the argument that the socialization of investment 'did not mean government control or influence over private investment'.

15. The 'socialization of investment' also has an impact on confidence. I return to this point below.

16. For a more detailed analysis, see Dequech (1995a).

17. One of my objectives here is to make people concerned with the logical coherence between policy and theory. I do not mean to imply that we should start from the policy proposals and then find a theory to support them. On the contrary, I believe that if the theory (which may be more or less influenced by political–ideological positions) does not support a certain policy, so much the worse for that policy.

18. People's optimistic disposition to face uncertainty (which, as mentioned above, is not exactly the same as animal spirits) is not irrational, but arational. Rather than being completely subjective, it is influenced by the cultural environment in which agents are located (Dequech 1995b; see also, on animal spirits, Davidson 1991b: 38; Matthews, 1991: 110). So is people's rationality (Dequech 1996b). Therefore, policy makers must pay attention to the cultural environment they deal with (see also Harcourt 1992: 30).

19. Keynes was concerned with the effect of public policy on confidence. See Bateman (1994).

20. The use of a notion of uncertain as gradable and reducible is clear in Minsky's (1996: 359, 364) defence of institutional reform.

21. Among these institutions, Davidson (1978: 388–9) highlights, first of all, contracts and especially the money wage contract, crucial for the 'conventionality of belief' in price stability. Market makers perform a similar function. Kregel (1980: 46; 1981: 69–70) clearly refers to 'uncertainty-reducing institutions', including not only wage and debt contracts but also supply and trading agreements.

22. See, for example, Vickers (1979–80: 244–5; 1994: 157–9), Harcourt and O'Shaughnessy (1985: 8–9), Earl and Kay (1985: 43), Hamouda and Smithin (1988: 163), Carabelli (1988: 220), Littleboy (1991: 30), Lavoie (1992: 11), Darity and Horn (1993: 30), Rotheim (1993: 199) and Crotty (1994).

23. Someone might argue that institutions act upon the effects of uncertainty (rather than upon uncertainty itself) by reducing the economic agents' anxiety in the face of uncertainty. I suggest that instead of some difference in psychological terms, the difference in terms of the existence and stability of some institutions provides a relatively objective basis for people to have a higher degree of belief in economic stability in Switzerland than in post-Soviet Russia, for example.

24. Policy makers may also need to persuade the public that such a long-term programme of public spending is not harmful to the economy. In other words, they may need to fight against a culture of anti-Keynesian ideas emanating from academia to other spheres.

25. The second type of measure is, of course, a particular way of reducing uncertainty. If the government announces a recessionist plan, this may also reduce uncertainty, but could make *pessimistic* expectations worthy of more confidence. As mentioned above, confidence *and optimism* are required for low unemployment.

REFERENCES

Bateman, B. (1994), 'Rethinking the Keynesian Revolution', in J. Davis (ed.), *The State of Interpretation of Keynes*, Boston: Kluwer: pp. 103–21.

Brown-Collier, E. and B. Collier (1995), 'What Keynes Really Said about Deficit Spending', *Journal of Post Keynesian Economics*, **17** (3), Spring: 341–55.

Camerer, C. and M. Weber (1992), 'Recent Developments in Modelling Preferences: Uncertainty and Ambiguity', *Journal of Risk and Uncertainty*, **5**: 325–70.

Carabelli, A. (1988), *On Keynes's Method*, London: Macmillan.

Carvalho, F. (1988), 'Keynes on Probability, Uncertainty, and Decision Making', *Journal of Post Keynesian Economics*, **XI** (1), Fall: 66–81.

Carvalho, F. (1992), *Mr. Keynes and the Post Keynesians*, Aldershot, UK: Edward Elgar.

Chick, V. (1987), 'Are *The General Theory*'s Central Contributions Still Valid?', *Journal of Economic Studies*, **4** (4): 5–12.

Crotty, J. (1994), 'Are Keynesian Uncertainty and Macrotheory Compatible? Conventional Decision Making, Institutional Structures, and Conditional Stability in Keynesian Macromodels', in G. Dymski and R. Pollin (eds) (1994), *New Perspectives in Monetary Macroeconomics*, Ann Arbor: University of Michigan Press: pp. 105–39.

Darity, W. and B. Horn (1993), 'Rational Expectations, Rational Belief, and Keynes's *General Theory*', *Research in the History of Economic Thought and Methodology*, **11**: 11–47.

Davidson, P. (1978), *Money and the Real World*, 2nd edn, London: Macmillan.

Davidson, P. (1982–83), 'Rational Expectations: a Fallacious Foundation for Studying Crucial Decision-making Processes', *Journal of Post Keynesian Economics*, **V** (2), Winter.

Davidson, P. (1988a), 'A Technical Definition of Uncertainty and the Long-run Non-neutrality of Money', *Cambridge Journal of Economics*, **12** (3), September: 329–37.

Davidson, P. (1988b), 'Financial Markets, Investment and Employment', in E. Matzner, J. Kregel and A. Roncaglia (eds) (1988), *Barriers to Full Employment*, London: Macmillan. Reprinted in P. Davidson (1990): pp. 611–28

Davidson, P. (1990), *Money and Employment – The Collected Writings of Paul Davidson*, Volume I, ed. by Louise Davidson, New York: NYU Press.

Davidson, P. (1991a), 'Is Probability Theory Relevant for Uncertainty? A Post Keynesian Perspective', *Journal of Economic Perspectives*, **5** (1): 129–43.

Davidson, P. (1991b), *Controversies in Post Keynesian Economics*, Aldershot, UK: Edward Elgar.

Davidson, P. (1993), 'Austrians and Post Keynesians on Economic Reality: Rejoinder to the Critics', *Critical Review*, **7** (2–3): 423–44.

Davis, J. (1992), 'Keynes on the Socialization of Investment', *International Journal of Social Economics*, **19** (10–12): 150–63.

Dequech, D. (1995a), 'Uncertainty, Conventions and Short-term Expectations', University of Cambridge, mimeo.

Dequech, D. (1995b), 'Toward a General Approach to Rationality and Conventions Under Uncertainty', University of Cambridge, mimeo.

Dequech, D. (1995c), 'Some Notes on Post Keynesianism and Institutionalism', University of Cambridge, mimeo.

Dequech, D. (1996a), 'Uncertainty in a Strong Sense: Meaning and Sources', University of Cambridge, mimeo.

Dequech, D. (1996b), 'Trying to Define Rational Behaviour Under Uncertainty', University of Cambridge, mimeo.

Dow, S. (1995), 'Uncertainty about Uncertainty', in Dow and Hillard (eds) (1995): pp. 117–27.

Dow, S. and J. Hillard (eds) (1995), *Keynes, Knowledge and Uncertainty*, Aldershot, UK: Edward Elgar.

Earl, P. and N. Kay, (1985), 'How Economists can Accept Shackle's Critique of Economic Doctrines without Arguing Themselves out of their Jobs', *Journal of Economic Studies*, **12** (1): 34–48.

Ellsberg, D. (1961), 'Risk, Ambiguity and the Savage Axioms', *Quarterly Journal of Economics*, **75**: 643–69.

Feltz, W. and L. Hoogduin (1988), 'Rational Formation of Expectations: Keynesian Uncertainty and Davidson's (Non)-ergodicity-criterium', *Metroeconomica*, **XXXIX** (2), June: 105–19.

Gärdenfors, P. and N.-E. Sahlin (1982), 'Unreliable Probabilities, Risk Taking, and Decision Making', *Synthese*, **53** (3), December: 361–86.

Gerrard, B. (1995), 'Probability, Uncertainty and Behaviour: A Keynesian Perspective', in Dow and Hillard (eds) (1995): 177–96.

Hamouda, O. and J. Smithin (1988), 'Some Remarks on "Uncertainty and Economic Analysis"', *Economic Journal*, **98**, March: 159–64.

Harcourt, G.C. (1992), 'A Post-Keynesian Comment', *Methodus*, **4** (1): 30.

Harcourt, G.C. (1995), 'A "Modest Proposal" for Taming Speculators and Putting the World on Course to Prosperity', in G.C. Harcourt (1995), *Capitalism, Socialism and Post-Keynesianism*, Aldershot, UK: Edward Elgar: pp. 32–38.

Harcourt, G.C. and T.J. O'Shaughnessy (1985), 'Keynes's Unemployment Equilibrium: Some Insights from Joan Robinson, Piero Sraffa and Richard Kahn', in G.C. Harcourt (ed.) (1985), *Keynes and His Contemporaries*, New York: St. Martin's Press: pp. 3–41.

Hicks, J. (1977), *Economic Perspectives*, Oxford: Oxford University Press.

Hoogduin, L. (1987), 'On the Difference between the Keynesian, Knightian and the "Classical" Analysis of Uncertainty and the Development of a More General Monetary Theory', *De Economist*, **135** (1): 52–65.

Keynes, J.M. (1936), *The General Theory of Employment, Interest and Money*, London: Macmillan. 1964 edn, Harvest/HBJ.

Keynes, J.M. (1973a), *The Collected Writings of John Maynard Keynes*, Vol. VIII, *A Treatise on Probability*, London: Royal Economic Society.

Keynes, J.M. (1973b), *The Collected Writings of John Maynard Keynes*, Vol. XIII, London: Macmillan.

Keynes, J.M. (1973c), *The Collected Writings of John Maynard Keynes*, Vol. XIV, London: Royal Economic Society.

Keynes, J.M. (1979), *The Collected Writings of John Maynard Keynes*, Vol. XXIX, London: Royal Economic Society.

Kregel, J. (1980), 'Markets and Institutions as Features of a Capitalistic Production System', *Journal of Post Keynesian Economics*, **III** (1), Fall: 32–48.

Kregel, J. (1981), 'On Distinguishing between Alternative Methods of Approach to the Demand for Output as a Whole', *Australian Economic Papers*, **20** (36), June: 63–71.

Kregel, J. (1985), 'Budget Deficits, Stabilisation Policy and Liquidity Preference: Keynes's Post-War Policy Proposals', in F. Vicarelli (ed.) (1985), *Keynes's Relevance Today*, London: Macmillan: 28–50.

Kregel, J. (1987), 'Rational Spirits and the Post Keynesian Macrotheory of Microfoundations', *De Economist*, **135** (4): 520–532.

Lavoie, M. (1992), *Foundations of Post-Keynesian Economic Analysis*, Aldershot, UK: Edward Elgar.

Lawson, T. (1985), 'Uncertainty and Economic Analysis', *Economic Journal*, No. 95, December: 909–27.
Lawson, T. (1988), 'Probability and Uncertainty in Economic Analysis', *Journal of Post Keynesian Economics*, **XI** (1), Fall: 38–65.
Littleboy, B. (1991), *On Interpreting Keynes*, London: Routledge.
Matthews, R. (1991), 'Animal Spirits', in Meeks (ed.) (1991): pp. 103–25.
McCann, C. (1994), *Probability Foundations of Economic Theory*, London: Routledge.
Meeks, J.G. (1991), 'Keynes on the Rationality of Decision Procedures under Uncertainty: The Investment Decision', in Meeks (ed.) (1991): 126–60.
Meeks, J.G. (ed.) (1991), *Thoughtful Economic Man*, Cambridge: Cambridge University Press.
Minsky, H. (1986), *Stabilizing an Unstable Economy*, New Haven: Yale University Press.
Minsky, H. (1996), 'Uncertainty and the Institutional Structure of Capitalist Economies', *Journal of Economic Issues*, **XXX** (2), June: 357–68.
O'Donnell, R. (1989), *Keynes: Philosophy, Economics and Politics*, London: Macmillan.
O'Donnell, R. (1991a), 'Keynes on Probability, Expectations and Uncertainty', in R. O'Donnell (ed.) (1991), *Keynes as Philosopher-Economist*, New York: St. Martin's Press: pp. 3–60.
O'Donnell, R. (1991b), 'Keynes's Weight of Argument and its Bearing on Rationality and Uncertainty', in B. Bateman and J. Davis (eds) (1991), *Keynes and Philosophy*, Aldershot, UK: Edward Elgar.
Pressman, S. (1987), 'The Policy Relevance of *The General Theory*', *Journal of Economic Studies*, **4** (4): 15–25.
Pressman, S. (1989), 'Keynes on Speculation', *Perspectives on the History of Economic Thought*, Vol. I, Aldershot, UK: Edward Elgar: pp. 97–110.
Rotheim, R. (1993), 'On the Indeterminacy of Keynes's Monetary Theory of Value', *Review of Political Economy*, **5** (2): 197–216.
Runde, J. (1990), 'Keynesian Uncertainty and the Weight of Arguments', *Economics and Philosophy*, **6**: 275–92.
Runde, J. (1991), 'Keynesian Uncertainty and the Instability of Beliefs', *Review of Political Economy*, **3** (2): 125–45.
Runde, J. (1993), 'Paul Davidson and the Austrians: Reply to Davidson', *Critical Review*, **7** (2–3): 381–97.
Rutherford, M. (1984), 'Rational Expectations and Keynesian Uncertainty: A Critique', *Journal of Post Keynesian Economics*, **VI** (3), Spring: 377–87.
Shackle, G. (1967), *The Years of High Theory*, Cambridge: Cambridge University Press.
Smithin, J. (1989), 'The Composition of Government Expenditures and the Effectiveness of Fiscal Policy', in J. Pheby (ed.) (1989), *New Directions in Post-Keynesian Economics*, Aldershot, UK: Edward Elgar: pp. 209–27.
Vercelli, A. (1991), *Methodological Foundations of Macroeconomics: Keynes and Lucas*, Cambridge: Cambridge University Press.
Vickers, D. (1979–80), 'Uncertainty, Choice, and the Marginal Efficiencies', *Journal of Post Keynesian Economics*, **II** (2), Winter: 240–245.
Vickers, D. (1994), *Economics and the Antagonism of Time*, Ann Arbor: University of Michigan Press.

6. Disequilibrium pricing, critical equilibrium and the real cycle

Etelberto Ortíz C.

1 INTRODUCTION

Keynesian results on equilibrium below full employment and instability have often been sustained on the basis of sticky prices. One of the important theses in post Keynesian economics is the notion that full employment and stability are not necessarily conditions attributable to 'a competitive economy', when considered in the context of a general equilibrium under perfect competition. The contention of this chapter is that equilibria below full employment and real cycles are the logical result of a successful competitive economy. The issues involved in this debate, as is well known, are highly relevant for the analysis of economic policy. Particularly, the standard neoclassical contention is that positions below full equilibrium or disequilibria are attributable to: price or other forms of rigidities, errors incurred by agents or to 'government failure', meaning price distortions induced by public policies, and/or difficulties involving the flow of information, or problems concerning the formation of expectations by relevant economic agents – generally speaking, to *market failure*. The consequence of such an approach is that economic policy is then directed towards correcting the ill function of markets. The core of the proposition is, then, that the notion of 'market failure' as the source of crises or cycles is at the heart of difficulties.

To deal with this issue, this chapter sustains the following proposition: from a classical view, it can be proved that a successful competitive process is fully consistent with a level of activity below full employment. Furthermore, considering an investment process on Keynesian lines, a successful competitive process necessarily develops into a real cycle, whose stability conditions may give rise to different patterns of adjustment.

Section 2 presents a disequilibrium model of pricing with classical–Keynesian features. Classical in terms of a model of prices of reproduction, Keynesian in terms of an investment function that responds to market expectations on profits. The concept of equilibrium within a dynamic framework is questioned, and the notion of a *critical equilibrium* is advanced to highlight its dynamic characteristics.

Section 3 discusses the stability characteristics that give rise to the possibility of a real cycle as a result of a successful competitive process. For this purpose, the model does not include any consideration about the relationship with financial and monetary issues, though we acknowledge they are essential for the overall analysis of the cycle and crisis theory. The emphasis is directed to the relationship of the competitive process and its limits within a classical model of pricing.

1.1 Background

Within classical–Marxist thought, there is the contention that the notion of competition is radically different, because it gives rise to a market process in which the sequence:

$$\text{disequilibrium} \rightarrow \text{adjustment} \rightarrow \text{disequilibrium}$$

leads to a process of highly consistent stabilization in order to explain a market economy's notable capacity for adjustment, while at the same time demonstrating the nature of the instability underlying its operation. Furthermore, the view of the market process itself may become considerably more coherent than the view from neoclassical theory.

In order to clarify this point, it is important to emphasize the difference between the concept of competition developed by classical economists in contrast to neoclassical thought. In classical models inspired by Sraffa, as well as neoclassical Walrasian models,[1] we find that the set of initial, starting conditions for production and demand determine the equilibrium result, although their theoretical elements differ. The adjustment process which takes place, leading towards equilibrium, is determined uniquely by the initial conditions. Therefore the point of equilibrium is not influenced by the type of disequilibrium initially present, or by the agents' patterns of reactions. Whatever the agents' perception of the initial disequilibrium is, the prior conditions suffice to establish the equilibrium point, independently of the agents' trial-and-error process in their attempts to reach equilibrium. Under such a notion, it is inconceivable that the position of any agent out of equilibrium should be identified. A truly disequilibrium model should give us the opportunity to identify any position out of equilibrium within a dynamic process. Therefore it demands the simultaneous identification of positions in equilibrium and out of equilibrium.

From 1983 there has been a continuous flow of papers on the modelling of a classical–Marxist conception of competition.[2] The results from this debate show that a consistent process of pricing can be reconstructed theoretically, from a model of production prices. Such models can prove that a recursive process of pricing, of independent agents, observing only rates of profit and prices, can lead to a highly stable process. There has been a general failure to identify the nature of the market process involved, with the exception of Kubin (1989).

One of the reasons for limited progress in this debate is that the classical theory of competition has been considered within a narrow time framework and without acknowledging the complexity and depth of the issues involved. For example, according to Nikaido (1983), we can present the problem as follows: the model of reproduction prices is conceived in terms of a sequence in which disturbances in market prices (P_t) tend to stabilize towards the production prices (P^*) as long as $|\mathbf{A}| < 0$ (with $\mathbf{A}$ representing the matrix of technical coefficients of production). The dynamic process may be represented as in the Cayley–Hamilton theorem:

$$(P^*) = \mathbf{e}^{At} (P_0) + \phi_t.$$

Obviously, when prices (P_t) are confronted with an external disturbance ϕ_t, they are unable to move towards equilibrium unless $\mathbf{A}$ generates a convergent succession, which in turn is only possible if: $|\mathbf{A}| < 0.$[3] Taking this into account, Nikaido views the classical and Marx models of competition based on production prices as resting on an overly narrow base, either on the characteristics of the production matrix or equivalently, that the organic composition of capital in the consumer goods sector should be greater than in the capital goods sector. In our view, Nikaido's conclusion may look correct with respect to the mathematical development of the problem. Not so in relation to the economic interpretation of classical–Marxist theories of competition, given that there are serious problems in the way this has been stated. As Kubin (1989) has clearly pointed out, the difficulty with Nikaido's critique rests in an inadequate representation of the way agents are able to resolve their position of disequilibrium. This basically refers to the way agents confront the perceived disequilibrium, and the resulting consequences on the adjustment pattern. Kubin's presentation proves that, if proper account is taken of a dynamic market process, where agents get involved in actual transactions, the process is highly stable, such that stability conditions do not depend at all on the structure of production.

Nevertheless, we have to recognize that there is a debate, and that there is not a unique approach to the problem. Two aspects require highlighting: one concerns the short-run stability conditions of the competitive process, the second, the long-run effect of competition on production. Restating the argument in Cayley–Hamilton terms, we find that no account has been taken of the scope of influence of ϕ on $\mathbf{A}$; certainly this is absent from all interpretations of classical–Marxist theories, with the notable exception of Schumpeter.[4]

One of the interesting features of this approach is that it generally depends on a market process that requires an effective demand function. That is, it depends on an investment function, operating out of equilibrium. This is the particular feature highlighted in this chapter.

1.2   Time and Competition

It is important to point out that the process of market adjustment that we have described rests on a theory of competition that leads to a 'selective process'. This phenomenon has a significant implication which is often overlooked. The model considers a process which, while selective in nature and having direct effects on the agents' reactions, cannot be identified as a 'simultaneous solution' or a 'general equilibrium' model. This is so because economic magnitudes and 'centres of gravity' are established through a sequential process. Thus, as agents react to disequilibrium, they make decisions to reallocate capital and prices, which alter not only the demand vectors but also the matrix of production conditions itself. For example, if the market price of sector i is higher than the production price: $P_i > P^*$, and the sectoral rate of profit is also higher than the homogeneous rate (r^*), there is room for the presumption that the rate of accumulation in this sector will be greater than the equilibrium growth rate $k_i > k^*$. Nevertheless, this movement will inevitably alter the matrix of production conditions. The withdrawal of the more vulnerable enterprises will alter the average (value). As a consequence, the process itself changes the centres of gravity for production prices.

At this point it would be worthwhile to take a look at the manner in which the dynamic problem of the competitive process has been formulated, from the viewpoint of various theories under consideration. In general, we have a time discrete system: $t_0, t_1, t_2, \ldots, t_n$. However, we must remember that in a dynamic process, there are in fact two kinds of fluctuations, one within each time period, and another throughout the succession of time periods. This behaviour can be diagrammed as follows:

	t_0	t_1	t_2	$\cdots$	t_n
begins:	$q_0 P_0$	$q_1 P_1$	$q_2 P_2$		$q_n P_n$
	$\downarrow$	$\downarrow$	$\downarrow$		$\downarrow$
finishes:	$q_0^r P_0^r$	$q_1^r P_1^r$	$q_2^r P_2^r$		$q_n^r P_n^r$

The models referred to earlier (in note 2), with the exception of Benetti (1986) and Kubin (1989), analyse a horizontal time sequence, but the results do not reflect the adjustments made by the agents within each time period. A case in hand can be observed in Flaschel and Semmler's second model (1988), where asymptotic stability is achieved by incorporating the agents' perceptions of the sign of the disequilibrium.

2 DISEQUILIBRIUM PRICING AND INVESTMENT WITHIN A MODEL OF REPRODUCTION

Disequilibrium is introduced through the reactions to the difference between the profit rate capitalists obtain in a particular sector r_i and the rate they generally view as the maximum attainable rate r'.[5]

The competitive process as conceived in classical–Marxist theories implies that when capitalists believe the profit rate they are obtaining in a given sector is smaller than the one they might obtain in other sectors r', then they will be impelled to reallocate their capital to the more profitable sectors. The underlying concept is that the fundamental objective for capitalists is to increase profits[6] and in fact, unlimited accumulation of capital becomes an overriding impulse.[7]

It is important here to define the rate r'. First, there is no a priori reason for associating this rate with a particular industrial sector. It may apply to one or various sectors. Only in a few cases would it correspond to objective data, although in general it may approach the average of the highest rates of profit achieved all over the economy. It cannot be identified exactly, however, because those obtaining the highest rates of profit do not necessarily make their results publicly available. Despite its ambiguous definition, the rate conceivably exists in the minds of all those desiring the best possible investment of their capital. It is a target rate which cannot be considered fictitious or disconnected from reality, and constitutes an important *leitmotif* in the accumulation process.

An alternative way to approach r', is to think about it as a proxy of the marginal efficiency of investment (MEI) ratio, in so far as it represents the prospective rate of return on investment. That is to say, it reflects the target yield of investment (see Arestis 1992). That means investment decisions are governed by the expected profitability of investment.

It should be noted that when capitalists consider moving their capital to an activity which they believe can obtain this target profit rate r', the money does not flow to only one sector. Rather it goes to those sectors which, as a group, are believed to offer the highest possible profit rate. In the same way, capitalists identify the less profitable sectors by the low rate of return on their investment and consequently, less and less capital is made available to these sectors.

The competitive process therefore rests on the following assumptions about capitalists' behaviour:

1. Not only are they constantly looking to obtain greater profits, but there is no a priori reason why they should be satisfied with some predetermined level of profit.[8]
2. Because of significant differences among profit rates, partly due to varying levels of efficiency among producers, investment behaviour leads to the reallocation of capital from one sector to another, sometimes as a result of simply copying the actions and technology of others.
3. In principle, the reallocation of capital does not modify the structure of technological relations, in other words it does not introduce technological changes. Matrix [A] may change, however, in a long-run process, because of the movement of capital and the resulting impact on the relative importance of each sector.[9]

To express these ideas formally: if capitalists in any sector of the economy observe that r_i, the rate which can be obtained in sector i, is such that $r^* < r_i < r'$ (with r^* corresponding to the standard profit rate[10]), then as a group they will be compelled to move capital to sector i. Therefore, we find a flow of capital to sector i, defined by the function: $\Phi_i (k) > 0$, such that:

$$\text{if } |r' - r_i| > \alpha, \text{ then } \Phi_i(k) > 0$$
$$\text{if } |r' - r_i| < \alpha, \text{ then } \Phi_i(k) < 0$$

with α representing the costs of changing from one sector to another. In the same way if a firm obtains a profit rate at the interval $r_i < r^* < r'$, an outflow of capital will be precipitated in accordance with the function $\Phi_i (k) < 0$. All we are assuming is a decreasing demand function, and producers are price makers.

We therefore find the following conditions in relation to the function $\Phi_i (k)$:

$$\text{if } \Phi_i (k) > 0, \text{ consequently: } \dot{q}_i > 0, \text{ and } \dot{r}_i < 0,$$
$$\text{if } \Phi_i (k) < 0, \text{ consequently: } \dot{q}_i < 0, \text{ and } \dot{r}_i > 0,$$

where: $\dot{q}_i = dq/dt$, $\dot{r}_i = dr/dt$.

These conditions simply indicate that an increase in the capital allocated to sector i will be followed by an increase in production q_i and a decrease in their respective profit rates; *mutatis mutandis* for a reduction in the capital invested in a given sector. These propositions will be tackled formally below.

The aggregated investment function is the addition of all firms' investment functions, such that: $I_{ti} = \int \Phi_i(r' - r_i)\, dt$; in so far as $\Phi_i(r' - r_i) > \alpha$; there is a positive flow of investment, that is, if $I' = \delta I / \delta \pi > 0$, where $\pi = (r' - r_i)$. Therefore $I_t > 0$, and $I'' = \delta I'/ \delta^2 \pi < 0$.

For the time being we assume that income effects of investment are dominant, and outweigh substitution effects due to the rate of interest. It is also assumed that all investment is backed by resources belonging to the enterprise, and ignores the operation of a financial system. This is so in order to highlight the real component of the internal cycle, and is not meant to minimize the financial issues involved.

When we look at the overall process, we start with the following production model:

$$q_1 = a_{11} q_1 + a_{12} q_2 + \ldots + a_{1n} q_n$$
$$q_2 = a_{21} q_1 + a_{22} q_2 + \ldots + a_{2n} q_n$$
$$\ldots$$
$$q_n = a_{n1} q_1 + a_{n2} q_2 + \ldots + a_{nn} q_n$$

which, in matrix form, for the period t, can be represented by: $[Q_i]_t = [A][Q_j]_t$ (with the capital letters inside brackets indicating matrixes and associated vectors).

Now, we shall examine the market process. Producers calculate demand based on past experience, and the growth rate determined by that experienced in each market. This is the equivalent to hypothesizing an adaptive process in which the expected demand is calculated on recent experience in market growth. Thus, producers will be willing to invest to produce quantity q_i^d, which does not exceed past sales plus an increase calculated from the experienced growth rate $q_i^d = (1 + g_i) q_{it-1}^d$. We can express formally this presumption for sector i as an equation of *effectual demand*:[11]

$$q_i^d = (1 + g_i) [a_{i1} q_{it-1} + a_{i2} q_{it-1} + \ldots + a_{in} q_{it-1}].$$

If we modify the equation for growth rates, the following is true for the case of two different commodities:

$$q_{1t} = a_{11} q_{1t-1} (1 + g_1) + a_{12} q_{2t-1} (1 + g_2)$$
$$q_{2t} = a_{21} q_{1t-1} (1 + g_1) + a_{22} q_{2t-1} (1 + g_2)$$

which can be expressed in matrix form as:

$$[Q_i^d]_t = [A'][Q_j]_{t-1} (1 + g_i).$$

The market process requires that $[Q_i] <=> [Q_i^d]$, with $<=>$ representing an exchange. The notion of effective demand considers that the advance of capital sets the structure and level of effective demand. The vector of final demand c_2, is added to the demand generated by the advance of capital for production:

$$a_{11}\,\dot{x}_1 + a_{12}\,\dot{x}_2 = x_1 - (\,a_{11}\,x_1 + a_{12}\,x_2\,)$$
$$a_{21}\,\dot{x}_1 + a_{22}\,\dot{x}_2 + c_2 = x_2 - (\,a_{21}\,x_1 + a_{22}\,x_2\,)$$

where: $\dot{x}_i = dx_i\,/dt$; and in matrix form: $\mathbf{A}\,\dot{\mathbf{X}} + \mathbf{Y} = (\mathbf{I} - \mathbf{A})\,\mathbf{X}$. This expression sets the relationship of production and effective demand.

We have, then, two problems to consider:

- the effect of investment decisions on the equation of effective demand, that is, the effect of $\Phi_i(k_i)$.
- the pattern of production decisions in the reproduction process, that is, the effect of production decisions in $(1 + g_i)$ and r_i.

The second problem may be analysed by solving the equations of effective demand for growth rates $(1 + g_i)$, such that:

$$1 + g_1 = \frac{1/\lambda - 1/\beta_2}{a_{11} - a_{12}/\beta_2}; \quad 1 + g_2 = \frac{\lambda - \beta_1}{a_{22} - B_1/a_{21}}$$

Where $\lambda = q_2/q_1$, $\beta_1 = a_{12}/a_{11}$ and $\beta_2 = a_{22}/a_{21}$.

This system of equations can be solved for the growth rate at which the system expands homogeneously: $(1 + g^*)$, which can be obtained by the eigenvalue associated with the system of equations of effective demand. The positive solution for both growth rates is obtained for g_1 as a decreasing function of λ and for g_2 as an increasing function of λ. The trajectories will be stable if the production relationship between the two sectors λ can be found in the interval $\beta_2 < \lambda < \beta_1$. But this is only a necessary condition.

The equilibrium growth path, $\mathbf{g}^*$, associated with the vector of equilibrium output $\mathbf{q}^*$, reflects the problem of the necessary proportions in production: $\mathbf{q}^*$. Nevertheless, there is no necessary relationship between this structure of production and the full-employment level of production: $\mathbf{Q}^* \cdot \mathbf{L}^* = F(\mathbf{Q}^*)$, given the labour requirements in $[\mathbf{A}]$. The differences from the actual $\mathbf{Q}$ and $\mathbf{Q}^*$, concern the disequilibrium of magnitudes and relates to the actual magnitude of total investment: $\mathbf{I}_t$.

Next we consider the effect of the functions of investment on growth levels and profit rates. If we look at the disturbances created by investment decisions, the system of equations of effective demand becomes:

$$q_{1t} = a_{11}\,q_{1t-1}\,(\Phi_1(k_1)) + a_{12}\,q_{2t-1}\,(\Phi_2(k_2))$$
$$q_{2t} = a_{21}\,q_{1t-1}\,(\Phi_1(k_1)) + a_{22}\,q_{2t-1}\,(\Phi_2(k_2)).$$

Let us now assume that capitalists believe they can obtain a higher profit rate in sector 1 than in sector 2, that is $\mathbf{r}_1 > \mathbf{r}_2$. Consequently, in disequilibrium this is expressed in the rates of accumulation of capital, such that we now have the following inequalities:

$$\Phi_1(k_1) = \frac{1/\lambda - 1/\beta_2}{a_{11} - a_{12}/\beta_2} > 0; \quad \Phi_2(k_2) = \frac{\lambda - \beta_1}{a_{22} - \beta_1 a_{21}} < 0.$$

In so far as $\mathbf{r}_1 > \mathbf{r}_2$, we find that $\Phi_1(k_1) > \Phi_2(k_2)$. It follows that we should then expect that q_1 increases at a faster rate than q_2, and consequently λ will tend to diminish. We can change the previous formulas to reflect this phenomenon as follows:

$$\Phi_1(k_1) = \frac{a_{11} - \lambda}{(\lambda a_{11})(\beta_2 - \beta_1)}; \quad \Phi_2(k_2) = (\lambda + a_{22})(\beta_2 - \beta_1).$$

In the particular case under consideration, assuming initially that the determinant of matrix $[\mathbf{A}']$ is negative, that is: $|\mathbf{A}| < 0$; then if $|\beta_2 - \beta_1| < 0$, Φ increases and consequently, due to the increased investment in sector 1, λ tends to decrease. Therefore the trajectories will have the following properties:

- Initially $(a_{11} - \lambda) < 0$, and $\Phi_1 > 0$.
- As λ decreases, $(a_{11} - \alpha)$ tends to become greater than zero, and Φ_1 will tend to decrease, even to the point of a negative figure.
- As well, we find that $(\lambda + a_{22}) > 0$, which will make Φ_2 negative, but as λ decreases, the contractive impact will tend to diminish.
- The condition $|\beta_2 - \beta_1| < 0$ is equivalent to saying that the trace of the matrix of technical coefficients $[\mathbf{A}]$ is equal to the trace of the matrix of fundamental solutions, that is, to the sum of the system's eigenvalues. This fulfils the condition that the sum of eigenvalues be positive and that the dominant eigenvalue be associated with a positive characteristic vector.

This case demonstrates that even when the condition of the negative determinant is fulfilled, the fluctuations in investment may not be limited, except in the case of $|\beta_2 - \beta_1| < 0$. If this last condition is not fulfilled, Φ_1 can only show a consistent trajectory if $|a_{11} - \lambda|$ is negative. If this is not the case, the fluctuations cease to be limited and Φ_2 increases permanently.

Now, we shall examine the market process under the condition that all agents must respect their budget constraint. This is possible if their income is equal to their costs plus the profit rate. The case of two different commodities can be expressed in the following way for any time period:

$$q_1 p_1 = a_{11} q_1 p_1 (1 + r_1) + a_{12} q_1 p_2 (1 + r_1)$$
$$q_2 p_2 = a_{21} q_2 p_1 (1 + r_2) + a_{22} q_2 p_2 (1 + r_2).$$

The solution of this system for the profit rate $(1 + r^*)$ associated with the dominant eigenvalue of matrix [A] permits us to identify the structure of production prices. Given that this system is a dual to the system of effective demand, the standard profit rate $(1 + r^*)$ corresponds to homothetic growth, for which production prices can be identified. This equation can be reformulated in the following manner:

$$(1 + r_1) a_{11} (1 + \beta_1 p_2) = p_1$$
$$(1 + r_2) \lambda a_{22} ((1/\beta_2) + p_2) = \lambda p_2$$

which can be resolved, respectively, for $(1 + r_i)$, and then, considering the fluctuations within a situation characterized by disequilibrium, the following equations may be obtained:

$$(1 + r_1) = \frac{p_1}{a_{11} + a_{12} p_2}; \quad (1 + r_2) = \frac{p_2}{a_{21} + a_{22} p_2}.$$

We then find that with an initial disequilibrium in which $r_1 > r_2$, if there is an increase of q_1 and a decrease of p_1, then $(1 + r_1)$ will tend to diminish. If, in addition, by reducing the amount of capital in sector 2 the production in this sector diminishes, we can expect P_2 to increase while r_1 will further diminish and r_2 will increase.

Price trajectories follow the same pattern of adjustment, except that the direction of change for particular values may be reversed,[12] depending on particular values of matrix [A].[13] Nevertheless, trajectories are convergent if the determinant of [A] < 0.[14] Consequently price trajectories are necessarily convergent, given that: $\lim P_t = P^*$ as $t \to \infty$. This case can be asserted under the same model and conditions, A < 0. But it can also be sustained under the conditions postulated by Kubin (1989), where convergence depends on the particular market structure and the actual adjustment path followed by producers in terms of quantities made available to the market.[15]

To summarize: if we analyse a process in which businesses reallocate capital to the sectors believed to have the highest possible rate (r') at a given moment, we may expect to find the following:

- In as much as sectoral growth rates indicate a production relationship between two sectors which is represented in the interval $\beta_1 < \lambda < \beta_2$, production will follow stable trajectories.
- Production trajectories following investment reallocation will be stable only if the resulting production rate λ does not fall outside the interval $\beta_1 < \lambda < \beta_2$. Therefore $\lambda \rightarrow q^*$, but not necessarily to Q^*. The reason is that even if we have the property that a lower wage entails a higher actual rate of profit **r**, such a change impacts all activities in differing degrees according to the structure of [**A**]. Nevertheless that does not mean a higher rate of capital accumulation or a higher rate of effectual demand. For a reduction in wages to have any impact on the rate of investment, it would be required that it has a positive effect on **r'**, that is, on the MEI. There is no a priori condition for this to apply.
- Even when we find stable trajectories in the flow of investment and production, the reallocation of capital to more lucrative sectors implies a decrease in the highest profit rates and an increase in profit rates in less lucrative sectors. These changes do not alter the standard rate **r*** but they do lower the potential profit rate **r'**.

The trajectories of the sectoral rate of profit may be represented by Figure 6.1.

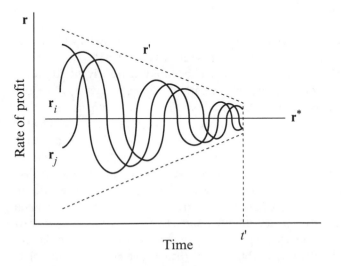

Figure 6.1   Trajectories of the rates of profit

The figure shows a convergent path of the particular (r_j) towards the standard rate (r^*) of the system. *The MEI or expected (r') profit rates corresponds to the upper envelop of all trajectories.* The model shows how the market process itself generates the fluctuations in the profit rate and also the way in which the standard rate appears as a rate characterizing the system of dynamic equations. The standard rate r^*, preserves a theoretical status of structural referent, and exists and operates concurrent to the market process. Although this does not mean that it influences the investment decision-making process. In a dynamic recursive context this process of reallocation of capital, given the production structure, generates fluctuations consistent with the variables under consideration – profit rates, prices and quantities – which tend towards their natural centres of gravity. In this case the natural variables operate as if they were a centre of gravity without having to be known by the agents. These natural rates are approached by market variables across time, however they are (posited) from the outset by the productive structure, and operate systematically as the centres of gravity for the market values.[16]

This interpretation conflicts with other readings of classical and Marx theories of prices, in which production prices appear as the 'determinants' of market prices. It is also at odds with those interpretations which refer to them as long-term equilibrium rates or averages. The difference is that in our approach we find that through a dynamic market process operating with a given production structure, a relationship is established which produces simultaneously both the gravitation of market variables as well as the expression of its structural elements: the natural or production prices, but characterizing a dynamic system, specifically the homogeneous profit rate and production prices, or what the classics call the natural variables.

At this point it is necessary to present another problem fundamental to the interpretation of the competitive process. If the agents base their decision to invest on the r' rate, it is because there is a benefit to be received, namely the difference between r' and the profit rate they are currently obtaining r_j: $|r' - r_j| > \alpha$. But this competitive process, as reliably successful as it may seem, has the effect of causing this difference to diminish, a fact which is clearly perceived by the agents. Therefore, is there any reason agents should continue to reallocate capital to the most lucrative sectors if by doing so they will cause a decrease in the profit rate r' which serves as the stimulus for the accumulation process? The conventional answer is limited to considering only the characteristics of asymptotic trajectories in profit rates and prices converging towards natural variables. From our point of view this is a limited answer. First of all, if the costs and risks associated with entering other sectors are higher than the difference between the profit rate currently obtained and the rate one believes is attainable, changing sectors will not be a profitable venture. Formally, for capitalists in sector

i we have: if $|\mathbf{r'} - \mathbf{r}_i| < \alpha$, then the competitive process is no longer driven forwards and accumulation may come to a halt.

The variation in $\mathbf{r'}$ demonstrates curiously that the competitive process as a whole is so intensive and efficient that as capital is reallocated in search of greater profit, market variables approach natural variables in terms of profit rates and prices. Paradoxically, this phenomenon brings to an end the competitive and investment process. The incentive to take risks in reallocating capital ceases to exist. The conventional interpretation of this problem is that a crisis would be faced at this point, because the prospects for capital accumulation in the medium term would be exhausted. The continuation of the accumulation process would require that the conditions under which the process operated until this point should be broken.

It is essential to identify that a falling $\mathbf{r'}$ does not necessarily imply that the standard theory of the falling rate of profit, which would correspond to an average rate, as the cause of a crisis. All through the process, the standard rate of profit $\mathbf{r}^*$ has remained at the same level. Therefore the argument is not for a falling rate of profit, but of a falling expected rate of profit on investment, $\mathbf{r'}$.

Above, the analysis of reallocation of capital takes place under the assumption that technological changes are not introduced. This is so because agents may enter other economic sectors simply because they could be copying the actions of others. Once the point $\mathbf{t'}$ is reached, in which $|\mathbf{r'} - \mathbf{r}_i| < \alpha$, this form of capital accumulation is no longer possible. From this point on, the continuity of the accumulation process demands that in order to continue investing, capitalists must introduce technological changes. In other words competition rests on the attempts to create differences among economic activities and, thereby, in profit rates. This effect operates for the medium term, and is associated with the creation of new prospects for accumulation.

It is important to observe the relationship between decision making regarding investment and the competitive process. According to the assumptions we have made about investment patterns, when investors discover there is no longer an economic incentive to change their investments' allocation (because the difference in the profit rates $|\mathbf{r'} - \mathbf{r}_i|$ is so small that it fails to cover the costs of changing sectors), one can expect a substantial reduction in investment.

This means that as long as point $\mathbf{t'}$ is not reached, investment will not necessarily affect the matrix of technical coefficients. On the contrary, once $\mathbf{t'}$ is reached, it becomes necessary to transform the technology being used in order to continue the reproduction–investment process.

This implies that, in the short term, competition generates low-level impacts, and even so, one can define a matrix $[\mathbf{B}]$ which has components derived from matrix $[\mathbf{A}]$ and the disturbances induced by Φ in such a way that these components will be $[\mathbf{B}] = \{a_{ij} + \varepsilon_{ij}\}$ where $|\varepsilon_{ij}| < \mu$, for a sufficiently small μ.

In this case matrix [**B**] brings together the same characteristics of stability as matrix [**A**], which is therefore recognized as a 'robust' structure.[17]

The difficulty in representing this process mathematically lies in the fact that the behaviour of **r'** shows a discontinuity that, until now, would be expected to behave with an asymptotic trajectory of the essential variables of the production process. We know that the discontinuity is introduced by α, the costs associated with changing the allocation of investment. However, in the present approach, this parameter is seen as part of the competitive process itself. What we are clearly unable to establish is the pattern of technological change that may follow. This is so because it is impossible to define beforehand the manner and time frame in which different agents will react to the need to introduce technological changes. All we can do is to predict a change to a new cycle of accumulation characterized by new conditions.

What becomes apparent is the limits of attempting to analyse the dynamic problems involved in the competitive process, by reducing it to the properties of asymptotic stability. Such an approach leads to the consideration of technological change as an exogenous phenomenon. Stability characteristics are certainly vital for understanding a model's basic operation. However, it is important to emphasize that the model presented here challenges the limitations of interpretation of the convergence process and redefines the problem of technological change as one fundamentally linked to the competitive process.

These results lead us to postulate that:

> The equilibrium associated with matrix **A**: $\{\mathbf{p^*}, \mathbf{q^*} \text{ and } \mathbf{r^*}\}$, is acknowledged as a *critical equilibrium* of the dynamic system represented, such that when the inequality $|\mathbf{r'} - \mathbf{r}_i| < \alpha$ is approached, investors will not continue to advance capital, and will consider investing to transform the matrix [**A**]. Therefore, the continuation of the reproduction process requires the incorporation of technological changes.

It is important to note that technological change can take place in almost any direction. There are no a priori restrictions placed on the form taken by a shift in the discontinuity, from point t' on, as represented in Figure 6.2.

Usually, within the terms of a model such as the one presented here, specific assumptions are established regarding the nature of technological change and competition.[18] The problem presented by this interpretation is that we are led to a point in which it is impossible to formally analyse all the aspects of the problems associated with structural change. Nevertheless, a new element that is particularly noteworthy has been introduced, which appears with the type of recursion analysed. It is the effect of the competitive process on matrix [**A**]. This leads us to introduce other considerations regarding the continuity of accumulation and change, that is, stability conditions.

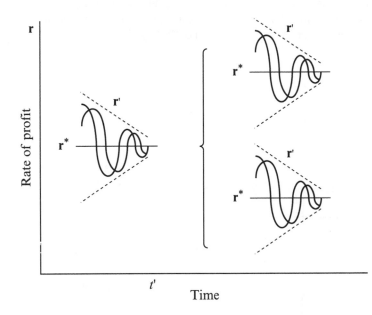

Figure 6.2   Alternative paths for structural change

3   COMPETITIVE ADJUSTMENT AND STABILITY CONDITIONS

Given that from time t', it is no longer possible to take for granted the linear continuity of expansion, there are five additional conditions to analyse:

1. While the variations on matrix [**A**] are bounded such that any disturbance fulfils the condition that matrix [**B**] = $\{a_{ij} + \varepsilon_{ij}\}$, such that $|\varepsilon_{ij}| < \mu$, for a sufficiently small μ, it is acceptable to consider that matrix [**B**], possesses the same characteristics of stability as matrix [**A**]. This means the eigenvalues of matrix [**B**], e_b, continue to fulfil the requirement of being understood as real, negative numbers. Expressed graphically, this means that in the presence of a disturbance such as ε_{ij}, the variations in the eigenvalues e_a and e_b, respectively, are such that they remain in quadrant I in Figure 6.3.

    The problem of passing from matrix [**A**] to another structure provided by matrix [**C**] lies in the transformations that are produced in the transition. Thus, even if [**C**] is stable, sudden but temporary shifts in an eigenvalue to quadrant II, such as $\mathbf{e}_c$, will be produced during the transition. In this case the transition cannot be viewed in terms of a linear model, since we cannot discard the possibility that the process could pass through a potentially unstable matrix which is neither [A] nor [B].

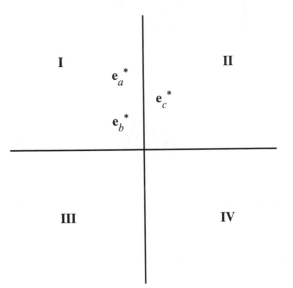

Figure 6.3   Phase diagram

2. As long as the model operates on matrix [A], it maintains the same speed of adjustment.[19] However, once the transition begins, changes in the model's set of parameters will automatically modify the system's subdominant eigenvalues, and therefore the speed of adjustment. If the modification of matrix [A] towards matrix [C] reduces the speed of adjustment, this can lead to alterations and disequilibrium in the stabilization process. The significant aspect in this case is not merely the characteristics of stability in matrices [A] and [C] given their dominant eigenvalues. Rather, we have that during the transition, the decisive element of a perturbation may be associated with one of the subdominant eigenvalues, a situation that may introduce a substantial difference in stability conditions. One possible result could be changes in the speed of adjustment. Nevertheless, we cannot discard the possibility that during the transition the conditions of stability may be dominated by the remaining eigenvalues (in other words by the 'transients'). For this reason, the transition from [A] to [B] may bring conditions of extreme fragility which are not evident to any of the agents involved.

3. The model prescribes stable growth as long as [A] corresponds to the homothetic growth vector $(1 + g^*)$.[20] Once the structural change begins, nothing indicates that the agents will be able to immediately identify the new production and demand vectors upon which their actions can be validated in the market, that is, the new homothetic vector of production and demand. Consequently, considerable disequilibrium between supply and demand can be expected during the transition. Therefore agents may not be able to determine the direction of adjustment which will lead to equilibrium. The reason is that in this phase, the conditions of stability may be dominated by subdominant eigenvalues that may produce non-linear cycles. Here, we confront the problem that stability is not reduced to 'proportions', and we have to admit that this situation may affect the stability with respect to 'magnitudes'. The fact that agents cannot easily determine the new relevant vector of demand and production has its repercussions. In our analysis, we find mistakes to be costly with the potential to create substantial adjustment problems. We can predict that in some sectors more than a few agents will find it increasingly difficult to sell their products while others will be unable to meet the demand. The impact of this magnitude in fluctuations of prices, quantities and profit rates may recreate an environment in which it will be very difficult to re-establish adequate conditions for a new cycle of accumulation. In the same way, this will undoubtedly have significant effects on payments and redemption of liabilities throughout the economy.[21] In this form, instability due to production proportions may bring in instability on magnitudes.

4. Once we have established that in a linear model it is impossible to foresee the direction of change in the process (in other words the form to be taken by new technology), or whether it will permit an increase or a decrease in the standard profit rate, the limitations of a conventional interpretation of the model become clear. This is true because at the critical equilibrium in a linear model, there is a possibility of a bifurcation, with an undetermined pattern of change that may take different paths. Furthermore, it is unknown whether the change will go through a potentially stable or unstable structure. One can begin by presuming that the bifurcation will take on the characteristics described by Hopf[22] or Van der Pol;[23] simply because these are two of the best-known models with regard to the stability problems under consideration. Under these conditions, the transition can no longer be viewed as linear.

5. The possibility that the expansion comes to a halt at t_m is not sustained on resource scarcity, growing labour costs, or difficulties of finding labour to handle the new equipment. It rests just on the incidence of the competitive drive on the MEI. Nevertheless it could be argued that there is reason to identify a relationship between the cost to switch investment from one

sector to another with full employment and growing marginal costs. Even under such conditions the impact would produce a growing α, not a decreasing **r**'. Therefore the critical equilibrium posited is not necessarily identified with a full equilibrium condition.

Returning to the aggregated investment function, once the differential profit rate is smaller than the cost to change allocation, π < α; then **I**' < 0 , and aggregate investment may face a contraction.[24] The discontinuity predicted by the model in fact breaks the nice movement of the cycle, and the phase of downward movements may consist of sudden deviations and shocks, as is represented by the curve x in Figure 6.4.

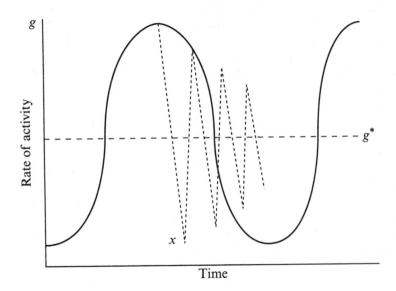

Figure 6.4   Growth cycle and crisis

4   CONCLUSIONS

To summarize, we have the following results:

- The concept of equilibrium relevant to the analysis of the competitive process and reproduction is one of a *critical equilibrium.*
- The concept of equilibrium generally used in models of production prices is unsatisfactory for representing the competitive process. The concept of

critical equilibrium permits a clear definition of the 'natural variables' as well as their relationship with market variables. Furthermore, a highly important reference is established with respect to the competition process and reproduction: an efficient competitive process permits the market variables to approach the natural variables. When market variables come close to the natural variables, the *leitmotif* of the competitive process ceases to function, triggering a turn in the direction of the cycle.

- The condition of equilibrium expresses fundamental relationships in the economy;[25] but it is necessary to put forward clearly the relationship between the agents' reactions to disequilibrium and equilibrium itself, which is precisely the problem of stability.

- A competitive equilibria is concerned with the relationship of an equilibrium position and variables out of equilibrium. The emphasis is on the process, not on the equality of both. Therefore the analysis of a competitive equilibria is not restricted to the fixed points where demand equals supply. In this form, stability conditions of the competitive process can prove that actual profit rates and market prices will be regulated by the equilibrium prices, that is, by production prices, namely the structural atractors of the system. None the less, this equilibria is not necessarily equal to the full-employment rate of production.

- Generally, problems of technological change are viewed on the basis of a long-term vision, considering structural changes and growth. From our point of view, this is not where the emphasis should be placed. When the need for technological change is incorporated as a significant component of the competitive process, it automatically becomes an ever present factor.

- One of the most interesting aspects of the non-linear model, which is particularly relevant in analysing long-term changes in a competitive economy, is that the model reflects a situation in which a stable process can be established at defined intervals with stationary solutions represented in cyclical movements, which have been called 'limit cycles'. It can be proved that the specific solution for the linearization of a non-linear model provides the possibility of utilizing the type of schemes used in the theory of production prices. Therefore, if we accept the notion that the fundamental dynamic problem is of a non-linear nature, this implies that the linear models of production prices are adequate, however incomplete, in representing fluctuations in a given phase. The obvious theoretical vacuum, for the moment, lies in the description of the relationship between stable phases and transition periods.

- One consequence of adopting a non-linear model is the introduction of a very important change in the way natural variables operate in classical–Marxist theory. It is hypothesized that the natural variables operate as a centre of gravity for market prices and profit rates. Referring to centres of gravity is equivalent to treating the proper values and vectors of the characteristic equation as 'attractors'[26] in the 'gravitational' process of market variables.

These attractors can operate within limited phases of a dynamic model similar to the form usually attributed to production prices in standard models. This is because in non-linear models, stability is maintained within a well-defined area of the phase plane.[27] Therefore, if we accept that the basic structural model is non-linear and bifurcations of the type previously presented may exist (especially those described by Hopf), this implies that the conditions of stability change in the attractor. This hypothesis suggests that although trajectories tend towards the centre of gravity, when they approach this centre, they come up against the stability conditions in the attractor, which is unstable. This occurs while preserving a space around the attractor where the conditions of stability are maintained. An equilibrium like this is recognized as a *critical equilibrium* (see Figure 6.5).

We emphasize that although this condition is viewed as typical of the stability conditions of a non-linear model, we can incorporate the concept of critical equilibrium as relevant to an analysis of fluctuation conditions of a competitive model established as a dynamic model developed from a linear model.

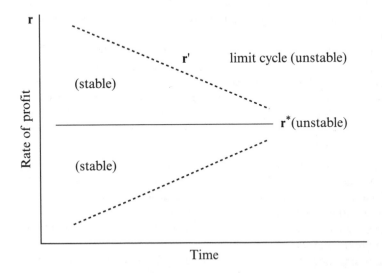

Figure 6.5   Limit cycle and critical equilibrium

NOTES

1. For example, the Sraffian perspective in Sraffa (1973) and Steedman (1984) and the Walrasian perspective in Arrow and Hahn (1971).
2. See Nikaido (1983), Duménil and Lévy (1987), Flaschel and Semmler (1986), Boggio (1985), Benetti (1986), Kubin (1989), and Ortíz (1994).
3. See Gandolfo (1985, Part II: Ch. 8); Luenberger (1979: 154–60); and Brock and Malliaris (1989).
4. See Semmler (1984).
5. This rate should not be confused with the maximum rate attainable if the wage rate were zero, that is, Sraffa's **R** (1973).
6. With respect to capitalists, Marx states: 'But as for personified capital, their motive is not use-value or enjoyment, but exchange value and its growth' (Marx 1981, Vol. I: 577).
7. 'Accumulate! Accumulate! This is the message of Moses and the prophets! Industry provides the material which accumulates by saving' (a reference by Marx to a passage in Adam Smith (1958, Book II: Ch. III)). Marx continues: 'Therefore, save! save! and reconvert into capital the greatest part possible of surplus value and surplus product. Accumulation for the sake of accumulation, production for the sake of production. Classical economy expresses in this way the historical mission of the bourgeois period' (Marx 1981, Vol. I: 681).
8. Marx proposes that the personified capital in the capitalist is aimed not at use-value 'but the untiring efforts at making a profit. (For the merchant the profits already made have little importance since the focus is always on future profits – Genovesi 1765)'. A reference is made in the same source to MacCulloch in *The Principles of Political Economy* 1830, London which emphasizes that 'the inextinguishable passion for profit, the [cursed hunger for gold] will always be what guides capitalists' (Marx 1981, Vol. I: 151).
9. Schumpeter states that when dealing with competition, we cannot simply take for granted the 'existing' conditions or structures, but rather we must search out the way the competition process itself creates and destroys those structures (Schumpeter 1947: 43).
10. The 'standard profit rate' corresponds with the dominant eigenvalue associated to matrix [**A**].
11. See Benetti (1986) on Torrens and the notion of 'effectual demand'.
12. Following Steedman's (1984) critique on the relationship between profit rates and prices.
13. This is so even under the conditions set by Steedman's (1984) critique, about the possibility that prices may not move in the direction of profit rates.
14. This point is considered in Duménil and Lévy (1987) and Flaschel and Semmler (1988).
15. Kubin's argument is set on a fixed point theorem for equilibrium and on the analysis of the stability conditions of the Jacobian obtained from the dynamic model.
16. In this sense it cannot be said that production prices are established over a long run, since they exist as part of a given production structure. In Marx's terminology, the standard rate is posited as an implicit assumption in the process of determining prices.
17. The term is a translation of 'systèmes grossiés' from the Pontriaguin–Andronov theorem (1930). This concept seems to have a great potential for analysing behaviour of complex structures.
18. For example, those which Marx uses to analyse this issue: fixed capital increases more than variable capital or its equivalent, as in the discussion found in Okishio (1984).
19. The adjustment speed of a dynamic model is given through a linear transformation of the subdominant eigenvalues.
20. Given that it corresponds to the eigenvalue on the left-hand side of matrix [**A**]. It is therefore a dual to the homogeneous profit rate.
21. It is possible at this time to propose only some of the relevant problems inherent in this situation. However, it is believed that a new line of research may be proposed, one that would establish a point of reference for discussing the disparities between structures of production and demand as well as the crisis of disproportions.
22. A bifurcation as described by Hopf is found in non-linear models characterized by structurally unstable phases which have nearly reached a critical point (Aulin 1989: 89–92). In this case the critical point is stable and surrounded by a stable limit cycle. A stable limit cycle 'can be thought of as a generalization of a point of equilibrium, as it is a complete cycle of behavior that is stable, not a particular set of values'.

23. In a bifurcation as described by Van der Pol, a stable equilibrium becomes unstable with a stable equilibrium on each side (Saunders 1980: 70).
24. One aspect of this situation has typically been addressed by making arbitrary assumptions about the moment in which there is a break in the tendency towards growth or decline, for example with a change in the level of the rate of interest or the availability of credit. This makes it easier to trace symmetrical fluctuations through a cycle.
25. Marx puts it this way: 'The exchange or sale of merchandise at its value is rational, based on the natural law of its equilibrium. Divergences can be explained on the basis of the law, however the law cannot be explained on the basis of divergences' (Marx (1881), Vol. III, C. X: 237).
26. The term 'attractor' to designate the equilibrium of a variable, is an equilibria that results from a confluent movement, which is not limited to physics or engineering, but whose usage is now standard in describing dynamic models.
27. The stability conditions can no longer be asymptotic for all $\mathbf{R}^n$, but may be considered to have local stability. Luenberger (1979: 322–7).

REFERENCES

Arestis, Philip (1992), *The Post-Keynesian Approach to Economics*, Aldershot: Edward Elgar.

Arrow, K.J. and F.H. Hahn (1971), *General Competitive Analysis*, San Francisco: Holden Day.

Aulin, Arvid (1989), *Foundations of Mathematical System Dynamics*, London: Pergamon Press.

Beavis, B. and I. Dobbs (1990), *Optimization and Stability Theory for Economic Analysis*, Cambridge: Cambridge University Press.

Benetti, Carlo (1981), 'La Question de la Gravitation de Prix de Marché dans la Richesse des Nations', *Cahiers d'Economie Politique*, Paris, No. 6: 9–33.

Benetti, C. (1986), 'La Théorie de la Demande Effective Chez Torrens', *Cahiers d'Economie Politique*, Paris, No. 12: 3–39.

Boggio, L. (1985), 'On the Stability of Production Prices', *Metroeconomica*, **XXXVII** (3): 3–25.

Brock, W.A. and A.G. Malliaris (1989), *Differential Equations, Stability and Chaos in Dynamic Economics*, Amsterdam: North-Holland..

Duménil G. and D. Lévy (1987), 'The Dynamics of Competition: A Restoration of the Classical Analysis', *Cambridge Journal of Economics*, No. 11: 133–64.

Duménil G. and D. Lévy (1989), 'The Competitive Process in a Fixed Capital Environment: A Classical View', *The Manchester School*, **LVII** (1): 38–53.

Flaschel, P. and W. Semmler (1986), 'The Dynamic Equalization of Profit Rates for Input–Output Models with Fixed Capital', in Semmler (1986a): pp. 1–34.

Flaschel, P. and W. Semmler (1987), 'Classical and Neoclassical Competitive Adjustment Processes', *The Manchester School*, **LV** (1), March, 13–37.

Flaschel, P. and W. Semmler (1988), 'The Dynamic Equalization of Profit Rates for Input–Output Models with Fixed Capital', in W. Semmler (ed.). *Lecture Notes in Economics and Mathematical Systems*, New York: Springer Verlag, No. 275.

Gandolfo, Giancarlo (1985), *Economic Dynamics: Methods and Models*, Amsterdam: North-Holland.

Hahn, Frank (1982), 'Stability', in K. Arrow and M. Intriligator (eds), *Handbook of Mathematical Economics*, Vol. II, Amsterdam: North-Holland, pp. 745–93.

Jorgenson, D.W. (1961), 'Stability of a Dynamic Input–Output System', *Review of Economic Studies*, **XXVIII** (2), 76: 5–22.

Kubin, Ingrid (1989), 'Stability in Classical Competition: An Alternative to Nikaido's Approach', *Zeitschrift für Nationalokonomie*, **50** (3).

Luenberger, D.G. (1979), *Introduction to Dynamic Systems. Theory Models, and Application*, New York: John Wiley & Sons.

Marx, K. (1973), *Grundrisse*, Introduction to the *Critique of Political Economy*, Harmondsworth: Penguin Books.

Marx, Karl (1975), *El Capital*, (Capital), Mexico. Siglo XXI Eds.

Morishima, Michio (1974), *Marx's Economics*, Cambridge: Cambridge University Press.

Nikaido, H. (1983), 'Marx on Competition', *Zeitschrift für Nationalokonomie*, **43** (4).

Nikaido, Hukukane (1985), 'Dynamics of Growth and Capital Mobility in Marx's Scheme of Reproduction', *Zeitschrift für Nationalokonomie*, **45** (3): 197–218.

Okishio, N. (1972), 'On Marx's Production Prices', *Keizaigaku Kenkyu*, **19**.

Okishio, Nuobo (1984), 'Progrès Technique et Taux de Profit', in Abraham Frois (ed.), *L'Economie Classique. Nouvelles Perspectives*, Paris: Economica: 110–126.

Ortíz, Etelberto (1994), *Competencia y Crisis en la Economía Mexicana*, Mexico: Siglo XXI. Edit.

Robles, Mario (1990–92), 'Trabajo Abstracto, Capital y Competencia en Marx. El modelo de la Transformacion', in *Competencia y Monopolio. Teoría y Práctica*, Numero especial revista ECONOMIA : TEORIA Y PRACTICA. U.A.M. México: 47–66.

Schumpeter, J.A. (1947), 'The Dynamics of Competition and Monopoly', in Alex Hunter (ed.), *Monopoly and Competition*, Harmondsworth: Penguin Books, 1969.

Semmler, Willi (1984), *Competition, Monopoly and Differential Profit Rates*, New York: Columbia University Press.

Semmler, W. (1986a) *Competition, Instability and Nonlinear Cycles*, New York: Springer Verlag.

Semmler, W. (1986b), 'On a Microdynamics of a Nonlinear Macrocycle Model', in Semmler (1986a).

Shaikh, Anwar (1990), *Valor, Acumulación y Crisis*, Ensayos de Economía Política. Bogotá, Colombia: Tercer Mundo Editores.

Sraffa, Piero (1973), *Production of Commodities by Means of Commodities. Prelude to a Critique of Economic Theory*, Cambridge: Cambridge University Press.

Steedman, Ian (1984), 'Natural Prices, Differential Profit Rates and the Classical Competitive Process', *The Manchester School*, **52** (2).

Uzawa, H. (1961), 'On a Two Sector Model of Economic Growth', *Review of Economic Studies*, **XXIX** (1), 78: 40–47.

C. Government Spending

7. The effects of the fiscal deficit on the composition of US GDP: an analysis of disaggregated data

Neil H. Buchanan

1 INTRODUCTION

The impact of the federal budget deficit on the economy is a source of continuing concern, both among macroeconomists and – even more urgently – among political decision makers. The old Keynesian consensus that budget deficits were generally good for the economy, in the sense of making it more prosperous (or, at least, in bringing it out of recessions), has been pushed aside by the fear that the apparently-large deficits that began in the 1980s in the United States have damaged the economy and are impoverishing future generations of Americans. The continuing debate over whether fiscal deficits make us better off or worse off – or some combination of the two – can, of course, best be addressed by returning to the data.

In previous work (Buchanan 1996a, 1996b), I have investigated various measures of the US fiscal deficit in terms of their potential uses in time-series empirical research. Those studies, based on previous work by Eisner (among many examples, see 1991, and Eisner and Pieper 1988, 1992), reached two major conclusions: (1) among alternative measures of the fiscal deficit, the so-called price-adjusted standardized-employment deficit (PASED) provides the most statistically significant time-series results in a variety of standard macroeconomic regressions (at least among federal-level deficit measures);[1] and (2) there is an identifiable, positive statistical correlation in annual data between the one-year-lagged deficit[2] and the annual growth rate of US gross domestic product (GDP) – but this correlation has widely varying statistical significance, depending upon the specification and sample period chosen.

Looking at the second conclusion (which concerns theoretical macroeconomic relationships as opposed to the definitions and derivations of particular deficit series), it is important to ask whether a robust specification of the growth/deficit relationship can be found where the relationship varies based on the state of the economy. It is also natural to ask whether the effect of fiscal deficits on GDP is a broad-based effect, or whether particular sectors of the economy or types of expenditure are more likely to respond positively (or negatively) to deficit spending than are others. This chapter will investigate those questions.

Section 2 presents the results of an expanded analysis of aggregate GDP growth as a dependent variable, including a description of the use of an interactive term in the regression. Section 3 describes the reasons for, and approach to, disaggregating of GDP growth for use in further regression analysis. Section 4 presents the results of the statistical and regression analyses of disaggregated data, emphasizing not merely the statistical results but also the macroeconomic implications of those findings. Section 5 concludes.

2   ANALYSING AGGREGATE GDP GROWTH

The econometric tests summarized below are based on a non-linear variant of equations found in Eisner (1991) and tested further in Buchanan (1996a, 1996b). Those results were based on a simple reduced-form equation, based on a standard Keynesian IS/LM framework,[3] with GDP growth as the dependent variable, and the monetary base, the exchange rate and the fiscal deficit as independent variables.

For the current study, this framework was enhanced to allow for the possibility that the effect of deficits varies with the state of the economy, consistent with (but not limited to) the logic of the multiplier/accelerator interaction concept, pioneered by Samuelson (1939). That is, if the response of private firms to increases in real GDP is to increase fixed investment (in a positive response to good economic news, *à la* 'animal spirits'), then this effect could be captured by a non-linear, interactive term which couples the GDP gap and the fiscal deficit.

The implications of the interactive term are potentially much broader than this, however, in that it would capture *any* response to deficits when the economy has a GDP gap, for example, changes in residential investment in housing, changes in consumption of any kind, or responses by any other component of GDP. Indeed, one of the main purposes of this chapter is to identify the disaggregated responses of GDP growth to deficits. Section 4 summarizes that analysis.

The interactive term, moreover, is designed to capture the effects of supply constraints in the economy, or what Keynes (1936) referred to as 'bottlenecks'. That is, when the economy is running at higher levels of capacity, the likelihood grows that increases in aggregate demand will have smaller effects. For example, in a deep recession, there are plenty of workers, machines, factories and farms that are not producing anywhere near their potential output. The real economic response to a deficit in such a situation is likely to be quite strong, as potential suppliers will readily respond to the demands from either government (if the deficit is a result of higher government spending) or consumers (if the deficit is, instead, a result of lower net taxes) by providing more goods and services. The response to multiplier effects (the spending by the workers and business owners who were the beneficiaries of the first round of deficit spending) is also likely to be strong and immediate.

As the economy strengthens, however, this effect naturally weakens. Since there are fewer workers available to produce more goods, and factories are running with little down time, the existence of a deficit does not (and most likely *cannot*) lead to increases in output – or, at best, it can only lead to smaller increases in output. The multiplier responses are similarly diminished.

Given this intuition, a statistical test which is based on the simple assumption that the response of the economy to deficits is always the same (independent of the state of the economy) will miss this potentially-important non-linearity. Separating the effects of deficits on the economy into linear and interactive effects will indicate whether this notion of bottlenecks, or supply constraints, is empirically supported.

In the larger sense, therefore, the results below will act as a consistency test of standard Keynesian theory as it relates to the macroeconomic impact of fiscal deficits. While there are many variations on the meaning of the term Keynesian, it is none the less true that the various groups (synthesis Keynesians, post Keynesians, new Keynesians and variations thereof) have a set of views of deficits and their effects on the economy that are broadly similar – although there is certainly disagreement even among adherents of individual schools of thought.

Each group would, with some qualifications, answer 'yes' to each of the following questions. Do deficits affect GDP at all? Do deficits raise GDP growth, at least in the short run? If there are effects, do they differ depending on the state of the economy? Do consumption and imports rise when the economy strengthens? Are government purchases independent of prior deficits? Are exports exogenous?

Perhaps most importantly, the results summarized below can also shed some light on the areas of controversy that exist even among Keynesians, especially on questions relating to fiscal deficits and investment. Do deficits crowd out investment at all? If so, do they crowd out investment more or less as the economy weakens? Which types of investment respond most strongly to deficits? For example, is equipment investment more responsive to deficits (especially during recessions) than investment in plant?

Finally, it is also possible to investigate questions about which some uncertainty exists even at the intuitive or theoretical level. For example, how do the components of consumption respond to deficits? Of particular interest for policy, is consumption of durables more responsive to deficits than are other types of consumption?

Each of these questions is addressed (although certainly not definitively answered) in the analysis below. Virtually all of the results which Keynesians would expect are confirmed, the most basic being that deficits do have real effects. For the controversial questions, the results show (among other things) that crowding out of investment is supported by the point estimates, but that those point estimates are not statistically significant at standard levels of confidence. Accelerator effects on equipment investment *are* supported, and the relevant coefficients are highly statistically significant. Overall, a believer in activist fiscal policy (especially as a countercyclical measure) will not be disappointed by these results.

2.1   The Growth Equation and the Meaning of the GAP

The dependent variable continues to be the GDP growth rate. (All variables were analysed using *real* values, expressed in fixed-weighted 1987 dollars, unless otherwise noted.) The independent variables are: a monetary variable, a deficit variable and an interactive variable (the product of the deficit and the GDP gap), with each entered as a distributed lag for one through four quarters.[4]

The equation to be estimated, therefore, is:

$$\%\Delta GDP_t = \alpha_0 + \alpha_1 Trend + \sum_{i=1}^{4}\beta_i \Delta MB_{t-i} + \sum_{i=1}^{4}\gamma_i DEF_{t-i} \sum_{i-1}^{4}\delta_i GAP_{t-i}DEF_{t-i} + \varepsilon_t$$

where MB is the real monetary base as a percentage of real GDP, DEF is the real structural deficit (nominal PASED divided by nominal GDP), and GAP is the GDP gap (which is defined as $[(GDP - GDP^*)/GDP^*]*100$, where GDP^* is the value of GDP when the unemployment rate is at NAIRU[5]).

I shall refer to the sum of the estimated coefficients on DEF_{t-1} through DEF_{t-4} (that is, $\gamma_1 + \gamma_2 + \gamma_3 + \gamma_4$) as the 'linear coefficient'. The term 'interactive coefficient', on the other hand, refers to the sum of the coefficients in the last term of the regression $(\delta_1 + \delta_2 + \delta_3 + \delta_4)$.[6]

What distinguishes the present analysis from the studies noted above (other than the use of quarterly data rather than annual data[7]) is the use of the interactive term. The theoretical reason for the use of this term was described earlier. The technical reason is that the γ_i's will provide an estimate of the response of GDP growth to the deficit when there is no gap (since a gap of zero makes the last term drop out). This isolates the response of GDP growth to a change in the deficit when the economy is at NAIRU. Therefore, the positive sum of the estimated γ_i's (as discussed below, and shown in the tables at the end of the chapter) reflects the surge in GDP growth as the level of GDP rises from the current level of GDP^* to a higher *level* of GDP^* after an increase in the deficit.[8]

The interactive coefficient can then identify the effects of deficits that arise only when there is a gap, with the weighted sum of the linear and interactive coefficients indicating the total effect of the deficit on GDP growth in any given state of the economy.

With a distributed lag, there is a question as to how to test the statistical significance of the coefficients on the four quarterly lagged independent variables. An 'exclusion test' indicates the probability value (or *p*-value, which is the same as the significance level, or one minus the confidence level) of the *F*-test that the coefficients of the four quarterly lags of the deficit variable are all zero, that is, the test of whether it would hurt the regression to 'exclude' the four lagged values of the deficit (as a group) from the list of independent variables.

An alternative test of the significance of the deficit variables is the *t*-test of whether the *sum* of the coefficients of the four lags of the deficit is significantly different from zero. However, this test is less meaningful than the exclusion test, because it is possible for the coefficients not to be of the same sign. In that case, even if all four coefficients are individually significantly different from zero, the sum of the coefficients might not significantly differ from zero, even though the inclusion of the four lags of the independent variable improves the regression results.[9] Therefore, the results below and in the tables at the end of the chapter test statistical significance using the exclusion test criterion.

For the sample period 1972:1 through 1994:4, using quarterly data, the above regression produces the following results (with the *p*-values of the significance tests – for individual parameters and for exclusion tests, as appropriate – in parentheses):[10]

$$\%\Delta GDP_t = 6.38 \qquad -0.05 \text{ Trend}+$$
$$\quad\quad (0.00) \qquad\quad (0.01)$$
$$\quad 19.94\ \Delta MB_{t-1} -6.84\ \Delta MB_{t-2} -2.32\ \Delta MB_{t-3} +22.73\ \Delta MB_{t-4}+$$
$$\quad (0.08) \qquad\quad (0.56) \qquad\quad (0.85) \qquad\qquad (0.06)$$
$$\quad 0.40\ DEF_{t-1} +0.73\ DEF_{t-2} +0.99\ DEF_{t-3} -1.88\ DEF_{t-4}+$$
$$\quad (0.51) \qquad\quad (0.25) \qquad\quad (0.12) \qquad\qquad (0.00)$$
$$\quad 0.04\ GAP_{t-1}{}^{*}DEF_{t-1} \qquad\quad +0.01\ GAP_{t-2}{}^{*}DEF_{t-2}+$$
$$\quad (0.70) \qquad\qquad\qquad\qquad\quad (0.92)$$
$$\quad 0.05\ GAP_{t-3}{}^{*}DEF_{t-3} \qquad\quad -0.27\ GAP_{t-4}{}^{*}DEF_{t-4}$$
$$\quad (0.65) \qquad\qquad\qquad\qquad\quad (0.02)$$

Linear coefficient $(\Sigma\gamma_i) = 0.24$, Interactive Coefficient $(\Sigma\delta_i) = 0.16$
$$\qquad\qquad\qquad (0.03) \qquad\qquad\qquad\qquad\qquad\qquad\qquad (0.21)$$
Adjusted $R^2 = 0.24$, Durbin–Watson = 1.47.

The critical values of the Durbin–Watson test statistic (DW), at a 5 per cent two-sided level of significance, are 1.72 and 2.28 for the beginning of the inconclusive range and 1.51 and 2.49 to reject the null hypothesis that there is no first-order serial correlation (AR(1)). The estimated DW value of 1.47 indicates that the equation needs to be re-estimated, correcting for AR(1).

Since the equation to be estimated is non-linear, however, the standard methods of correcting for serial correlation (the Cochrane–Orcutt procedure and the Hildreth–Lu procedure being the most common) cannot be used. Therefore, an analogous generalized least squares procedure (using non-linear least squares), described in more detail below, was used.

The corrected equation was:

$$\%\Delta GDP = \rho\%\Delta GDP_{t-1} + \alpha_0 + \alpha_1 Trend + \sum_{i=1}^{4} \beta_i(\Delta MB_{t-i} - \rho\Delta MB_{t-i-1}) +$$

$$\sum_{i=1}^{4} \gamma_i DEF_{t-i} - \rho DEF_{t-i-1}) + \sum_{i=1}^{4} \delta_1(GAP_{t-1}DEF_{t-i} - \rho GAP_{t-1}DEF_{t-i-1}) + u_t.$$

The results of that regression are shown below:

$\%\Delta GDP_t = 4.61$ -0.03 Trend +
     (0.01)   (0.06)
     $19.44\ \Delta MB_{t-1} -6.06\ \Delta MB_{t-2} -2.04\ \Delta MB_{t-3} +20.10\ \Delta MB_{t-4}+$
     (0.08)   (0.58)   (0.86)   (0.08)
     $0.36\ DEF_{t-1} +0.75\ DEF_{t-2} +1.00\ DEF_{t-3} -1.88\ DEF_{t-4}+$
     (0.54)   (0.20)   (0.09)   (0.00)
     $0.05\ GAP_{t-1}{}^{*}DEF_{t-1}$ $+0.02\ GAP_{t-2}{}^{*}DEF_{t-2}$ +
     (0.63)   (0.86)
     $0.05\ GAP_{t-3}{}^{*}DEF_{t-3}$ $-0.29\ GAP_{t-4}{}^{*}DEF_{t-4}$
     (0.64)   (0.01)

Linear coefficient $(\Sigma\gamma_i) = 0.23$, interactive coefficient $(\Sigma\delta_i) = 0.17$
           (0.02)   (0.13)
Adjusted $R^2 = 0.27$, Durbin–Watson = 1.93, $\rho = 0.25$ (0.03)

In the results immediately above, note that the values of the linear coefficient and the interactive coefficient (0.23 and –0.17, respectively) are very close to the estimates in the OLS regression (0.24 and –0.16).[11]

(I also estimated the model with eight quarterly lags of the linear deficit and interactive terms. The results were roughly consistent with the results here, with the sum of the coefficients of the eight linear DEF variables almost exactly double the sum of the four linear coefficients shown above (0.49 versus 0.23). The sum of the eight coefficients on the interactive terms, on the other hand, was almost exactly half of that shown above (–0.09 versus –0.17). This indicates that two years of a 1 per cent deficit is twice as stimulative as one year (when there is no gap), and the interactive response is both absolutely and relatively less important when the deficit persists for that long. The statistical significance of each of the coefficients, however, was markedly worse than the results here, with the *p*-value of the exclusion test on the (eight-lag) linear coefficient rising above 0.07 (versus 0.02 for four lags) and that for the interactive coefficient ballooning to more than 0.41 (from 0.13). The adjusted R^2 fell to 0.22. Therefore, the analysis below proceeds from a model using four lags of all independent variables.)

2.2   The GAP and the Interactive Term

The interactive term indicates the response of GDP growth to the deficit when the economy is in a boom (a positive GAP) or a recession (a negative GAP). If the δ_i's are significantly different from zero, therefore, the GDP growth rate would respond differently to the deficit, depending on the condition of the economy.

Even before initiating the regression tests of the specified equation, however, it was important to ensure that inclusion of the GAP variable was justified on statistical grounds. That is, if it turned out that DEF and GAP were highly correlated (for example, if the deficit were only positive when GAP was negative, a case of pure countercyclical spending), then the collinearity between the two right-hand-side variables would compromise the statistical results – and the economic implications of the specification would be seriously brought into question as well.

Therefore, I measured the gap in two ways: as an income gap (as described above) and as an unemployment gap (where GAPU is defined as the actual unemployment rate minus the NAIRU unemployment rate). The results of simple correlations were quite definitive. Not only does neither GAP nor GAPU have a strong correlation with DEF, but the correlation coefficients are *extremely* low. For the 1972:1–1994:4 period, GAPU and DEF had a correlation coefficient of 0.20, while GAP and DEF had a correlation of 0.03. GAP also had a correlation of 0.03 with the other explanatory variable, ΔMB. Since GAP was almost perfectly non-collinear with either of the other exogenous variables, therefore, it was both economically meaningful and statistically legitimate to include the interactive term in the regression equation.

While the exclusion test for the interactive coefficient in the AR(1) regression summarized above does not achieve the usual 95 per cent level of confidence, it will turn out that some of the components of GDP do have significant interactive coefficients; so the interactive term will be extremely important in understanding the overall response of GDP and its components to deficits. Also, it is worth looking at the point estimate of the interactive coefficient in the aggregate growth equation to understand how to interpret it – both econometrically and macroeconomically.

Since a value of unity for the GAP variable means that the economy is 1 per cent above GDP* (and since the DEF variable is also measured in full per cent at an annual rate), the interactive coefficient indicates the response of the economy to a 1 per cent real structural deficit (in the preceding year) when GDP is 1 per cent above GDP*. If the coefficient were found to be positive, therefore, this would imply that there is a positive response of GDP growth to the deficit (in addition to the response measured by the linear coefficient) when the economy is booming. A negative coefficient, on the other hand, would mean that the response of GDP growth to deficits is less than the response would be at NAIRU (as measured by the linear coefficient).

For the estimates obtained from the GLS regression summarized above, the positive sum of the γ_i's (0.23) indicates that there is a stimulative effect of deficits when the economy is at GDP*, so that a 1 per cent deficit causes GDP growth to be 0.23 per cent higher than it would otherwise be. If the economy is in a 1 per cent recession (that is, GAP = –1.0), and DEF is 1.0, then the negative sum of the δ_i's (–0.17) indicates that GDP growth rises (since the two negative signs cancel out) *more than* indicated by the γ_i's alone, or a total of 0.40 per cent of extra growth due to the deficit. On the other hand, adding together the γ_i's and δ_i's would tell you that GDP growth is only 0.06 per cent higher when there is a 1 per cent deficit and the economy is 1 per cent above GDP*.

This is shown graphically in Figure 7.1, which shows that there is a linear relationship between deficits and growth with a slope of 0.23. This relationship pertains when GAP = 0. When GAP = 1, however, the response of GDP growth to the deficit becomes much weaker, as indicated by the flatter line in the graph. When GAP = –1, the line becomes steeper, reflecting the greater responsiveness of growth to the deficit. The lines for GAP = –3 and GAP = –5 are steeper still, with the response to DEF = 1 in the latter case being a rise in GDP growth of 1.08 per cent.

Note that it is possible for the deficit to have a net negative impact, since when GAP = 2 (which has only been exceeded from 1972:4–1973:2 and from 1979:1–1979:3 during the sample period), the effect of a 1 per cent deficit is to lower GDP growth by 0.11 per cent. This would mean that the economy is so strong that any positive impact of the deficit is being more than crowded out by some combination of responses among consumers, businesses and the foreign sector.

Also, although it is not shown on the graph, as the gap becomes more and more negative (which means that the economy is weaker and weaker), the stimulative effect of deficits is further enhanced by the strong responses of private actors to the stimulus to the economy. In other words, the weaker the economy, the more underutilized resources there are to respond to any stimulus, and the more likely is the stimulus to be re-spent and thus provide further stimulus to income.

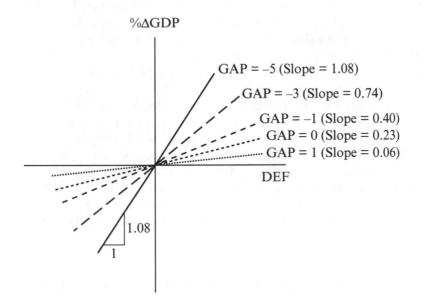

Figure 7.1 The effects of the interactive coefficient

This is analogous to arguments dating back at least to *The General Theory*, that deficits are much less stimulative when the economy is near or above capacity and more so when the economy is in a recession. In fact, although the current model is specified differently from the aggregate supply/aggregate demand model (in that this model does not have prices in it, and it includes both the *level* of GDP and the *growth rate* of GDP in different variables), these results tend to confirm the 'Keynesian version' of the short-run aggregate supply curve in that model. That is, rather than a constant upward slope of the short-run aggregate supply curve, this suggests that the curve is steeper to the right of GDP^* and flatter to the left.

2.3 Looking for Asymmetric Effects

This method of estimation, however, assumes that the effect of deficits varies symmetrically around GDP^*, that is, that the effect of deficits when there is a positive 1 per cent GDP gap is the same in absolute value as the effect when there is a negative 1 per cent GDP gap. Clearly, this need not be true. Therefore,

I also performed a test which attempted to allow for an asymmetric effect of deficits, depending upon whether GAP is positive or negative. This was done by adding a new interactive variable, where each of the four lags of the new interactive term is multiplied by a dummy variable, with the dummy equal to 1 when GAP was positive and zero otherwise. This would allow the effect of being above or below GDP* to differ (although it still assumes linearity).

However, the statistical results were disappointing in two ways. First, the exclusion test of the four coefficients on the dummied interactive terms had very low statistical significance, with a confidence level of only 52 per cent that all four coefficients were significantly different from zero. Second, the numerical sum of those variables was positive and more than three times greater in absolute value than the interactive coefficient without a dummy (1.11 versus −0.29). Also, the linear coefficient became negative, −0.30.

This would mean that the effect of deficits on GDP growth is negative when there is no gap, near zero when GAP = −1, and *very* positive as the economy gets stronger. Since this result is both unfounded in theory and statistically weak, the analysis was limited to a simple symmetric interactive relationship, as described above.

3   WHAT CAN BE LEARNED FROM DISAGGREGATING GDP?

The above results indicate that there is an interesting set of statistical relationships that tend to confirm certain well-known theoretical macroeconomic propositions. A positive fiscal deficit raises the rate of GDP growth, and the effect is greater in a weak economy and lesser (and perhaps even negative) in a strong one. This indicates that it would be useful to know just what it is in the GDP that responds to the deficit when there is no gap, and what creates the interactive response to the gap. In order to pursue those questions, it will be necessary to disaggregate the left-hand side of the equation.

Before describing the specific empirical tests and the estimates obtained from disaggregating GDP, however, it will be useful to explore further what might be learned by separating GDP into its components. This will provide a preview of the issues that are raised by such an analysis, and it will also offer a glimpse of the types of results that might be found.

3.1   Macroeconomics and Disaggregation

Having found a robust statistical relationship between an aggregate variable such as GDP and any explanatory variable(s), it is sensible to ask whether less-aggregated series which add up to that aggregate dependent variable are similarly correlated with the explanatory variable(s). For example, if there were fifty separate series of state domestic product, and those fifty series summed in each time period to GDP, then it would be natural to ask how the variables that statistically correlate to GDP correlate to each of the fifty state output series.

More to the point for the analysis below, it is natural to ask in what way the variables that affect GDP growth also affect the growth of the different types of expenditures and production that make up GDP. If the deficit increases GDP, does it increase C, I, G and NX proportionately, or does one of those variables (or a subset of them) correlate more strongly than the others with the deficit? On the supply side, does the increase in GDP show up as proportionate increases in goods, services and structures? For either question, of course, there are further potential disaggregations made possible by the official statistics; so each of these questions can be asked about different types of consumption, investment, goods production, and so on.

The answers to these questions, of course, have direct import for macroeconomic policy. If higher deficits were found to correlate with higher business investment in structures, for example, that would lead to quite different attitudes about deficit spending than a finding that nearly all of the increase in GDP was accounted for by increases in the production and purchase of nondurable goods. In the latter case, concerns about deficits 'impoverishing our grandchildren' would tend to gain credibility, whereas the former case would tend to diminish such concerns.

Of course, the relationships described above between the deficit and GDP growth have to carry over to at least one of GDP's components (or a combination of components), simply as a matter of mathematical fact. The challenge is to find those components (or relationships among components) that account for the robust statistical relationship between deficits and GDP growth.

The most basic question that can be asked is: are each of the four major components of expenditure as responsive as GDP itself is to deficits, or does the deficit lead only to (for example) higher investment spending – which, as noted, would tend to alleviate fears that public dissaving is compromising the economy's future growth? Or, do other types of expenditure respond?

If one found, on the other hand, that consumer expenditure was the most responsive element of total expenditures, it would be useful to know whether this rise is for immediate consumption or is based on a more investment-like motivation. That is, as argued by, among many examples, Gordon (1993) and Fuhrer (1992), consumer expenditure on durable goods can potentially be better understood as an accumulation of assets for future consumption, and is thus a different way of saving for the future. Clearly, then, knowing that consumption spending responds to deficits would argue for further disaggregation of the consumption series.

Therefore, if one finds a strong relationship between deficits and a particular type of expenditure, one would then want to know how the expenditures in that category break down: for example, is the higher investment composed of higher inventories, residential construction, or plant and equipment spending? Is higher consumption concentrated in durables, nondurable, services, or all three?

More questions can be addressed. Do the presumably exogenous components of GDP, federal government purchases and exports, display weak statistical correlation to the right-hand-side variables, or is their presumptive exogeneity brought into question by the results? Do imports and consumption respond similarly to deficits, or do deficits seem to cause a greater response in the purchases of domestic goods over foreign goods (or vice versa)?

Finally, do results regarding demand-side responses correspond with those regarding supply-side responses: for example, if there is a strong response of both business plant expenditures and residential construction to an increase in the deficit, is there also a strong increase in the production of structures?

3.2 Disaggregated Data in the NIPA

While there are a theoretically limitless number of ways to break down the GDP into component parts, the statistical method used for this analysis will exploit two of the disaggregations which are provided as part of the National Income and Product Accounts (NIPA), each of which sums to total GDP. These are: (1) the expenditures method, which separates GDP into the four familiar spending categories (private consumption, private investment, government purchases and net exports) as well as subcategories (and, in some cases, sub-subcategories) of those four aggregates, for a total of eighteen series; and (2) the major products method, which separates GDP into the various types of output produced (such as nondurable goods and structures), for a total of thirteen series.

Eisner and Pieper (1988) perform a similar analysis on disaggregated expenditures, but not at a significant level of disaggregation (for example, only breaking investment into fixed investment and inventories), and using annual data and a simpler specification of the growth equation. Their results are contrasted with the results of this analysis in Section 4.

3.3 Disaggregation and Statistical Correlation

The simplest relationship between an aggregate variable and its components would be one in which each component individually mirrors the variance of the aggregate. This is shown in Figure 7.2, which displays what I call Type 1 Disaggregation, where a variable Y and each of its component series ($Y1$, $Y2$ and

Y3, which add up to Y) are similarly correlated to each other and to an independent variable, X.

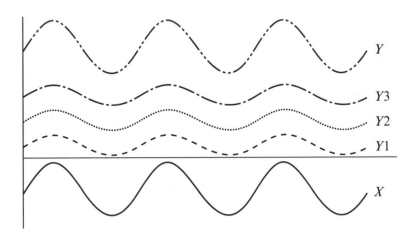

Figure 7.2   Type 1 Disaggregation

However, it clearly will not always be the case that each of the component series is significantly correlated with the explanatory variable(s) in question. For example, if the explanatory variable that showed statistical significance in the GDP equation were 'tourist visits into the United States', it might well be the case that the regressions for only a few states (most likely New York, Maryland, Virginia, Florida, California and Hawaii) would show a strong relationship between state domestic product and that explanatory variable.

This possibility is shown in Figure 7.3, which displays Type 2 Disaggregation, the situation where an independent variable (X) has a strong correlation with an aggregate series (Y) but with only one of Y's components (Y3, in this case). The robust statistical relationship is between Y3 and X, with Y1 and Y2 clearly showing no correlation with X (and, in this case, simply showing diverging linear trends). In the aggregate, therefore, Y3 is the part of Y that accounts for the strong statistical relationship between Y and X.

It is also possible, however, to find that there is no strong relationship between *any* single component series and the explanatory variable(s). Figure 7.4 shows an example of Type 3 Disaggregation, which shows that none of the three subseries is well correlated with X over their entire range, but the three summed together produce a good (actually, a perfect) statistical fit.[12] Clearly, there are a limitless number of ways in which this situation can be drawn (including cases where no single subseries tracks X even for a short time period), with the common factor being merely that the summed components must correlate to X.

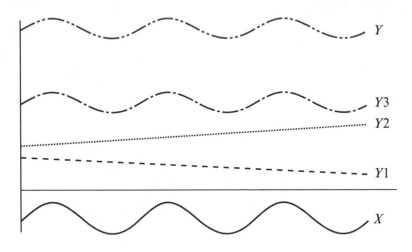

Figure 7.3   Type 2 Disaggregation

In the case of Type 3 Disaggregation, moreover, the relationship among the components might be either 'systematic' or 'independent'. That is, the relationship among the components could be driven by a causal process ('systematic') and would therefore continue to be found over different sample periods, or it could simply be a statistically random coincidence ('independent').

An example of a systematic relationship among components would be a regression of total crop yield against rainfall with quarterly data. One is likely to discover, upon looking at disaggregated data on particular crop yields, that some crops only respond to rainfall in certain quarters. (That is, a crop which is planted in April and harvested in June would respond to rainfall in only one quarter of the year – with no output response to any exogenous variables at other times of the year.) Aggregate crop yield would, of course, none the less be reliably related to rainfall.

Thus, while one most likely could not identify any component of total crop yield which is significantly correlated with rainfall in *every* quarter, it is undoubtedly true that aggregate crop yield is statistically correlated with rainfall each quarter, year after year. The robust statistical relationship, therefore, would not be a historical anomaly.

On the other hand, it could be that the component series are essentially independent, in which case the visible statistical relationship between the aggregate dependent variable and the exogenous variable(s) is merely fortuitous for the time period under study. For example, one might find that the results of US presidential elections (the left-hand-side variable) are correlated with major leaguers' batting averages (the right-hand-side variable) in the baseball season preceding the election. In that case, trying to find a sub-aggregate of voting patterns (disaggregated by state, or congressional district, or gender of voters, for example) that is correlated with batting averages would likely prove futile.

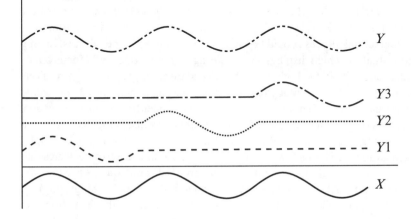

Figure 7.4   Type 3 Disaggregation

In such a case, the aggregate results are statistically unlikely to repeat themselves over different sample periods; so none of the individual components, or any combination thereof, is likely to be correlated with batting averages. It would not be reliable, therefore, to assume that the statistical correlation will continue; and it would be dangerous at best to make predictions about the results of policy based on such a relationship!

Thus, the possible results of investigating the components of GDP are: (1) Type 1 Disaggregation, where each component series is correlated to the explanatory variable(s) in similar ways; (2) Type 2 Disaggregation, where only some of the underlying series are so correlated; (3) Type 3 Disaggregation which is systematic, where the particular components will continue to interact in the same way over different time periods; and finally (4) Type 3 Disaggregation which is independent, where the overall statistical correlation among the aggregated series and the independent variable is not likely to continue, because the components and the exogenous variable are moving independently of one another.

Realistically speaking, of course, Type 1 is highly unlikely for any serious amount of disaggregation. Type 2, on the other hand, is simultaneously desirable (in the sense of implying a meaningful statistical relationship to study) and at least reasonably likely to be found in real data (as opposed to Type 1). Type 3 Disaggregation is certainly possible; but it raises more questions than it answers. Upon finding Type 3 Disaggregation, it would be necessary to design further tests to determine whether the statistical relationship is systematic or independent.

Furthermore, in the case under study here, for even the most basic forecasting of the effects of policy changes on disaggregated series, Type 2 Disaggregation allows one to infer the effects of a change in the deficit on at least some of the components of GDP, whereas Type 3 would not allow such a direct inference.

Of course, this process could be taken to an absurd extreme. That is, having found a situation which displays Type 2 Disaggregation, one could focus on the relevant series ($Y3$ in the Figure 7.3 above) and disaggregate once again. If one were then to find Type 1 Disaggregation among the components of $Y3$, this would argue for analysing each of the separate series at a further level of disaggregation. This could continue in principle indefinitely, since any disaggregated series can be disaggregated further not only in the same dimension (for example, disaggregating the United States into fifty states, and then each of the states into its counties) but along an entirely different dimension (for example, disaggregating state data by industry or gender, rather than by geography).

Therefore, the point is not simply to disaggregate as far as the data allow, but to disaggregate when there is an interesting economic question to be answered by the disaggregation. Section 3.1 described some of the potentially interesting questions that analyses of disaggregated GDP data might help to answer.

Finally, the entire logic of this section can be reversed. That is, rather than starting from a robust relationship between Y and X and analysing whether disaggregation of Y identifies further robust relationships with X, it is possible for Y and X to be uncorrelated while some of the components of Y might be strongly correlated with X in ways that are masked in the aggregation. I call this Type 4 Disaggregation.

One example of this is displayed in Figure 7.5, in which Y and X are uncorrelated, while $Y1$ is perfectly correlated with X. Neither $Y2$ nor $Y3$ is correlated with X over their entire range,[13] but the sum of $Y1$, $Y2$ and $Y3$ results in Y being a straight line. Thus, disaggregation reveals a robust statistical relationship that aggregation had obscured.

As noted earlier, both Type 2 and Type 4 Disaggregation are present in the statistical analysis summarized here. One of the exogenous variables (the deficit alone) is significantly correlated with real GDP growth, while another (the product of the GDP gap and the deficit) is not – at least, at standard cut-off levels of statistical significance. Disaggregating GDP reveals that the former variable is correlated with only a few of the components and subcomponents of GDP growth (Type 2 Disaggregation), while the latter is correlated in economically important ways to some of the subcomponents, even though it is not correlated to GDP growth at a high level of statistical significance (Type 4 Disaggregation).

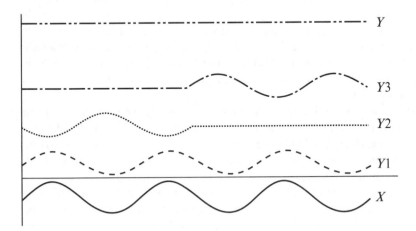

Figure 7.5   Type 4 Disaggregation

4   ANALYSING DISAGGREGATIONS OF GDP GROWTH

The exercise here asks the following question. If we take the GDP growth equation specified above seriously, what do regressions of exactly the same form but substituting components of GDP growth for the dependent variable tell us?

4.1   The Adding-up Property

The econometric tests summarized below are based on separate regressions with each component of GDP as the dependent variable and with the same regressors used for each regression. Since each of the component breakdowns of GDP is based on a simple additive disaggregation method, it is a matter of computational certainty that – using ordinary least squares estimation – the coefficients of the fiscal deficit (or of any exogenous variable) for each of the separate component regressions must sum to the coefficient of the fiscal deficit in the regression with total GDP as the dependent variable.

This can be seen most easily in Figure 7.2 above (Type 1 Disaggregation). Clearly, the coefficient on X in the regression $Y = a + bX$ is equal to 1. The b_i

coefficient on X in each of the disaggregated regressions ($Y1 = a_1 + b_1X$, $Y2 = a_2 + b_2X$, $Y3 = a_3 + b_3X$) is equal to 1/3, so that the b_i's sum to 1. Also, while each of the intercept terms is different, it is still true that $a_1 + a_2 + a_3 = a$.

Therefore, the estimates of the coefficient on the deficit variable from a set of four regressions (with the same exogenous variables and functional form) which take consumption, investment, government purchases and net exports as the dependent variable in turn will sum to the estimated coefficient on the deficit variable in a regression where GDP is the dependent variable. If further regressions are run with smaller subdivisions of each aggregate used as dependent variables, the coefficients on each independent variable must still add up to the overall estimate (just as, in any given year, the levels of these components must sum to total GDP).

The above discussion requires one clarification, however. The dependent variable in the regressions summarized above is the *growth rate* of GDP, which is simply the change in GDP divided by the lagged GDP. Therefore, the division of GDP into separate components must be in a form which will allow the disaggregated components of GDP to add up to the GDP growth rate.

However, the growth rate of GDP is obviously *not* equal to the sum of the growth rates of consumption, investment, government purchases and net exports; rather, it is equal to 'the change in consumption divided by lagged GDP' plus 'the change in investment divided by lagged GDP', and so on.[14] In the discussion below, these variables are designated in lower-case, bold-face type. For example: c_t represents the change in consumption from quarter $t - 1$ to quarter t, divided by the value of GDP in quarter $t - 1$, with the result multiplied by four to express the quarterly change at an annual rate. The precise definition of any variable x_t, therefore, is $4\Delta X_t / \text{GDP}_{t-1}$.

In each of the complete sets of regressions tested, ordinary least squares estimation produced at least two regressions whose Durbin–Watson statistics (DW) indicated the presence of serial correlation (at a 5 per cent two-sided level of significance), as well as many more with inconclusive tests (see Tables 7.2 and 7.5).

The first recourse in such a situation is to perform a regression with correction for first-order serial correlation, such as the Cochrane–Orcutt procedure, which is a generalized least squares approach, using quasi-differencing.[15] This involves transforming an equation of the form:

$$Y_t = \beta_0 + \beta_1 X_t + \varepsilon_t, \text{ where } \varepsilon_t = \rho\varepsilon_{t-1} + u_t.$$

where ρ is the coefficient of serial correlation, into an equation that can be estimated using ordinary least squares regression. Simple manipulation of those equations results in:

$$Y^*_t = \beta^*_0 + \beta_1 X^*_t + u_t,$$

where

$$Y^*_t = Y_t - \rho Y_{t-1}, X^*_t = X_t - \rho X_{t-1},$$

and

$$\beta^*_0 = \beta_0 - \rho\beta_0.$$

Note that β_1 is unchanged by the transformation. If a value for ρ is given, the Y^*_t equation is then estimated using OLS. Otherwise, the value of ρ is determined through an iterative procedure, which is what the Cochrane–Orcutt algorithm performs. The equation discussed in Section 2 above was derived by adapting this method to the non-linear equation under investigation.

Performing this procedure equation by equation on a set of disaggregated variables will, however, generally prevent the estimated coefficients on the deficit from adding up appropriately, since each new corrected regression will generate a different estimate of ρ, which will then cause the adding-up property to be violated. Another way to see this is to note that the dependent variables no longer add up according to the disaggregation pattern, because each variable has been quasi-differenced using a unique estimate of ρ.

In order to preserve the adding-up property of a set of regressions, one possibility is to impose the same value of ρ for all regressions within the set. Choosing that value of ρ is, however, not straightforward. One possible approach is to choose the minimum absolute value of ρ which would bring the most extreme DW value into the acceptable range.

However, in each set of regressions there was at least one component of GDP that had a Durbin–Watson statistic on the opposite side of 2.0, indicating serial correlation of the opposite sign. Imposing the appropriate value of ρ (to move the lowest or highest DW into the acceptable range) in many cases pushed the opposite DW statistic so high or low as to indicate that the imposed value of ρ had actually created (or worsened) serial correlation in the regression associated with that DW statistic.

The available data could not, therefore, simultaneously be used to produce estimates which preserved the adding-up property and in which every equation was corrected for serial correlation. Given that, it would still be possible to report regression results (after correcting for serial correlation) for only the most disaggregated series and to add up the resulting coefficients into more-aggregated results, culminating in the GDP regression. This would, however, produce no standard test statistics for the more-aggregated regressions, making it difficult to infer whether the sum of two regression results – one with very significant results and one with insignificant results – is in the aggregate significant.

Fortunately, however, tests of the data showed that simply using a generalized least squares technique (with quasi-differencing) on each equation separately (each with its own estimated value of ρ) provided estimates which added up surprisingly well. Thus, for example, the estimated sums of the coefficients on the lagged deficit variables from the GLS estimates of the **c, i, g** and **nx** regressions (Table 7.3) sum to 0.24, while the linear coefficient in the **gdp** regression itself is 0.23. Therefore, Tables 7.3 and 7.6 simply report the results of AR(1) regressions for each component of GDP, with the differences between the more- and less-aggregated components obvious by inspection.

4.2   Averages and Average Growth

It will be useful to analyse the historical changes in the components of GDP, in order to compare the changes in these components induced by deficits with the average changes over the sample period. Tables 7.1 and 7.4 summarize some basic statistics within each accounting method for the 1972:1–1994:4 sample period.

The first column, labelled 'First', indicates the ratio of each component of GDP to aggregate GDP, in the first quarter of the sample (1972:1). Similarly, 'Last' indicates the ratio of each component to GDP in the last quarter. 'Average' is the ratio of the average value of the component for the twenty-three-year sample period to the average value of aggregate GDP for that period.

The final column is labelled 'Ave. growth'. This takes the average growth rate for a component of GDP (that is, the change in the component divided by lagged GDP, as defined above) for the sample period and divides it by the average growth rate of total GDP for that time period. For example, for total consumption, the entry in the last column is calculated as follows:

$$\text{Ave. growth of consumption}_t = \frac{\text{average}\,\dfrac{C_t - C_{t-1}}{GDP_{t-1}}}{\text{average}\,\dfrac{GDP_t - GDP_{t-1}}{GDP_{t-1}}}$$

$$= \frac{\dfrac{\sum \dfrac{C_t - C_{t-1}}{GDP_{t-1}}}{n}}{\dfrac{\sum \dfrac{GDP_t - GDP_{t-1}}{GDP_{t-1}}}{n}} = \frac{\sum \dfrac{C_t - C_{t-1}}{GDP_{t-1}}}{\sum \dfrac{GDP_t - GDP_{t-1}}{GDP_{t-1}}}$$

Thus, this column in each table allows one to compare the relative importance of each component of GDP in over two decades of economic growth.

The entries in Table 7.1 highlight several important trends in the expenditure data over the sample period. First, both consumption and gross investment became larger parts of total GDP,[16] while government purchases became smaller, and net exports ended where they started.

Therefore, while the 'Last' column indicates that consumption was 66.8 per cent of overall GDP at the end of 1994, the growth of consumption had constituted a markedly larger share of GDP growth during the period, 70.6 per cent of the average growth in GDP. A similar difference appears for total investment, which accounted for 18.2 per cent of GDP at the end of the sample period but had accounted for 20.4 per cent of GDP growth over the twenty-three-year period.

The story for government purchases is quite the opposite. While it continued to constitute 17.0 per cent of GDP in 1994:4, and an average of 19.0 per cent for the period, its contribution to the growth of GDP for those years was a paltry 11.0 per cent. Moreover, looking at the two subcomponents of government purchases makes it clear that virtually all of this shrinkage occurred at the federal level, which contributed only 2.2 per cent of that 11.0 per cent average growth, with the slightly-shrunken state and local government sector responsible for the remainder of the diminished governmental contribution to the average GDP growth rate.

Other important patterns in the components show that: (1) in the consumption sector, durables and services were growing in importance while nondurables were shrinking; (2) fixed investment was the major force behind the growth in the investment sector, with growth of investment in equipment (which nearly doubled over the period) constituting roughly 90 per cent (14.6 per cent out of 16.3 per cent) of the growth accounted for by fixed investment as a whole; and (3) both exports and imports grew significantly, with the 2 per cent difference in their growth rates equal to the difference in their levels (as a percentage of GDP).

Separating the output of the economy into its major products focuses attention on the total quantities of goods, services and structures produced, as well as separating inventories from sales.

Table 7.4 shows the overall historical patterns in the production of these categories of goods. The data confirm that production of goods has become a slightly larger part of overall output and output growth, while production of services has constituted more than half of the growth in output, and production of structures has been shrinking. Within the goods category, production has been shifting from nondurables to durables, while inventories appear to have been volatile over this time period (as indicated by the 'Average' being smaller than either the 'Last' value or the 'First' value).

4.3   Results of Regressions on Disaggregated GDP Components

Tables 7.2 and 7.5 report the results of ordinary least squares regressions. These tables are produced for several purposes: to demonstrate which regressions show evidence of serial correlation, to demonstrate the adding-up property of the estimated coefficients (subject to rounding errors), and to allow the corrected regressions (in Tables 7.3 and 7.6) to be compared with the OLS regressions. Tables 7.2 and 7.5 make it clear that most of the interesting statistical results are already evident even in the OLS regressions. Correction for serial correlation only strengthens those results. Therefore, in the discussion of regression results below, I will refer exclusively to Tables 7.3 and 7.6, which summarize the results of the AR(1) regressions.

The expenditure disaggregation
Based on the patterns discerned in Table 7.1, and turning to the regression results in Table 7.3, the places to look for impact on GDP growth would seem to be consumption (especially durables and services) and investment (especially equipment investment).

One way to analyse these results is to look only at those estimates that are statistically significant, concentrating on the most detailed level of disaggregation possible. When there is not a gap, the only subcomponents of GDP that one can be highly confident will respond to deficits are durables consumption and state and local government purchases, since no other linear coefficients are statistically significant at even a 90 per cent level of confidence. Among the interactive coefficients, the response of durables consumption, equipment investment and imports are significant, and nondurables consumption is near the borderline of the 95 per cent level of confidence.

Viewed in this way, the statistical support for a positive effect of deficits on GDP growth at NAIRU is supported, as are the additionally positive effects of deficits during recessions – although the size of the interactive coefficient in the import equation diminishes the overall impact of deficits during recessions. Crowding out is not supported by any of these results, while the accelerator hypothesis on equipment investment is supported.

The simple Keynesian consumption function appears to be operative as well, with consumption rising in response to deficits (which means that consumption is higher when GDP is higher). Finally, the fact that much of the response to deficits comes from durables consumption lends support to the consumption-as-investment view.

These results support an activist Keynesian view of the effects of deficits on the economy. The numerical estimates, and their meanings in the context of the theoretical questions at issue here, are discussed below.

The point estimates tell some interesting stories; but, as noted, most of the results are not statistically significant. Following this discussion of point estimates, therefore, a more complete description of statistical significance will be useful. First, however, a discussion which takes the point estimates seriously will facilitate a discussion of the implications of the various estimated coefficients.

In the course of that discussion, in order to alert the reader to those results that are statistically significant, the following convention will be adopted: for those results that are significant at a 90 per cent level of confidence (that is, with a *p*-value of 0.10 or less), I will put an asterisk in parentheses (*) immediately after first mentioning the estimate. For estimates which are significant at a 95 per cent level of confidence, I will put two asterisks in parentheses; and for a 99 per cent level of confidence, I will put three asterisks in parentheses.

According to the linear coefficients in Table 7.3, running a deficit while the economy is at NAIRU raises the growth of consumption (***), government purchases (**) and net exports. Indeed, each of those three components individually responds by at least two-thirds as much as the total response of aggregate GDP growth (which outweighs the large drag created by the response of investment, discussed at some length below).

Among types of consumption, each of the three categories accounts for roughly one-third of the overall impact on consumption, with durables consumption increasing by 0.07 per cent (***) due to a 1 per cent deficit and nondurables and services each increasing by 0.08 per cent. For government spending, the state and local sector accounts for two-thirds of the growth (**). Interestingly, exports seem to respond quite strongly, while imports paradoxically *decrease* as the deficit rises (and, therefore, as the economy strengthens).

Investment, and nearly every category of investment, is crowded out. Indeed, the linear coefficients in **c** and **nx** barely compensate for the decrease in investment growth. Since investment's average growth rate over this time period (from Table 7.1) was 20.6 per cent of the GDP growth rate, and the GDP growth rate averaged 2.6 per cent over this time period, this means that we might have expected that investment growth (as a percentage of GDP) would have been about 0.52 per cent. Subtracting 0.34 per cent from that (the point estimate of the linear coefficient in the **i** equation) means wiping out two-thirds of average investment growth for the sample period.

This result takes on a somewhat different interpretation, however, if one looks for the source of the crowding out. The only component of investment that is not crowded out at all is residential construction, which shows a very small increase due to the strengthening economy. Perhaps more important, though, the estimates show that two-thirds of the crowding out is actually a decrease in inventory accumulation growth, a result that could quite easily be reconciled with a surge in all types of consumption (private, government and foreign) in an economy that is already at GDP*. However, equipment investment growth shows a large decline of 0.11 per cent of GDP, which is precisely the type of investment that is most important for future economic growth. Investment in plant, on the other hand, is not affected by the deficit.

Overall, the analysis of the linear coefficients indicates that, when a deficit is incurred while the economy is at NAIRU, all types of private consumption rise (with the inexplicable exception of imports), government spending and exports rise, residential construction rises by a small amount, and inventories and equipment investment are significantly crowded out. Imports aside, there is nothing else in those results that runs counter to standard Keynesian assumptions about consumer or investor behaviour, with the crowding-out result supporting those who believe that deficits are harmful at NAIRU. The logic of the standard Keynesian textbook consumption function also is supported, with consumption of all types responding positively to the deficit at the same time that income rises due to the deficit.

It is not unimaginable that state and local governments respond to higher federal deficits with greater spending of their own, in a case of spending complementarity. On the other hand, there is little reason to believe that exports or federal spending should be increased by real federal structural deficits; so there are definitely some mysteries to be explored.

Looking at the p-values of the exclusion tests for the linear coefficients in Table 7.3 begins to shed light on some of these mysteries, and to bring into question some of the seemingly believable results discussed above. While the p-value of the **c** equation is 0.01, this appears to be a textbook case of Type 2 Disaggregation, with the p-value in the **cdur** equation estimated at 0.00 (that is, a level of confidence greater than 99.5 per cent) while **cnon** and **cser** have relatively low p-values (0.24 and 0.18, respectively). This indicates that we can only have high confidence that durables consumption responds to deficits, while nondurables and services consumption are much less likely to respond at all.

Looking at the p-values in the disaggregations of investment is even more interesting. While the **i** equation shows a p-value of 0.14, which is not statistically significant at standard levels of the tests, it is interesting to note that even this level of confidence apparently derives from three basic components of investment: investment in plant (which has a point estimate of –0.00 and a p-value of 0.14), residential investment (which appears to respond positively to deficits, with a p-value of 0.12), and inventories (with a p-value of 0.11). The p-value for the large, negative coefficient in the **ie** equation is 0.60, indicating that there is only a two-in-five chance that equipment investment falls (that is, that the linear coefficient is non-zero) in response to deficits at NAIRU.

The only element of investment that has both a large negative point estimate and an even moderately significant exclusion test, therefore, is inventories. The crowding-out story, therefore, looks less compelling and gives less reason for concern about the impact of deficits on future macroeconomic performance, since the most important parts of investment for future economic growth (plant and equipment investment) seem – for different reasons – to be relatively impervious to deficits.

This result contrasts markedly, however, with the reported results in Eisner and Pieper (1988). Using annual data and a somewhat different specification of the growth equation (the most important difference being the lack of an interactive term), they report that regressions for **i** and **ifix** show a strong *positive* response to deficits. The increase in aggregate investment due to higher deficits comprises more than 80 per cent of the overall effect on GNP growth[17] (although that is somewhat of an overstatement since their results, which are based on regressions with Cochrane–Orcutt correction, do not add up to the estimates for the aggregate **gnp** equation nearly as closely as the results summarized here); and the increase in fixed investment comprises nearly 69 per cent of the change in GNP growth.

Moreover, their reported results are statistically significant: the *t*-statistics for the two estimates (that is, for the coefficients on the deficit variable in the **i** and **ifix** equations) are 3.25 and 3.74, respectively, indicating significance levels in excess of 99 per cent. The difference with the results reported here is attributable in the first instance to the use of quarterly data rather than annual data, since preliminary tests for this chapter showed that a linear equation similar to that used in Eisner and Pieper (that is, excluding the interactive term) confirmed their results in tests with annual data but failed to detect significant coefficients on the deficit variable in tests with quarterly data. (This was true for the overall **gdp** regression as well as for the **i** and **ifix** regressions.)

Inclusion of the interactive term, however, showed that a statistically significant effect of deficits can be found, even using quarterly data. Therefore, the estimated coefficients on the interactive term (the δ_i's) lend confirmation to standard Keynesian results, but with the added information that the Keynesian effect of deficits arises due to a weak economy.

Looking at the *p*-values in the government and foreign sectors also helps to clarify some of the mysteries discussed above. While the linear coefficient in the **g** equation is significant at the 95 per cent level, it turns out that the source of that statistical correlation is the state and local government sector. Since the *p*-value in the **gfed** equation is 0.26, while that in the **gsl** equation is 0.03, this tends to support the notion that state and local government purchases follow federal deficits, whereas federal purchases very likely do not. While it is imaginable that a deficit in one year could lock in federal spending the following year, the complementarity story at the state and local level is much more plausible, given the explicit links between federal spending and state and local spending (seed money, in-advance matching grants, and so on).

In the foreign sector, both of the puzzles mentioned above are fairly definitively put to rest by the levels of the *p*-values. In the **ex** equation, the *p*-value of the linear coefficient is an astounding 0.91, indicating that exports almost certainly do not respond to domestic economic conditions. Similarly, the negative coefficient on imports has a *p*-value of 0.46. When the economy is at GDP*, therefore, it appears that the foreign sector does not create a significant part of the response of GDP growth to the deficit.

Turning now to the interactive coefficient, and again concentrating on the point estimates, the most obvious result in Table 7.3 is that only three point estimates are positive: for the **gsl**, the **nx** (***) and the **ex** equations. The **gsl** result can be ignored based both on its size (0.01) and its *p*-value (0.58), while the **ex** result can be ignored mostly on the basis of theory (that the export sector should not respond to domestic events) – but again also because of the relatively statistically insignificant *p*-value. The positive value of the interactive coefficient (and its low *p*-value) in the **nx** equation, therefore, derive from the **im** equation (**), which will be discussed below.

The negative value of the interactive coefficient in each of the other equations tested supports the notion described earlier, in which a negative value of GAP (a recession) means that a positive deficit is more stimulative (or less contractionary) than it would be at GDP*. In the **c** equation, for example, a 1 per cent DEF and a –1 per cent GAP would indicate a 0.28 per cent increase (***) in consumption growth (rather than the 0.20 per cent growth predicted at NAIRU), while a +1 per cent GAP would cause consumption's response to the deficit to be only 0.12 per cent. Therefore, for each of the components and subcomponents of GDP (with the exception of the three already discussed), the interactive coefficient indicates a greater response to deficits (or a less negative response) during a recession than otherwise.

Looking at the range from a –1 per cent GAP to a 1 per cent GAP, therefore, the response of consumption growth to a 1 per cent deficit is 0.20 ± 0.08, while investment growth's response is –0.34 ± 0.24, government purchases growth's response is 0.22 ± 0.04, and net exports growth's response is 0.16 minus-or-plus 0.19.[18]

Applying similar arithmetic to the possibility of a –2 per cent GAP, the most notable change is that aggregate investment now responds positively to a deficit, since –0.34 + 0.48 = 0.14, which means that a 1 per cent DEF with a –2 per cent GAP creates 0.14 per cent of extra investment growth, with the acceleration effect now so strong that it wipes out the crowding-out effect. Businesses and new home buyers respond so positively to having a surge in GDP growth, therefore, that they expand their capital stock in anticipation of better times. The composition of that investment growth is extremely interesting, as the discussion now turns to the sub components of consumption, investment, government purchases and net exports.

The results for consumption and its components are very similar for the interactive coefficient to the results for the linear coefficient, in that the point estimates are about equal to each other (with the estimate equal to -0.02 for **cdur** (**), -0.03 for **cnon** (*) and -0.03 for **cser**). The overall story for consumption indicates that people respond to expansionary fiscal policy even at NAIRU; and they respond even more strongly during a recession, quite likely due to a consumer confidence effect, with consumers responding to positive movements in their income (and in the economy in general) by buying more goods.

The breakdown of the investment statistics shows that the various types of investment respond to deficits during a recession or a boom in theoretically-plausible ways. Starting at the bottom of the table and working up, the results for the inventories regression show that the interactive response is positive during a recession, which means that businesses start thinking about building up their inventories when they see a positive movement in a weak economy. Thus, while inventories are drawn down when there is a deficit at GDP*, the sum of the linear coefficient and the interactive coefficient indicates that this response is dampened during a recession – and it is even reversed if the recession is deep enough. Conversely, during a boom, businesses apparently view the good times as temporary, as they draw down inventories at an even faster rate.

The response of residential investment was already positive, even with no gap. Therefore, the interactive coefficient (*) indicates that new home buyers become conservative during a boom (where the net effect of a 1 per cent DEF with a +1 per cent GAP is -0.08 per cent) and more confident during a recession. One potential explanation for this is that the initiation of expansionary fiscal policy during a recession brings new home buyers into the market who had been holding back because of the weak state of the economy.

The results for plant and equipment investment (together and separately) tend to confirm an accelerationist story. When GAP is positive, the economy is operating above some concept of capacity, in which case higher deficits will further crowd out investment spending. On the other hand, during a recession, the slack in the economy causes the deficit to act as an impetus to demand and subsequently investment, which is what the concept of acceleration describes.

If, for example, the economy is in a recession at 2 per cent below potential (as it was in the third quarter of 1993), raising the deficit by 1 per cent of GDP (roughly \$51 billion at that time) would have caused equipment investment growth to be 0.06 per cent higher as a percentage of GDP (**), or approximately \$3 billion more than the \$16.6 billion increase in equipment investment that actually occurred during that quarter (at an annual rate, from the previous quarter).

Based on the point estimates, however, it will take a deep recession (on the order of a -2.25 per cent GAP) for the total of plant and equipment investment to have a net positive response to deficits. The necessary size of GAP to turn the growth in **ie** positive is larger still (in absolute value). Note also that plant investment remains largely unresponsive to deficit spending (given its linear coefficient estimate of –0.00 and its interactive coefficient estimate of –0.01), leaving the majority of the response of plant and equipment investment to be explained by equipment alone.

As discussed above, it is generally not appropriate to infer any meaning from the government purchases regression (**g**) or the federal government regression (**gfed**). It is not surprising that the estimated coefficients and adjusted R^2 for those two regressions (especially **g**) are insignificant.[19] Again, these results are provided for completeness, simply to show that the estimated coefficients come close to adding up appropriately.

In the **ex** equation, the interactive coefficient is positive, which would mean (if exports were not likely – based on most theoretical models – to be exogenous) that the response of exports to deficits is weakened during a recession. In the **im** equation, the interactive coefficient is negative (**), which would mean that deficits during recessions cause increases in imports, and vice versa. Since higher imports are a drag on GDP, however, this means that both exports and imports respond to deficits so as to weaken overall economic growth. With a –1 per cent GAP, the foreign sector becomes a net drag on the economy, as the negative response of exports and the positive response of imports to deficits during a recession overwhelm their otherwise-expansionary impact (based on their linear coefficients).

Looking at the p-values of the interactive coefficients, the estimate for the **cdur** equation is statistically significant at a 98 per cent level, while the **cnon** equation almost meets the benchmark 95 per cent level of confidence and the **cser** estimate is insignificant. Note that only the **cdur** equation has statistically significant estimates for both the linear and interactive coefficients, indicating that people respond to deficits by increasing their purchases of durable goods and that this effect is even stronger during a recession. Moreover, the positive impact of deficits on durables consumption growth is not wiped out entirely unless the GAP is more than +3.5 per cent.

In the investment equations, the significant p-values for **ifix** and **ipe** appear to arise from Type 2 Disaggregation in which the significance of the estimate in the **ie** equation carries over into the more-aggregated regressions. Note also that the linear coefficient in the **ie** equation had a very low level of confidence in rejecting the null hypothesis that it was equal to zero. On the other hand, the interactive coefficient is very statistically significant. Thus, if the linear coefficient really were equal to zero, the interactive coefficient would indicate that equipment investment responds positively to a deficit during a recession, rather than merely 'less negatively'. This is an even stronger confirmation of the accelerator process.

None of the estimates of the interactive coefficients in the government purchases equations are statistically significant, while the significance of the estimate in the **nx** equation appears to be created mostly by the response of imports. The lack of a significant estimate for **gfed**, **gsl** and **ex** confirms theoretical expectations, as does the significance of the interactive coefficient in **im**, as discussed above.

The major conclusion from the expenditures disaggregation is that standard Keynesian predictions about consumption and investment are largely supported. When there is not a gap, the statistical results indicate support for the simple consumption function as a function of income, as well as support (without strong statistical significance) for crowding out of certain types of investment (mostly inventory investment). When the economy is below NAIRU, consumer confidence and accelerator effects appear to be operative.

The major products disaggregation
The results in Table 7.6 show that the most statistically significant results for the linear coefficient are those for the **goodsale** and **struc** regressions. However, neither the sale of durable goods nor of nondurable goods shows a significant linear coefficient; so it is hard to determine the source of the statistical strength in the aggregate series for sales of goods (and overall sales).

What is somewhat surprising, however, is that the durable goods regressions have such insignificant estimates. Given the results in the expenditures regressions (specifically, **cdur**), it is somewhat disappointing that durables output is not significantly affected by deficits.

The interactive coefficient, however, in the **dursale** regression does indicate statistical significance. Since durable goods are sold both to consumers and as equipment investment, this coefficient ought to mirror the statistical significance of the regression on the expenditures side of the accounts. However, the interactive coefficient has the opposite sign from the sign in those two regressions, deepening the mystery rather than resolving it.

There is also a large, significant linear coefficient in the **durinv** equation, which is of the opposite sign and larger in absolute value than the estimate for the linear coefficient in the **gdp** regression! This is inconsistent with virtually every other statistical estimate summarized here.

The results on Table 7.6 clearly do not match up well with those on Table 7.3. Given the differences in the two methods of disaggregation, this is (at least in retrospect) not surprising. The expenditures method separates purchases by particular groups of economic actors, and then further summarizes how each group divided their purchases among each type of good. The major products method, on the other hand, summarizes in each category the total production of each type of good, no matter the ultimate buyer.

For example, the variable CNON (under the consumption category) includes only the nondurable goods which were actually purchased by households; but the NONDUR variable includes nondurable goods which were sold to businesses

Consumption, investment and government spending

Table 7.1   Components of GDP relative to total GDP, in levels, averages and rates of growth – disaggregation by expenditure

Component of GDP				First	Last	Average	Ave. growth
GDP				100.0	100.0	100.0	100.0
C				63.5	66.8	66.0	70.6
	CDUR			7.1	10.2	8.3	13.5
	CNON			24.2	20.6	22.4	16.2
	SER			32.2	35.9	35.3	40.8
I				16.8	18.2	16.3	20.4
	IFIX			16.2	17.3	15.8	18.5
		IPE		9.9	13.0	11.2	16.3
			IP	4.1	2.9	3.8	1.7
			IE	5.8	10.2	7.3	14.6
		IRES		6.4	4.3	4.6	2.2
	IINV			0.6	0.9	0.5	2.0
G				21.7	17.0	19.0	11.0
	GFED			9.6	6.1	7.8	2.2
		GSL		12.1	10.9	11.2	8.8
	NX			–2.0	–2.0	–1.3	–2.0
		EX		5.6	12.8	8.7	20.8
		(IM)		7.6	14.8	9.9	22.8

Notes
COM = component of GDP.
First = COM/GDP, in per cent, for first quarter of sample.
Last = COM/GDP, in per cent, for last quarter of sample.
Average = average(COM)/average(GDP), in per cent.
Ave. growth = average(ΔCOM$_t$/GDP$_{t-1}$)/ave.(%ΔGDP$_t$), in per cent at annual rate.
Component definitions:
GDP = Gross Domestic Product, in 1987 fixed-weight dollars
    C = Personal Consumption Expenditures
        CDUR = Consumption of Durable Goods
        CNON = Consumption of Nondurable Goods
        CSER = Consumption of Services
    I = Gross Private Domestic Investment
        IFIX = Fixed Investment
            IPE = Plant and Equipment Investment
                IP = Investment in New Plant
                IE = Investment in New Equipment
            IRES = Residential Construction
        IINV = Inventory Accumulation
    G = Government Purchases of Goods and Services
        GFED = Federal Government's Purchases of Goods and Services
        GSL = State and Local Governments' Purchases of Goods and Services
    NX = Net Exports
        EX = Exports
        (IM) = Imports
(Parentheses) indicate that component is subtracted from identity.

Sources: Author's calculations. Sample period: 1972:1–1994:4; data sources: NIPA, Flow of Funds.

(for example, meals in an executive dining room), governments (for example, janitorial supplies for the Smithsonian Institution), and foreign buyers (for example, sales of American beer in Germany), in addition to those sold to households. This creates a fundamental difference between the similarly-named categories in the two methods of disaggregation. Looking for similar responses by similar-named variables to deficits would nevertheless have been fruitful, had the variation in the pairs of series also been similar (that is, if the variation in NONDUR were similar to the variation in CNON, in this example). Unfortunately, the results here clearly indicate that they are not.

The major products disaggregation, therefore, is not at all helpful in confirming or contradicting the results in Table 7.3. Those results in Table 7.6 that are statistically significant are either of the wrong sign, too large to make sense (as in the linear coefficient for **durinv**), or too small to matter (as in the linear coefficient for **struc**). Therefore, this provides little or no information to complement what was learned from the Expenditures disaggregation.

Table 7.2   Regression results for the expenditures method of disaggregation ordinary least squares

$$\mathbf{com_t} = \alpha_0 + \alpha_1 \text{trend} + \sum_{i=1}^{4} \beta_i \Delta \text{MB}_{t-i} + \sum_{i=1}^{4} \gamma_i \text{DEF}_{t-1} + \sum_{i=1}^{4} \delta_i \text{GAP}_{t-i} \text{DEF}_{t-i} + \varepsilon_t$$

Component of GDP	Linear coefficient $\Sigma\gamma_i$	p-value of exclusion test: $\gamma_i = 0$	Interactive coefficient $\Sigma\delta_i$	p-value of exclusion test: $\delta_i = 0$	Durbin–Watson statistic	Adjusted R^2
gdp	0.24	(0.03)	−0.16	(0.21)	1.47	0.24
c	0.22	(0.00)	−0.08	(0.01)	1.76	0.31
cdur	0.06	(0.00)	−0.02	(0.01)	2.11	0.30
cnon	0.08	(0.20)	−0.03	(0.06)	1.50	0.19
cser	0.08	(0.18)	−0.03	(0.27)	2.10	0.14
i	−0.37	(0.11)	−0.24	(0.11)	1.67	0.17
ifix	−0.18	(0.12)	−0.13	(0.01)	1.11	0.25
ipe	−0.18	(0.39)	−0.05	(0.01)	1.17	0.18
ip	−0.05	(0.10)	−0.02	(0.02)	1.34	0.07
ie	−0.13	(0.41)	−0.03	(0.02)	1.48	0.29
ires	−0.00	(0.17)	−0.08	(0.20)	1.23	0.23
iinv	−0.19	(0.18)	−0.11	(0.10)	2.46	0.05
g	0.22	(0.04)	−0.04	(0.11)	1.94	0.06
gfed	0.07	(0.26)	−0.05	(0.12)	1.99	0.03

Table 7.2   continued

Component of GDP	Linear coefficient $\Sigma\gamma_i$	p-value of exclusion test: $\gamma_i = 0$	Interactive coefficient $\Sigma\delta_i$	p-value of exclusion test: $\delta_i = 0$	Durbin–Watson statistic	Adjusted R^2
gsl	0.15	(0.01)	0.01	(0.53)	1.67	0.06
nx	0.18	(0.39)	0.19	(0.00)	1.69	0.24
ex	0.08	(0.90)	0.07	(0.27)	2.01	0.07
im	−0.10	(0.44)	−0.12	(0.02)	1.65	0.20

Notes
All coefficients are expressed in per cent (i.e., 0.23 means 0.23%) at annual rates.
Definitions of variables:
Dependent
COM = component of GDP.
Component definitions: see Table 7.1.
All dependent variables are computed as follows: $\mathbf{com_t} = [4(COM_t - COM_{t-1})/GDP_{t-1}]*100$.
Independent
MB = end-of-period real monetary base, as a percentage of real GDP.
DEF = Price-Adjusted Standardized-Employment Deficit, as a percentage of nominal GDP.
GAP = GDP gap = [(actual GDP – GDP at NAIRU)/(GDP at NAIRU)]*100.

Source: Author's calculations. Sample period: 1972:1–1994:4; data sources: NIPA, Flow of Funds.

Table 7.3   Regression results for the expenditures method of disaggregation, corrected for serial correlation

$$\mathbf{com_t} = \alpha_0 + \alpha_1 trend + \sum_{i=1}^{4}\beta_i\Delta MB_{t-i} + \sum_{i=1}^{4}\gamma_i DEF_{t-1} + \sum_{i=1}^{4}\delta_i GAP_{t-i}DEF_{t-i} + \varepsilon_t$$

Component of GDP			Linear coefficient $\Sigma\gamma_i$	p-value of exclusion test: $\gamma_i = 0$	Interactive coefficient $\Sigma\delta_i$	p-value of exclusion test: $\delta_i = 0$	Adjusted R^2
gdp			0.23	(0.02)	−0.17	(0.13)	0.27
c			0.20	(0.01)	−0.08	(0.01)	0.31
	cdur		0.07	(0.00)	−0.02	(0.02)	0.29
	cnon		0.08	(0.24)	−0.03	(0.06)	0.23
	cser		0.08	(0.18)	−0.03	(0.28)	0.13
i			−0.34	(0.14)	−0.24	(0.12)	0.18
	ifix		−0.08	(0.17)	−0.14	(0.01)	0.39
	ipe		−0.09	(0.68)	−0.04	(0.04)	0.33
		ip	−0.00	(0.14)	−0.01	(0.30)	0.21
		ie	−0.11	(0.60)	−0.03	(0.02)	0.32

Table 7.3   continued

Component of GDP		Linear coefficient $\Sigma\gamma_i$	p-value of exclusion test: $\gamma_i = 0$	Interactive coefficient $\Sigma\delta_i$	p-value of exclusion test: $\delta_i = 0$	Adjusted R^2
	ires	0.01	(0.12)	−0.09	(0.10)	0.35
	iinv	−0.21	(0.11)	−0.11	(0.12)	0.09
g		0.22	(0.05)	−0.04	(0.12)	0.05
	gfed	0.07	(0.26)	−0.05	(0.11)	0.02
	gsl	0.14	(0.03)	0.01	(0.58)	0.07
nx		0.16	(0.49)	0.19	(0.00)	0.26
	ex	0.08	(0.91)	0.07	(0.19)	0.08
	im	−0.09	(0.46)	−0.12	(0.02)	0.20

Note: Definitions of variables: see Tables 7.1 and 7.2.
Source: Author's calculations. Sample period: 1972:1–1994:4; data sources: NIPA, Flow of Funds.

Table 7.4   Components of GDP relative to total GDP, in levels, averages and rates of growth – disaggregation by major products

Component of GDP	First	Last	Average	Ave. growth
GDP	100.0	100.0	100.0	100.0
SALES	99.4	99.1	99.5	98.0
INVEN	0.6	0.9	0.5	2.0
GOOD	39.7	42.1	40.2	44.7
GOODSALE	39.1	41.2	39.8	42.8
INVEN	0.6	0.9	0.5	2.0
DURABLE	14.7	20.8	17.3	28.4
DURSALE	14.4	20.3	17.0	26.5
DURINV	0.3	0.6	0.3	1.9
NONDUR	25.0	21.2	22.9	16.3
NONDSALE	24.7	20.9	22.8	16.3
NONDINV	0.3	0.3	0.2	0.1
SERV	47.2	49.0	49.4	51.1
STRUC	13.1	8.9	10.3	4.2

Notes
COM = component of GDP.
First = COM/GDP, in per cent, for first quarter of sample.
Last = COM/GDP, in per cent, for last quarter of sample.
Average = average(COM)/average(GDP), in per cent.
Ave. growth = average(ΔCOM/GDP_{t-1})/ave.($\%\Delta GDP_t$), in per cent at annual rate.
Component Definitions:
GDP = Gross Domestic Product, in 1987 fixed-weight dollars
    SALES = Final Sales of Domestic Product
        INVEN = Change in Business Inventories
    GOOD = Total Goods Produced

Table 7.4   continued

```
GOODSALE = Final Sales of Goods
INVEN = Change in Business Inventories (same as INVEN above)
    DURABLE = Total Durable Goods Produced
        DURSALE = Final Sales of Durable Goods
        DURINV = Change in Business Inventories of Durable Goods
    NONDUR = Total Nondurable Goods Produced
        NONDSALE = Final Sales of Nondurable Goods
        NONDINV = Change in Business Inventories of Nondurable Goods
SERV = Total Services Produced
STRUC = Total Structures Produced
```

Source: Author's calculations. Sample period: 1972:1–1994:4; data sources: NIPA, Flow of Funds.

Table 7.5   Regression results for the major products method of disaggregation, ordinary least squares

$$\mathbf{com_t} = \alpha_0 + \alpha_1 \text{trend} + \sum_{i=1}^{4} \beta_i \Delta MB_{t-i} + \sum_{i=1}^{4} \gamma_i DEF_{t-i} + \sum_{i=1}^{4} \delta_i GAP_{t-i} DEF_{t-i} + \varepsilon_t$$

Component of GDP	Linear coefficient $\Sigma\gamma_i$	*p*-value of exclusion test: $\gamma_i = 0$	Interactive coefficient $\Sigma\delta_i$	*p*-value of exclusion test: $\delta_i = 0$	Durbin–Watson statistic	Adjusted R^2
gdp	0.24	(0.03)	–0.16	(0.21)	1.47	0.24
sales	0.43	(0.02)	–0.05	(0.01)	1.62	0.27
inven	–0.19	(0.18)	–0.11	(0.10)	2.46	0.05
good	0.02	(0.13)	–0.06	(0.45)	1.90	0.15
goodsale	0.21	(0.03)	0.05	(0.00)	2.16	0.25
inven	–0.19	(0.18)	–0.11	(0.10)	2.46	0.05
durable	–0.11	(0.17)	–0.07	(0.17)	1.89	0.18
dursale	0.13	(0.12)	0.03	(0.01)	2.26	0.20
durinv	–0.24	(0.04)	–0.09	(0.04)	2.36	0.11
nondur	0.14	(0.72)	0.00	(0.64)	2.30	–0.04
nondsale	0.09	(0.29)	0.02	(0.06)	2.10	0.06
nondinv	0.05	(0.99)	–0.02	(0.51)	2.58	–0.08
serv	0.24	(0.16)	–0.00	(0.59)	2.25	0.11
struc	–0.02	(0.02)	–0.10	(0.07)	1.31	0.21

Table 7.5   continued

Notes
All coefficients are expressed in per cent (i.e., 0.23 means 0.23%) at annual rates.
Definitions of variables:
Dependent
COM = component of GDP.
Component definitions: see Table 7.4.
All dependent variables are computed as follows: $\mathbf{com_t} = [4(\text{COM}_t - \text{COM}_{t-1})/\text{GDP}_{t-1}]*100$.
Independent
MB = end-of-period real monetary base, as a percentage of real GDP.
DEF = Price-Adjusted Standardized-Employment Deficit, as a percentage of nominal GDP.
GAP = GDP gap = [(actual GDP – GDP at NAIRU)/(GDP at NAIRU)]*100

Source: Author's calculations. Sample period: 1972:1–1994:4; data sources: NIPA, Flow of Funds.

Table 7.6   Regression results for the major products method of disaggregation, corrected for serial correlation

$$\mathbf{com_t} = \alpha_0 + \alpha_1 \text{trend} + \sum_{i=1}^{4} \beta_i \Delta \text{MB}_{t-i} + \sum_{i=1}^{4} \gamma_i \text{DEF}_{t-1} + \sum_{i=1}^{4} \delta_i \text{GAP}_{t-i} \text{DEF}_{t-i} + \varepsilon_t$$

Component of GDP	Linear coefficient $\Sigma\gamma_i$	p-value of exclusion test: $\gamma_i = 0$	Interactive coefficient $\Sigma\delta_i$	p-value of exclusion test: $\delta_i = 0$	Adjusted R^2
gdp	0.23	(0.02)	–0.17	(0.13)	0.27
sales	0.39	(0.02)	–0.06	(0.00)	0.28
inven	–0.21	(0.11)	–0.11	(0.12)	0.09
good	0.02	(0.13)	–0.06	(0.45)	0.13
goodsale	0.22	(0.03)	0.05	(0.00)	0.24
inven	–0.21	(0.11)	–0.11	(0.12)	0.09
durable	–0.12	(0.17)	–0.07	(0.16)	0.17
dursale	0.15	(0.11)	0.03	(0.02)	0.20
durinv	–0.24	(0.05)	–0.09	(0.07)	0.14
nondur	0.11	(0.65)	–0.00	(0.71)	–0.02
nondsale	0.08	(0.30)	0.02	(0.06)	0.05
nondinv	0.02	(0.88)	–0.03	(0.45)	0.01
serv	0.25	(0.06)	0.00	(0.71)	0.11
struc	0.01	(0.01)	–0.10	(0.09)	0.29

Note: Definitions of variables: see Tables 7.4 and 7.5.

Source: Author's calculations. Sample period: 1972:1–1994:4; data sources: NIPA, Flow of Funds.

5 CONCLUSIONS

This analysis was based on a specification of a GDP growth equation with an interactive term – the product of the GDP gap and the fiscal deficit. This equation separates the response of GDP growth to deficits when the economy is at NAIRU from those responses that only arise when there is a recession or a boom. The results indicate that deficits are expansionary when there is no gap, more expansionary during a recession, and potentially contractionary during a strong enough boom – although the estimated effects during a recession and a boom have only an 87 per cent level of confidence.

The methods of disaggregating GDP in the National Income and Product Accounts provide an arithmetic framework for analysing the effects of fiscal deficits on growth of the gross domestic product. This chapter isolated the effects of federal fiscal deficits on individual components of output, which can then be evaluated relative to the overall responsiveness of GDP to deficits. While this arithmetic framework is somewhat compromised by statistical methods designed to correct for serial correlation, the differences are relatively trivial in the tests summarized here.

For the expenditure method of disaggregating GDP, the most notable inferences from the statistical tests are that consumption, particularly of durable goods, contributes strongly to the growth in output in response to deficits – both when the economy is at potential, and even more strongly when the economy is in a recession. This indicates that public dissaving is followed by an increase in private 'investment' in the form of accumulation of durable goods – although this increase is numerically smaller than the deficit itself.

When the economy is at NAIRU, the 'crowding out' of investment by deficits (which is not a statistically significant result, with only an 86 per cent level of confidence) is largely comprised of a draw-down of inventories, which is most likely caused by the increases in consumption that follow an increase in the deficit. When there is a gap, the statistically significant response is from equipment investment, with the results confirming the theoretical prediction that equipment investment is crowded out by deficits in booms but accelerated by deficits in recessions. Imports also appear to respond positively to deficits during recessions, weakening the expansionary impact of fiscal policy.

Overall, these results indicate that deficits are (as predicted by standard Keynesian theory) expansionary, that they are countercyclical, that durables consumption responds to deficits even when the economy is at GDP* (and even more strongly when it is below GDP*), and that business fixed investment is most likely to respond positively to deficits during a recession. While there is even some indication that deficits at NAIRU are not necessarily damaging to investment at all, at the very least the use of deficits as a countercyclical fiscal policy tool is supported by these results.

In the major products method of disaggregating GDP, the results are weak and inconsistent with both theory and the other statistical results. Little statistical support is lent even to the most basic theoretical insights.

NOTES

1. A related series (used in the cited studies by Eisner, and Eisner and Pieper) is called the price-adjusted *high*-employment deficit, based upon a different (and, unfortunately, discontinued) structural deficit series from the Bureau of Economic Analysis. The two series can be thought of as essentially interchangeable, although an extensive investigation of their similarities and differences can be found in Buchanan (1996a). Both measure the structural deficit at the federal level only.
2. In all regressions discussed in this chapter, the deficit variable was derived by dividing nominal PASED by nominal GDP (to create a 'real structural deficit' variable).
3. An example of such a model, and the derivation of the reduced-form equations, is summarized in Buchanan (1996a).
4. In some of the equations tested in the referenced works, an exchange rate variable (specifically, the change in the real trade-weighted US exchange rate) is included as a right-hand-side variable. For the specification used in this chapter, however, inclusion of this variable not only indicated that the coefficients on the exchange rate variable itself were not significantly different from zero, but the other diagnostic tests (adjusted R^2, and so on) were slightly degraded by inclusion of the exchange rate on the right-hand side. Even a regression with import growth alone as the dependent variable was not improved by the exchange rate explanatory variable. Therefore, the exchange rate was dropped from the list of exogenous variables.
5. Definitions of NAIRU and GDP* are the same as those used by the Congressional Budget Office in estimating the standardized-employment deficit. Use of NAIRU-based series here should not be construed as acceptance or endorsement of the concept, but rather as an attempt to see what can be learned from using this official series. See Staiger et al. (1996) and Eisner's contribution to this volume for interesting empirical analyses of some shortcomings of the NAIRU concept.
6. While this is inaccurate grammatically, in that I am using singular terms to describe plural concepts, greater clarity and simplicity are ultimately achieved by referring to each distributed lag as if it were a single estimate.
7. The CBO only publishes the standardized-employment deficit (SED) for fiscal years, computed on a budget basis. (See, for example, Congressional Budget Office 1995.) This series was the basis of most of the variants of the structural deficit in Buchanan (1996b) and of half of those series in Buchanan (1996a). However, CBO also computes (but does not publish) quarterly, NIPA-based estimates of the SED. The results analysed here are based on those quarterly, NIPA-based estimates.
8. Since GDP's long-term growth rate is determined by such variables as population growth and productivity growth, it is unlikely that an increase in the deficit will affect the permanent long-run GDP growth rate, unless the federal deficit is comprised largely of a very particular type of productivity-enhancing spending – a possibility that is the subject of future work. (If growth is path dependent, that could also create a link between long-run growth rates and current deficits.) In any case, the deficit can certainly affect the level of GDP at any point in time.
9. One can even imagine a special case in which the actual values of the four coefficients add up to exactly zero. In that case, testing a null hypothesis on the sum would be entirely misleading.
10. The displayed values of the δ_i's add up to –0.17, with the difference due to rounding error.
11. Having a negative coefficient on one of the lags of the deficit need not imply that the relationship between the deficit and GDP growth is inverse. Rather, it can simply mean that there is a combination of effects that involves both levels and changes of the deficit. For example,

the AR(1) regression above has estimated values of γ of 0.36, 0.75, 1.00, and -1.88, as the lag increases. As only one of many examples, this could imply the following relationship:

$$\%\Delta\text{GDP} = 0.23\text{DEF}_{t-1} + 0.13(\text{DEF}_{t-1} - \text{DEF}_{t-2}) + 0.88(\text{DEF}_{t-2} - \text{DEF}_{t-3})$$
$$+ 1.88(\text{DEF}_{t-3} - \text{DEF}_{t-4})$$

In this example, moreover, the *p*-values of the *t*-tests for the four estimated coefficients individually are 0.54, 0.20, 0.09 and 0.00. However, running a regression with only the fourth lag of the deficit degrades the results significantly (and has no apparent theoretical justification). Therefore, including the four lags as a group, and testing them for exclusion as a group, is the most appropriate statistical method.

12. For the particularly simple example displayed here, the test statistics for equations using the disaggregated variables would pass virtually any common test of statistical significance. For example, in a regression of *Y*1 on a constant term and *X*, the estimated coefficient on *X* has a *t*-statistic greater than 6.0. While this could be made to shrink with a sufficiently large number of subseries of *Y* that mimic this pattern of disaggregation, such a numerical example would be diagramatically uninformative.

13. The caveat in the previous note is also relevant here.

14. This is based on nothing more than the simple algebraic rule that:

$$\frac{x+y}{x+y} = \frac{x}{x+y} + \frac{y}{x+y}$$

15. The following discussion is based on Studenmund (1992: 349–50).

16. Net investment (gross investment minus depreciation), on the other hand, had the following values: First =7.1%, Last = 7.8%, Average = 5.4%, Ave. growth = 8.2%. This indicates that net investment as a percentage of GDP stayed below both the first and the last values for long stretches of the sample period, such that the average value for the entire period was low (and the average growth rate was high due to the high growth rates during the period when net investment was climbing back to 7.8 per cent of GDP).

17. Since their study was undertaken before the 1992 NIPA revisions, they use data on gross national product rather than gross domestic product.

18. The estimates here ignore the theoretical reasons to ignore the estimated responses of **gfed** and **ex** described above, describing instead the straightforward implications of the point estimates.

19. The point estimates are fairly large, however, reflecting the historical pattern of deficits and spending, that is, the fact that both spending and deficits increased for a large part of this time period.

REFERENCES

Buchanan, Neil H. (1996a), 'Comparing Alternative Methods of Adjusting U.S. Federal Fiscal Deficits for Cyclical and Price Effects', Working Paper No. 169, The Jerome Levy Economics Institute.

Buchanan, Neil H. (1996b), 'Which Deficit? Comparing Thirteen Measures of the U.S. Fiscal Deficit on Theoretical and Empirical Grounds', Working Paper No. 170, The Jerome Levy Economics Institute.

Congressional Budget Office (1995), *The Economic and Budget Outlook: Fiscal Years 1996–2000*, January, Washington, DC.

Eisner, Robert (1991), 'Deficits and Us and Our Grandchildren', in James M. Rock (ed.), *Debt and the Twin Deficits Debate*, Mountain View, CA: 81–107.

Eisner, Robert (1997), 'A New View of the NAIRU', in Paul Davidson and Jan Kregel (eds), *Growth in Output and Employment in a Global Economy*, Brookfield, VT.

Eisner, Robert and Paul J. Pieper (1988), 'Deficits, Monetary Policy, and Real Economic Activity', in Kenneth Arrow and Michael Boskin (eds), *The Economics of Public Debt*, 3–38.

Eisner, Robert and Paul J. Pieper (1992), 'Real Deficits and Real Growth: a Further View', *Journal of Post Keynesian Economics*, Fall: 43–9.

Fuhrer, Jeffrey C. (1992), 'Do Consumers Behave as the Life-Cycle/Permanent-Income Theory of Consumption Predicts?', *New England Economic Review*, September/October: 3–14.

Gordon, Robert J. (1993), *Macroeconomics*, 6th edn, New York.

Keynes, John Maynard (1936), *The General Theory of Employment, Interest and Money*, New York: Macmillan.

Samuelson, Paul A. (1939), 'Interactions Between the Multiplier Analysis and the Principle of Acceleration', *The Review of Economics and Statistics*, 75–8.

Staiger, Douglas, James H. Stock and Mark W. Watson (1996), 'How Precise are Estimates of the Natural Rate of Unemployment', Working Paper No. 5477, National Bureau of Economic Research.

Studenmund, A.H. (1992), *Using Econometrics: A Practical Guide*, 2nd edn, New York: HarperCollins.

PART II

Roundtable: Can Keynes's Employment
Policies Reach the Underclass?

8. The problem of the 'extremely poor' in Brazil: are aggregate demand management policies enough?

Fernanda Lopes de Carvalho*

1 INTRODUCTION

At the close of this century, the creation of jobs has again become one of the most important questions facing our societies. One is concerned not only that the number of new labour posts being created may be insufficient but also that their quality may fall short of what would be needed to allow the poorer sections of the population to better their lives. In Brazil, as elsewhere, the 'employment question' is at the heart of the problem of social exclusion and extreme poverty. The deterioration of the situation of the poor in recent years, on the other hand, has become a point of widespread concern in that country. Since 1993, as a result of a national campaign to mobilize society against extreme poverty, the demand for the government to take immediate action to create jobs has gathered momentum, becoming a strong influence on the shaping of its political agenda.

Creating new jobs is undoubtedly a key initiative to reduce poverty to levels acceptable in a civilized society. However, economic growth in itself is a necessary but not a sufficient condition to solve the problem of the extremely poor in Brazil, to improve their living conditions, and to bring them up from below the absolute poverty line. Makeshift jobs alone will not be sufficient to achieve these goals. We need productive jobs that will pay enough to sustain a family decently. Moreover, the other side of extreme poverty, in the case of Brazil, is privilege, that is, extreme inequality in the distribution of income. As Brazilian President Fernando H. Cardoso has recently put it, 'Brazil is not a poor country; it is unfair'.

The problem of the extremely poor in Brazil is, thus, very complex and demands complex solutions. Economic growth *is* necessary and full employment policies are necessary as well. Nevertheless, some large sections of the underclass do not benefit, or benefit only marginally, from a general rise in national income. For them, *structural* policies are needed to prepare them so that they

175

can benefit from overall growth. On the other hand, structural policies, not just economic, are also necessary to overcome extreme inequality, which helps to generate extreme poverty. In what follows, I begin by giving background data on the underclass problem in Brazil. Thus, Section 2 gives not only some general information on the Brazilian economy and society, but tries, in particular, to answer the question: who are the poor in Brazil and with what factors is extreme poverty associated? Section 3 discusses the relationship between the characteristics of the Brazilian employment market and social inequality, to show that combating poverty in Brazil requires deeper public intervention than just creating jobs. Section 4 examines some of the structural policies that may be adopted in order to allow extreme poverty to be eliminated, and gives examples of initiatives being adopted either by local governments or by grassroots groups.

SOCIAL INEQUALITY AND EXTREME POVERTY

According to many analysts the most pervasive feature of Brazilian society is *inequality*. Both income and wealth are heavily concentrated, whether we are considering social strata or size distribution. Income is also unequally distributed among geographical regions, ethnic groups, in terms of gender, and so on. After a long period of economic growth since the mid-1930s, which received a strong impetus from the rapid industrialization programmes in the 1950s, 1960s and 1970s, Brazil cannot be, and is not, considered, at this point, a poor country: according to the United Nations Development Programme, per capita income in 1991 reached US$5,240. Data about food production point in the same direction.[1] Until inflation accelerated and stagnation set in in the early 1990s, the Brazilian economy was counted among the ten largest western economies. Some data are reasonably favourable: in 1991, 87 per cent of the urban population had access to treated water supplies and 62 per cent to sewage systems, although only 9 per cent of the rural population had access to the same services. Knowing this, it is all the more shocking to find poverty at such extreme levels as we see even in the southern (richer) regions of the country. Extreme poverty is explained by equally extreme income and wealth concentrations rather than by low national income. The latest report on Brazilian human development, sponsored by the United Nations Development Programme (PNUD/IPEA 1996), points out that the average income of the richest 10 per cent of the population is approximately 30 times bigger than the average income of the poorest 40 per cent. Table 8.1 shows how income concentration has grown from 1960 to 1990. This is to be compared with equivalent groups in a sample of 36 countries where the average income of the richest is 10 times that of the poorest. The latter situation is found, for instance, in Argentina, which has a per capita income slightly larger than Brazil's.

Table 8.1   Income shares (percentages)

	Richest 20%	Poorest 50%
1960	54	18
1970	62	15
1980	63	14
1990	65	12

Source: PNUD/IPEA (1996).

Extremely inequality in Brazilian society has deep historical roots. The IMF-inspired adjustment processes adopted since the 1980s to overcome balance of payments disequilibria and to face the external debt crisis, made the situation very much worse from the distributive point of view. Data from the World Bank show that, *ceteris paribus*, the Brazilian economy has to grow at 3 per cent a year just to avoid an increase in the number of people below the poverty line and at least 7 per cent to reduce extreme poverty. Average growth has been much lower than 7 per cent, first because of the attempts to prevent the inflation rate from exploding and, after the Real Plan,[2] to prevent inflation from firing up again. On the other hand, the fall in the inflation rate in the last year and a half has had some favourable impact through the reduction in the inflation tax, which used to fall mainly on the poorer social groups who had no access to the financial investments that allowed higher-income groups to defend their purchasing power. As a result of the combination of stagnation plus high inflation, large extreme poverty pockets emerged, which did not get worse simply because of a long-term fall in fertility rates which had been initiated in the 1970s.[3] The improvements verified after the fall of the inflation rate represented an important respite but it consisted of a one-off gain, and was not sufficient, by itself, to eliminate, or even to reduce significantly, the extreme poverty pockets.

2.1   Poverty and Extreme Poverty

To address this problem and devise solutions, we have first to characterize the situation of those living in poverty. We shall not use, however, the term *underclass*.[4] A more complex concept of poverty will be required, that is, one taking into consideration multiple facets of the quality of life, such as income levels, good consumption patterns, general consumptions patterns, access to education, health care and public infrastructure, and so on. In a society in which inequality reaches extreme levels it is more useful to use these indicators to classify social groups in terms of degrees of poverty, down to the extreme poverty level.

Unfortunately, most of the systematically available data refer only to income levels which serve to define poverty in terms of per capita income in household units. In these circumstances, *poverty* is defined by the possession of only enough purchasing power to buy a limited basket of goods satisfying basic needs in terms of feeding, clothing, housing and transportation to work. *Extreme poverty*, on the other hand, is defined when per capita income in household units is, at best, only enough to buy a limited basket of food, sufficient to satisfy the minimum nutritional requirements set by the United Nation's Food and Agriculture Organization and World Health Organization.

A study by IPEA, a federal government think-tank, based on data researched by the Brazilian Central Statistical Office (IBGE), revealed that, in March 1993, a population of 31,679,095, representing 22 per cent of the total Brazilian population, was living in a state of extreme poverty (see Peliano 1993). These individuals, more or less equally distributed among urban and rural areas,[5] would be the closest equivalent in Brazil to the concept of underclass.[6]

As we see in Table 8.2, slightly more than half (54.6%) of the extremely poor live in the northeast of Brazil: a population of 17.3 million, which represents 41 per cent of the region's total population. In particular, if we consider only the extremely poor living in rural areas, we find 63 per cent of them in the same region.

Table 8.2   Incidence of extreme poverty, 1990

Areas	Poor population	Share of total of the poor (%)	Share of total population (%)
Metropolitan	4,396,421	13.88	9.58
Non-metropolitan urban	11,228,228	35.44	18.41
Rural	16,054,447	50.68	42.79
Total	31,679,095	100.0	21.94
Incidence by geographical region			
North*	685,204	2.16	
Northeast	17,288,528	54.57	
Southeast	7,982,453	23.20	
South	4,082,314	12.89	
Central–western	1,640,597	5.18	
Total	31,679,095	100.0	

Note: Excluding rural population.

Source: Peliano (1993)

While the northeast has been a historically depressed area in Brazil, it may be, at first sight, more surprising to learn that the second-highest concentration of extreme poverty, in absolute numbers, is to be found in the southeast: a population of 7,982,453, representing, though, 12.4 per cent of total regional population. Poverty here is concentrated in urban rather than in rural areas. As is clear from the data, poverty is not only a social problem, but it is also a regional problem: while per capita income in the northeast reached, in 1991, US$2,559, it was US$7,212 in the south. In Piaui, one of the poorest among Brazilian states, it was US$1,339, while it was US$8,896 in São Paulo (the most industrialized state) and US$10,202 in Brasilia, where federal government activity is concentrated.

2.2 Labour Market and Poverty

Employment figures in Brazil suggest that the central problem in that country may not be the creation of jobs. In fact, comparatively low rates of open unemployment have been registered in the Brazilian economy for a long period. The highest unemployment rate reached between April 1994 and May 1996, according to this survey, was 6.4 per cent, in March 1996. Even if we ignore for a moment the methodological pitfalls of such surveys, we cannot avoid recognizing that behind these numbers is hidden the reality of low wages, precarious working conditions, high rates of job turnover and little or no access to the (already limited) welfare benefits.

In fact, recent surveys show a comparatively low incidence of long-term unemployment: in 1995, according to IBGE, two-thirds of the unemployed workers has been less than six months without a job. The meaning of these numbers is ambiguous though: a hard to measure number of people remain unemployed for a short time not because they are able to find other jobs but because they are discouraged from searching for work of an equivalent nature to the one lost. With unemployment benefits severely limited, these workers just tended to accept anything to survive. This is reflected in Table 8.3, where it is shown that in the six largest metropolitan areas of the country, the share of people working under labour contracts (which given them access to welfare benefits) fell from 56 per cent (1990) to 48 per cent (1995). This fall is matched by the increase in the number of workers who do not have labour contracts (and, thus, no protection from labour laws) or who are self-employed. These two groups already comprise about 48 per cent of the labour force. What these data show, therefore, is the loss of quality in the supply of jobs and the increasingly precarious nature of labour relations in Brazil.

To have a more complete picture of the labour market, it is important to keep in mind some further aspects. First, the situation is much worse in rural areas, where a significant fraction of the population and of the workforce remains. In

Table 8.3   Types of employment (percentages) in the six largest metropolitan
areas

	Employed		Self-employed	Employers
	With contract	Without contract		
1990	55.7	19.7	20.3	4.4
1991	52.5	21.4	21.8	4.3
1992	50.6	22.5	22.7	4.3
1993	49.6	23.1	23.1	4.2
1994	48.0	24.2	23.8	4.0
1995	47.9	24.3	23.8	4.0

Source: Urani (1996).

the agricultural sector, 74 per cent of those employed had no formal contracts
of any nature (see PNUD/IPEA 1966). To this picture, one should also add gender
and racial discrimination. Although the participation of women in the labour force
has been increasing in recent years, reaching 35 per cent in 1990, their average
wages are still only 63 per cent of those earned by men. If one considers the
increasing importance of the women's contribution to household incomes,
even becoming, in many cases in poor families in metropolitan areas, the main
breadwinner, gender discrimination becomes a powerful influence in
impoverishing the population and increasing inequality. As for racial
discrimination, black and *mulatto* men earned on average only 63 per cent and
68 per cent, respectively, of the earnings of white men. Black and mulatto women
were, if anything, in an even worse situation, earning only 68 per cent of the
average income of white women. Despite a widespread myth about the non-
existence of racial discrimination in Brazil, one should keep in mind that even
after controlling for factors such as level of education, significant differences
in income levels remain (see PNUD/IPEA 1966).

As much as these data in themselves tell a story of structural imbalances that
strengthen existing patterns of inequality, there are other ways in which the labour
market serves as a means of perpetuating poverty instead of allowing people to
rise above it. Key among these factors is child labour. A survey made in the
northeast state of Pernambuco, reported in a Brazilian newspaper, found that
in sugar-cane plantations, one of the most important economic activities in the
state, more than 50 per cent of the children working there are responsible for
about 30 per cent of their family's total income. Not surprisingly, the United
Nations Development Programme's report mentioned above states that 23 per
cent of the children between the ages of 10 and 14 in families earning incomes

up to half a legal minimum wage (which was about 100 dollars in 1996), work. The share rises to 54 per cent of the teenagers between 14 and 17 years old (see PNUD/IPEA 1966).

In Brazil as a whole, in 1990, children between 10 and 14 years old represented 5.2 per cent of the workforce, a high rate even according to Latin American standards, especially when one considers that the Federal Constitution outlaws child labour. Teenage workers (between 15 and 17 years old) represented 6.5 per cent of the workforce (4.3 million people). These numbers, nevertheless, do not tell the whole story. If adult labour is precarious, child and teenage labour is extremely so: no rights, very low wages and long hours – 46.6 per cent of the children and 77.3 per cent of the teenagers employed work 40 hours or more a week (see PNUD/IPEA 1966). Among teenagers, who are legally allowed to work, only 33 per cent had any kind of formal link with the employer. Needless to say, these children and teenagers are unable to attend school or to achieve anything like a satisfactory standard of education. In fact, 46 per cent of the total group has less than four years of schooling.

The picture gets worse, again, when we detail the data in terms of regions or gender. About 35 per cent of the girls between the ages of 10 and 17 work as domestic servants, frequently in semi-slavery conditions. In the northeast, this is the situation of more than 50 per cent of the girls of those ages. Still in the northeast, the International Labour Organization calculates that about 120 thousand children are employed in the sugar-cane plantations, doing very dangerous and painful work. Data for the State of Pernambuco indicate that 56 per cent of the children working in sugar-cane harvesting suffered accidents at some point. In the production of manioc flour, the number rises to an incredible 97 per cent. The Agricultural Workers' Union (*Confederação Nacional dos Trabalhadores na Agricultura*) reports that in the State of Bahia, children are employed in large numbers for average weekly wages of US$5. The same situation is witnessed in many sectors and regions, such as coal, tobacco and kitchen salt production. Even modern sectors, such as orange production for export, have been noted to employ children.

Norms concerning the employment of children and teenagers have been violated repeatedly both in traditional and in modern activities. In fact, modern trends in the reorganization of productions, such as the contracting out of some ancillary activities, allow firms to pretend not to know how some of these are actually accomplished.

The importance of child labour in supplementing household incomes is visible not only in organized activities, but also in the large cities, at every corner or every traffic light where children sell newspapers, fruit, gum, and so on, or polish shoes, wash cars, offer to help carry packages and to do practically any other task one can think of. Working for tips, sometimes late at night, many of these children are not counted in official statistics because frequently they are less than ten years old.

We could offer an endless list of sectors where child labour is used, always in the most hazardous conditions. Of course, this situation, rooted in the extreme poverty in which the families of these children live, becomes itself a factor of further impoverishment. As in nineteenth-century England, classically described by Engels, child labour competes with that of adults and helps to keep wages low, forcing the families to send more children to work, in a really vicious circle. In addition, children entering the labour market at an early age will never have the chance to go to school and improve their skills. The survey of living conditions made by IBGE in 1990 shows that 12.3 per cent of the children between 10 and 14 of families earning up to one-quarter of the legal minimum wage spend their time working and never go to school. The index falls precipitously to 1.2 per cent in the case of families earning more than two minimum wages (see PNUD/IPEA 1966). Again, we face a vicious circle in which misery breeds misery.

2.3   Other Factors

The patterns described above are strengthened by the poor supply of public goods to the lowest-income groups of the population. Lack of education condemns them to low-skill jobs, where remuneration is insufficient to survive, forcing the families to send their children to the labour market at an early age. In fact, it is not so much a problem of lack of schools as it is of quality. Existing schools are unable to help the poor to develop their skills and improve their situation. On the other hand, as we saw, a large fraction of the children and of the teenagers are under enormous pressure to work and begin supporting the household without waiting to get a better qualification (which the educational system is unlikely to offer, anyway). Again, if the picture is bad in the large towns such as São Paulo or Rio de Janeiro, it is not nearly as bad as it becomes when we see the data on the northeast.

Inadequate health care and access to treated water, sewage systems, and so on, exacerbate this state of affairs. All these factors contribute to the emergence of unskilled labour on a scale that would be very difficult to absorb with the low growth rates that have characterized the Brazilian economy in recent years, even if the other barriers we described were not operative. Unskilled workers can get only low-paid jobs that force them to look for other sources of income. All this contributes to generating patterns of extreme poverty. What is more serious, a vicious circle is created that cannot be broken just by expanding the economy. Growth is needed and is, in the long term, a *sine qua non* condition for prosperity. In the more immediate term, however, deeper measures, such as structural policies or other actions to break the poverty circle, are needed.

3   COMBATING EXTREME POVERTY

Combating poverty in a country like Brazil requires concerted action on many fronts. Keynesian demand management policies to promote full employment and growth are, without a doubt, an essential element of any anti-poverty struggle. On the one hand, income can be redistributed more easily when it is growing than when it is stagnated. In the later situation, redistribution means absolute reductions in someone's income, something that is much more likely to provoke adverse reactions than the redistribution of income additions. On the other hand, to incorporate larger and larger fractions of society into the labour market, allowing them to benefit from contractual and legal rights, is tantamount to recognizing their citizenship. Nevertheless, extreme poverty in the dimension that this problem assumes in Brazil cannot be effectively attacked only by recourse to aggregate employment policies. These policies affect the extremely poor only indirectly and in insufficient proportions to actually change their status. In addition, even these kinds of macropolicies sometimes fall short of their possible impact when they are planned without a larger perspective. Thus, for instance, when a sewage system is built, the authorities should aim at using labour-intensive construction techniques so one can have the benefit not only of better sanitary conditions but also of a larger number of workers in employment.

In fact, even the kind of social policies that have been implemented in Brazil have generally affected the poor, that is, those near the poverty line, but not the extremely poor. Initiatives such as the creation of unemployment insurance reach those who are in the lowest strata of the *formal* labour market. Those working informally, without officially-recognized contracts, are simply excluded from these initiatives. To attack extreme poverty, it is necessary to define clearly the target groups to be helped.

Extremely poor families are locked in a vicious circle that must be explicitly taken into consideration when devising policies to improve their situation. In principle, *if there is the necessary political will to do it*, attacking extreme poverty should not be beyond the Brazilian economy's means. Two of the more serious restrictions, absolute scarcity of resources and rapid population growth, are simply absent in the case of Brazil. On the other hand, extreme poverty is not just a problem for the state: it is also a *citizenship problem*, and there are ways through which the Brazilian society can act on its own initiative. In what follows, we want to outline measures that can be (and, in some regions, are already being) adopted by governments, at any of the three levels, federal, state and local. But, we also want to discuss some initiatives that are being taken by the Brazilian society itself.

3.1   Governmental Action Against Poverty

We have repeatedly pointed out the twin problems of the low skills of a large group of workers and of the poor quality (and low remuneration) of many of the working opportunities that are created. Thus, low productivity and low remuneration combine to breed poverty. To attack this problem, it is necessary to bring about a deep change in the Brazilian education system, aiming at a much better elementary cycle. As mentioned before, it is less a problem of opening new schools or of material conditions (although transportation to school and back may be a problem in certain areas) but of improving the quality of teaching, focusing not only on the development of basic skills but also on the adequacy of what is being taught to the needs of poor households. Not surprisingly, schools fare worse precisely where poverty is more acute. These children need more attention, better-trained teachers and teaching methods adapted to their realities. These schools are marked by student absenteeism and withdrawal. Obviously, an important part of the problem is the families' pressures on the children to get jobs, making it difficult for them to remain in school, even if they want to.

To meet the challenge of changing these habits, some initiatives have been successfully implemented by local administrations to encourage the families to keep their children in school. In the city of Brasilia, the Federal District, a monthly minimum wage is guaranteed to each poor family that has resided in the town for at least five years if their children, between the ages of 7 and 14, attend school regularly. In Rio de Janeiro city, again, the local government is beginning to implement a programme in which a basket of staple food is distributed to families whose children may be being forced to leave school. The target children are identified by their teachers, who are also responsible for controlling their attendance. The project involves very low costs and has had success, and will now be extended to other areas of the town. Other towns are also implementing guaranteed-income programmes that would lower the pressure on children to work prematurely. The most successful of them, however, are the programmes that make the benefit conditional on school attendance.

Keeping the children in school no matter how important, is still just a first step. Of course, the schools themselves have still to be improved and this may be a long-term goal. Immediate action, however, is imperative lest the schools be improved only when we shall all be dead, as Keynes wrote. On the other hand, there is already a generation of low-skilled adult workers who should be trained to increase their productivity. Unfortunately, governmental initiatives in this field, specially on the part of the federal government, have been rather perfunctory.

Some degree of intervention is also necessary to generate job opportunities for unskilled labour. It is widely expected in Brazil that the end of high inflation will stimulate a recovery of private investment, modernizing productive facilities and favourably affecting the quality of jobs being created. Current developments suggest that this may be overoptimistic. On the one hand, economic growth in other countries has not been followed by a proportionate expansion of employment. Moreover, high real interest rates and credit restriction to prevent inflation from re-accelerating has been the cornerstone of the Brazilian stabilization policy since early 1995. It is argued that balancing the federal budget should allow the easing of monetary policy, but it is very uncertain if and when this will take place.

Be this as it may, I am not directly concerned with these jobs because they are out of reach of the large number of workers living in deep poverty. Those who succeed in finding a 'regular' job usually find it either as employees in small firms or as small entrepreneurs, running what is called 'backyard firms' in Brazil. In large towns, many of these are microfirms, like the so-called *camelos*, people who set up little tents in the street to sell all sorts of merchandise. We find also repair shops, itinerant plumbers, electricians, and so on. These activities are very important from the point of view of employment, if not in terms of income. A large part of them, however, are illegal. Initiatives to legalize these activities, simplifying bureaucratic procedures, and even of financial support, facilitating the access to credit, would go along way to reduce poverty. In fact, some programmes have already been devised, both by governments and by non-governmental organizations, to supply credit to small and microfirms to improve skills, offer better services, and so on. For these initiatives to succeed, however, it is necessary to have organizers from within the target communities themselves, to spread information about the programmes and to stimulate the community to take initiatives on their own behalf. In addition it is also necessary to offer complementary programmes to upgrade labour skills and to give the projects technical assistance.

3.2 An Essential Step: Agrarian Reform

There is a wide consensus in Brazil nowadays that a change in the agrarian structure is a pre-condition to any successful programme of income redistribution. Only 5 per cent of the agricultural estates occupy 67 per cent of all available land, an area of approximately 403 million hectares. The 18 biggest rural establishments occupy an area that is equivalent to the total area of Portugal, Switzerland and Holland. A large part of these properties are kept unused, as stores of value, or are utilized in activities that economize labour, such as cattle raising. As a result, many families are expelled from the tracts of land where they live. It is believed that breaking up the large unproductive properties, which comprise most of the land in Brazil, would be essential to regulate the flow of migrants from rural areas to the cities, which is today, and has been for a long time, the main depressing influence on urban lower incomes. Wandering landless families in rural areas migrate to the cities constantly, feeding one of the largest 'industrial reserve armies' in the world. Endowed with skills that are in fact useless in urban environments, these workers can only compete for the most menial jobs, thus contributing to keep the remunerations for these tasks at a minimum survival level. Past attempts at reform have been largely ineffective because redistribution of property is not enough: technical assistance and access to credit to buy inputs are also necessary to make small agricultural enterprises viable. Increasing pressures of public opinion and of landless rural families, however, have given a new urgency to the problem, although political action to solve it has still been very slow.

3.3   The Activities of Non-governmental Organizations and Grassroots Initiatives

A new feature in the struggle against extreme poverty in Brazil (as, in fact, in many other countries) has been the emergence of non-governmental organizations and the mobilization of society itself to contribute to the solution of problems much beyond the simple pressure on governments to act. In Brazil, a national movement called *Citizens' Action Against Hunger and Misery and for Life*, created in 1993, has been very successful in organizing non-governmental initiatives to combat extreme poverty.[7]

Citizens' Action itself sprang from the large mass movement that emerged to demand the impeachment of former President Collor de Mello in 1992. The corruption charges made against his administration led to a popular demand for 'ethics in politics' as a condition for the consolidation of democracy, then recently restored in Brazil after more than 25 years of military dictatorship. It was soon realized that social exclusion on the scale that we described in the first section was not compatible with democracy and with the rights of citizenship. In 1993, an appeal was made to Brazilian society to mobilize against hunger, attacking the immediate manifestations of extreme poverty without losing sight of the need for longer-term measures. The response to the appeal of Citizen's Action, led by Mr Herbert de Souza (known as Betinho), was overwhelming, allowing the organization of literally thousands of committees, all over the country, where people from diverse social classes could devise actions ranging from distribution of food in extremely poor communities to the support of productive initiatives to generate income in these areas. These committees are independent of government and, in fact, of any central power. Citizens' Action serves as a channel to inform and to organize but not to control: its main goal is to promote a change in the political culture of the country, trying to reawaken a sense of initiative and of national solidarity and to give concrete meaning to terms such as citizenship and human rights, in a country long used to alienation and passiveness. Its strategy was first to lead a campaign against hunger, to alleviate the most immediate problem plaguing the extremely poor. After the emergency campaign gathered momentum, a new banner was raised: the generation of new jobs, not only by pressuring governments into implementing full-employment policies, but also by stimulating the communities to create job opportunities themselves.

Citizens' Action has catalogued a long list of spontaneous initiatives that show much creativity in the search for local solutions to the problems of employment and extreme poverty. Basically, these groups search for ways to improve the skills of poor community workers at the same time as productive activities are organized to absorb them. These groups eventually received the support of university teachers and researchers, who have given technical assistance to some of the projects. Most of the initiatives consist in the setting up of small manufactures to produce consumption goods that do not demand significant investment in plant and equipment. There are bakeries, groups producing clothing, shoes and sandals, bricks, toys, furniture, handicrafts, and so on. In rural or suburban areas, community vegetable gardens are very common. Less common but particularly successful have been enterprises where unused land is made available, either by private owners or by state-owned firms that control them, to grow staples such as rice or corn. Agricultural technicians have volunteered to assist these activities and the results have been impressive in terms of productivity and quality. One should note that most of the activities are not innovative in themselves. What is really new is the concept of partnership in which different social groups are called together to collaborate in the generation of jobs and income. Nevertheless, some truly new ideas may be identified in some cases. Two of these experiences may be worth reporting.

The first case is a project implemented by a group composed basically of bank clerks in the interior of the state of Ceara, a very poor region, plagued by constant droughts, with high indices of malnutrition and infant mortality. This committee found a way to combat hunger and to generate income at the same time. Through several devices, the committee members were able to purchase some nanny- and billy-goats to act as procreators. The herd is lent for two years to poor communities, during which period the herd triples in number, allowing the community to consume the milk (reducing infant mortality) and to sell surplus production and byproducts. After two years the community returns as many goats as were lent to them, which are then re-lent to another community. The same system, but with chickens, is now being implemented in another northeastern state.

The second case is in Rio de Janeiro City, where a group of middle-class women have organized sewing classes for slum women. It took quite a long time to organize and train the women, who did not have appropriate working practices, such as discipline, hygiene habits, and so on. After two and a half years of work, however, the women have made much progress and have been able to produce very sophisticated pieces of clothing. Again, partnership has been essential: the local church offered space for the women to work; the middle-class neighbourhood financed the building of a small barn to house the equipment, bought with the contributions of workers of an airline company and of a local firm; another firm helped by supplying instructors to train the workers and to upgrade their skills; and many other groups have given support in many different forms.

4   CONCLUSION

The main point of this chapter is that aggregate demand policies to promote full employment may not be enough to solve the problem of poverty when a significant fraction of the workforce is locked out in a vicious circle of extreme poverty, low skills and marginality. This does not mean, of course, that full-employment policies are useless or undesirable. Nothing could be farther from the truth. Full employment and economic growth are necessary conditions for long-term sustained prosperity. These policies, however, are not sufficient because they do not reach, or do so only marginally, the extremely poor. In countries where extreme poverty is not a significant problem, paternalist initiatives may suffice to eliminate it. In countries such as Brazil, it is necessary to target those social groups that are excluded from the market mechanisms. Two ways of attacking extreme poverty were shown: on the one hand, government, federal, state or local, can implement structural policies and institutional reforms to remove the deeper causes of exclusion; on the other hand, society itself can be organized to implement projects to help the poor communities to help themselves. Government and society are not competitors. In fact, the mobilization of society should be seen as a condition for a successful government programme of income redistribution, since it takes mostly *political will* to eliminate extreme poverty.

NOTES

*   The opinions expressed here are the author's and do not necessarily represent the views of the Brazilian Institute of Social and Economic Analyses or the Rio de Janeiro State Committee of the Citizens' Action.
1.   According to the Brazilian Central Statistical Office (IBGE), grain production in 1995–96 reached 86 million tons.
2.   The 'Real Plan' was the most recent, and so far the most successful stabilization plan adopted in Brazil. It was implemented in July 1994 and has brought monthly inflation rates to less than 2 per cent in late 1995, down from more than 40 per cent earlier in 1994.
3.   The population growth rate fell from 2.9 per cent in the 1960s to 1.9 per cent in the 1990s. See PNUD/IPEA (1996).

4. Besides, as pointed out by Gans (1993: 328), the term itself can carry inappropriate pejorative meanings.
5. One has to note that 'in the rural areas, food consumption is higher than in urban areas (about 7.5% higher), which is explained by the easier access to items that are not marketed (the occurrence of higher malnutrition indices in those regions are due to lesser access to health care and to sewage systems)' (Peliano 1993: 5).
6. Brazil has gone through a rapid urbanization process in the period since the Second World War. Thus, rural population constituted 70 per cent of total population in 1950. In 1991, the share had fallen to 24 per cent.
7. For a more detailed discussion of the origins and experience of the Citizens' Action, see Carvalho (1994).

REFERENCES

Carvalho, Fernanda (1994), 'Citizens in Action for Life, Against Hunger and Deprivation', Rio de Janeiro: IBASE, mimeo.

Gans, Herbert (1993), *People, Plans and Policies*, New York: Columbia University Press.

Peliano, A.M.T.M. (1993), *O Mapa da Forme: Subsídios à Formulação de uma Política de Segurança Alimentar* (The Map of Hunger: Elements for the Formulation of a Food Security Policy), Documents de Política IPEA no. 14, Brasília.

PNUD/IPEA (1996), *Relatório sobre o Desenvolvimento Humano no Brasil* (Report on Human Development in Brazil), Brasília: IPEA.

Urani, Andre (1996), 'Desemprego no Brasil em Meados dos Anos 90' (Unemployment in Brazil in the Mid-90s), Monitor Público, **8** (3), January–March.

9. Keynes, employment policy and the underclass

William Darity Jr

Given Keynes's vision of social change and his stated attitudes towards Britain's working class, I speculate that he would have displayed a cautious paternalism towards the condition of the contemporary underclass in the more affluent nations. About fifteen years ago, two coauthors and I, in trying to unwrap the ideological content of Keynes's work in the 1930s, described Keynes as 'one of the most sophisticated representatives of the managerial class on the eve of its flowering [who] recommended a "socialization" of investment'. We went on to observe that 'Keynes' *General Theory* can be read as a studied expression of the desires of the managerial class to stake out a territory for action independent of [the capitalist class] through the state' (Darity et al. 1982: 191).[1]

While Keynes's preference was for a social order organized and dominated by the judgement of the *deserving* members of the intelligentsia, he did not propose or desire destruction of the hierarchical structure of a society premised on a tripartite scheme of classes: his own, which I refer to as the managerial class, the business or capitalist class, and the working class. Keynes sought to rationalize that social order, to make it more humane, and to make it more stable. Often characterized as 'the savior of capitalism', even by his most astute biographer, Robert Skidelsky (1992), it is more accurate to view him as a brilliant stalking horse for the ascension of the managerial class.

Skidelsky's (1992: 232–3) own observations about Keynes's political sympathies suggest that the latter's intention was to seek a modification of capitalism that would prevent it from being susceptible to the onslaught of Bolshevism. But that modification would involve the construction of an aristocracy of the academically credentialled intellectuals:

> It is easy to imagine Keynes [the Liberal] at home, or as at home as he ever would be, in the Conservative Party of Macmillan and Butler – both of whom became personal friends, unlike any Labour leaders. He admired Conservatism's elitism: 'the inner ring can almost dictate the details and technique of policy,' he remarked admiringly. It was only to stupid elitism he objected. Keynes believed that ability was innate, and deplored only the fact that, in its attachment to the hereditary principle, Conservatism prevented natural ability from rising to the top. A Conservative Party

led by Oxford and Cambridge men would not have been so objectionable to him as one which still stuffed Cabinets with dukes. As he became older and started his own ascent to the peerage, the stupidity and class prejudice associated with the hereditary principle came to seem less noxious to him than parallel manifestations of those same tendencies in the Labour Party. Keynes emphatically rejected the class basis of socialist ideology and politics. 'It [the Labour Party] is a class party, and the class is not my class. If I am going to pursue sectional interests at all, I shall pursue my own.'

Of course, Keynes favoured decreased inequality in the income distribution, although stopping far short of endorsing complete equalization. In an intriguing passage in *The General Theory*, Keynes (1936: 374) can be found making the following comment about economic inequality in Great Britain:

> For my own part, I believe that there is a social and psychological justification for significant inequalities of incomes and wealth, but not for such large disparities as exist to-day. There are valuable human activities which require the motive of money-making and the environment of private wealth-ownership for their full function. Moreover, dangerous human proclivities can be canalised into comparatively harmless channels by the existence of opportunities for money-making and private wealth, which, if they cannot be satisfied in this way, may find their outlet in cruelty, the reckless pursuit of personal power and authority, and other forms of self-aggrandisement. It is better that a man should tyrannise over his bank balance than his fellow-citizens; and whilst the former is sometimes denounced as being but a means to the latter, sometimes at least it is an alternative. But it is not necessary for the stimulation of these activities and the satisfaction of these proclivities that the game should be played for such high stakes as at present. Much lower stakes will serve the purpose equally well ...

Thus, for Keynes significant economic inequality was needed, just considerably less of it than prevailed in Britain in the 1930s. But Keynes had no desire to overturn the British structure of class stratification. At most he desired greater empowerment of those he would have identified as possessing the intellectual and artistic wherewithal, the managerial class.

Keynes's managerial class consists of expert 'professionals with portfolios' (Darity 1996: 124). Like all dominant classes it, too, has displayed a tendency to preserve status for its own offspring. The hereditary principle for class replication has come strongly into play. Becoming one of the 'Oxbridge men' (or Harvard/Yale men) is not an opportunity equally open to all from all walks of life. For access to the managerial class largely depends upon demonstration of academic merit, inclusive of successful performance on standardized tests. As Richard Weinberg (1989: 100) has observed about so-called intelligence tests in particular:

> The standardized IQ test has become an important part of American life. Performances on individual and group tests of intellectual abilities – the 'magical' numbers – continue to be an important basis for selection, placement and other decision making in the psychoeducational and employment arenas across the life span. The scores

determine who is adopted quickly or accepted in the top-tier preschools, who is labeled retarded or gifted or is tracked to receive special education placement and programming, who is placed in the bluebird learning group or the cardinals, who goes to elite colleges or is offered other educational opportunities, and who serves in the military as an officer or gets into a management-training program. IQ tests have played a pivotal role in allocating society's resources and opportunities.

Moreover, academically high-achieving youths, who presumably have scored high on these standardized tests of cognitive ability, increasingly are likely to be the children of academically high-achieving parents (Morgan 1980: A1–A2). Unlike the conceit of the genetic determinists (see for example, Herrnstein and Murray 1994), this is not due to biology.[2] It is due to systematic differentiation in opportunities for cognitive development and quality schooling.

Robert Reich (1992: 227) has described the process of the development of the 15–20 per cent of American youths who are prepared for the socially elite careers involving 'symbolic analytical' work. In so doing he has listed a host of advantages bestowed upon these children by their parents, none of which need be linked to genetic endowments:

> The formal education of the budding symbolic-analyst follows a common pattern. Some of these young people attend elite private schools, followed by the most selective universities and prestigious graduate schools; a majority spend childhood within high-quality suburban public schools where they are tracked through advanced courses in the company of other similarly fortunate symbolic-analyst offspring and thence to good four-year colleges. But their experiences are similar: Their parents are interested and involved in their education. Their teachers and their professors are attentive to their academic needs. They have access to state-of-the-art science laboratories, language laboratories, interactive computers and video systems in the class-room, and high-tech school libraries. Their classes are relatively small; their peers are intellectually stimulating. Their parents take them to museums and cultural events, expose them to foreign travel, and give them music lessons. At home are educational books, educational toys, educational videotapes, microscopes, and personal computers replete with the latest educational software. Should the children fall behind in their studies, they are delivered to private tutors. Should they develop a physical ailment that impedes their learning, they immediately receive good medical care.

In the US context, 80–85 per cent of youths do not have these advantages, primarily because of the politics of public schooling and the politics of provision of comprehensive social support to those families in poverty-induced distress. In short, neither are provided; it is not in the collective interest of the managerial class to do so, since it would alter radically the intergenerational and racial/ethnic opportunity structure.

Jonathon Kozol (1991) has documented with devastating detail the disparities in school funding that separate school districts and schools within districts that serve populations from different social classes. But Kozol's emphasis on funding differentials does not address the content of schooling for particular groups, given high or low relative levels of expenditure. The matter of content has been the subject of Jewell Mazique's (1992) research.

In an essay published originally in 1969 in *Triumph* magazine under the pseudonym Martha White Washington, Mazique described in detail the mechanisms whereby public schooling was transformed in the early 1960s into a scheme of programmed retardation, rather than education, for the predominantly black student population of the relatively well-funded District of Columbia school system. Mazique exposed in particular the 'educational "innovation" racket' which eliminated the teaching of fundamentals from the early grades. Earlier Mazique (1965: 270) had presented evidence to the US Congress of teachers being actively discouraged from developing competency in their students in mathematics and reading on the grounds that this would be 'pushing' children who were not yet ready to learn such material.

Today those denied the advantages most systematically are the children of the underclass, the children of 'the most deprived and least utilized fraction of the working class [which is d]isproportionately black and spatially concentrated in communities beset by intense degrees of poverty [and] conceptually equivalent to Marx's "lumpen" element of the proletariat' (Darity 1996b: 129). An operational definition of the underclass that identifies it as consisting of persons who experienced poverty for five years or more over a seven-year interval suggests that the underclass constitutes between 5 and 10 per cent of the US population (Levy 1977).[3]

A macroeconomic stabilization policy, derived from Keynes's analysis, to maintain full employment will not alter the relative social status of members of the underclass. Nor would it be designed to do so. Part and parcel of Keynes's sensible rationalization of a social order that periodically wastes productive resources, including human resources, full employment policy is not an antipoverty policy nor is it a policy geared towards a fundamental transformation of social relations:

> If real wages are not sufficiently high to insure that employment eradicates pauperization, poverty will persist. An employed underclass can still be an underclass. Social hierarchy will focus even more plainly on occupational differentiation in a fully employed economy. Distribution of income and the quality of life will depend explicitly on the distribution of jobs and the structure of wages. (Darity 1986: p. 222)

For the poles of distance between overclass and underclass are no longer merely matters of income and wealth. Now they are primarily a matter of possession of expert knowledge coupled with possession of advanced educational credentials. A full-employment policy or more generally an employment guarantee does not bridge that gap. The genuinely revolutionary social policy that 'will reach' the underclass is one that produces a widespread diffusion of opportunities for cognitive development and quality schooling for all children. That is the social policy that will effectively undermine the privileged position of the offspring of the new overclass.

This goes far beyond Keynes's desire for 'wise' selection of the intelligentsia. For Keynes still perceived the mental gifts that would justify social leadership as being confined to a small minority. In his view that small minority simply did not overlap exactly with those persons in possession of hereditary titles (which I understand are now marketable items in Britain). The key then was to find that 'talented tenth' regardless of its class origins.

The perspective advanced here is far more optimistic about the distribution of human cognitive talent. What should make the selection of the managerial class difficult is not how hard it is to find those with talent but how easy it should be! Instead of 15–20 per cent of America's population possessing the symbolic analytic skills to take elite positions, consider the social environment if 80–85 per cent of America's youth were qualified to do so. The elimination of the politically induced scarcity of youths with the prospect for becoming symbolic analysts would radically alter the social landscape of the post-industrial order. It would 'reach' the underclass by changing dramatically how high the members of the underclass can reach.

NOTES

1. For a more comprehensive discussion of the managerial class and its rise to power during the Great Depression, see Darity (1996b).
2. For a critique of the biogenetic explanation of social stratification, see Darity (1996a).
3. For a more comprehensive discussion of definitions of the underclass, both conceptual and empirical, see Darity and Myers (1994).

REFERENCES

Darity Jr, William (1986), 'The Managerial Class and Industrial Policy', *Industrial Relations*, Spring: 212–27.

Darity Jr, William (1996a), 'Race, Intelligence, Poverty and Social Stratification', Paper prepared for the American Psychological Association's Task Force on Poverty.

Darity Jr, William (1996b), 'The Undesirables, America's Underclass in the Managerial Age', in Obie Clayton (ed.), *An American Dilemma Revisited: Race Relations in a Changing World*, New York: Russell Sage Foundation: pp. 112–37.

Darity Jr, William, Ronald Johnson and Edward Thompson (1982), 'The Political Economy of U.S. Energy and Equity Policy', in Hans Landsberg (ed.), *High Energy Costs: Assessing the Burden*, Washington, DC: Resources for the Future: 170–219.

Darity Jr, William and Samuel Myers Jr, with Emmett Carson and William Sabol (1994), *The Black Underclass: Essays on Race and Unwantedness,* New York: Garland Publishing.

Herrnstein, Richard and Charles Murray (1994), *The Bell Curve: Intelligence and Class Structure in American Life*, New York: The Free Press.

Keynes, John Maynard (1936), *The General Theory of Employment, Interest and Money*, London: Macmillan.

Kozol, Jonathon (1991), *Savage Inequalities: Children in America's Schools*, New York: Crown Publishers.

Levy, Frank (1977), 'How Big Is the American Underclass?', Working Paper 0090–1 Washington DC: The Urban Institute.

Mazique Jewell (1965, 1966), 'Testimony on Behalf of the League for Universal Justice and Goodwill', *Investigation of the Schools and Poverty in the District of Columbia of the Committee on Education and Labor*, House of Representatives, 89th Congress, 7, 8, 12, 26 October 1965 and 13 January 1966: 255–306.

Mazique, Jewell (1992), 'Betrayal in the Schools', in Floyd Hayes III, *A Turbulent Voyage: Readings in African–American Studies*, San Diego: Collegiate Press: pp. 468–78.

Morgan, Dan (1980), 'A Mixed Message on Education from the Home of the Bomb', *The Washington Post*, 19 October: A1–A2.

Reich, Robert (1992), *The Work of Nations: Preparing Ourselves for 21st Century Capitalism*, New York: Vintage Books.

Skidelsky, Robert (1992), *John Maynard Keynes: The Economist As Savior, 1920–1937*, London: Macmillan.

Weinberg, Richard A. (1989), 'Intelligence and IQ: Landmark Issues and Great Debates', *American Psychologist*, February: 98–104.

10.   A new view of the NAIRU

Robert Eisner*

1   INTRODUCTION

Tied to the notion of a 'natural rate of unemployment', introduced by Milton Friedman (1968) and almost simultaneously propounded by Phelps (1968), the NAIRU variously indicates that increasing aggregate demand cannot reduce unemployment permanently below some minimum, usually short of previous targets of 'full unemployment', or that this could be done only at the cost of accelerating inflation.

This concept was thus a sharp departure not only from the old Keynesian argument that there would be little to fear from inflation unless increases in demand pressed against a supply that, under conditions of full or close-to-full unemployment, could not be augmented with additional workers. It also rejected the old 'Phillips Curve', which indicated a tradeoff, becoming more and more expensive as full unemployment was approached, so that increased demand could reduce and maintain lower unemployment but only at the cost of higher, *but constant* inflation.

The new argument was that this old Phillips curve was a 'short-run' relation that shifted with changes in expectations of future inflation. Reductions in unemployment, which raised actual inflation as they moved us up the short-run Phillips curve, would then raise expectations of future inflation and thus raise the curve so that the rate of inflation corresponding to any given rate of unemployment would be higher. If fiscal or monetary policy aimed at keeping aggregate demand sufficiently high to maintain any rate of unemployment below the natural rate, the short-run curve would keep rising and with it actual inflation. As agents came to perceive such a policy regime, they would adjust their expectations more and more quickly. Inflation would rise more and more rapidly and ultimately the higher nominal aggregate demand would translate into no change in real demand or the policy makers would give up in the face of the run-away inflation.

Unemployment would then be back at its natural rate and inflation would stop accelerating – but would stay at its new, higher rate until unemployment was raised above the natural rate and the process was, painfully, reversed. The long-run Phillips curve was thus in effect vertical at the natural rate of unemployment or NAIRU. Unemployment less than the NAIRU would set up not merely higher but continuously increasing inflation. Unemployment above the NAIRU would bring constantly decreasing inflation, presumably leading eventually to sharp *de*flation.

The only way to reduce unemployment, except possibly in the very short run, was then to improve supply and thus reduce the NAIRU. This might be done by eliminating or softening minimum wage restrictions and taxes on labour and restrictions on firing and discriminatory or other impediments to hiring, by reducing or eliminating unemployment benefits, by increasing wage flexibility, by improving labour markets, by upgrading education and training of workers and perhaps by offering subsidies to new hiring. Many of these measures have considerable merit in their own right, others are more dubious or bring serious welfare costs. But in any event, if the NAIRU is taken seriously, these supply-side measures are the *only* ways that long-run or average unemployment can be reduced. Fiscal stimulus packages or easier money and lower nominal interest rates will not work. And if unemployment is deemed already at or close to the NAIRU, the monetary authority must take prompt anti-inflationary action to prevent the economy from 'over-heating'. Otherwise, inflation will not only be higher but will be launched on its accelerating course, from which it can be diverted only by the medicine of excess unemployment, that is, unemployment above the NAIRU.

The results of this view were clearly reflected in policy decisions of the Federal Reserve in the United States. The Fed tightened the reins and raised interest rates six times in 1994. It was seen by many as likely to raise rates again – until GDP growth slowed substantially in the first quarter of 1995 – even though inflation had been generally running at a constant or slowing rate of less than 3 per cent. But unemployment was falling and by September 1994 had fallen below 6 per cent. To most of our central bankers, that was the natural rate, or already below it. Hence more unemployment had to be brooked before it was too late.[1]

There have been growing theoretical and statistical criticisms of the NAIRU.[2] The main differences among policy-oriented macroeconomists, however, most of whom seem to accept the concept, is that conservatives tend to put the NAIRU higher, at say 6.5 or 7 per cent, while liberals put it lower, at 6 or perhaps 5.5 per cent. A few brave souls suggest that, since our estimates do have standard errors[3] and we are not quite sure exactly where the NAIRU is, we should cautiously try to drive unemployment lower until demand pressures have clearly resulted in at least the beginnings of that much-feared accelerating inflation. But still fewer have risen to challenge the basic concept.

In this chapter, I shall do just that, arguing that the NAIRU has never had any sound base in theory and has not found support in the historical data. I shall debate the issues on the home grounds of supporters of the NAIRU, using their usual basic specifications of the model. I shall show that their estimates of the impact of low unemployment depend critically on their inclusion of high-unemployment observations in their regressions. And I shall show that what meaningful relation may exist is apparently asymmetric. Estimates of a variant of the conventional model that permits such a distinction suggest that while unemployment above the NAIRU may have lowered inflation in the United States, unemployment *below* the NAIRU has had little or no lasting effect in increasing inflation.

2   THE USUAL FORMULATION OF THE NAIRU

There are two crucial assumptions necessary to arrive at the usual concept of the NAIRU. One is that, left to itself, any given rate of inflation is somehow self-perpetuating. The mechanism would appear to involve the equality of expected future inflation to some weighted average of past inflation, although it is not at all clear why rational agents should always form their expectations in this way. Then, given these expectations, they act in such a manner that somehow expected future inflation is realized in actual future inflation, unless again some other variables intervene to affect the result. The second crucial assumption is that unemployment lowers inflation and that lower unemployment raises the rate of inflation. The combination of these two assumptions generates the result that increases in demand that may lower unemployment can do so only in the short run. And rational agents recognizing the truth of these assumptions make the short run very short indeed – soon becoming infinitesimal in length.

The dynamic process that supposedly effectuates all this has been elaborated in various fashions. Most frequently involved are more or less ignorant workers who initially mistake increases in nominal wages associated with inflation as increases in real wages and hence increase their supply of labour. In fact, the argument goes, prices have initially risen more than wages so that employers, faced with an actual decline in the real wage, move down their marginal labour productivity curves and hire more workers. But when workers sooner or later note that prices have gone up at least as much as wages, they withdraw their 'excess' labour and employers are left hiring the same number of workers as before, at the initial real wage. Workers are always on their supply curves, so that what unemployment exists is voluntary. No ugly shortages of effective demand prevent markets from clearing.

I have long been puzzled why many economists should take this contrived scenario or others, involving island parables or what have you, seriously. There is little evidence that fluctuations in real wages or changes in labour supply account for much if any of the fluctuations in unemployment observed in the United States. And much of the evidence, on quits for example, indicates that lower unemployment is associated with reductions in labour supply, as more workers voluntarily give up their jobs. Higher unemployment is correspondingly associated with fewer quits, as workers are fearful that they will not easily find other jobs if they give up the ones they have.

There is at best an important ellipsis in the argument, not easily papered over. The NAIRU after all relates not to changes in prices and wages, but to changes in inflation.[4] Agents are somehow assumed to adjust current labour supply and demand, in terms of levels of prices and wages, to perceived changes in rates of change of those variables. And when we come to changes in inflation, we somehow assume that expectations are single valued and held, accurately or not, with certainty. As all of us know, we are faced with at best rather uncertain probability distributions of expected future inflation, and we do not even have a good idea of the parameters of those probability distributions. Why, under these circumstances should agents be concerned only with their first moment? Is it only the single-valued mean that should affect their actions? Or is it also the variance of the distribution or higher moments yet? Might those other moments not be expected to influence behaviour under conditions of risk aversion and costs of planning and decision making for an uncertain future? And what other variables might affect all of these moments and affect them differently under different circumstances? How clear and how stable then is the path from past inflation to future inflation?

The general mathematical formulation leading to the NAIRU might be written:

$$IN = b_1 \, IN_{-1} + b_2 \, (U - \text{NAIRU}) + \Sigma_{bg} \, Z_g, \tag{10.1}$$

where IN = inflation, IN_{-1} is lagged inflation or an average of past inflation rates, U = unemployment, and Z_g represents other factors that might affect the rate of inflation. The value of b_2 is expected to be negative; U less than the NAIRU will raise inflation. If the value of b_1 is less than one we are faced with the proposition that inflation is not self-sustaining. Left to itself, any given rate of inflation would then decay, a devastating blow to the NAIRU and the vertical long-run Phillips curve. The model is thus frequently put in its strong form, with b_1 assumed equal to one, or the sum of regression coefficients in estimates relating to a series of lagged values of inflation constrained to equal unity. If we further ignore any other factors (not necessarily independent of rates of inflation) which may affect inflation, we are left with the formulation:

$$\Delta IN = b_2 \, (U - \text{NAIRU}), \quad b_2 < 0. \tag{10.2}$$

Inflation will remain constant, that is, $\Delta IN = 0$ if, and only if, $U - \text{NAIRU} = 0$, that is, if unemployment is at the NAIRU. Higher unemployment will reduce inflation, but unemployment below the NAIRU will increase inflation, and keep increasing it; we shall have that accelerating inflation.

3   ESTIMATES OF THE CONVENTIONAL MODEL

There has been something of a cottage industry of estimates of the NAIRU over the years. I shall take as exemplary a recent formulation by the CBO (1994), similar to the early influential work of Gordon (1982).[5] Coefficients are estimated from what are called 'Phillips curve regressions' of quarterly time series of the form:

$$IN_t = C + \Sigma b_i \, IN_{t-i} + \Sigma b_j \, U_{t-j} + b_f FAE_{t-1}$$
$$+ \, b_p \, PRD_t + b_c \, NIXON_t + b_o \, NIXOFF_t. \tag{10.3}$$

The lagged inflation variables, IN, run variously from $t-1$ to $t-12$, $t-18$ and $t-20$. The lagged unemployment variables, U, are taken from t to $t-4$ (not $t-1$ to $t-4$, as erroneously indicated in CBO 1994). FAE is a measure of inflation in food and energy prices, defined as the difference between the rates of change of the fixed-weight price index for personal consumption expenditures (PCE) and the fixed-weight index for PCE less food and energy.[6] PRD is the difference between the rates of change of labour productivity in the non-farm business sector and segmented trends of labour productivity. $NIXON$ is a dummy variable for the quarters of Nixon price controls, 0.8 for the five quarters from 1971.3 to 1972.3, and zero otherwise. $NIXOFF$ is a dummy variable for the termination of wage and price controls in 1974, 0.4 in 1974.2 and 1975.1 and 1.6 in 1974.3 and 1974.4, and zero otherwise.

CBO estimates its basic regressions with unemployment for married males, which I dub UNMM, and then attempts to convert its estimate of the NAIRU for married males to a NAIRU for total unemployment on the basis of the demographic composition of the labour force. I replicate the CBO estimates for married-male unemployment but also estimate directly sets of NAIRUs for total unemployment, which I label simply UN. CBO estimates the lagged inflation coefficients with a third-degree polynomial distributed lag (PDL, n, 3) where n is the number of lagged variables, with the far end point restricted to zero and the sum of the coefficients constrained to equal one. The unemployment coefficients are estimated directly with no restrictions.

I have replicated the CBO estimations both with PDL formulations and with independent estimates of each of the lagged inflation coefficients and with and without the constraint that the sum of the inflation coefficients be unity. The

NAIRU is estimated simply enough, by the CBO, by assuming that $\Sigma b_i = 1$, so that for constant IN, or $IN_t = IN_{t-i}$ for all i, $IN_t - \Sigma b_i IN_{t-i} = 0$, and that the means of FAE_{-1} and PRD are their expected values of zero. Ignoring the quarters where $NIXON$ and $NIXOFF$ are non-zero, we then have for constant or non-accelerating inflation:

$$\Delta IN_t = 0 = C + \Sigma b_j U_{t-j} \qquad (10.4)$$

The constant rate of U which satisfies this equation is the estimated value of the NAIRU. Hence, we have:

$$\text{NAIRU} = -C / \Sigma b_j. \qquad (10.5)$$

The CBO's 'preferred equation', that for the benchmark-years-weighted GDP price index (INE), gave a NAIRU for married males (NAIRU–MM) of 3.55 per cent. This was reported to translate into an overall NAIRU of about 5.8 per cent in 1993.[7]

In Table 10.1, I offer replications of the CBO estimates for the CPI–U (INC) and the benchmark-weighted GDP price index (INE) and add estimates for the changes in the GDP implicit price deflator (INF), but do not constrain the sum of the inflation coefficients to equal unity.[8] Equation (10.4) is then replaced by

$$0 = C - IN_t + \Sigma b_i IN_{t-i} + \Sigma b_j U_{t-j}. \qquad (10.6)$$

This would reduce to (10.4) if the constant, non-accelerating rate of inflation were zero. I have rather taken it to equal 3 per cent. Where the sum of the estimated inflation coefficients is not necessarily unity, we hence have:

$$\text{NAIRU} = -(C + 3^* \{\Sigma b_i - 1\}) / \Sigma b_j. \qquad (10.7)$$

It may be noted first that, despite my not imposing the constraint that the sum of the inflation coefficients equal unity, my results for the married-male-unemployment regression are virtually identical with those of the CBO. For one thing, the unconstrained estimates of that sum in fact come out close to unity: 1.038 for the CPI–U deflator and 1.037 for the GDPIPD.[9] And the critical sums of unemployment coefficients, reported by the CBO to be –0.77 for INC, for example, are –0.742 in my replication. My NAIRU estimates are 3.611 per cent for the CPI–U deflator, against the CBO's 3.72 per cent, and 3.566 per cent (as reported in Eisner 1995a) against 3.55 per cent for the CBO estimate for benchmark-weighted GDP deflator (based on 117 observations ending in 1993.4), and 3.424 per cent for the new GDP implicit deflator, calculated from current-dollar and chained 1992-dollar measures of GDP.[10]

Table 10.1   Inflation and married-male and total unemployment sums of inflation coefficients not constrained to equal unity. Replication of CBO (August 1994)

Variable or statistic	Regression coefficients and standard errors			
	Married males		Total unemployment	
	CPI–U	GDP implicit price deflator	CPI–U	GDP implicit price deflator
	(INC)	(INF)	(INC)	(INF)
Constant	2.565	2.766	3.671	3.521
	(0.593)	(0.429)	(0.848)	(0.608)
ΣIN_{t-i} coeff. ($1 \leq i \leq 20$)	1.038	1.037	1.194	1.151
	(0.059)	(0.048)	(0.080)	(0.070)
ΣU_{t-j} coeff. ($0 \leq j \leq 4$)	−0.742	−0.840	−0.728	−0.704
	(0.177)	(0.136)	(0.174)	(0.135)
FAE_{t-1}*	0.216	0.130	0.087	0.614
	(0.238)	(0.112)	(0.369)	(0.192)
PRD_t	−0.035	−0.084	−0.021	−0.080
	(0.038)	(0.027)	(0.038)	(0.028)
$NIXON_t$	−1.666	−1.386	−1.718	−1.010
	(0.843)	(0.615)	(0.799)	(0.613)
$NIXOFF_t$	0.873	3.455	1.154	3.002
	(0.731)	(0.515)	(0.757)	(0.575)
$\hat{R}^2$	0.764	0.843	0.787	0.842
DW	2.040	2.139	1.950	2.099
NAIRU	3.611	3.424	5.844	5.641

Note: * Or ΣFAE_{t-f} $1 \leq f \leq 4$, for total unemployment.

Table 10.2 Projections of percentage inflation in CPI–U and GDPIPD for one percentage point reduction in unemployment rates beginning in 1996.1, for one quarter, four quarters, eight quarters and permanently, conventional model (from equations in Table 10.1)

Married-male unemployment

	Consumer price index					GDP implicit price deflator				
Period	3.55%	2.55% 96.1	2.55% 96.1–96.4	2.55% 96.1–97.4	2.55%	3.55%	2.55% 96.1	2.55% 96.1–96.4	2.55% 96.1–97.4	2.55%
1996.1	3.15	3.87	3.87	3.87	3.87	2.24	3.37	3.37	3.37	3.37
1996–Av	2.73	3.01	3.62	3.62	3.62	2.37	2.41	3.02	3.02	3.02
1997–Av	2.81	3.03	3.65	4.54	4.54	2.18	2.50	2.81	3.47	3.47
1998–Av	2.71	2.82	3.18	4.03	4.91	2.14	2.26	2.67	3.31	3.96
2002.4	2.87	3.05	3.54	4.18	7.81	1.78	1.85	2.30	2.89	5.90

Total unemployment

	Consumer price index					GDP implicit price deflator				
Period	5.70%	4.70% 96.1	4.70% 96.1–96.4	4.70% 96.1–97.4	4.70%	5.70%	4.70% 96.1	4.70% 96.1–96.4	4.70% 96.1–97.4	4.70%
1996.1	3.33	4.07	4.07	4.07	4.07	2.20	3.30	3.30	3.30	3.30
1996–Av	2.87	3.09	3.74	3.74	3.74	2.20	2.23	2.86	2.86	2.86
1997–Av	2.99	3.25	3.88	4.74	4.74	2.11	2.38	2.53	3.19	3.19
1998–Av	2.90	3.13	3.62	4.51	5.37	2.04	2.15	2.53	2.95	3.61
2002.4	3.39	3.88	4.75	5.92	10.71	1.56	1.67	2.13	2.80	5.50

While my parameter estimates, using the conventional model, then, correspond predictably to the CBO (and presumably other similar) estimates, some of the implications usually drawn for policy purposes are not supported. In particular, it is often argued that we must not let the genie of inflation out of the bag; even a brief, inflation-accelerating experience of low unemployment will be disastrous because it will be so difficult to correct. I have tested that proposition initially by simulating dynamic projections using married-male unemployment with the Table 10.1 equations for INC, inflation in the consumer price index, and INF, inflation in the GDP implicit price deflator (see Table 10.2). Assuming no effects of food and energy price inflation, $FAE(-1)$, or PRD, deviation of productivity from trend, I have experimented with projections of the quarters from 1996.1 to 2002.4 on the basis of varying assumptions:

1. UMM, unemployment of married males is constant at the NAIRU of 3.55 per cent.

2.   UMM falls to 2.55 per cent for one quarter and then returns to the NAIRU.
3.   UMM falls to 2.55 per cent for one year and then returns to the NAIRU.
4.   UMM falls to 2.55 per cent for two years and then returns to the NAIRU.
5.   UMM falls to 2.55 per cent and stays there.

With married-male unemployment held steady at 3.55 per cent, the forecast value of CPI–U inflation is 3.15 per cent in 96.1 and remains trivially below that throughout the forecast period, ending at 2.87 per cent in 2002.4. Lowering the unemployment figure to 2.55 per cent for one quarter and then returning it to 3.55 per cent drives inflation up by 0.7 percentage points in the first quarter but by only 0.3 percentage points over the entire first year; by 2002.4 inflation is at 3.05 per cent, about 0.2 percentage points higher than if there had been no initial fall in unemployment. Unemployment at 2.55 per cent for four quarters raises inflation by 0.9 percentage points in the first year but, after seven years, inflation in 2002.4 is only at 3.54 per cent, less than 0.7 percentage points more than the forecast value for 3.55 per cent unemployment. Holding unemployment at 2.55 per cent for eight quarters raises inflation in 2002.4 by 1.3 percentage points over baseline. Unemployment of 2.55 per cent over the entire period raises CPI–U inflation by about 5 percentage points, to some 7.8 per cent.

Forecasts of the conventional model with the GDP implicit price deflator show even less-inflationary consequences of lower unemployment. The first quarter of unemployment at 2.55 per cent, one percentage point below the NAIRU, does cause a jump of 1.1 percentage points in inflation, from 2.24 per cent to 3.37 per cent. By 2002.4, however, inflation of 1.85 per cent is less than 0.1 percentage points above the forecast on the basis of unemployment staying always at the NAIRU. Four quarters of lower unemployment leaves inflation at 2.3 per cent in 2002.4, still only 0.5 percentage points higher than that generated by the steady NAIRU path, and eight quarters of 2.55 per cent unemployment brings inflation in 2002.4 to 2.89 per cent, 1.1 percentage points higher than baseline. Married-male unemployment kept indefinitely one percentage point below its NAIRU does appear to bring continuously accelerating inflation – all the way to 5.9 per cent by the end of 2002.

Since the lower unemployment would be expected to generate huge increases in output, some might think a few extra percentage points of inflation, even if there were not large standard errors to the forecasts so that we could predict them accurately, and even if they could not be counteracted by means other than by slowing the economy, would offer a pretty good bargain, or tradeoff, as it used to be called. (By 'Okun's Law', each percentage point of *total* unemployment translates into at least 2 percentage points of output – more than $150 billion of GDP this year – and the figure for married-male unemployment would presumably be even greater.) And simulations with this conventional model, and others to be presented later, indicate that a mere return to the NAIRU, let alone a slight increase of unemployment above it, would quickly eliminate most of the increase in inflation that had occurred.

Simulations based on total-unemployment regressions, indicating departures from a 5.7 per cent total-unemployment rate are similar. Lowering unemployment by one percentage point does increase inflation, but slowly. The initial 5.7 per cent baseline inflation of 2.2 per cent in the GDPIPD is 0.6 percentage points higher in 2002.4 if unemployment is kept lower for one year, and only 1.2 percentage points higher if unemployment is lower for a full two years. And inflation is only 5.5 per cent by 2002.4 even if unemployment is kept permanently at 4.7 per cent.

But that is only the beginning of my story. The conventional model, it will be shown, constrains the unemployment and inflation parameters in ways that are in fundamental conflict with the data.

4   AN ALTERNATIVE MODEL WITH ASYMMETRICAL EFFECTS OF DEPARTURES FROM THE NAIRU

As equation (10.1) indicates, there are certainly in principle other variables, there dubbed Z_g, which may affect inflation. The CBO, as do others, acknowledges this in adding variables for food and energy price inflation (*FAE*), presumably at least in part exogenous, deviations of productivity from trend (*PRD*), and the imposition and removal of price controls. May there not be others and may they not have different impacts when unemployment is low and when unemployment is high? When unemployment is high, more unemployment may lead to more competition for limited markets, which may check inflation. But when unemployment is low, reducing unemployment further may have little impact on inflation. Let me suggest several hypotheses pointing to a theoretical formulation in which low unemployment tends to hold inflation in check.

First, low measured unemployment is usually associated with greater, more efficient utilization of all resources as fixed factors of labour, management and capital are put to fuller use. This may entail increases in productivity and decreases in average costs (not necessarily captured fully by the *PRD* variable) which militate against price increases.[11] Second, persistent low unemployment may set up forces of capital–labour substitution and further increases in anticipated future productivity (also not necessarily captured in the *PRD* variable) which curb inflation. Third, some game-theoretical considerations suggest that, in a collective bargaining situation, real wages may tend to move countercyclically, so that in periods of low unemployment upward wage pressure may be less.[12] And fourth, with profits high and overhead costs spread broadly, various oligopolistic considerations – such as a desire to discourage new entry – may become more important. Firms that are flush with profits are threats to move into new areas. Firms already there may well hesitate to offer greater invitation to would-be interlopers with moves for additional price increases.

This is of course just a sketch of a theory as to why low unemployment and the high profits usually associated with it may militate against inflation. Possible causes of asymmetry in the relation between inflation and unemployment are myriad. Yet, the issue has not to my knowledge, except summarily in Eisner (1994), been explored. We shall in this section indicate a formulation to examine it, and offer some dramatic results of our empirical analysis.

To do so, initially we replace equation (10.3) by

$$IN_t = CH + CL + \Sigma b_i IN_{t-i} + \Sigma b_{jH} UH_{t-j+1} + \Sigma b_{jL} UL_{t-j+1}$$
$$+ \Sigma b_f FAE_{t-f} + b_p PRD_t \tag{10.8}$$
$$+ b_c NIXON_t + b_o NIXOFF_t, \quad i = 1 \text{ to } 20, j = 1 \text{ to } 5, f = 1 \text{ to } 4,$$

where $UH = U$ when $U \geq$ NAIRU and zero otherwise, $UL = U$ when $U <$ NAIRU and zero otherwise,[13] and CH and CL are the constant terms corresponding respectively to UH and UL. They are calculated as the regression coefficients of dummy variables defined as: UHD = 1 when $U \geq$ NAIRU and zero otherwise, and ULD = 1 when $U <$ NAIRU and zero otherwise. In an alternate formulation, we constrained the constant term to be the same for all observations. The NAIRU for married males was taken, as estimated by CBO and closely confirmed in my regression, as 3.55 per cent. The NAIRU for total unemployment is the CBO series, derived from its 3.55 per cent married-male NAIRU, but varying on the basis of demographic changes between 5.5 and 6.3 per cent over the observation period.

Our reformulation of the conventional model will raise two critical questions. (1) Will the estimated values of Σb_{jL} in equation (10.8) differ consistently from Σb_{jH} and differ significantly from zero? (2) Will Σb_i, the sum of the inflation coefficients, remain at or above unity?

Results for regressions with separate constant terms for high- and low-unemployment observations, as seen in Table 10.3, show absolute values of the Σb_{jL} sharply less than those of the Σb_{jH}. For total unemployment, the differences were highly statistically significant, with t-statistics of 2.60 and 2.25 for the CPI–U and GDPIPD regressions, respectively. Unemployment above the NAIRU did appear to reduce inflation. The sums of the negative coefficients differed very significantly from zero. But for unemployment below the NAIRU, the Σb_L were much closer to zero and were never significantly negative.

Table 10.3 *Inflation and married-male and total unemployment, unemployment above NAIRU (UH) and unemployment below NAIRU (UL), separate constants*

Variable or statistic	Regression coefficients and standard errors			
	Married males		Total unemployment	
	CPI–U	GDP implicit price deflator	CPI–U	GDP implicit price deflator
	(INC)	(INF)	(INC)	(INF)
UH constant	−0.966	−0.866	−1.862	−1.423
	(0.371)	(0.314)	(0.468)	(0.440)
UL constant	0.560	0.393	0.181	0.041
	(0.258)	(0.209)	(0.292)	(0.269)
$\sum IN_{t-i}$ coeff. $(1 \leq i \leq 20)$	1.046	1.021	1.216	1.136
	(0.059)	(0.050)	(0.080)	(0.075)
$\sum UH_{t-j}$ coeff. $(0 \leq j \leq 4)$	−0.701	−0.749	−0.833	−0.830
	(0.314)	(0.244)	(0.266)	(0.235)
$\sum UL_{t-j}$ coeff. $(0 \leq j \leq 4)$	−0.416	−0.419	−0.039	−0.240
	(0.313)	(0.242)	(0.265)	(0.220)
$\sum UL_{t-j} - \sum UH_{t-j}$ Coeff.	0.285	0.330	0.794	0.590
	(0.395)	(0.303)	(0.305)	(0.262)
FAE_{t-1} *	0.138	0.151	−0.451	0.432
	(0.244)	(0.118)	(0.399)	(0.214)
PRD_t	−0.031	−0.059	−0.007	−0.054
	(0.036)	(0.027)	(0.035)	(0.028)
$NIXON_t$	−2.066	−1.687	−2.512	−1.609
	(0.881)	(0.675)	(0.848)	(0.708)
$NIXOFF_t$	0.786	3.531	1.386	3.315
	(0.753)	(0.560)	(0.758)	(0.622)
$\hat{R}^2$	0.764	0.833	0.796	0.832
DW	2.019	2.016	1.982	1.946

Note: * Or $\sum FAE_{t-f} 1 \leq f \leq 4$, for total unemployment.

Let us spell out that critical asymmetry. Turning to inflation in the GDP implicit price deflator in Table 10.3, we find that the sum of the coefficients for total unemployment above the CBO NAIRU was a highly significant −0.830. This suggests an even greater anti-inflationary impact of high unemployment than the coefficient sum of –0.704 estimated in the conventional relation, shown in Table 10.1. But the coefficients for the low-unemployment variable summed to only –0.240. Results were even more striking when inflation was measured by the CPI–U. The high-unemployment coefficients summed to –0.833 while the low-unemployment coefficients summed to only –0.039. The sums of the inflation coefficients, however, were greater than unity in both regressions, indicating that a considerable amount of unemployment would be necessary to keep inflation from getting out of hand.

When we do not allow separate constant terms for high- and low-unemployment observations, results are somewhat different, but again most damaging to the conventional NAIRU model. Now the sums of the inflation coefficients are less than unity, suggesting that inflation, left to itself, would decay to some equilibrium value, depending on the level of unemployment. At 5.7 per cent unemployment these would be about 6 per cent for the CPI–U and 1.9 per cent for the GDPIPD on the basis of the low-unemployment coefficients of the total-unemployment regressions.

The sums of the high-unemployment coefficients are considerably less in absolute value than in the regressions with separate constant terms, coming to only about –0.3 in the total-unemployment regressions, as shown in Table 10.4. They indicate a lesser anti-inflationary impact of high unemployment. The sums of the low-unemployment coefficients are again less in absolute value and, for the CPI–U regression, non-negative (actually a trivially positive 0.03). Thus, the low-unemployment CPI–U coefficients indicate that unemployment below the NAIRU will not raise the 6 per cent equilibrium rate and would even, if we could believe the point estimate, *reduce* it about 0.7 percentage points for each percentage point less of unemployment. Each percentage point reduction in unemployment would raise that equilibrium GDPIPD inflation by about 1.8 percentage points. Hence, 4 per cent unemployment would generate equilibrium rates of inflation of about 4.8 per cent in the CPI–U and 4.9 per cent in the GDPIPD.[14]

So far we have been constraining parameters other than those of the unemployment variables to be the same. Of most importance, what will happen to our estimates of the sum of the inflation coefficients when those constraints are removed? We have therefore estimated completely separate, independent, high-unemployment and low-unemployment regressions.

Results of the separate regressions for the CPI–U and the GDPIPD for married males are presented in Table 10.5. In each of the separate regressions the sums of the inflation coefficients are less than unity; for the GDPIPD regressions the *t*-statistics for the departure from unity are 2.0 or more. The sums of unemployment coefficients are negative in all cases and do not now differ consistently in the high-unemployment and low-unemployment regressions.

These results point again to constant equilibrium rates of inflation, reduced by increased unemployment, but offering no place for accelerating inflation. This implies that, even if it did raise inflation, unemployment below the NAIRU would effect an old Phillips curve relation.

Table 10.4   Inflation and married-male and total unemployment, unemployment above NAIRU (UH) and unemployment below NAIRU (UL), single constant

Variable or statistic	Regression coefficients and standard errors			
	Married males		Total unemployment	
	CPI–U	GDP implicit price deflator	CPI–U	GDP implicit price deflator
	(INC)	(INF)	(INC)	(INF)
Constant	0.299	0.280	0.230	0.288
	(0.271)	(0.226)	(0.328)	(0.288)
$\sum IN_{t-i}$ coeff. $(1 \leq i \leq 20)$	0.938	0.913	0.958	0.910
	(0.059)	(0.049)	(0.074)	(0.064)
$\sum UH_{t-j}$ coeff. $(0 \leq j \leq 4)$	−0.548	−0.521	−0.307	−0.297
	(0.337)	(0.260)	(0.280)	(0.226)
$\sum UL_{t-j}$ coeff. $(0 \leq j \leq 4)$	−0.507	−0.459	0.030	−0.161
	(0.337)	(0.263)	(0.297)	(0.239)
$\sum UL_{t-j} - \sum UH_{t-j}$ Coeff.	0.041	0.062	0.336	0.135
	(0.422)	(0.323)	(0.330)	(0.266)
$FAE_{t-1}{}^{*}$	0.207	0.293	−0.016	0.751
	(0.263)	(0.124)	(0.440)	(0.222)
PRD_t	−0.035	−0.075	−0.031	−0.086
	(0.039)	(0.029)	(0.039)	(0.029)
$NIXON_t$	−0.765	−0.557	−1.075	−0.460
	(0.901)	(0.689)	(0.909)	(0.727)
$NIXOFF_t$	0.463	3.003	0.537	2.362
	(0.809)	(0.597)	(0.835)	(0.643)
$\hat{R}^2$	0.726	0.802	0.743	0.801
DW	2.016	2.011	1.922	1.900

Note: * Or $\sum FAE_{t-f}$, $1 \leq f \leq 4$, for total unemployment.

Table 10.5   Inflation and married-male unemployment, unemployment above NAIRU (UH) and unemployment below NAIRU (UL), separate regressions

Variable or statistic	Regression coefficients and standard errors			
	CPI–U		GDPIPD	
	High-unemployment regression UH	Low-unemployment regression UL	High-unemployment regression UH	Low-unemployment regression UL
Constant	0.345	0.431	0.343	0.413
	(0.267)	(0.265)	(0.226)	(0.225)
$\sum IN_{t-i}$ coeff.	0.928	0.905	0.899	0.882
$(1 \le i \le 20)$	(0.058)	(0.057)	(0.049)	(0.048)
$\sum U_{t-j}$ coeff.	−0.419	−0.477	−0.432	−0.355
$(0 \le j \le 4)$	(0.324)	(0.329)	(0.254)	(0.265)
FAE_{t-1}	0.146	0.273	0.237	0.274
	(0.254)	(0.260)	(0.125)	(0.128)
PRD_t	−0.037	−0.036	−0.081	−0.082
	(0.038)	(0.039)	(0.029)	(0.029)
$NIXON_t$	−0.873	−0.804	−0.677	−0.488
	(0.879)	(0.907)	(0.684)	(0.718)
$NIXOFF_t$	0.353	0.549	3.031	3.066
	(0.772)	(0.803)	(0.582)	(0.614)
$\hat{R}^2$	0.729	0.721	0.795	0.785
DW	2.008	2.009	1.966	1.969

Turning to the total-unemployment regressions shown in Table 10.6, we find that the sums of the unemployment coefficients in the low-unemployment regressions are close to zero, and less in absolute value, but not significantly less than the high-unemployment coefficients, which are considerably less than in the composite regressions. The sum of the unemployment coefficients in the CPI–U regression is in fact again slightly positive. Even lesser inflationary effect or greater deflationary effect of low unemployment is suggested for recent years in regressions with a shift dummy for the quarters from 1990.1 to 1995.4.

The GDPIPD regressions point to constant 'NAIRU' rates of inflation of 6.9 per cent and 3.1 per cent, respectively, in the high-unemployment and low-unemployment cases. Each increase of one percentage point of unemployment above the NAIRU would then lower inflation by 2.2 percentage points. But each reduction of unemployment by one percentage point below the NAIRU would raise inflation by only 0.65 percentage points (0.092 ÷ {1–0.858}). At 4 per cent unemployment the steady rate of inflation would settle at 4.2 per cent. On the basis of the 1990–95 observations, it would settle at 2.6 per cent. The corresponding equilibrium inflation rate in the CPI–U at 4 per cent unemployment would be all of 0.8 per cent!

Table 10.6   Inflation and total unemployment, unemployment above NAIRU (UH) and unemployment below NAIRU (UL), separate regressions

Variable or statistic	Regression coefficients and standard errors					
	CPI–U			GDPIPD		
	High-unemployment regression	Low-unemployment regressions		High-unemployment regression	Low-unemployment regressions	
	UH	UL	UL	UH	UL	UL
Constant	0.267	0.430	0.498	0.365	0.510	0.593
	(0.299)	(0.269)	(0.280)	(0.261)	(0.234)	(0.253)
C9095	—	—	–0.295	—	—	–0.237
	—	—	(0.337)	—	—	(0.277)
$\sum IN_{t-i}$ coeff.	0.949	0.910	0.905	0.894	0.858	0.848
($1 \leq i \leq 20$)	(0.067)	(0.058)	(0.058)	(0.058)	(0.050)	(0.052)
$\sum U_{t-j}$ coeff.	–0.252	0.083	0.134	–0.238	–0.092	–0.043
($0 \leq j \leq 4$)	(0.252)	(0.266)	(0.273)	(0.210)	(0.221)	(0.229)
$\sum FAE_{t-f}$ coeff.	0.070	0.040	0.010	0.695	0.788	0.770
($1 \leq f \leq 4$)	(0.397)	(0.425)	(0.427)	(0.217)	(0.221)	(0.222)
PRD_t	–0.032	–0.046	–0.047	–0.081	–0.088	–0.090
	(0.037)	(0.037)	(0.037)	(0.028)	(0.029)	(0.029)
$NIXON_t$	–1.218	–1.144	–1.248	–0.560	–0.283	–0.376
	(0.861)	(0.894)	(0.902)	(0.700)	(0.731)	(0.740)
$NIXOFF_t$	0.374	0.412	0.403	2.232	2.203	2.214
	(0.809)	(0.814)	(0.814)	(0.642)	(0.641)	(0.642)
$\bar{R}^2$	0.749	0.747	0.747	0.795	0.794	0.794
DW	1.914	1.919	1.926	1.946	1.930	1.934

5   SIMULATIONS AND FORECASTS

One way to reveal the effects of the various, interacting coefficients is to simulate or forecast ahead, as we did for the conventional model with results shown above in Table 10.2, with different assumed values of unemployment.

With equations estimated with observations ending in 1995.4, we have forecast ahead the 28-quarter period from 1996.1 to 2002.4. For these quarters we have first assumed total unemployment to remain constant at the 5.7 per cent that we have taken to be the NAIRU on the basis of our estimates of the conventional model; this is close to the 5.83 per cent CBO estimate of the current NAIRU noted above.

Table 10.7   Projections of percentage inflation in CPI–U and GDPIPD for one percentage point reduction in total unemployment rates beginning in 1996.1, for one quarter, four quarters, eight quarters and permanently, based on separate high and low unemployment regressions (from equations in Table 10.6)

High-unemployment regression

	Consumer price index					GDP implicit price deflator				
Period	5.70%	4.70% 96.1	4.70% 96.1– 96.4	4.70% 96.1– 97.4	4.70%	5.70%	4.70% 96.1	4.70% 96.1– 96.4	4.70% 96.1– 97.4	4.70%
1996.1	3.94	4.36	4.36	4.36	4.36	2.66	3.00	3.00	3.00	3.00
1996–Av	3.30	3.37	3.56	3.56	3.56	2.81	2.92	3.12	3.12	3.12
1997–Av	4.20	4.32	4.59	4.85	4.85	3.27	3.31	3.48	3.79	3.79
1998–Av	4.83	4.92	5.17	5.57	5.83	3.68	3.72	3.85	4.06	4.38
2002.4	7.01	7.07	7.21	7.42	9.02	4.99	5.00	5.09	5.22	6.29

Low-unemployment regression

	Consumer price index					GDP implicit price deflator				
Period	5.70%	4.70% 96.1	4.70% 96.1– 96.4	4.70% 96.1– 97.4	4.70%	5.70%	4.70% 96.1	4.70% 96.1– 96.4	4.70% 96.1– 97.4	4.70%
1996.1	3.38	3.67	3.67	3.67	3.67	2.02	2.34	2.34	2.34	2.34
1996–Av	3.07	3.20	3.25	3.25	3.25	2.28	2.36	2.52	2.52	2.52
1997–Av	3.55	3.48	3.43	3.61	3.61	2.41	2.41	2.45	2.69	2.69
1998–Av	3.78	3.71	3.60	3.48	3.67	2.57	2.58	2.59	2.63	2.88
2002.4	4.67	4.54	4.62	4.53	4.11	2.83	2.83	2.88	2.89	3.31

We present in Table 10.7 results for the separate high-unemployment and low-unemployment regressions (of Table 10.6) for total unemployment, which are analogous to those from the conventional model shown in Table 10.2 (on the basis of the equations in Table 10.1). We note now that the high-unemployment regressions indicate that, even at the NAIRU, inflation would rise some over seven years, but that lowering unemployment a percentage point would make little difference. At the worst, with a permanent reduction in unemployment of one percentage point, inflation would have increased only 2 percentage points more in the CPI–U and 1.3 percentage points in the GDPIPD. In the case of the low-unemployment regressions, as would be predicted by the positive sum of unemployment coefficients, a permanent one percentage point reduction in unemployment actually left CPI–U inflation lower in 2002.4, by 0.65 percentage points, than it would have been with continuation at the 5.7 per cent NAIRU baseline. It raised GDP inflation by about 0.5 percentage points.

Table 10.8   *Projections of percentage inflation in CPI–U and GDPIPD for total unemployment rates above and below NAIRU, based on conventional model regression and on separate high unemployment and low unemployment regressions (from equations in Tables 10.1 and 10.6)*

Conventional model regression

Period	Consumer price index				GDP implicit price deflator			
	Unemployment							
	4.7%	5.7%	6.7%	7.7%	4.7%	5.7%	6.7%	7.7%
1996.1	4.1	3.4	2.6	1.9	3.3	2.2	1.1	0.0
1996–Av	3.7	2.9	2.0	1.1	2.9	2.2	1.5	0.9
1998–Av	5.4	3.0	0.4	–2.0	3.6	2.0	0.5	–1.1
2000–Av	7.3	3.1	–1.2	–5.4	4.3	1.8	–0.7	–3.2
2002–Av	9.9	3.2	–3.4	–10.1	5.3	1.6	–2.2	–5.9
2002.4	10.7	3.4	–3.9	–11.2	5.5	1.6	–2.4	–6.3

High-unemployment regression

Period	Consumer price index				GDP implicit price deflator			
	Unemployment							
	4.7%	5.7%	6.7%	7.7%	4.7%	5.7%	6.7%	7.7%
1996.1	4.4	3.9	3.5	3.1	3.0	2.7	2.3	2.0
1996–Av	3.6	3.3	3.0	2.8	3.1	2.8	2.5	2.2
1998–Av	5.8	4.8	3.8	2.8	4.4	3.7	3.0	2.3
2000–Av	7.4	5.9	4.4	2.9	5.4	4.3	3.3	2.3
2002–Av	8.6	6.7	4.8	2.9	6.2	4.9	3.6	2.4
2002.4	9.0	7.0	5.0	3.0	6.3	5.0	3.7	2.4

Table 10.8   continued

Low-unemployment regression

	Consumer price index				GDP implicit price deflator			
	Unemployment							
Period	2.7%	3.7%	4.7%	5.7%	2.7%	3.7%	4.7%	5.7%
1996.1	4.3	4.0	3.7	3.4	3.0	2.7	2.3	2.0
1996–Av	3.6	3.4	3.3	3.1	3.0	2.8	2.5	2.3
1998–Av	3.4	3.6	3.7	3.8	3.5	3.2	2.9	2.6
2000–Av	3.1	3.5	3.8	4.2	4.0	3.5	3.1	2.7
2002–Av	3.0	3.5	4.0	4.5	4.2	3.8	3.3	2.8
2002.4	3.0	3.6	4.1	4.7	4.3	3.8	3.3	2.8

Low-unemployment regression based on 1990–95 observations

	Consumer price index				GDP implicit price deflator			
	Unemployment							
Period	2.7%	3.7%	4.7%	5.7%	2.7%	3.7%	4.7%	5.7%
1996.1	4.0	3.7	3.4	3.2	2.8	2.5	2.2	1.9
1996–Av	3.2	3.0	2.9	2.7	2.7	2.5	2.3	2.1
1998–Av	1.9	2.2	2.6	2.9	2.7	2.5	2.3	2.2
2000–Av	1.0	1.7	2.3	3.0	2.8	2.6	2.4	2.1
2002–Av	0.5	1.4	2.2	3.0	2.9	2.6	2.4	2.1
2002.4	0.4	1.4	2.3	3.2	2.9	2.6	2.4	2.2

In Table 10.8 we compare projections over the 1996–2002 period for unemployment rates at, above, and below the 5.7 per cent NAIRU. The conventional model offers the expected stability of inflation at the NAIRU, increasing inflation at lower unemployment and deceleration, turning to price declines, at higher unemployment. Simulations with the separate high-unemployment regressions also indicate faster, and increasing inflation with lower unemployment, although each percentage point of unemployment, as anticipated above, is associated, even at the end of seven years, with only 2.0 percentage points more of inflation in the CPI–U and only 1.3 percentage points more in the GDPIPD. And as again anticipated in Table 10.6, the NAIRU for the high-unemployment observations is about 7.7 per cent, rather than 5.7 per cent.[15]

The low-unemployment simulations indicate only 0.5 percentage points more of GDP inflation by 2002.4 for each percentage point reduction in unemployment. Even 2.7 per cent unemployment would raise average annual inflation from 3 per cent in 1996 to 4.2 per cent in 2002, as compared to an increase from 2 per cent to 2.8 per cent if unemployment were left at 5.7 per cent.

Table 10.9   *Projections of percentage inflation in CPI–U and GDPIPD, from conventional, all-unemployment and low-unemployment regressions (from equations in Table 10.6)*

A. 1985.4, 1990.4, 1995.4, based on simulations over 64 quarters from 1980.1 to 1995.4

Conventional, all-unemployment regression

	Consumer price index			GDP implicit price deflator		
Unemployment	85.4	90.4	95.4	85.4	90.4	95.4
Actual	4.14	6.96	1.93	3.64	4.23	1.82
Baseline	5.25	6.87	5.51	3.79	2.95	0.71
1% Lower	11.21	21.57	37.36	7.16	10.10	13.47
1% Higher	−0.70	−7.84	−26.34	0.41	−4.19	−12.05

Low-unemployment regression

	Consumer price index			GDP implicit price deflator		
Unemployment	85.4	90.4	95.4	85.4	90.4	95.4
Actual	4.14	6.96	1.93	3.64	4.23	1.82
Baseline	7.31	7.32	4.74	4.23	2.47	0.16
1% Lower	7.25	6.70	4.86	4.28	3.09	1.23
2% Lower	7.18	6.07	4.99	4.33	3.71	2.30

B. 1965.4, 1980.4, 1995.4, based on simulations over 160 quarters from 1956.1 to 1995.4

Conventional, all-unemployment regression

	Consumer price index			GDP implicit price deflator		
Unemployment	65.4	80.4	95.4	65.4	80.4	95.4
Actual	1.90	9.02	1.93	1.97	10.62	1.82
Baseline	−0.28	−1.20	−69.38	4.40	15.10	21.96
1% Lower	12.36	112.50	768.92	10.97	46.37	132.31
1% Higher	−12.91	−114.90	−907.69	−2.16	−16.17	−88.39

Low-unemployment regression

	Consumer price index			GDP implicit price deflator		
Unemployment	65.4	80.4	95.4	65.4	80.4	95.4
Actual	1.90	9.02	1.93	1.97	10.62	1.82
Baseline	3.14	6.06	4.35	3.46	7.11	2.58
1% Lower	2.81	5.16	4.44	3.69	7.26	2.98
2% Lower	2.48	4.26	4.54	3.93	7.41	3.38

On the basis of the 1990–95 observations, inflation would remain virtually constant regardless of the unemployment rate, averaging 2.1 per cent or 2.2 per cent for each of the years from 1996 to 2002 with 5.7 per cent unemployment, and rising from 2.7 per cent to 2.9 per cent with 2.7 per cent unemployment. The CPI–U, low-unemployment simulations suggest again that lower unemployment actually *reduces* inflation. With 5.7 per cent unemployment, inflation would have risen from 3.1 per cent in 1996 to 4.5 per cent in 2002. With 2.7 per cent unemployment it would have *fallen* from 3.6 per cent to 3 per cent. On the basis of the 1990–95 observations average inflation would have fallen from 3.2 per cent in 1996 to 0.5 per cent in 2002.

We have finally compared simulations of the total-unemployment regressions of the conventional model and the low-unemployment regressions over the estimation period, beginning unemployment changes either in 1980.1 or in 1956.1, at the beginning of the estimation period. Noting the results of the shorter simulation, shown in Table 10.9A, for 1985.4, 1990.4 and 1995.4, we see that the baseline simulations kept inflation constant or mirrored its lower actual figure at the end of the period. In the conventional model, unemployment 1 per cent less each quarter did indeed eventually bring greatly accelerated inflation. Unemployment 1 per cent more brought the predicted huge deceleration of inflation, eventually to prices falling at a cataclysmic rate. The low-unemployment simulations, however, showed little or no increase in inflation for one or two percentage point reductions in unemployment.

Results of simulations over the entire period, shown in Table 10.9B, are even more striking. Even the baseline simulations with the conventional all-unemployment regressions eventually generate hugely decelerating or accelerating inflation. Unemployment one percentage point lower explodes the system in hyperinflation, while one percentage point of higher unemployment would drive the price level negative! The low-unemployment simulations, by contrast, show baseline inflation fairly constant, fluctuating some with actual inflation, and show virtually no indication of accelerating inflation with lower rates of unemployment. Inflation in the GDPIPD actually came down slightly in the 30 years from 1965 to 1995 both in the baseline simulation and in the two simulations with lower unemployment. Some of the contrasting results of the low-employment regressions and the conventional, all-employment regressions are illustrated in Figure 10.1. Complete lack of support for the NAIRU is shown clearly in Figure 10.2, based on low-employment regressions reflecting the shift in the 1990–95 observations.

In all cases, it should be acknowledged, standard errors of forecasts are considerable, running over 2 percentage points. Confidence levels, even at the 5 per cent probability level, would run 4 or 5 percentage points above and below the projections.

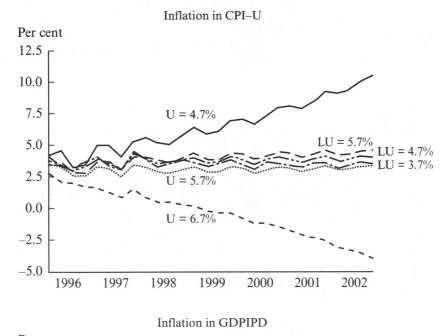

Inflation in CPI–U

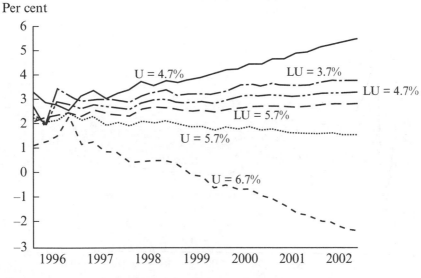

Inflation in GDPIPD

Notes:
U = 6.7%, 5.7% (NAIRU) and 4.7%; LU = 5.7%, 4.7% and 3.7%.

*Figure 10.1 Conventional model all-unemployment (U) and low-unemployment
(LU) regression forecasts of inflation, 1996.1–2002.4*

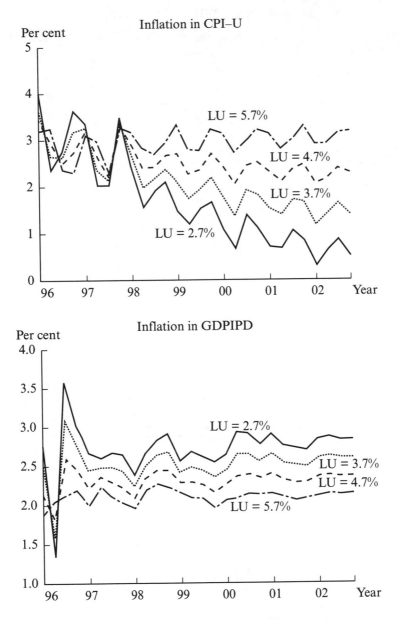

Notes: LU (Low unemployment) = 5.7%, 4.7%, 3.7% and 2.7%.

Figure 10.2   Low-unemployment regression forecasts of inflation, 1996.1–2002.4, reflecting shift in 1990–1995 observations

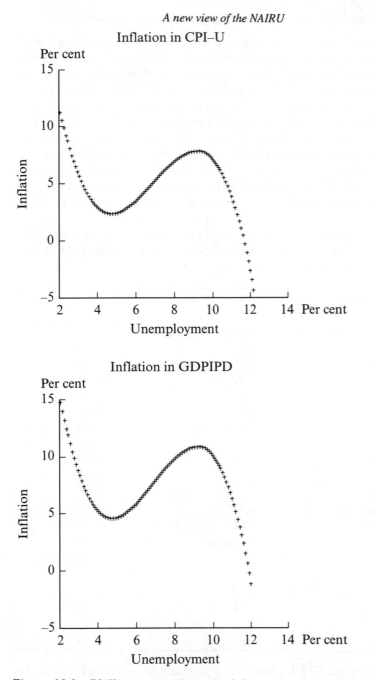

Figure 10.3 Phillips curves from third-degree regressions, based on 160 observations from 1956.1 to 1995.4

What these simulations may reflect is a set of observations generating a short-run Phillips curve quite different from its original hyperbolic shape. Phillips curves calculated and plotted from cubic equations relating inflation to current and four lagged values of unemployment over our 1956–95 estimation period, shown in Figure 10.3, appear rather to confirm the original suggestion by Tobin (1955) that they are S-shaped. *Very* low unemployment is indeed associated with considerably more rapid inflation, but the curves do not turn upwards, as we reduce unemployment, until inflation reaches minima at 4.8 per cent unemployment, as shown in Table 10.10. Higher unemployment is associated with *higher* inflation until it reaches maxima, at 9.1 per cent unemployment for the CPI–U and 9.3 per cent unemployment for the GDPIPD.

Table 10.10   Phillips curve from third degree regression, inflation in CPI–U and GDPIPD, based on observations over 160 quarters from 1956.1 to 1995.4

Unemployment	Inflation in CPI–U (percentages)	Inflation in GDPIPD
0.0	37.08	44.52
1.0	22.20	27.31
2.0	12.09	15.62
3.0	5.97	8.51
4.0	3.02	5.10
4.8	2.41(min)	4.40(min)
5.0	2.44	4.45
6.0	3.44	5.67
7.0	5.21	7.83
8.0	6.94	10.02
9.0	7.84	11.34
9.1	7.85(max)	11.39
9.3	7.83	11.43(max)
10.0	7.10	10.87
11.0	3.91	7.69
12.0	−2.52	0.90
13.0	−13.00	−10.42

Looking at the CPI–U, lower unemployment is associated with higher inflation then, but only when unemployment is above 9.1 per cent or below 4.8 per cent. At the old target of 4 per cent unemployment, inflation is 3 per cent, little above its minimum of 2.4 per cent. Much higher unemployment would be associated with the end of inflation but these data suggest unemployment would have to be in the neighbourhood of 12 per cent before prices actually began to come down.

6   CONCLUSION

I would not bet the family farm or the nation's economy on any set of econometric estimates, even my own, and these have substantial standard errors, as just pointed out. I welcome further tests and estimates of the relations that I have presented. However, for those committed to the concept of a NAIRU – which I find poorly based to begin with – its breakdown when we distinguish between responses to high and low unemployment may not easily be dismissed.

I do not claim a robust basis for a new dogma that says that lowering unemployment will reduce inflation. There may indeed be no stable, universal relation among unemployment and all the various factors that may contribute to inflation, let alone accelerating inflation. But there is no robust empirical support for holding down economic growth to avoid unemployment less than the presumed NAIRU.[16]

NOTES

*   I am indebted to the Congressional Budget Office and to Robert Arnold, in particular, for the series that they used in preparing their estimates of the NAIRU. I have also benefited from the fine research assistance of James Gill, Jay Hoffman, Suken Shah and Daniel A. Pasini. I am grateful to participants in the Northwestern macroeconomics seminar, and particularly to Robert J. Gordon, for helpful comments and for corrections to an earlier draft. And I am also grateful to participants in seminars at the Congressional Budget Office, the Federal Reserve Bank of Chicago and the University of Wisconsin, and to Robert S. Chirinko, Martin Eichenbaum, Allen Sinai, Robert M. Solow, Daniel Sullivan, Mark W. Watson and Kenneth D. West for further helpful comments. An earlier and longer version of this chapter was presented at the 7th World Congress of the Econometric Society in Tokyo (Eisner 1995a). Some of the conclusions from the earlier paper have been published in Eisner (1995b, 1996a and 1996b). A French translation of this chapter is now published in Eisner (1997b) and a further analysis of the subject of this chapter has been presented in Eisner (1997a).
 1.   Stock and bond markets crashed in the United States the day it was reported that the February 1996 unemployment rate had fallen to 5.5 per cent. Investors concluded that the Fed would now certainly not move to lower interest rates as it had been expected to do in response to previous evidence of a slowing economy. The markets plummeted again in early May 1996 after reports that first-quarter real GDP growth was at 2.8 per cent, deemed too high to leave unemployment constant, and that the April unemployment rate was back down 0.3 percentage points to 5.4 per cent.
 2.   See, for example, Blanchard (1990), Tobin (1967, 1972, 1993 and 1995), Solow (1987), Setterfield et al. (1992), Setterfield (1996), and Hahn (1995), Cross (1995b) and other chapters

in Cross (1995a) and most recently Fair. (1997a and 1997b), Blanchard and Katz (1997), Gordon (1997) who now has a varying NAIRU, Rogerson (1997), and Staiger, Stock and Watson (1997).

3.   See Staiger et al. (1996).

4.   Ray Fair (1996), working with data for 29 other countries and the United States, has argued that the NAIRU is 'two derivatives' off. He found unemployment to be associated with higher prices but not rising prices, let alone rising inflation.

5.   Other recent similar work has been done by Weiner (1993).

6.   I have responded to a suggestion (by Dean Baker of the Economic Policy Institute) that general levels of prices might react to changes in food and energy prices over some period of time. I have hence introduced the *FAE* variable with four distributed lags in later regressions reported upon below and found their explanatory power to be superior to that of the single-lagged *FAE* variable used by the CBO.

7.   In later estimates (CBO 1995, Table E-1: 91, footnote b), it was judged 0.2 percentage points higher to correspond to new estimates of actual unemployment, so that the NAIRU for 1994 was put at 6.0 per cent. The earlier increases suggested by the new estimates were subsequently thought to be exaggerated and the CBO's estimates for 1996 were 5.83 per cent.

8.   I estimated parameters of lagged inflation variables both independently and with the CBO's PDL, *n*, 3 specification. Results were very similar but I will report on the independent lag parameters regressions which I used in the forecast simulations.

9.   It was 0.994 for the old benchmark-weighted GDP deflator for observations from 1955.1 to 1993.4 used in the original CBO estimates.

10. I have calculated inflation in the GDPIPD deflators from the series in current dollars and the new real gross domestic product in chained 1992 dollars, for the quarters beginning in 1959.1, for which these are presently available. I have used the old series in 1992 benchmarked dollars for the quarters before 1959.1.

11. Chirinko (1995), seeking to explain procyclical movements in productivity, finds evidence that marginal cost is below average cost and falls relative to average cost in expansions. Robert Hall (1988 and 1991) has contended that price is frequently well above marginal costs and capacity constraints not binding, which might suggest that there is little reason to raise prices as employment increases. Rotemberg and Summers (1990) have presented evidence of countercyclical movement in markups. Chirinko and Fazzari (1994), while not supporting a general finding of countercyclical markups, do find substantial evidence of increasing returns. Decreasing marginal costs, increasing returns and countercyclical or even acyclical markups would all be consistent with a finding that upward pressure on prices is less under conditions of low unemployment.

12. See Eberwein and Kollintzas (1995) and the works cited therein.

13. To prevent any bias from the differences between the differences of the means of the high- and low-unemployment variables and these assigned values of zero, I normalized these variables around zero. Thus, for each sample, the means of UNH and UNL, and similarly UNMMH and UNMML, for the married-male regressions, were subtracted from each valid observation.

14. Assuming exogenous factors not operative (that is, in our formulation, $FAE = PRD = 0$), the change in the steady rate of inflation, IN, resulting from a permanent change in the rate of unemployment, U, is calculated as

$$\Delta IN = \Delta U^* \Sigma b_j \div (1 - \Sigma b_i)$$

where Σb_j is the sum of the unemployment coefficients and Σb_i is the sum of the inflation coefficients. Designating the constant term as C, the equilibrium rate of inflation for the mean values of unemployment, which was normalized to zero for the high and low unemployment variables, UVH2 and UVL2, is

$$IN_{EQ} = C \div (1 - \Sigma b_i).$$

Since UVH2 = 0 corresponds to an unemployment rate of 7.272 per cent and UVL2 = 0 corresponds to an unemployment rate of 4.951 per cent, the equilibrium rate of inflation as a function of the rate of unemployment may be written:

$$INH_{EQ} = (C + \Sigma b_{jH}^* \{U - 7.272\}) \div (1 - \Sigma b_i),$$

for the high-unemployment relations, and

$$INL_{EQ} = (C + \Sigma b_{jL}^* \{U - 4.951\}) \div (1 - \Sigma b_i),$$

for the low-unemployment relations.

15. The NAIRUs calculated from the regression coefficients, shown in Table 10.6, were 7.722 for the CPI–U and 7.463 for the GDPIPD; on the basis of the shift in the 1990–95 observations, the current NAIRUs would be 6.577 for the CPI–U and 6.474 for the GDPIPD.

16. Results of vector autoregression, shown in the appendix, with accompanying tables and figures, appear generally consistent with the least square regressions shown in the text and with this conclusion.

REFERENCES

Blanchard, O.J. (1990), 'Unemployment: Getting the Questions Right and Some of the Answers', in J.H. Drèze and C.R. Bean (eds), *Europe's Unemployment Problem*, Cambridge, MA: MIT Press: pp. 66–89.

Blanchard, Olivier and Lawrence F. Katz (1997), 'What We Know and Do Not Know About the Natural Rate of Unemployment', *The Journal of Economic Perspectives*, **11** (1), Winter: 51–72.

Chirinko, Robert S. (1995), 'Non-Convexities, Labor Hoarding, Technology Shocks, and Procyclical Productivity: A Structural Econometric Approach', *Journal of Econometrics*, **66** (1–2), March–April: 61–78.

Chirinko, R.S. and S.M. Fazzari (1994), 'Economic Fluctuations, Market Power, and Returns to Scale: Evidence from Firm-Level Data', *Journal of Applied Econometrics*, **9**: 47–69.

Congressional Budget Office (CBO) (1994), *The Economic and Budget Outlook: An Update*, Washington, DC: Congressional Budget Office, August.

Congressional Budget Office (CBO) (1995), *The Economic and Budget Outlook: Fiscal Years 1996–2000*, Washington, DC: Congressional Budget Office, January.

Cross, Rod (ed.) (1995a), *The Natural Rate of Unemployment; Reflections on 25 Years of the Hypothesis*, Cambridge: Cambridge University Press.

Cross, Rod (ed.) (1995b), 'Is the Natural Rate Hypothesis Consistent with Hysteresis?', in Cross (ed.) (1995a): pp. 181–200.

Eberwein, Curtis J. and Tryphon Kollintzas (1995), 'A Dynamic Model of Bargaining in a Unionized Firm With Irreversible Investment', *Annales d'Economie et de Statistique*, 37/38: pp. 91–115.

Eisner, Robert (1994), *The Misunderstood Economy: What Counts and How to Count It*, Boston: Harvard Business School Press.

Eisner, Robert (1995a), 'A New View of the NAIRU', Northwestern University, January and, as presented in a somewhat shorter version to the 7th World Econometric Congress in Tokyo, August 1995.

Eisner, Robert (1995b), 'Our NAIRU Limit, The Governing Myth of Economic Policy', *The American Prospect*, Spring: 58–63. Reprinted in *Macroeconomics*, 1996/1997 Annual Edition, Dushkin Publishing Group: 134–9.

Eisner, Robert (1996a), 'Deficits and Unemployment', in *Reclaiming Prosperity: A Blueprint for Progressive Economic Reform*, (1996), Washington, DC: Economic Policy Institute: 27–38.

Eisner, Robert (1996b), 'The Retreat From Full Employment', in *Employment, Economic Growth and the Tyranny of the Market: Essays in Honour of Paul Davidson*, Volume 2, 1996 106–30.

Eisner, Robert (1997a), 'The Decline and Fall of the NAIRU', presented to the 1997 annual American Economic Association Meetings, Northwestern University, January.

Eisner, Robert (1997b), 'Une Autre Interprétation du NAIRU', *Cahiers de l'Espace Europe*, March: 9–37.

Fair, Ray C. (1996), 'Testing the Standard View of the Long-Run Unemployment–Inflation Relationship', Cowles Foundation, Yale University, March.

Fair, Ray C. (1997a), 'Testing the NAIRU Model for 27 Countries', Cowles Foundation, Yale University, March.

Fair, Ray C. (1997b), 'Testing the NAIRU Model for the United States', Cowles Foundation, Yale University, March.

Friedman, Milton (1968), 'The Role of Monetary Policy', *American Economic Review*, **58**, March: 1–17.

Galbraith, James K. (1997) 'Time to Ditch the NAIRU', *The Journal of Economic Perspectives*, **11** (1), Winter: 93–108.

Gordon, Robert J. (1982), 'Inflation, Flexible Exchange Rates, and the Natural Rate of Unemployment', in M.N. Baily (ed.), *Workers, Jobs and Inflation*, Washington, DC: Brookings Institution: pp. 89–158.

Gordon, Robert J. (1997), 'The Time-Varying NAIRU and its Implications for Economic Policy', *The Journal of Economic Perspectives*, **11** (1), Winter: 11–32

Hahn, Frank (1995), 'Theoretical Reflections on the "Natural Rate of Unemployment"', in Cross (ed.) (1995a): pp. 43–56.

Hall, Robert E. (1988), 'The Relation Between Price and Marginal Cost in U.S. Industry', *Journal of Political Economy*, **96**, October: 921–47.

Hall, Robert E. (1991), 'Labor Demand, Labor Supply, and Unemployment Volatility', in Olivier Jean Blanchard and Stanley Fischer (eds), *NBER Macroeconomics Annual 1991*, Chicago: NBER: pp. 17–47.

Phelps, Edmund S. (1968), 'Money-Wage Dynamics and Labor-Market Equilibrium', *Journal of Political Economy*, **76**, August, Part 2: 678–711.

Rogerson, Richard (1997), 'Theory Ahead of Language in the Economics of Unemployment', *The Journal of Economic Perspectives*, **11** (1), Winter: 73–92.

Rotemberg, J.J. and L.H. Summers (1990), 'Inflexible Prices and Procyclical Activity', *The Quarterly Journal of Economics*, **105**: 851–74.

Setterfield, M.A. (1996), 'Using the NAIRU as a Basis for Macroeconomic Policy: An Evaluation', in B. Maclean and L. Osberg, *The Unemployment Crisis: All for Nought?*, McGill-Queen's, pp. 56–72.

Setterfield, M.A., D.V. Gordon and L. Osberg (1992), 'Searching for a Will o' the Wisp: An Empirical Study of the NAIRU in Canada', *European Economic Review,* **36**: 119–36.

Solow, Robert M. (1987), 'Unemployment: Getting the Questions Right', *Economica*, **53**: S23–34.

Staiger, Douglas, James Stock and Mark Watson (1996), 'How Precise are Estimates of the Natural Rate of Unemployment?', National Bureau of Economic Research Working Paper 5477, March.

Staiger, Douglas, James H. Stock and Mark W. Watson (1997), 'The NAIRU, Unemployment and Monetary Policy', *The Jounal of Economic Perspectives*, **11** (1), Winter: 33–49.

Tobin, James (1955), 'A Dynamic Aggregative Model', *Journal of Political Economy*, **63** (1), April: 103–15.

Tobin, James (1967), 'Unemployment and Inflation: The Cruel Dilemma', in A. Phillips (ed.), *Price Issues in Theory, Practice and Policy*, Philadelphia: University of Pennsylvania Press: pp. 101–7.

Tobin, James (1972), 'Inflation and Unemployment', *American Economic Review*, **62** (1), March: 1–18.

Tobin, James (1993), 'Price Flexibility and Output Stability: An Old Keynesian View', *Journal of Economic Perspectives*, **7**, Winter: 45–65.

Tobin, James (1995), 'The Natural Rate as New Classical Economics', in Cross (ed.) (1995a): pp. 32–42.

Weiner, Stuart E. (1993), 'New Estimates of the Natural Rate of Unemployment', *Economic Review*, Federal Reserve Bank of Kansas City, Fourth Quarter: 53–69.

APPENDIX: RESULTS OF VARS

Results of vector autoregressions with eight lagged values of unemployment and inflation, along with the exogenous variables *PRD*, *FAE*(–1), *NIXON* and *NIXOFF*, as shown in Tables 10A.1 and 10A.2 and Figure 10A.1, would appear consistent with those of the ordinary least squares regressions present in the text.

Noting first the VARs involving the CPI–U, we find that a one percentage point (positive) shock to the regression of UN, the series for all unemployment, is associated with an immediate decline in inflation. The reduction reaches a maximum of 2.69 per cent in quarter 6 and is persistent throughout the 28 periods of forecast. The one percentage point shock in the high-employment VAR reduces inflation by a maximum of only 0.57 percentage points, in quarter 5, and subsequent quarters indicate a considerable easing of that effect.

The low-unemployment VAR results are quite different. A one percentage point shock here is associated with a 0.27 percent reduction in inflation in quarter one, followed immediately by a cancelling increase. From quarter 6 on we see *in*creases in inflation. A *re*duction in unemployment below the NAIRU would seem to reduce inflation.

Results of the VARs relating to the GDP implicit price deflator are similar in that again the shock in the all-unemployment regression is associated with a substantial though lesser reduction in inflation and the shock in the high-employment regression is associated with only a very modest reduction in inflation. The low-unemployment shock here is not followed by generally higher inflation but again it is not associated with markedly lower inflation.

Table 10A.1   VAR percentage response of INC2 (inflation in CPI–U) to one
percentage point shocks of UN (all unemployment), UVH2 (high
unemployment) and UVL2 (low unemployment)

	All unemployment		High unemployment		Low unemployment	
Quarter	UN	INC2	UVH2	INC2	UVL2	INC2
1	1.00	−0.48	1.00	−0.43	1.00	−0.27
2	1.58	−1.95	0.66	−0.07	0.93	0.26
3	1.81	−1.83	0.37	−0.14	0.92	−0.03
4	1.72	−1.33	0.31	−0.20	0.79	−0.22
5	1.40	−2.60	0.34	−0.57	0.76	−0.37
6	1.08	−2.69	0.25	−0.09	0.71	0.13
7	0.83	−2.61	0.00	0.14	0.68	0.22
8	0.60	−2.14	−0.03	0.03	0.52	0.67
9	0.38	−2.35	−0.04	−0.41	0.38	0.56
10	0.14	−2.26	−0.07	−0.36	0.27	0.53
11	−0.05	−1.95	−0.13	−0.03	0.17	0.67
12	−0.22	−1.95	−0.12	−0.17	0.11	0.92
13	−0.37	−1.90	−0.11	−0.38	0.03	0.99
14	−0.48	−1.71	−0.12	−0.36	−0.03	0.89
15	−0.56	−1.46	−0.09	−0.18	−0.08	0.89
16	−0.62	−1.45	−0.06	−0.26	−0.10	0.89
17	−0.67	−1.42	−0.06	−0.34	−0.11	0.87
18	−0.71	−1.23	−0.07	−0.24	−0.11	0.81
19	−0.73	−1.12	−0.04	−0.18	−0.10	0.77
20	−0.74	−1.09	−0.02	−0.24	−0.09	0.69
21	−0.74	−1.02	−0.03	−0.23	−0.07	0.59
22	−0.74	−0.90	−0.04	−0.13	−0.05	0.53
23	−0.72	−0.84	−0.02	−0.13	−0.03	0.49
24	−0.71	−0.81	−0.01	−0.18	−0.01	0.42
25	−0.69	−0.73	−0.03	−0.14	0.00	0.35
26	−0.67	−0.65	−0.03	−0.06	0.02	0.30
27	−0.65	−0.62	−0.02	−0.09	0.03	0.27
28	−0.62	−0.59	−0.02	−0.13	0.04	0.23

Note: * Eight quarter lags of INC2 and unemployment variables with *PRD*, *FAE*(−1), *FAE*(−2),
FAE(−3), *FAE*(−4), *NIXON*, and *NIXOFF* exogenous.

*Table 10A.2 VAR percentage response of INF2 (inflation in GDPIPD) to
one percentage point shocks of UN (all unemployment), UVH2
(high unemployment), and UVL2 (low unemployment)*

	All unemployment		High unemployment		Low unemployment	
Quarter	UN	INF2	UVH2	INF2	UVL2	INF2
1	1.00	−1.14	1.00	−0.41	1.00	−0.32
2	1.58	−1.55	0.67	−0.15	0.93	0.26
3	1.85	−1.51	0.35	−0.17	0.93	−0.59
4	1.80	−0.57	0.28	−0.27	0.77	−0.18
5	1.50	−1.29	0.34	−0.41	0.78	−0.18
6	1.21	−0.86	0.26	−0.20	0.73	0.27
7	1.01	−1.33	0.02	0.05	0.69	0.10
8	0.79	−1.12	−0.05	−0.17	0.55	0.09
9	0.57	−1.20	−0.04	−0.15	0.43	−0.12
10	0.34	−0.99	−0.05	−0.04	0.32	−0.14
11	0.13	−0.80	−0.11	0.04	0.25	−0.24
12	0.00	−0.62	−0.13	−0.06	0.18	−0.24
13	−0.08	−0.70	−0.09	−0.10	0.11	−0.26
14	−0.13	−0.63	−0.07	−0.01	0.04	−0.26
15	−0.18	−0.60	−0.06	0.00	−0.01	−0.27
16	−0.23	−0.56	−0.05	−0.04	−0.05	−0.27
17	−0.27	−0.54	−0.03	−0.07	−0.08	−0.27
18	−0.29	−0.52	−0.01	−0.03	−0.10	−0.28
19	−0.30	−0.47	0.00	−0.02	−0.11	−0.28
20	−0.30	−0.44	0.00	−0.05	−0.11	−0.28
21	−0.30	−0.42	0.00	−0.05	−0.11	−0.26
22	−0.30	−0.39	0.01	−0.04	−0.10	−0.24
23	−0.30	−0.36	0.01	−0.03	−0.09	−0.23
24	−0.30	−0.34	0.00	−0.04	−0.08	−0.21
25	−0.30	−0.33	0.00	−0.04	−0.07	−0.19
26	−0.30	−0.32	0.00	−0.03	−0.06	−0.18
27	−0.29	−0.29	0.00	−0.03	−0.05	−0.16
28	−0.28	−0.27	−0.01	−0.03	−0.04	−0.15

Note: [*] Eight Quarter Lags of INF2 and unemployment variables with *PRD, FAE(−1), FAE(−2),
FAE(−3), FAE(−4), NIXON,* and *NIXOFF* exogenous.

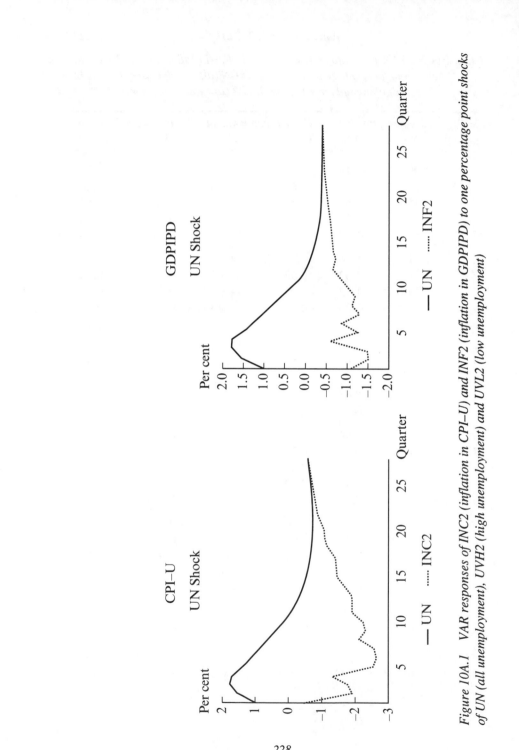

Figure 10A.1   VAR responses of INC2 (inflation in CPI–U) and INF2 (inflation in GDPIPD) to one percentage point shocks of UN (all unemployment), UVH2 (high unemployment) and UVL2 (low unemployment)

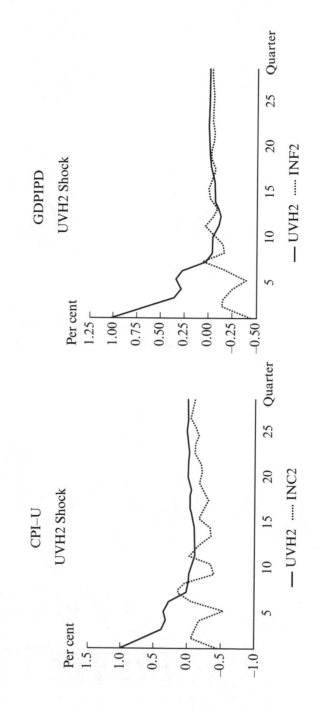

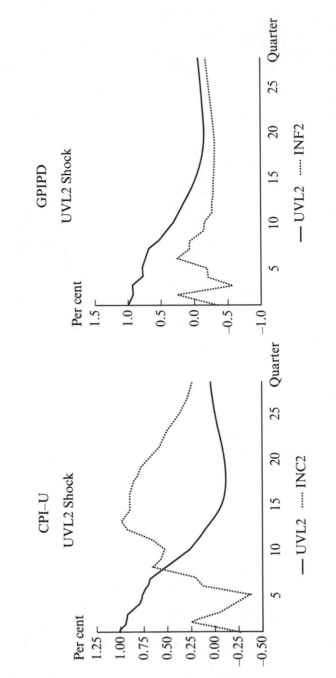

Note: * Eight Quarter Lags of INC2, INF2 and unemployment variables with *PRD, FAE(−1), FAE(−2), FAE(−3), FAE(−4), NIXON,* and *NIXOFF* exogenous.

11.   It's time to ditch the NAIRU*

James K. Galbraith

1   INTRODUCTION

The concept of a natural rate of unemployment, or non-accelerating inflation rate of unemployment (NAIRU), has ruled macroeconomics for about 25 years. Yet it is still controversial. There is still a wide range of view over how the NAIRU should be estimated. These facts in themselves raise questions about the practical usefulness of the concept.

This chapter presents a brief for no-confidence, in four parts. First, the theoretical case for the natural rate is not compelling. Second, the empirical evidence for a vertical Phillips curve and the associated hypothesis that lowering unemployment past the NAIRU leads to unacceptable acceleration of inflation is weak, and has become much weaker in the past decade. Third, that attempts to estimate the location of the NAIRU or natural rate have been, viewed collectively, a professional embarrassment. Fourth, that adherence to the concept as a guide to policy has major costs and negligible benefits. Conversely, the risks of dropping the natural rate hypothesis are minor; both the American economy and the discipline of economics will survive.

2   UNRESOLVED THEORETICAL QUESTIONS

The idea of the 'natural rate of unemployment' is usually traced to the work of Milton Friedman (1968) and Edmund Phelps (1968). Specifically, the natural rate was born in Friedman's remarkable 1968 presidential lecture to the American Economics Association, as close as economists get to delivery from Olympus. Perhaps no other presidential address has ever been so influential.

Before Friedman's lecture, most American economists accepted a stable Phillips curve as the best concise statement of the relationship between the unemployment rate and inflation. Friedman introduced an expectations function into the Phillips curve, so that the inflation rate would now depend on both unemployment and past inflation expectations. Friedman showed that in his model the expected rate of inflation predicts the actual rate of inflation only when unemployment is held at an equilibrium value, the natural rate.

Thus, Friedman drew the distinction between the short run, when variations of unemployment could affect inflation, and the long run, when by construction unemployment could not vary. Within the terms of this thought experiment, efforts to reduce unemployment below its natural rate equilibrium would appear successful in the short run, but would soon generate accelerating inflation whose intolerability would force a retreat to the natural rate.

This argument swept the field, yet it is open to questions that were not widely raised at the time. First among these concern the shortcomings of the Phillips curve itself, and specifically its lack of theoretical justification. The Phillips curve had always been a purely empirical relationship, patched into IS–LM Keynesianism to relieve that model's lack of a theory of inflation.[1] Friedman supplied no theory for a short-run Phillips curve, yet he affirmed that such a relationship would 'always' exist. And Friedman's argument depends on it. If the Phillips relationship fails empirically – that is, if levels of unemployment do not in fact predict changes in the rate of inflation in the short run – then the construct of the natural rate of unemployment also loses meaning. This empirical issue, which is more troubling than most suppose, will be discussed in the next section. For the moment, it is sufficient to note that a theoretical argument that rests on an atheoretic foundation is likely to run into trouble sooner or later.

Friedman may have sensed this. For while his core argument was macroeconomic, a gloss on then-prevalent Keynesianism and the Phillips curve, he also phrased a version of it in microeconomic terms. According to this alternative version, the natural rate of unemployment is the point of intersection of supply and demand curves in an aggregative, classical market for labour. The two versions are quite distinct. If the main line of Friedman's argument concerning a vertical Phillips curve led towards a non-accelerating inflation rate of unemployment, the notion of an aggregate labour market pointed the way towards the new classical model. Friedman (1968: 8, emphasis added) said:

> At any moment of time, there is some level of unemployment which has the property that it is consistent with equilibrium in the structure of *real* wage rates. At that level of unemployment, real wage rates are tending on the average to rise at a 'normal' secular rate. ... *A higher level of unemployment is an indication that there is an excess supply of labor that will produce downward pressure on real wage rates.* The 'natural rate of unemployment' in other words, is the level that would be ground out by the Walrasian system of general equilibrium equations, provided there is embedded in them the actual structural characteristics of the labor and commodity markets ...

Such a labour market is free of money contracts and money illusion. Employment is purely a function of the real wage, acting on the marginal physical productivity of labour and on the marginal disutility of work. In such a market, nominal shocks can have only nominal, not real, effects: money (for which read, macroeconomic policy) is neutral, perhaps even in the short run. Friedman's formulation states explicitly that persistent unemployment below the natural rate must lead through the labour market to rising real wages, whose nominal element is at least the proximate cause of rising prices.

This story is pre-Keynesian in all its essentials. And the essential theoretical objections to it were set forth by Keynes (1936) in the *General Theory*. First, labour supply and demand cannot be modelled in terms of the real wage, for workers care about relative wages as well as real wages; this introduces an asymmetry between nominal wage cuts and nominal price increases. Second, workers cannot actually negotiate for their own real wages, because of an interdependency between money wages and the price level. These two objections, which are the foundations of the *General Theory*, undermine the concept of the labour supply curve (the 'second classical postulate', as Keynes called it) and hence the very construct of an aggregative 'labour market'. The neoclassical synthesis buried these objections long ago, but never actually resolved them.

If there is no aggregative labour market in any sense meaningful to economics, then theories based on shifts in wages clearing labour markets will fail to hold. From a proper Keynesian perspective, the correct response to the neo-Walrasian formulation of the natural rate hypothesis is simply, 'Sorry, but the "labour market" is a misconception; it doesn't exist'. Aggregate demand for output, and not supply and demand for labour, determine employment. By these lights the aggregate labour market, lacking a defensible supply curve as well as any internal clearing mechanism, is simply a failed metaphor, unsuitable for use as the foundation of a theory.

A further line of objection to the theory of the natural rate also has its roots in Keynes. Is long-run equilibrium really a good guide to macroeconomic policy? Friedman's NAIRUvian long run and the more strictly classical natural rate, based on rational expectations, are certainly beguiling. But are they relevant? Information may be asymmetric. Competition may be monopolistic. Non-linearities and even chaos are possible. Equilibria may be multiple or continuous. In such cases, the long-run equilibrium may be undetermined or incalculable or beyond achievement. To put it another way, the future may be inherently unpredictable. Here, the political scientists with their concept of 'rational ignorance' may have something to teach economists. In a world of rational indifference, of a principled refusal to compute, surely all significant change is essentially unexpected, the short-run relationships are what matter, and policies will usually work in the short run. As Robert Lucas (1981) once observed, the long run is no more than a sequence of steps which each occur in the here and now. If short-run policies necessarily fail – the Lucas position – you must live by the long run. But if short-run policies actually work – the Keynes position – it is fruitless to look that far ahead and what you have to do is work from one short run to the next. The point is that one must choose one construct or the other, rather than trying to split the differences or otherwise base policy on both at the same time.

To be sure, these objections are easier to make in retrospect. In 1968, mainstream American Keynesians were committed to Samuelson and Solow's (1960) version of the Phillips curve, so they could not object to Friedman's specification that inflation was a function of unemployment and other factors. Being neoclassical synthetists, they could also hardly deny a role for expectations, or that expectations must be satisfied in the long run, or the policy relevance of the long run, nor that there existed a Walrasian aggregate labour market – a concept they had themselves resurrected in defiance of Keynes. Thus rhetorical power of Friedman's argument was especially great against his American Keynesian targets. And so the game Friedman started, which was the search for a macroeconomics with suitably orthodox 'microfoundations' in a proper classical labour market, has been going on ever since. Only the truest Keynesians – such as Nicholas Kaldor (1983) in the UK, Robert Eisner in the US, and the post Keynesians generally speaking – could escape Friedman's trap.

3   THE MISMEASURE OF NAIRU

Supporters of the natural rate and the NAIRU tell an enticing story about how the inflation of the 1970s proved their theory correct. Robert Lucas (1981: 560) summarizes the story well:

> Now, Friedman and Phelps had no way of foreseeing the inflation of the 1970s, any more than did the rest of us, but the central forecast to which their reasoning led was a conditional one, to the effect that a high inflation decade should not have less unemployment on average than a low-inflation decade. We got the high inflation decade, and with it as clear-cut an experimental discrimination as macroeconomics is ever likely to see, and Friedman and Phelps were right.

This sweeping conclusion has been widely accepted, and has had the effect of bolstering a weak theoretical argument with the authority of unpleasant fact. But is it right? Do the data still support the claim 15 years further on?

Figure 11.1, similar to diagrams in many textbooks, shows the breakdown of the short-run Phillips curve after 1969. In Figure 11.1, the dots represent monthly moving averages (over twelve months), with yearly labels inserted at mid-year. At a glance, Figure 11.1 does resemble a shifting set of short-run Phillips curves. For example, one can pick out a constellation in the lower left for the 1960s, and another constellation in the upper centre representing the late 1970s, after the second oil shock. But on average, taking the data as a whole, there is only a very modest inverse relation between inflation and unemployment.

Clearly, the range is very wide, with much horizontal movement; it is hard to look at this data and visualize a vertical long-run Phillips curve running down the middle. Moreover, the main upward thrusts were contributed by a fairly small number of inflationary months – in the late 1960s, in 1973 and in 1979.

Figure 11.1 Inflation and unemployment, 1990–1996 (monthly moving averages)

More important, the figure is not symmetric. (Eisner (1996) explores this issue in persuasive detail.) Leftward movements, when unemployment is falling, are substantially horizontal. In each expansion from the late 1960s to the mid-1990s, inflation rose little as unemployment fell. However, rightward movements as unemployment rises do result in a fall in inflation. Recessions are indeed disinflationary, as no one disputes, and the disinflation is strong in the early phases, while unemployment remains comparatively low. However, additional very high unemployment adds little extra to disinflation.[2]

For further evidence, consider the results of a too-simple regression, offered purely for the purpose of illustration, where unemployment and a constant term are used to explain the acceleration of inflation in monthly data. Table 11.1 presents the results of this regression for 1960–96, and for three subsets of that period: 1960 to 1967 (ante-Friedman); 1968 to 1983 (the years of monetarist ascension); and 1984 to the present. The first two periods provide nearly identical, small-but-significant support for the hypothesis that lower unemployment leads to accelerating inflation. The third period offers no such connection.

Table 11.1   Simple OLS regressions of inflation acceleration on unemployment (monthly data)

Sample Period	Constant	Coefficient	R-Squared
1960–1996	0.121	–0.019 (3.58*)	0.029
1960–1967	0.132	–0.020 (2.49*)	0.063
1968–1983	0.132	–0.021 (2.31*)	0.027
1984–1996	0.017	–0.003 (0.30)	0.0006

Notes
t-statistics in parentheses; * indicates significant at 0.01 level.
Independent variable is monthly unemployment; dependent variable is monthly change in CPI–U inflation rate, taken as a twelve-month moving average for the following year. These regressions are offered for purposes of illustration only.

Even when the relationship between unemployment and inflation was statistically significant, the very low R-squareds in Table 11.1 make clear that unemployment explained only a small part of the variation in inflation. The coefficient estimates also argue that even if a persistently low unemployment rate would have accelerated inflation, it would have done so quite slowly, with plenty of time to reverse policy if need be. (This point does not depend on whether one accepts the NAIRU as a theoretical device or not). The fundamental policy implication of the natural rate hypothesis is that of tight limits on the rate of economic growth, lest inflation accelerate beyond control. The empirical evidence, however, is in almost uniform agreement that inflation is highly inertial and that whatever limits may exist are at worst highly elastic.

The NAIRU hypothesis is related to the older Keynesian idea, introduced in the 1962 *Economic Report of the President*, of potential GDP and the GDP gap (GAP). As an empirical matter, Gap analysis is often still used for rough-and-ready assessments of distance to the NAIRU. Here too, there are reasons to treat the evidence with caution.

A typical method of calculating the growth rate of potential GDP is to look at, say, the peak-to-peak annual growth rate from 1973 to 1989 to show that 2.5 per cent, or thereabouts, represents the long-run growth ceiling of the economy. But this extrapolation from one business cycle peak to the next interjects a fatal assumption: that the peaks are exogenous. All a peak means is that something happened to slow down productivity growth; the economy hit a new set of limits. Just what those limits were and why they changed remains a professionally troublesome mystery – unresolved at present after 25 years of research – as troublesome as the estimation of the NAIRU and, I believe, for a closely related reason.

To understand the potential difficulty, suppose that erring policy makers have in the past reacted imprudently to 'supply shocks' in ways that prematurely and systematically curtailed economic expansion. In that case, the business cycle peak is endogenous to policy. Suppose they did this because of the rise of a false doctrine of limits – such as the natural rate hypothesis. It is then possible that if growth policies had been more sustained, disciplined and aggressive, then the perceived decline in the trend productivity growth rate would have been smaller than it was, and the estimated natural rate would also have been lower than it has appeared to be.

The point is not that I can offer proof of such a hypothesis, but that economists cannot distinguish this possibility from the idea of an exogenous peak. We cannot reject the possibility that macroeconomic policy has been in thrall to the illusion of a supposedly objective, but in fact self-induced, decline in the trend rate of productivity growth, and that we have been running from the phantom of accelerating inflation for more than two decades. The result: a self-inflicted wound, a socio-psychological disability, of colossal proportions.

One disquieting clue in all of this, which like the productivity slowdown is usually treated as an empirical puzzle, concerns the behaviour of wages. Surely, if the natural rate hypothesis means anything at all, it must imply that inflation stems from pressure in the labour market and is therefore wage driven. As noted earlier, Friedman's formulation states this explicitly, arguing that a link exists from persistently low unemployment in the aggregate labour market to higher wages, which in turn lead to rising prices. While Gordon (1996) argues that including wages in the model is a mistake, it is very hard to understand what the theory of a special link between unemployment and inflation can be, if it does not involve pressure through the labour market on wages and costs.

But the US has not experienced wage-led inflation since the 1950s, except briefly in 1973, as shown in Figure 11.2. Since 1973, average real wages have by most measures been stable or falling. All accelerations of inflation have been led by commodities, especially oil, or by import prices via devaluation. Why not therefore conclude that the economy has almost always been *above* the NAIRU during this time, and that the inflation rate should have been falling and even negative, but for these other factors? For that matter, why are no general-equilibrium theorists proposing the NAIROP, or non-inflation accelerating rate of oil production, or the NAIRODD, non-inflation accelerating rate of dollar devaluation? What we seem to hear, instead, is an argument that NAIRU estimates ignoring wages 'work better', leaving us in the dark as to *why* the unemployment rate should be connected to the price level, and with the suspicion that, as with the old unexplained Phillips curve, the empirical good times (such as they are) must sooner or later come to an unexplained end.

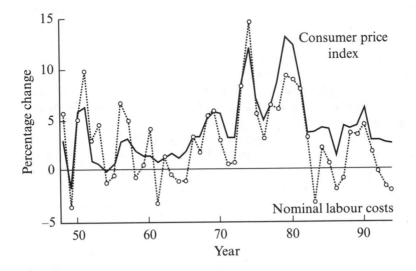

Figure 11.2   Inflation and labour costs, 1948–1994

4   THE SHIFTING NAIRU

A large literature now exists on estimating the natural rate of unemployment, or the NAIRU. For a stationary NAIRU, simple expressions can be derived. In general, these rest on a regression framework which explains inflation with unemployment, some proxy for inflationary expectations such as lagged inflation, and other economic variables. In this approach, when the other factors are held constant, and the coefficient on the past inflation is such that inflation is not changing, then all that is left is to find the unemployment rate which matches this stable rate of inflation. One alternative approach rests on the individualized ratio of job-separation to job-finding – a structural characteristic of the labour market in steady state (Hall 1979).

When these studies have specified that the natural rate be fixed, the estimates have had rather large statistical error terms. When the studies have allowed the natural rate to move, it has shifted considerably. For example, according to characteristic estimates by Adams and Coe (1990):

> The natural rate of unemployment is estimated to have increased steadily from 3.5 percent in the mid-1960s to a peak of 7.25 percent in 1980, and then to have fallen back to about 5.75 percent in 1988 ... Thus, roughly half of the increase in actual unemployment rates from the mid-1960s to their peak in the early 1980s can be attributed to increases in the natural rate.

Estimates of the NAIRU were at six per cent or so for the overall unemployment rate following the recession of 1990, and many insisted they would stay there. At present writing, they have generally fallen to 5.5 per cent or lower.[3] As in the past, the present estimates and re-estimates seem largely a response to predictive failure, though models are now emerging that incorporate time variation (Gordon 1996). Yet since the general abandonment of Perry-weighting for the changing demographic composition of the workforce some years ago (compare Perry 1970), we still have no theory, and no external evidence, governing the fall of the estimated NAIRU. We simply observe that inflation has not occurred and so the previous estimate must have been too high.

In general, the estimated NAIRU in a variety of studies has tracked the actual unemployment rate, sluggishly. When unemployment rises, analysts tend to discover that the demographic characteristics of workers are deteriorating, or that the job-wage and wage-price dynamic have become unstable (Gordon 1988). And then the unemployment rate drifts down again, those flaws mysteriously begin to disappear, and a lower NAIRU is estimated. Recent empirical studies, such as Eisner (1996) and Fair (1996), have confirmed this instability, both across time and in transnational comparisons.

It is often necessary to revise a parameter once or twice in the light of new information. Differences of specification are also normal in the early stages of scientific inquiry. But to hold to a concept in the face of decades of unexplained variation and failure of the profession to coalesce on procedural issues is quite another matter. This record has become an embarrassment to the reputation of the profession. In saying this, I do not disparage any individual's work. My point is that momentous decisions of public policy cannot depend on the track record of any one individual theorist or econometrician, however reliable his or her individual work. It is necessary for the issue to be settled. If professional economists want to be taken seriously on the NAIRU, they have to come to agreement. Judging from the recent literature, agreement on even the present location of the NAIRU or its confidence interval remains far away. Nothing remotely resembling the unified policy view of the 1960s Keynesians, with their commitment to the pre-NAIRU Phillips curve, exists today.

The innovation of a time-varying NAIRU (Gordon, 1996), though attractive in the face of the record of stationary models, seems unlikely to resolve the practical problem. For now we need agreement not only on a value, but on the process generating the value. How likely is this, given for instance the present disagreement over so basic an issue as whether wages belong in a price equation? Or, consider what time-variation adds to policy discussion. If the implication of TV–NAIRU models is that unemployment can be pushed down slowly, well past previously imagined limits, with the NAIRU in tow, well and good. But you can reach that conclusion without a NAIRU model; nobody argues for a crash programme to achieve 3 per cent unemployment next year. If, on the other hand, the implication is that one must base interest-rate policy on the ever-changing output of a computer model, I think policy makers will wisely assign TV–NAIRU estimates a low weight. And if the implication is that next year's NAIRU is a random walk from this year's, the practical consequence is not different from that of abandoning NAIRU models altogether.

Can you imagine a petition from a broad spectrum of economists, calling on the Federal Reserve to raise interest rates sharply at the present 5.1 per cent unemployment in order to ward off imminent inflation? If you cannot imagine such a thing – for a contrast, one thinks of Einstein's 1939 letter to Roosevelt on the possibility of the bomb, something that conveyed definite information from a figure of authority backed by his colleagues – then we as a scientific profession have not advanced this concept to the point where it is suitable for practical use. After 29 years, it is a fair question whether we shall ever do so.

5   THE COSTS OF NAIRUVIANISM

Speaking politically, the natural rate hypothesis has served a conservative cause. Ever since Friedman's speech, orthodox macroeconomics has virtually always leaned against policies to support full employment. In spite of stagnant real wages, it has virtually never leaned the other way.

For strict new classicals, this effect must be forgiven. The logic of their case imposes opposition to all policies affecting employment through aggregate demand. But for NAIRUvians, who believe that demand policy may have an appropriate role in engineering 'soft landings' at the NAIRU, it seems to be a matter of curiously irrational, systematic error. Some economists have been more eager to raise their estimate of NAIRU than to cut it. The NAIRU, like the wage rate, is downwardly sticky.

When a higher NAIRU accompanies higher unemployment, it cuts against the case for a policy of expansion, since a higher proportion of the existing unemployment is seen as necessary to preserve stable inflation. When unemployment is falling, a downwardly sticky NAIRU bolsters the natural caution of many economists concerning pro-growth policy intervention. In consequence, policy makers are almost *never* presented with a clear case, based on natural rate analysis and supported by a consensus of NAIRU-adhering economists, for a pro-employment policy.[4] This pattern continues right up to the present, as some economists who a year ago insisted that the natural rate was 6 per cent now insist on 5.5 per cent, or perhaps 5 per cent. Lower estimates will be forthcoming, after the fact, if unemployment continues to fall and inflation does not increase. But by then it will be too late, and potential gains from having the estimates in hand now will have been lost.

Economics has in this way talked itself out of a role in solving the central macroeconomic problems of unemployment and stagnation. Taxonomy – the empty art of labelling existing unemployment as 'structural', 'frictional' or 'cyclical' – has substituted for the development of theory bearing on action. The theories that have developed reinforce the message implicit in the taxonomy chosen: once frictional, structural and cyclical unemployment are allowed for, there is truly nothing left to be done. The cost of unnecessarily high unemployment itself must therefore, to some extent, rest on the conscience of the economics profession.

There is a second cost to this style of thinking, one that falls on the economists rather than on the economy. This is a loss of influence. It is one thing to position oneself in the centre of gravity of a national political debate, where one can condition theory with circumstance, address important problems, and recommend now one thing, now another, as conditions change. It is something else again to be always singing the same note, always revisiting the same issue, always revising past estimates, coming up with the 'new NAIRU' and the 'new new NAIRU' as though it were a matter of a political makeover. People stop paying attention, and rightly so.

All of this matters, of course, only if the unemployment itself is truly costly, all things considered. If a 5.1 per cent unemployment rate is no improvement over 5.5 per cent, why not go back to the estimated NAIRU and play it safe?

Analyses of the costs of unemployment typically focus on the unemployed themselves or on their immediate families and neighbourhoods. When the actual unemployment rate falls to its present 5 per cent range, opinions differ. Seven million citizens continue to seek work they cannot find. Another 700,000 or so are counted as discouraged, and some four million more are working part-time involuntarily. Millions more are working full-time in jobs that they would like to change if alternatives existed.

I believe these numbers remain far too high, particularly given the maldistribution of unemployment and the social pathology of having high rates of it concentrated in inner cities or among minority groups. Other economists obviously take a more sanguine view. But my point here is that the effects of unemployment are not isolated or confined to the unemployed; rather they extend throughout the economy, to a matter that affects us all. Specifically, empirical researchers are now increasingly finding a link between unemployment and economic inequality generally speaking (Danziger and Gottschalk 1995; Karoly 1996).

My own work strongly confirms the link between unemployment and inequality in the structure of wages. In recent and forthcoming work, Ferguson and Galbraith (1996) and Galbraith (forthcoming) have examined this relationship for the periods 1920–47 and 1958–92, for fairly comprehensive wage datasets covering manufacturing, agriculture, utilities and transportation in the earlier period and all of manufacturing in the later one. The focus on the wage structure is a departure, with the virtue that it disregards the influence that unemployment undoubtedly has on inequality of income between those who are employed and those who are not. Our data isolate the change in dispersion of hourly wages among those who remain employed, when unemployment varies.

We find that unemployment is a predominant cause of increased hourly wage dispersion in both periods, though the picture is somewhat more complicated in recent years than in the earlier ones – inflation and the exchange rate also play a role in increasing inequality in the modern wage structure. The underlying intuition is straightforward. In periods of high unemployment, low-paid and weakly protected workers suffer wage erosion, relative to those in better-paid, better-organized and more skill-intensive occupations. In the pre-Second World War data, this effect occurs mainly through the co-occurrence of mass unemployment and price/income depression in agriculture.

My conclusion is that high measured unemployment reflects conditions that have pernicious effects throughout the structure of wages and incomes. These conditions work to split the wage structure. They undermine the middle-class character of society and they separate the comfortable from the poor. The relationship between unemployment and inequality is therefore an additional reason for devoting intellectual and material resources to the pursuit of full employment. It also makes it reasonable to ask that advocates of speed-limit theorems and natural rate hypotheses prove their cases convincingly and in a unified way, something that in three decades they have not done.[5]

6   WHAT TO DO ABOUT INFLATION?

If we are stuck in the short run with a still-serious unemployment-cum-inequality problem, and if we reject the practice of using an estimated NAIRU as a serious guide to where to stop the reduction of unemployment, then what theory of inflation should we hold and what should we do about that risk?

I have devoted most of this chapter to an attack on the NAIRU as it often enters the policy discussion, in the post-Friedmanian or new classical versions under which inflation begins to accelerate promptly once the barrier is breached.

Almost no one working seriously on this issue appears to believe in this hair-trigger version of the NAIRU any more. Instead what we have are analyses showing very slow increases in the inflation rate over many years following a reduction of unemployment. And of course with 'time varying' estimates there is always the possibility that the NAIRU will fall even more.

If this is what is now meant by the NAIRU research, then the basic argument of this chapter is already non-controversial. It hardly matters whether the NAIRU continues to play a role in models, so long as all agree that the benefits of moving below the estimated NAIRU by moderate amounts vastly exceed the costs. This, of course, was never the intention of Milton Friedman or of most of the theorists and textbook writers who have belaboured the natural rate hypothesis over the past three decades.

At the same time, we need to recognize that almost no one seems to think that the major risks of accelerating inflation come from low unemployment. Gordon's estimates, once again, are exemplary: they show a minor risk. But since we observe that major inflations have occurred in the past, we do need to ask ourselve why that was so and what might possibly be done to prevent a recurrence.

Looking at history and again at the very few strongly inflationary episodes of the last thirty years as shown in Figure 11.1, one may reasonably argue that our most serious inflations hit, more or less unpredictably, as a result of war (Vietnam in 1967–69, Yom Kippur in 1973 and the subsequent OPEC oil embargo) and revolution (Iran in 1979 and the second oil crisis).

These events sharply destabilized existing patterns of wage, price and cost relations. Businesses and organized workers reacted, understandably, by trying to re-establish the previous patterns. They therefore set off a spiral, passing price and wage increases around the economy, igniting an essentially non-accelerating but highly inertial inflation that lasted in each case until a recession broke the spiral and forced all of the players to accept a changed arrangement.[6]

What was needed, in these cases, was an inflation policy which addressed problems of wartime supply management and commodity shocks. Vietnam was fought as a peacetime war; the massive civilian mobilizations and control mechanisms that stifled inflation during the Second World War were not imposed. That was a mistake: wars should be fought on a war footing or not at all. In the case of the oil shocks, the situation is more complex, since the events were abrupt and their genesis remains in some ways mysterious. In any event not every natural or man-made disaster can be predicted.

It would therefore be reasonable to approach anti-inflation policy in general as a matter, first and foremost, of designing circuit-breakers for shock episodes, so as to reduce the cost of adjusting to a new pattern of relative prices and therefore the need to do it through the brute-force method of mass unemployment. Some simple steps, such as coordinating the timing of wage bargains and providing the President with limited discretion over cost-of-living adjustments in Social Security, federal pensions and other payment streams might help a great deal, as I once proposed (Galbraith 1989).[7] Sterner measures could be held in reserve.

If this were done, then the very slow increases in inflation that might or might not happen as a result of pressure from low unemployment might be mitigated in benign ways. To decide what to do, it would be useful first to have some judgement from economists as to the exact mechanism at work. If it is pressure from wages, then a guideposts policy (together with some coordination of wage-bargain timing) might again be useful. If some other sector responding to low unemployment is somehow the villain, then perhaps a TIP or MAP proposal might be resurrected.[8] There is time for experiment here, and it should begin while the problem is not serious. The point is that the Federal Reserve need be brought into action only as a last resort, when all else fails (including patience), and not as the first line of defence.

The assignment of sole responsibility for anti-inflation policy to the Federal Reserve, a de facto development that is technically illegal under the Full Employment Act of 1978, is a serious underlying problem. Nothing in the law prevents the President and Congress from exerting leadership in this area, which they largely abandoned in 1981 for political reasons and have been prevented mainly by political cowardice from re-entering ever since. One of the serious unintended consequences of economists' preoccupation with NAIRU has been to convey a message to political leaders that they need not feel any responsibility in this area, that the inflation–unemployment tradeoff can be fine-tuned with interest rates by the Fed. It is not so.

7   CONCLUSION: A WORLD WITHOUT THE NAIRU?

Can economics live without the aggregative labour market, the natural rate and the NAIRU? Could physics survive without ether? Surely the measure of scientific maturity lies in a willingness to match theory with evidence, to discuss anomalies with an open mind, and to move on when it is appropriate to do so. Occasionally, this may mean reconstructing one's thinking from the ground up.

I believe that the case for basing anti-inflation policy primarily around the rate of unemployment was never persuasive – not in 1960 when the short-run Phillips curve came on to the American scene, or when Friedman introduced the vertical version he called the natural rate. The evidence since that time weighs further against drawing implications for policy from either confection, and equally against drawing implications from modern versions. One need not object to the NAIRU as a purely mathematical construct. After all, a steady-inflation unemployment rate is merely an implication of models specified in a certain way. The problem comes when one is asked whether to raise interest rates, *today*, based on the fact that the actual unemployment rate has dropped below the estimate of such a rate in someone's model. The uncertainty and dissensus among the best economists working on this issue, and the persistent failure of inflation to accelerate in recent years despite transgressing past NAIRUs, makes this an easy call.

Of course, when inflation hits it can be repressed by recession and stifled by stagnation. The test of policy, however, is to reconcile reasonable price stability with acceptable growth at the highest achievable levels of employment, and to manage shocks with the least disruption.

To abandon the NAIRU as a construct in policy discussion is essentially to abandon the pretext of impossibility of this task. This would open the way to the pursuit of a lower unemployment rate. Accelerated growth is one means towards this end – and Okun's Law, a much more reliable empirical rule than the Phillips curve, reminds us that an extra point of growth could bring unemployment down by a half-point or so per year. It is a reasonable bet that lower interest rates, combined with a somewhat less restrictive budget policy, could bring a growth acceleration.[9]

Surely a period of moderately accelerated growth is in order, mainly to recover ground lost to overly restrictive policies in the past. On the other hand, I do believe it would be a mistake to base policy *exclusively* on aggregate monetary and fiscal measures. Dispassionately reviewed, history makes a fair case that targeted employment policies, public capital investment programmes, and wage-price – but especially wage – guidelines have useful supporting roles in times of general prosperity.[10] I would especially argue for innovation now to establish circuit-breakers and other institutional mechanisms that would make handling a future exogenous inflation shock an easier and less costly task.

Economists have been a bit too quick to reject such policies outright, on the ground that they have no role in the idealized world of the model, where an assumed market already functions with perfect flexibility. We have also spent too little time discussing how to make such policies as effective, unobtrusive and sustainable as possible. When theory and histories conflict – as they do in the case of the natural rate and as they also do here – we should perhaps pay more attention to history. And we should be less easily tempted, than we sometimes have been, by the siren songs of the gods.

NOTES

*   This chapter first appeared in the Winter 1997 issue of the *Journal of Economic Perspectives*, and is copyright by the American Economics Association. Reprinted by permission of the editors.

Parts of this chapter draw on research supported by the Jerome Levy Economics Institute and on a research project supported by the Twentieth Century Fund. I thank Robert Eisner, William Darity jr, Alan Krueger, Brad DeLong and Timothy Taylor for comments, with special thanks to Taylor for his editorial work on the earlier drafts.

1. James Tobin once elegantly described the Phillips curve as a set of empirical observations in search of a theory, like Pirandello characters in search of a plot.
2. The slope is such that a 1 per cent fall in unemployment means nearly a 1 per cent rise in inflation. For the sake of the Phillips curve, at least the sign is correct, but the estimate is not statistically different from zero. As unemployment rises, a 1 per cent rise in employment brings a 2.75 per cent fall in inflation. This estimate has a 95 per cent confidence interval of about 1.6, and thus is significantly different from zero.
3. Mercifully, Akerlof et al. (1996: 43, Table 5) have produced estimates of the NAIRU ranging from 4.6 to 5.3 per cent, in good time for the September 1996 reduction of the actual unemployment rate to 5.1 per cent.
4. Come to think of it, if the process were symmetric, new Keynesian economists would be expected to take this position about half the time? An interesting hypothesis, suitable for further research.
5. Linking the estimates of wage dispersion from separate datasets going back to 1920, I find that unemployment accounts for some 55 per cent of the variation in inequality over 72 years of data. Using a method similar to that used to calculate the NAIRU, we can determine that rate of unemployment below which inequality declines and above which it rises. This, the 'ethical rate of unemployment' is estimated quite stably to be 5.5 per cent.
6. Adrian Wood's *A Theory of Pay* (1978) provides the best theoretical discussion of this process with which I am familiar.
7. To be specific, my idea was that the President be allowed to set a single, uniformly-applied, forward-looking rate of indexation for cost of living in the year ahead. This single rate of discretionary prospective indexation would affect all recipients of Federal transfer payments to individuals. It would compensate for expected inflation and serve as a signal to the wage process around which inflation expectations might coalesce. Losses in the real value of such transfers due to unanticipated shocks would not be compensated, as indeed they should not be.
8. Tax-based incentive policies originated with Sidney Weintraub and Henry Wallich, the market anti-inflation plan was an idea of Abba Lerner and David Colander (see Colander (ed.) 1986).
9. Friedman's (1968) argument against such policy is aptly inept: 'If [the monetary authority] ... takes interest rates or the current unemployment percentage as the immediate criterion of policy, it will be like a space vehicle that has taken a fix on the wrong star. No matter how sensitive and sophisticated in its guiding apparatus, the space vehicle will go astray'. But surely, a space vehicle can fix a course by any star whatsoever. It is only necessary that the star be fixed and visible; the 'natural rate of unemployment' is neither.
10. See Galbraith and Darity (1994) and Rockoff (1984) for discussions of this history and related references.

REFERENCES

Adams, Charles and David Coe (1990), 'A Systems Approach to Estimating the Natural Rate of Unemployment and Potential Output for the United States', *IMF Staff Papers*, **37** (2), June: 232–93.

Akerlof, George, William T. Dickens and George Perry (1996), 'The Macroeconomics of Low Inflation', *Brookings Papers on Economic Activity*, No. 1.

Colander, David (ed.) (1986), *Incentive Based Incomes Policies: Advances in TIP and MAP*, Cambridge, MA: Ballinger Publishing.

Danziger, Sheldon and Peter Gottschalk (1995), *America Unequal*, Cambridge, MA: Harvard University Press.

Economic Report of the President (1962), Washington: Government Printing Office.

Eisner, Robert (1996), 'A New View of the NAIRU', mimeo, Northwestern University, 4 June. (Early version presented to the 7th World Econometric Congress, Tokyo, August 1995.)

Fair, Ray (1996), 'Testing the Standard View of the Long-Run Unemployment–Inflation Relationship', mimeo, Yale University, April.

Ferguson, Thomas and James K. Galbraith (1996), 'The Wage Structure, 1920–1947', mimeo.

Friedman, Milton (1968), 'The Role of Monetary Policy', *American Economic Review*, **LVIII** (1), March: 1–17.

Galbraith, James K. (1989), *Balancing Acts: Technology, Finance and the American Future*, New York: Basic Books.

Galbraith, James K. (1994), 'The Surrender of Economic Policy', *The American Prospect*, March–April: pp. 60–67.

Galbraith, James K. (1996), 'Inflation, Unemployment and the Job Structure', Jerome Levy Economics Institute Working Paper.

Galbraith, James K. (forthcoming), *The Wage Structure and the Inequality Crisis*.

Galbraith, James K. and William Darity jr (1994), *Macroeconomics*, Boston: Houghton Mifflin.

Gordon, David M. (1988), 'The Un-Natural Rate of Unemployment: An Econometric Critique of the NAIRU Hypothesis', *American Economic Review Papers and Proceedings*, May: 117–23.

Gordon, Robert J. (1996), 'The Time-Varying NAIRU and its Implications for Economic Policy', Northwestern University, Mimeo, Version of 5 July.

Hall, Robert E. (1970), 'Why is the Unemployment Rate So High at Full Employment', *Brookings Papers on Economic Activity*, No. 3: 369–402.

Hall, Robert E. (1979), 'A Theory of the Natural Unemployment Rate and the Duration of Unemployment', *Journal of Monetary Economics*, **5**, April: 153–70.

Juhn, Chinhui, Kevin M. Murphy and Robert H. Topel (1991), 'Why Has the Natural Rate of Unemployment Increased over Time', *Brookings Papers on Economic Activity*, No. 2: 75–41.

Kaldor, Nicholas (1983), *Economics Without Equilibrium*, Armonk: ME Sharpe.

Karoly, Lynn A. (1996), 'Anatomy of the U.S. Income Distribution', *Oxford Review of Economic Policy*, **12** (1): 77–96.

Keynes, John Maynard (1936), *The General Theory of Employment, Interest and Money*, London: Macmillan.

Lucas, Robert (1981), 'Tobin and Monetarism: A Review Article', *Journal of Economic Literature*, **29** (2), June: 558–85.

Perry, George (1970), 'Changing Labor Markets and Inflation', *Brookings Papers on Economic Activity*, No. 3: 141 ff.

Phelps, Edmund S. (1968), 'Money-wage Dynamics and Labor Market Equilibrium', *Journal of Political Economy*, **76** (2): 678–711.

Rockoff, Hugh (1984), *Drastic Measures: A History of Wage and Price Controls in America*, New York: Cambridge University Press.

Samuelson, Paul A. and Robert M. Solow (1960), 'Analytical Aspects of Anti-Inflation Policy', *American Economic Review*, **L**, May: 177–94.

US Department of Commerce (1995), *Census Reports*.

Wood, Adrian (1978), *A Theory of Pay*, Cambridge: Cambridge University Press.

12. Employment policy, community development and the underclass

Dimitri B. Papadimitriou

1 INTRODUCTION

The difficulties in achieving a consensus regarding the definition of the *underclass* cannot be minimized. The term was first coined by *The New Yorker* writer Ken Auletta (1982) who used it broadly to include individuals with 'behavioral and income deficiencies'. Other definitions have been advanced by the seminal works of William Julius Wilson (1987), Erol Ricketts and Isabel Sawhill (1986), Douglas Glasgow (1980), William Darity (1980), and finally Christopher Jencks (1992) who draws fine distinctions of the underclass by classifying its members into various subgroups, that is, *impoverished underclass*, *jobless underclass*, *reproductive underclass*, *educational underclass* and *violent underclass*. In this chapter, I consider as members of the underclass, individuals residing in urban centres, mostly in inner city areas. Their neighbourhoods experience concentrated poverty and joblessness, and violence, and lack community-supporting institutions. Those individuals who are employed are 'working poor' and their education is at the high-school level or below; and, a good number of them are single parents, either male or female heads of households. Finally, I include as members of the underclass, a significant fraction of the more than 45 per cent of children under 6 years of age and individuals under the age of 18, who live below the poverty line. Even though only a fraction of those living in poverty reside in these neighbourhoods – about 21 per cent of all persons and 34 per cent of blacks residing in inner city areas were below the poverty line in 1994 – escaping from there requires confronting and dealing with a plethora of insurmountable obstacles. It should be noted that the members of the underclass are not likely to include Jews, Irish or Italians (Duster 1995: 479), nor are they only African-Americans. If it were only a 'black problem', it would disregard the two-thirds of African-Americans who are not poor, and the two-thirds of the poor residing in inner city areas who are not black (Blank 1992). African-Americans are, however, overrepresented in the underclass. This chapter focuses specifically on the issue of urban poverty and the changes in the urban-poor population, and relates these changes to changes in the economic and policy landscape that has evolved over the last fifteen years. Policy lessons drawn from other industrialized countries are also reviewed. At the end, consideration is given to various proposals for public action to alleviate the problems of the underclass, including community development that can be achieved via a network of community development financial institutions.

2   URBAN POOR AND THE UNDERCLASS: 1980–1996

Over the years, the number of people living in these conditions has risen, and alarmingly so, despite the economic vitality of the Reagan and Clinton years. Early research on the relationship between the macroeconomy and poverty gave credence to the 1960s experience that 'a rising tide lifts all boats' (Blank and Blinder 1986), that is, it showed that economic growth can be expected to produce a fall of poverty via the trickle-down mechanism. The paradox of the economic turnaround is that both the fall in unemployment and the rise of GNP devoted to government transfers appear to have had 'perverse' effects on poverty over the 1980s (Blank 1993; Cutler and Katz 1991) and early 1990s. In particular, Rebecca Blank's calculations revealed that during the years 1983–89, 'for every 1 point fall in unemployment, poverty increased by 0.42 points' while 'a 1 point rise in the share of transfers in GNP was associated with a 1.58 point rise in poverty' (Blank 1993: 25). These findings contrast with other evidence indicating that at times of recession, unemployment is unequally distributed (Blank and Card 1991) and that, generally, the disadvantaged bear a larger share of the economic decline (Cutler and Katz 1991: 2). Thus, there have been a number of attempts to use the above to reinforce the view that public policy responses cannot reach the underclass, and they are wrongheaded. Tables 12.1–3, give profiles of various population groups for selected years including the Carter, Reagan, Bush and Clinton presidencies. It will be noticed, for example, in Table 12.1 that although the trend of the overall unemployment rate is declining, the corresponding rate of black unemployment is consistently two to three times higher that of white. Similarly, the rate for Hispanics is about 60 to 70 per cent higher, the rate of whites. In Table 12.2 poverty rates of various segments of the US population residing in inner city areas, outside central cities and in non-metropolitan areas are shown to experience increasing trends with the more pronounced for blacks and Hispanics. These rates document the depth of poverty among the various groups especially those belonging to the underclass. In addition, Table 12.3 relates poverty rates to the level of education for similar population groups as in Tables 12.1 and 12.2. In summary, what Tables 12.1–3 demonstrate is that the 'vulnerable' (to use a common phrase) are the jobless; they mainly reside in inner city areas and have either dropped out of high school or have just finished high school; and overwhelmingly, the corresponding trends for blacks or Hispanics have consistently been higher by more than two to three times those of whites. Finally, Table 12.4 documents the dramatically increasing trend of the 'most vulnerable' of all population groups, that is, children under 6 years and individuals under age 18. What are we to make of all this evidence? From the outset the following should be clear: neither Tables 12.1–3 nor Blank's regression analysis should be used to draw causal conclusions. Indeed, such conclusions would be misleading, if they were to be interpreted as implying that rising unemployment would be associated with decreasing poverty rates (Blank 1993: 25) or that reducing government transfers would be associated with decreasing poverty. To this, I shall return later.

Table 12.1   Unemployed workers

	1980	1985	1989	1990	1991	1992	1993	1994	1995
Unemployment rate (%)									
Total (all persons)	7.1	7.2	5.3	5.5	6.7	7.4	6.8	6.1	5.6
White									
16 to 19 years old	15.5	15.7	12.7	13.4	16.4	17.1	16.2	15.1	14.5
20 to 24 years old	9.9	9.2	7.2	7.2	9.2	9.4	8.7	8.1	7.7
25 to 34 years old	6.1	5.9	4.3	4.6	6.0	6.6	6.0	5.2	4.6
Black									
16 to 19 years old	38.5	40.2	32.4	31.1	36.3	39.8	38.9	35.2	35.7
20 to 24 years old	23.6	24.5	18.0	19.9	21.6	23.9	22.0	19.5	17.7
25 to 34 years old	13.3	14.5	11.5	11.7	12.7	14.2	12.6	11.1	9.0
Hispanic									
16 to 19 years old	22.5	24.3	19.4	19.5	22.9	27.5	26.2	24.5	24.1
20 to 24 years old	12.1	12.6	10.7	9.1	11.6	13.2	13.1	11.8	11.5
25 to 34 years old	9.1	10.0	7.0	7.3	9.2	10.4	9.3	9.9	8.2
Women maintaining families (total)								8.9	8.0
White	7.3	8.1	6.1	6.3	7.2	7.8	7.7	n/a	n/a
Black	14.0	16.4	13.0	13.1	13.9	14.7	13.7	n/a	n/a
Married men, wife present									
White	3.9	4.0	2.8	3.1	4.2	4.7	4.1	3.4	3.0
Black	7.4	8.0	5.8	6.2	6.5	8.3	7.2	6.0	5.0

Note: n/a – not available.

Sources: U.S. Bureau of Labor Statistics, Employment and Earnings Reports, and unpublished data.

Table 12.2 Persons below poverty level in metropolitan and non-metropolitan areas by race and Hispanic origin

	1980	1985	1989	1990	1991	1992	1993	1994
All persons								
Metropolitan	11.9	12.7	12.3	12.7	13.7	14.2	14.6	14.2
Central cities	17.2	19.0	18.5	19.0	20.2	20.9	21.5	20.9
Outside central cities	8.2	8.4	8.2	8.7	9.6	9.9	10.3	10.3
Non-metropolitan	15.4	18.3	15.9	16.3	16.1	16.2	17.2	16.0
White								
Metropolitan	8.8	10.1	9.4	9.9	10.6	11.1	11.4	11.1
Central cities	12.1	14.9	13.6	14.3	15.4	16.2	16.4	15.9
Outside central cities	7.0	7.4	7.1	7.6	8.2	8.5	8.9	8.9
Non-metropolitan	12.9	15.6	13.2	13.5	13.6	14.4	14.8	13.8
Black								
Metropolitan	30.1	29.1	29.1	30.1	31.6	32.1	31.9	29.8
Central cities	32.3	32.1	33.2	33.8	35.3	35.4	35.8	34.2
Outside central cities	24.3	21.7	20.3	22.2	24.4	25.5	24.6	22.3
Non-metropolitan	40.6	42.6	39.7	40.8	38.9	40.7	40.3	35.4
Hispanic								
Metropolitan	n/a	n/a	25.6	27.8	28.3	29.0	30.4	29.8
Central cities	n/a	n/a	29.8	31.7	32.9	34.0	35.0	35.0
Outside central cities	n/a	n/a	20.2	22.8	22.6	22.5	24.6	24.5
Non-metropolitan	n/a	n/a	34.6	32.0	33.9	37.2	33.4	39.7

Notes: n/a – not available. All figures are in percentages; 1994 data are not directly comparable to data from earlier years.

Sources: US Bureau of the Census, Current Population Reports, and unpublished data.

In the 1960s and earlier, the neighbourhoods in the inner cities were vibrant in terms of economic activity and social interaction, since families of various ethnic groups including African-Americans lived in these communities. As Wilson pointed out in 1987 and in his recent book (1996), there were middle-class, working-class and lower/underclass families whose values were transmitted from group to group because they all used more or less the same commercial establishments and community organizations, that is, grocery stores, banks, post offices, public schools and other public spaces. In the beginning of the 1970s, this was changed, with businesses moving from the inner city areas to the suburbs; the middle class followed, leaving the lower class behind to compete for the few left-over jobs. With the departure of the middle class, the dissolution of these communities in terms of economics and social behaviour was inevitable. Today, there are 'overwhelming obstacles that many ghetto residents have to overcome just to live up to mainstream expectations involving work, the family, and the law [which] are taken for granted in middle-class society' (Wilson 1996: xviii). The disappearance of work, Wilson argues, has had the most aggravating effect on the social and cultural life in the inner-city underclass (ibid.: xix).

Table 12.3   Poverty rates related to education for householders 25 years old and over by race and Hispanic origin

	1980	1985	1989*	1990	1991	1992*	1993	1994
All persons								
One or more yrs of college	3.7	4.0	3.6	3.8	4.3	4.7	5.2	5.2
HS graduate	8.0	9.9	9.1	9.3	10.5	11.2	11.7	10.9
Did not complete HS	18.0	20.6	20.9	21.8	24.2	24.5	25.1	24.8
White								
One or more yrs of college	3.0	3.1	2.6	2.9	3.4	3.7	4.1	4.2
HS graduate	6.4	7.9	7.0	6.9	7.8	8.5	8.6	8.5
Did not complete HS	14.1	17.2	16.8	17.6	20.0	19.7	20.6	20.6
Black								
One or more yrs of college	12.0	13.7	12.3	12.0	12.2	14.3	15.0	10.3
HS graduate	22.7	25.0	23.4	26.2	30.0	28.7	31.4	26.0
Did not complete HS	37.0	36.4	39.3	40.6	41.4	44.7	44.4	40.1
Hispanic								
One or more yrs of college	8.1	8.6	8.2	9.3	9.6	10.9	10.5	10.7
HS graduate	14.1	15.0	16.4	15.0	18.8	19.8	23.5	20.7
Did not complete HS	31.0	34.0	31.4	34.0	36.1	35.8	37.2	38.0

Notes: All figures are in percentages.
       *Revised data.

Sources: US Bureau of the Census, Current Population Reports, and unpublished data.

Table 12.4   Children under age 6 and individuals under 18 below poverty level by race and Hispanic origin

	1980	1985	1989	1990	1991	1992	1993	1994
All persons								
Under age 6	20.7	23.0	22.5	23.6	24.6	25.7	25.6	24.5
Under age 18	18.3	20.7	20.1	20.6	21.8	22.3	22.7	21.8

Table 12.4   continued

	1980	1985	1989	1990	1991	1992	1993	1994
White								
Under age 6	16.0	18.3	16.9	18.4	19.2	20.1	20.1	19.0
Under age 18	13.9	16.2	15.1	15.9	16.8	17.4	17.8	16.9
Black								
Under age 6	45.8	47.7	49.8	51.0	51.7	53.1	51.7	49.1
Under age 18	42.3	43.6	43.8	44.8	45.9	46.6	46.1	43.8
Hispanic								
Under age 6	34.6	41.4	38.8	40.7	44.6	42.7	43.4	43.9
Under age 18	33.2	40.3	36.2	38.4	40.4	40.0	40.9	41.5

Notes: All figures are in percentages; 1994 data are not directly comparable to data from earlier years.

Sources: US Bureau of the Census, Current Population Reports, unpublished data, March 1995, prior reports.

3   CHANGING ECONOMIC LANDSCAPE

There is more or less a general understanding that the American economy is offering fewer and fewer high-paying jobs, and very grim prospects for the unskilled. In the new structure of an increasingly integrated international economy, where capital, technology and even labour are becoming mobile, our living standards may depend on the American factories of foreign corporations, the non-domestic factories of American corporations, foreign workers employed by American corporations or foreign corporations operating outside America. Our economy is global and we are global citizens. Until recently, the only American manufacturer of televisions produced them in Mexico; while a significant number of our engineers and designers involved in R&D relating to new generations of televisions, who work in America, do not work for American manufacturers. Their employers are Japanese, French or Dutch firms. The McDonnell–Douglas airplane is not an American plane and the Airbus is not a European plane. The evolving structure of the US economy does not necessarily imply that the educated and technically adept are immune from dislocation, as technological advances in automation, new work processes and spatial conditions dramatically change how work is performed. But it does mean that those educated beyond high school and prepared for careers in managerial, professional and technical occupations are and will be the beneficiaries of opportunities and rewards which will be further increased by continued on-the-job training and experience. In contrast, the less prepared are finding an unwelcoming job market. This is especially prevalent among the residents of inner city areas where the old-fashioned factory system and other employment opportunities have either moved out to the suburbs or disappeared altogether, with the remaining jobs for the unskilled being much too few to match the number of those seeking to fill them (Newman 1996).

Robert Reich, Labor Secretary in the Clinton Administration, talks frequently about the existence of an anxious class and the need for government activism to combat it. This anxiety, as the recently published CED report on 'American Workers and Economic Change' (CED 1996) suggests, is the result of the realization that a number of our social and economic institutions, whether they be those that prepare us for work, sustain us during our working lives or provide for our retirement, are obsolete. There is, therefore, a need to rethink the institutional structures of the public and private sectors. The report also urges that 'opportunities to acquire and develop skills [cannot be] unequal, [since] those without such opportunities will be left further and further behind'. And 'this is ... an enormous waste of human resources' (ibid.: 12). It is apparent, then, that both the private and public sectors recognize the necessity to implement policies that expand economic opportunity, promote and ensure equal access to education and professional development, and provide resources required to do so effectively.

Stimulative government policies usually involve a multitude of goals in addition to employment growth. These include the balance in the federal budget and international payments, the maintenance of price stability and the fostering of investment. We have witnessed that policies enacted to enhance macroeconomic activity have not always achieved prosperity for all segments of our citizenry. We are left, then, with the question of whether national policy can ameliorate poverty and improve the human condition of low-income households or the underclass. If so, what would be the sort of policy levers that can be effectively used? Darity and Myers (1994: 36) suggest that policies can be effective if, and only if, 'members of the underclass have attitudes that are completely adaptable to changes in their economic circumstances' while Wilson (1987, 1996) is unequivocal in that an expanding economy is the requisite for eliminating the underclass. An expanding economy, however, without specifically targeted policies, is not necessarily a guarantee to address the needs of the underclass; as was mentioned earlier, the decade of the 1980s may have been a time of relative prosperity, but the evidence shows it has had no impact on the disadvantaged. A different interpretation of the lessons to be drawn from the 1980s, as suggested by David Cutler and Lawrence Katz (1991), 'may well be that appropriate transfer policies for the disadvantaged can be important in enhancing outcomes for the poor, in times of both weak and strong macroeconomic performance'.

4   EXPERIENCE FROM OTHER COUNTRIES

Policy lessons drawn from the experiences of other industrialized countries may not be very straightforward, but, nevertheless, may be instructive. The evidence taken from the experience of government programmes in other developed countries is overwhelmingly positive. For example, Table 12.5 details the effect of government programmes in ameliorating child poverty. These programmes include: (i) broader child tax allowances than in the United States, including cash allowances to low-wage-earning families, (ii) subsidized paid-for child care, (iii) universal health care, and (iv) child support when fathers will not pay. Clearly, the statistics on the condition of children in poverty show that the US has the worst record of any of the other industrialized countries. It should be noted that in concert with the American experience many other countries also have a high incidence of single parents. In Sweden, France and the Netherlands, for example, single-mother families as a percentage of all families with children for the years shown in Table 12.5 were 15 per cent, 7 per cent, and 10 per cent respectively, while in the US single mothers represented 19 per cent of families with children.

Table 12.5   Children under age 6 at poverty level and effect of government programmes

Country	Before (%)	After (%)
United States (1991)	25.9	21.5
Australia (1989)	19.6	14.0
Canada (1991)	22.5	13.5
Ireland (1987)	30.2	12.0
Israel (1986)	23.9	11.1
United Kingdom (1986)	29.6	9.9
Italy (1991)	11.5	9.6
Germany (1989)	9.0	6.8
France (1984)	25.4	6.5
Netherlands (1991)	13.7	6.2
Norway (1991)	12.9	4.6
Luxembourg (1985)	11.7	4.1
Belgium (1992)	16.2	3.8
Denmark (1992)	16.0	3.3
Switzerland (1982)	5.1	3.3
Sweden (1992)	19.1	2.7
Finland (1991)	11.5	2.5

Note: Dates of latest data used in parentheses; government programs include: child tax credits, day care credits, health care and child support when fathers will not pay.

Sources: Luxembourg Income Study, 1995.

Table 12.6*   Estimated effect of 'average' Canadian transfer system on US poverty

	Poverty rate (%)
All families	
Actual	13.5
Simulated under average	
Canadian transfer system	
assuming least-elastic	9.4
labour-supply responses	
assuming most-elastic	9.5
labour-supply responses	
Single-head families with children	
Actual	45.3
Simulated under average	
Canadian transfer system	
assuming least-elastic	15.8
labour-supply responses	
assuming most-elastic	16.2
labour-supply responses	

Notes: 'Average' Canadian transfer system is a population-weighted average of systems in various Canadian provinces. Labour-supply response parameters are taken from range of estimates obtained in the Seattle–Denver Income Maintenance Experiment. Estimates assume that programme participation rates for eligible families equal actual participation rates among eligible Canadian families.

Source: Blank and Hanratty (1993: Table 10).

Acknowledgement: * Table 6.4 reprinted from *Working Under Different Rules*, Richard B. Freeman, editor, © 1994 Russell Sage Foundation, New York, New York. Reprinted with permission of Russell Sage Foundation.

The Canadian experience is also instructive because it shows convincingly that positive outcomes of income support programmes can be obtained. The Canadian transfer system raises more people out of poverty than does the American income maintenance system. In Table 12.6, the simulations by Blank and Hanratty (Card and Freeman 1994), quantify the effects that the Canadian transfer system would have on American poverty. It will be noticed that the simulations show that

1. the poverty rates among all American families would be reduced by 30 per cent, and

2. the poverty rates among single-parent families with children would be reduced by 60 per cent (Card and Freeman 1994: 212).

Obviously, one would want to know the cost of the Canadian transfer system. This is given in Table 12.7, which compares both the Canadian and American transfer payments programmes in terms of GNP for needs-based cash and non-cash transfers to non-elderly, unemployment insurance, and cash-based child support programmes. The differences in costs throughout the period covered in the table are dramatic, but so are the results in income and poverty outcomes (ibid.: 217).

Table 12.7* *Transfer programme expenditures in the United States and Canada, 1960–1990*

	Programme expenditures as a percentage of GNP						
	1960	1965	1970	1975	1980	1985	1990[a]
1. Needs-based transfers, including for disabilities[b] Can.:	0.66	0.98	1.37	1.69	1.76	2.15	2.20
US:	0.80	0.89	1.10	1.72	1.70	1.40	1.30
2. Unemployment insurance Can.:	1.22	0.54	0.78	1.81	1.28	2.13	1.77
US	0.59	0.44	0.38	0.87	0.68	0.46	0.32
3. Child programmes: tax credits and family allowance[c] Can.:	1.36	1.05	0.63	1.06	0.86	0.82	0.77
US	—	—	—	0.06	0.05	0.04	0.09
4. Sum of three programmes Can:	3.24	2.57	2.78	4.56	3.90	5.10	4.74
US	1.39	1.33	1.48	2.65	2.43	1.90	1.71

Notes
[a] 1990 data for Canada; 1989 data for US.
[b] Canadian data includes expenditures under Canada Assistance Program and earlier programmes for disabled people, as well as provincial and municipal welfare. US data include Aid to Families with Dependent Children (AFDC), Supplemental Security Income (SSI), Food Stamps, general assistance and other categorical payments under the Social Security Act, *excluding* Medicaid expenditures.
[c] Canadian data includes Family Allowance and Child Tax Credit. US data include refunded portion of Earned Income Tax Credit.

Sources: Statistics Canada, *Canada Year Book*, Ottawa: Statistics Canada, 1980–81, 1991 editions; Social Security Administration, *Social Security Bulletin Annual Statistical Supplement*, Washington, DC: GPO, 1991; Committee on Ways and Means, US House of Representatives, *1992 Green Book*, Washington, DC: GPO, 1992.

Acknowledgement: * Table 6.5 reprinted from *Working Under Different Rules*, Richard B. Freeman, editor, © 1994 Russell Sage Foundation, New York, New York. Reprinted with permission of Russell Sage Foundation.

5   POLICY INITIATIVES AND COMMUNITY DEVELOPMENT

Anti-poverty policies aimed at the problems of the urban underclass are needed to supplement traditional fiscal policies. Notwithstanding the need to create jobs, policies must be directed towards enhancing human capital and encouraging work effort among those in poverty. These policies should include public assistance programmes that prepare individuals for work or provide incentives for work and income support, such as an expanded EITC (Earned Income Tax Credit), wage subsidies and children allowances; other policies should promote early childhood development and assistance, and preschool and compensatory education. All these strategies can be achieved if, and only if, the present trend of reducing the spending on existing and new social programmes is reversed. Proposals for new initiatives have ranged from Danziger and Gottschalk's creation of a low-skill and jobless workers' minimum-wage public sector jobs programme (1995) to Edward V. Regan's public-investment infrastructure maintenance programme for unskilled and jobless workers (1994). These and other similar proposals, that is, Mickey Kaus's Works Progress Administration (WPA-like) public works jobs programme, can match the demand side of jobs to the supply side of disqualified welfare recipients in the 'ending welfare as we know it' debate, and help reverse the economic and social decay of the inner city (Kaus 1992).

Finally, targeted neighbourhood programmes, such as community development banks, are essential for the revitalization of economically distressed communities. Commercial banks are unwilling to provide financial services for low-income, low-wealth businesses and households. There is evidence suggesting that traditional banks perceive loans to micro-sized businesses and low-income households as risky especially if there is no previous banking relationship. Furthermore, as the costs of attracting deposits rise, so do the fees on non-interest-bearing cheque accounts (from about $27 to $35 in 1977 at 1991 prices to $60 to $66 by 1991). Rising fees and no access to credit have forced a segment of the population, especially those residing in inner cities, out of the traditional banking system.

Many of those who have left the banking system have turned to 'fringe banking' – primarily pawnshops and cheque-cashing facilities. John Caskey (1993) reports that in 1993, about 41 per cent of households with income below $12,000 had no deposit account (up from 9.5 per cent in 1977). Most users of cheque-cashing outlets are low-income workers or recipients of government transfers, and they tend to be young and non-white. In a study of three New Jersey counties, it was found that almost half of all AFDC (Aid to Families with Dependent Children) cheques issued in the counties were cashed at cheque-cashing facilities. The fees charged vary, but they can be exorbitant –1.5 per cent to as high as 15 per cent – and depend on the type of cheque cashed, location and whether the cheque-cashing facility operates in a state that regulates such fees (Caskey 1993). Since these individuals do not usually have credit cards or any access to other type of credit, they are forced to pawn their valuables as collateral against loans. The typical user of a pawnshop earns $8,000 to $16,000 per year, lives from 'hand to mouth', has no credit card, and borrows less than $50 at an interest rate that commonly reaches 240 per cent per year; 80 per cent of the customers are repeat users, caught in this costly cycle of pawning valuables at very high interest rates.

A community development bank (CDB) could provide an efficient and equitable alternative to expensive fringe banking. It would also offer a safe and secure repository for small savings, and it could use the funds of the community as a basis for loans to the community, playing a most important role in that community's stabilization and economic development. The establishment of a nationwide network of CDBs would provide the means to enhance the welfare of low-income citizens, inner-city minorities, and entrepreneurs seeking small-scale financing for their business. Shorebank Corporation is a successful community development bank, and the oldest. It is a holding company that includes South Shore Bank, a real estate development corporation, a small venture capital firm, and the Neighborhood Institute, which offers among its services low-income housing development, remedial education and vocational training. Many more Community Development Financial Institutions (CDFIs) have been established, some more successful than others, but all providing needed financial services to targeted communities.

The plight of communities suffering because of job loss, deteriorating housing, lack of private enterprise and declining 'economic and social infrastructure' has been labelled a central concern by Washington. The enacted 'Community Development Financial Institutions Act of 1994' tacitly implies the inability of the private sector to independently alter the downward slide of poor communities. Private investors and would-be entrepreneurs are leery about making financial commitments to areas burdened by chronic poverty and social volatility. There is an urgent need to carry out the provisions of the CDFI Act, especially in the provision of adequate funding. Access to lending and other banking services is an essential missing link to the revitalization of distressed communities. Although CDBs cannot be seen as a major factor in the growth of the economy they are, nevertheless, appropriate responses that fill the gap in the current institutional structure, and may well provide part of the setting in which a climate of opportunity replaces despair for many segments of the population, including the underclass.

Robert Reischauer the former CBO director, quoted in Darity and Myers (1994), has noted: '[Americans] are a nation attracted to the quick fix, to policies that promise instant solutions to difficult problems. The complexity of the underclass problem suggests that this is a dilemma that will not disappear soon. Nor will it wither in response to a single policy intervention'.

Do I believe that targeted policies can be, in general, successful, if policy makers are prepared to wait for incremental positive outcomes? I think so. The lessons from other countries and the incremental improvement resulting from tried policies in years past, seem to call rather convincingly for the adoption and implementation of the proposed policy initiatives.

REFERENCES

Auletta, K. (1982), *The Underclass*, New York: Random House.

Blank, R.M. (1992), 'Social Scientists and the Problem of Poverty', *The Chronicle of Higher Education*, 5 August: B1–2.

Blank, R.M. (1993), 'Why were Poverty Rates so High in the 1980s?', in Papadimitriou and Wolff (eds) (1993): pp. 21–5.

Blank, R.M. and A.S. Blinder (1986), 'Macroeconomics, Income Distribution, and Poverty', in S. Danziger and D. Weinberg (eds), *Fighting Poverty*, Cambridge, MA: Harvard University Press: pp. 180–208.

Blank, R.M. and David Card (1991), 'Recent Trends in Insured and Uninsured Unemployment: Is There An Explanation?', *Quarterly Journal of Economics*, **106**, November: 1157–90.

Card, D. and R.B. Freeman (1993), 'Small Differences that Matter: Canada vs. the United States', in R.B. Freeman (ed.), *Working Under Different Rules,* New York: Russell Sage Foundation: pp. 189–222.

Caskey, John (1993), 'Banks, Check-Cashing Outlets, Pawnshops, and the Poor', manuscript, January.

Committee on Economic Development (CED) (1996), 'American Workers and Economic Change: A Statement by the Research and Policy Committee of the Committee for Economic Development', New York.

Cutler, D.M. and L.F. Katz (1991), 'Macroeconomic Performance and the Disadvantaged', *Brookings Papers on Economic Activity*, (1991) 2.

Danziger, Sheldon H. and Peter Gottschalk (1995), *America Unequal*, Cambridge, MA: Harvard University Press.

Darity jr., William A. (1980), 'The Class Character of the Black Community: Polarization Between the Black Managerial Elite and the Black Underclass', *The Black Law Journal*, **7**: 21–30.

Darity jr., William A. and Samuel L. Myers jr. (1994), *The Black Underclass*, New York: Garland Publishing, Inc.

Duster, Troy (1995), 'Postindustrialization and Youth Unemployment: African Americans as Harbingers', in K. McFate, R. Lawson and W.J. Wilson (eds), *Poverty, Inequality and the Future of Social Policy*, New York: Russell Sage Foundation: pp. 461–85.

Glasgow, D.G. (1980), *The Black Underclass: Poverty, Unemployment and the Entrapment of Ghetto Youth*, San Francisco: Jossey-Bass.

Gornick, Janet, Marcia K. Meyers and R. Katherin Ross (1996), 'Supporting the Employment of Mothers: Policy Variation Across Fourteen Welfare States', Luxembourg Income Study, Working Paper No. 139, October.

Gornick, Janet, Marcia K. Meyers and R. Katherin Ross (1996), 'Public Policies and the Employment of Mothers: A Cross-national Study', Luxembourg Income Study, Working Paper No. 140, June.

Jencks, Christopher (1992), *Rethinking Social Policy: Race, Poverty, and the Underclass*, Cambridge, MA: Harvard University Press.

Kaus, Mickey (1992), *The End of Equality*, New York: Basic Books.

Newman, Katherine S. (1996), 'Working Poor: Low Wage Employment in the lives of Harlem Youth', in J. Graber, J. Brooks-Gunn and A. Petersen (eds), *Transitions Through Adolescence: Interpersonal Domains and Context*, Mahwah, NJ: Erlbaum Associates Publishers: pp. 323–44.

Papadimitriou, D.B. (ed.) (1994), *Aspects of Distribution of Wealth and Income*, New York: St. Martin's Press.

Papadimitriou, D.B., R. Phillips and L.R. Wray (1993), 'A Path to Community Development', *Public Policy Brief*, No. 6, Jerome Levy Economics Institute.

Papadimitriou, D.B. and E.N. Wolff (eds) (1993), *Poverty and Prosperity in the USA in the Late Twentieth Century*, New York: St. Martin's Press.

Regan, E.V. (1994), 'Infrastructure Investment for Tomorrow', *Public Policy Brief*, No. 16, Jerome Levy Economics Institute.

Ricketts, Erol and Isabel Sawhill (1986), *Defining and Measuring the Underclass*, Washington, DC: Urban Institute Press.

Russell, Cheryl and Margaret Ambry (1993), *The Official Guide to American Incomes*, Ithaca, NY: New Strategist Publications.

Sawhill, Isabel (1994), 'Income Inequality and the Underclass', in Papadimitriou (ed.) (1994): pp. 194–8.

US Bureau of the Census (1992), Current Population Reports, Poverty in the United States: 1991, Series P–60, No. 181, Washington: US Government Printing Office.

US Bureau of the Census (1996), Current Population Reports, Income, Poverty and Valuation of Noncash Benefits: 1994, Series P–60, No. 189, Washington: US Government Printing Office.

US Bureau of the Census (1996), Current Population Reports, Dynamics of Economic Well-Being: Poverty, 1992–1993, Series P–70, No. 55, June, Washington: US Government Printing Office.

US Bureau of the Labor Statistics (1992), Employment and Earnings, January, Washington: US Government Printing Office.

US Bureau of the Labor Statistics, Current Population Survey, unpublished tabulations, annual averages for 1994 and 1995.

Wilson, William Julius (1987), *The Truly Disadvantaged: The Inner City, The Underclass, and Public Policy*, Chicago: University of Chicago Press.

Wilson, William Julius (1996), *When Work Disappears*, New York: Alfred A. Knopf.

PART III

Keynes and Economic Development

13. Imported capital goods and the small open economy

Penny Hawkins[*]

1 INTRODUCTION

In a Keynesian model of a closed economy, investment determines the level of employment. Investment is exogenous to the model; income and employment adjust to investment. Hence in a closed Keynesian model, investment is the *causa causans*, to which other variables adjust. In a small open economy, which is reliant on imported capital goods, such as South Africa, adjustment to a current account deficit on the balance of payments takes place via a dampening of investment (Kahn 1992: 81). Hence, in a small open economy, investment adjusts to the balance of payments. This appears to turn the Keynesian causality on its head.

The chapter attempts to show that the causal role of investment is dependent on the income adjustment process which follows a change in investment. The nature of the income adjustment process depends on the openness of the model, and on whether the domestic capital goods sector meets the requirements of investors.

Section 2 will begin by presenting a definition of a small open economy, thereafter, the role of investment in a small open economy where investment involves imported capital goods will be examined. It emerges that a multiplier different from the traditional foreign trade multiplier is needed to explain the income adjustment process in the open model and that the influence of the balance of payments cannot be ignored. In Section 3, the model developed in section 2 will be related to the South African economy.

2 INCOME ADJUSTMENT IN A SMALL OPEN ECONOMY WHICH IMPORTS CAPITAL GOODS

The term SOE (small open economy) is often employed in the monetarist approach to the balance of payments. In the monetarist model, an SOE cannot influence its terms of trade but, like a perfectly competitive firm, can sell all it wants at the going price. In the monetarist model, the adjustment of the domestic price level or exchange rate ensures the neutrality of the balance of payments in the long run. In this view, a deficit on the current account of the balance of payments may be the desirable consequences of capital movements based on the decisions of rational individuals (Pitchford 1990: 76). This is essentially a microeconomic approach – private transactions are assumed to be self-financing, and the potential cost to the level of output and employment in the economy are ignored (Coutts and Godley 1992: 66). The importance of the balance of payments to the sustainable growth rate is well established in post Keynesian theory (Thirlwall 1979 and McCombie 1993) and it is from this viewpoint that a definition of the small open economy is sought.

Definitions of country size can be divided into two groups: those that classify small countries by virtue of a physical resource and those that identify economic features associated with smallness. These shall be referred to as the resource constraint and the analytic approaches, respectively.

In the resource constraint approach, production is seen as resource or supply constrained. A country is small because its resource endowment is small. The aim is to identify those resources which limit the country's production potential. Most often, population size is used as a classifier. Population limits of five million (Lloyd and Sundrum 1982: 19) to twenty million (Harberger 1988: 249) are employed in the literature. However, the use of population is not always the most appropriate measure of country size and the resource constraint perspective of the economic problem may be considered inadequate.

An alternative approach, the analytic approach, aims to identify economic features associated with smallness. Both Bhaduri et al. (1982: 49–68) and Prachowny (1975: 1) use openness as the basis for identifying small countries. Openness refers to the degree to which countries engage in international trade and are affected by the vagaries of world trade, that is, it is the ratio of foreign trade to national income. Openness may be seen as a manifestation of the supply and demand limitations of a small economy. Hence small economies are open economies. The SOE faces externally determined prices for its exports and imports, as it is considered to contribute only a negligible proportion to the world demand or supply of any commodity. Although some small countries may exert a degree of monopoly power in the export market for certain goods, they are unlikely to exert monopsony power in the import market, and are thus far more likely to be price takers than makers (Prachowny 1973: 215).

The analytic approach emerges as the most appropriate classification approach for this study, for two reasons: first, it identifies *economic* characteristics of the small economy; second, South Africa is the focus of study. Although South Africa has been grouped with small open economies (see, for example, Mohr, 1993: 26 and Nattrass 1991: 30), with a population of forty million in 1992, the resource-constraint definition discussed above would clearly not accommodate South Africa.

As background to the SOE model where imports are capital goods, the role of investment in a closed economy and an open economy where imports are for consumption, will be briefly sketched. In a closed economy, an increase in autonomous investment will result in the expansion of income (and by implication, employment) by virtue of the multiplier. The income adjustment process is the playing out of the multiplier set off by the initial impetus in autonomous expenditure, in this case, investment.

An autonomous increase in domestic expenditure in an economy open to trade will stimulate expenditure on both domestic and imported goods. The greater the propensity to import from new income, the smaller will be the impact on domestic output, and hence the smaller the foreign trade multiplier. The stimulation of domestic expenditure will lead to the multiplier process resulting in a new level of income and employment. The increase in imports will raise income and output abroad, encouraging employment in the foreign trade partners (Keynes 1936: 120). This stimulus of foreign employment by our import expenditure may encourage secondary export demand for domestic goods and services. These are referred to as feedback effects. There are two distinctions between a large economy trading with the rest of the world and a small open economy which imports only consumption goods. First, the foreign sector plays a larger role in the SOE (it is relatively more open), and the feedback effects from exporting the multiplier effects to trading partners are negligible (as the SOE is likely to export primary, and hence income-inferior, goods – so the feedback effects from higher world income are likely to be small).

If investment in an SOE which imports only consumption goods increases, and the multiplier effect results in imports for consumption growing faster than exports, the balance of payments will come under pressure. Pressure on the balance of payments can be dealt with by expenditure-switching and expenditure-absorbing policies. Expenditure switching involves a devaluation of the domestic currency so that home produce is cheap relative to foreign produce. This should encourage a shift of consumption away from foreign goods. The success of the policy will depend on the relative elasticities of import and export demand. For this reason, expenditure switching is often accompanied by an expenditure-absorbing policy where fiscal and monetary policy are used to dampen economic expansion.

In both the closed economy and the small open economy which imports only consumption goods, an increase in autonomous investment results in a new higher level of income and employment. Hence investment is stimulatory. Both of these models neglect imports of capital goods. This means, as Serven (1995: 80) suggests, that the impact of import prices on investment decisions is ignored. In addition, as this chapter would like to show, the income adjustment process resulting from these investment decisions is different from that promised by the closed model, or the open model, where only consumption goods are imported.

The neglect of imports of capital goods may be seen as a reflection of the absorption of conventional macroeconomics with 'large country' theory. Openness, in the sense of reliance on the foreign sector, and the composition of imports are neglected in many undergraduate texts (Dornbusch and Fischer 1984; Lipsey et al. 1987: 508; McConnell 1987: 240–66; and Stiglitz 1993: 753). This neglect persists in spite of the criticism levelled at the appropriateness of the foreign trade multiplier for open economies (Kennedy and Thirlwall 1979). In the traditional conception of the foreign trade multiplier, imports are viewed as a function of income, with the marginal propensity to import given by m. Hence the change in income resulting from an initial change in autonomous expenditure is of the form: $1/(1 - c + m)$; where c represents the marginal propensity to consume. Kennedy and Thirlwall (1979: 173) argue that this formulation is only appropriate in the unlikely event that the import coefficients are the same for all components of autonomous expenditure. In the traditional foreign multiplier, imports often implicitly represent consumption imports alone, as the explanation for induced import expenditure is associated with increased consumption demand. Even in cases where the explanation for induced imports includes intermediate inputs of the production process (as seen in Galbraith and Darity 1994: 352), imports are still depicted as a function of income, and the foreign trade multiplier remains unaltered.

Kennedy and Thirlwall (1979: 175) relate imports to each item of autonomous expenditure. If autonomous consumption-, investment-, government- and export expenditure each have an import component, the import content of the muliplicand becomes explicit in the multiplier. For example, change in income resulting from an autonomous change in investment is of the form: $1 - mi /(1 - c (1 - mc))$; where mi represents the import coefficient of investment and mc the import coefficient of induced consumption. The input–output formulation of the open economy multiplier makes it explicit that the income effects of changes in different items of autonomous expenditure may differ (ibid.: 173). This challenges the implicit assumption in the foreign trade multiplier that these coefficients are the same.

In the empirical examination of their model, Kennedy and Thirlwall suggest that small open countries are more likely to have import coefficients which differ substantially for different items of expenditure and that imports of these countries are less likely to be restricted to consumption goods alone (ibid.: 179). This suggests that although the foreign trade multiplier may be used in discussions of open economies which import only consumption goods, the input–output formulation of the multiplier more accurately reflects the (potentially less stimulatory) multiplier effects of autonomous investment expenditure when capital goods are imported.

In a small open economy which imports its capital goods, investment may be self-defeating rather than stimulatory (Casar and Ros 1983: 257). The process of importing capital goods fails to stimulate domestic effective demand and the effect of investment on the level of employment is not realized. Casar and Ros base their analysis on a country without a fully developed capital goods sector, and whose exports are largely primary goods. The primary goods export sector is seen as slow growing of stagnant (ibid.: 259). The lack of a domestic capital goods sector means that capital goods have to be imported. As capital goods are imported, the investment sector of the trading nations is stimulated. This sets up a multiplier process in the trading nation since income and employment increase, prompting an increase in consumption, and hence an increase in the production of the consumption sector. A new equilibrium level of income is established in the trading nation. This suggests that the stimulation resulting from the increase in investment expenditure benefits the trading nation. Back home, the imported capital goods increase future productive capacity, but effective demand for this capacity is not forthcoming. In the closed economy model, an increase in investment stimulated the demand for currently produced consumption goods. This demand emanated from those employed in the investment sector. However, in the small open economy, where capital goods are not ordered from the domestic investment sector, such demand is not forthcoming. Investment expenditure fails to stimulate effective demand for current production. Utilization of productive potential is deficient. To the degree that investment involves imported capital goods, the multiplicand of the multiplier process is exported (Stolper 1964: 132).

If investment involves some purchases from the domestic capital goods sector, and domestic demand is stimulated, part of this demand is lost to trading nations in the form of imports for consumption purposes; so the input–output formulation of the multiplier applies. Furthermore, repercussion effects resulting from the stimulation of trading partners are assumed to be minimal, as it is unlikely that demand for domestic primary goods will grow as a result of increased foreign income. Hence, when imports are capital goods, investment fails to stimulate employment and short-term expectations will be disappointed, which may result in the revision of production and employment plans. To the extent that short-term disappointment affects long-term expectations and animal spirits (Kregel 1976: 221), orders for investment goods will decline. The increase in the capital stock resulting from investment, tends to depress the rate of profit (Casar and Ros 1983: 262). The fall in the rate of profit can be stemmed by the government – if it stimulates effective demand without increasing productive capacity. The cost of this intervention, however, is a worsening of trade and fiscal deficits – implying that the intervention cannot continue indefinitely. The problem which initially appeared to be a lack of effective demand resulting from investment in imported capital goods is now transformed into a balance of payments crisis (ibid.: 263).

Casar and Ros's model of an open economy, resembles the problem identified in the Harrod–Domar growth theories. The Harrod–Domar growth models identify the problem of the dual role of investment. While investment adds to aggregate demand, it also increases productive capacity. The Keynesian model is essentially restricted to the short term; but Harrod and Domar seek to investigate the long-term results of investment (Jones 1975: 65), and so are compelled to face the effects of capital accumulation on employment. Domar (1946: 139) argues that the Keynesian system recognizes the income-generating capacity of investment, but ignores its productive capacity.

Although Harrod and Domar are concerned with the long-term growth process, and Casar and Ros with the implications of importing capital goods on the income adjustment process, they are essentially concerned with the same problem. In both models, effective demand may not be adequate. In the Harrod–Domar model, effective demand is seen as potentially inadequate to buy the products which may be produced if productive capacity is used to its full potential. In Casar and Ros's model, investment expenditure fails to stimulate domestic effective demand, while productive capacity is imported. In both models, investment is endogenous.

When investment involves capital good imports, the potential for conflict between the balance of payments equilibrium and other national policy objectives becomes apparent. Investment is necessary for full employment, but investment requires imports. In this case, the importation of the means by which expansion can be made possible causes the current account deficit.

Consider a small open economy which import capital and intermediate goods. Autonomous investment expenditure increases. This stimulates imports, and the import bill increases relative to export receipts, resulting in a current account deficit. A deficit will result in adjustment: under a *floating exchange rate* system, a current account deficit will put pressure on the exchange rate, since there will be excess demand for foreign exchange. The value of the domestic currency will fall. Depending on the elasticity of demand for imports, demand for imports may drop off as the price of foreign exchange continues to increase. Where investment decisions depend on the availability and price of imported capital goods, investment expenditure may fall. This suggests that it is not the exchange rate alone which adjusts to shocks on the balance of payments, but that investment also adjusts. In a situation of a *managed float*, the exchange rate may be supported by the intervention of the monetary authorities. Intervention is possible only if the reserve bank has stocks of foreign currency to sell to the market to attempt to meet the excess demand. If stocks are sufficient to meet the current flow demand, intervention in the market may be successful. If stocks are deemed to be inadequate, then the monetary authorities may resort to contractionary policy. This often implies an increase in the interest rate.

As Dow (1986: 252) suggests, short-term capital flows work to exacerbate the depreciation in the exchange rate or deterioration in foreign exchange reserves. As imports grow, relative to exports, short-term capital will flow out, in response to an expected currency depreciation, or an expected downturn in the economy. In either case, the very time that economies require international liquidity to sustain the income adjustment process triggered by the increased investment, is when it is least likely to be available (ibid.: 255). The forced adjustment will affect all planned investment, including that which may not involve imported capital goods. Although all domestic expenditure may be affected by an increase in the interest rate, the major effect will be borne by investment, as of the components of aggregate demand, it is the most sensitive to interest rates, and second, since it is investment expenditure which caused the deficit, investment is the target of policy measures. As investment starts falling, pressure on the current account will be relieved.

Under both exchange rate regimes, investment is dampened as the current account comes under pressure; either by price effects as the domestic currency depreciates, or by an increase in the interest rate. If one assumes that investment expenditure would involve some domestic input, then stimulation of the economy is preempted by the reduction in investment expenditure. If domestic orders are cancelled, expectations of entrepreneurs will be negatively affected and jobs will be lost, or not created, resulting in lower income levels. The contraction in investment demand also has negative implications for technological progress and export competitiveness (Thirlwall 1979: 46), but these effects are not examined here.

3 IMPORTED CAPITAL GOODS AND INVESTMENT IN SOUTH AFRICA

Openness, like size, is a relative concept. There is no clear-cut measure of classifying economies as closed or open, there is simply a continuum of openness (Prachowny 1985: 235). An economy is closed if it does not have external trading partners. Openness reflects the foreign proportion of a country's economic activity, or the foreign product value in domestic expenditure (Davidson 1994: 204). This may be measured by the ratios of imports to gross domestic expenditure (GDE), and exports to gross domestic product (GDP). The comparison of imports to GDE arises from the convention that excludes imports from GDP, but includes imports in the value of GDE. In some cases, the *sum* of exports to GDP and imports to GDE is used as an indication of the extent to which the foreign sector influences the domestic economy. Mohr and Rogers

(1991: 53), however, suggest that the *average* of the ratios of exports to GDP
and imports to GDE should be used as the measure of openness. The export and
import values should include both goods and services, since the foreign
involvement in both these areas affects the measure of openness. An economy
may be regarded as open if this average ratio is greater than 20 per cent
(Prachowny 1985: 235).

Figure 13.1 shows the ratios of exports to GDP and imports to GDE in
nominal prices for South Africa during the period 1970–95; as well as the
average of the two ratios. Non-factor services have been used in the calculation
of these ratios since the denominators, GDP and GDE, are domestic concepts.

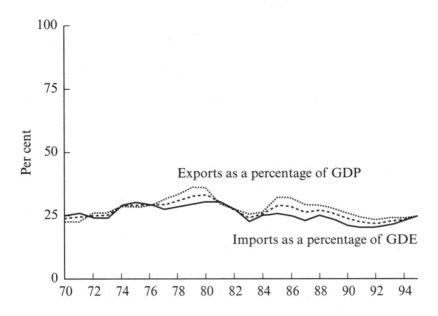

Source: SARB, *Quarterly Bulletin*.

Figure 13.1   The openness of the South African economy (at current prices)

The stability of the share of imports in GDE, seen in Figure 13.1, has been
a feature of the South African economy since the 1920s. This is despite a
policy of import substitution being implemented from as early as 1924 (McCarthy
1988: 9). Since the ratio of imports to GDE has not changed, the composition
of imports may have changed. Over the past two decades, the foreign sector has
accounted for about 25 per cent of South African domestic activity and on this
score, South Africa may be considered a small open economy.

Small open economies are seem as 'dependent' (Swan 1960: 51). Dow (1986: 253) refers to the 'export-dependent' economy. The most important feature of dependency in this study is the reliance of SOEs on imports, particularly imports of capital goods. Many SOEs are unable to engage in import substitution of capital goods because of scale difficulties. For this reason, SOEs tend to export

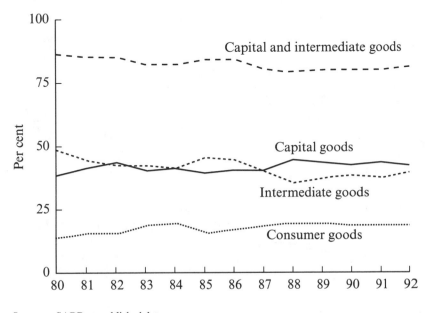

Source: SARB, unpublished data

Figure 13.2   Composition of imports as a percentage of merchandise imports (at current prices)

primary goods and import capital and intermediate goods (Streeten (1993: 197), Mohr and Rogers (1991: 54) and Taylor (1969: 238)). The composition of exports questions the validity of the monetarist assumption that SOEs can export as much as they desire, since demand for primary goods is limited.

An examination of the composition of South African merchandise imports reveals the reliance of South African on imported capital goods. In Figure 13.2, merchandise import are classified into capital, intermediate and consumer goods. Merchandise imports account for about 80 per cent of the total import bill over the period 1970–94. Capital and intermediate goods each make up about 40 per cent of the total merchandise import bill; together, they make up more than 80 per cent of the merchandise import bill.

Figure 13.2 emphasizes the high percentage of capital and intermediate goods in the import bill. The question remains as to the degree that imports represent investment expenditure. Gross domestic fixed investment (GDFI) and merchandise imports in current prices are shown in Figure 13.3. GDFI represents expenditure on new, durable and productive assets which have a life expectancy

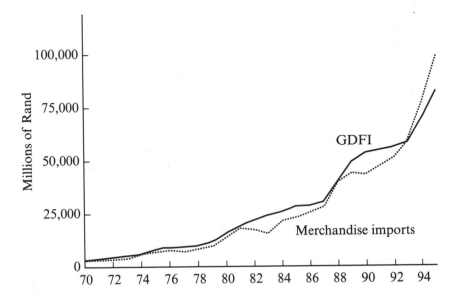

Source: SARB, *Quarterly Bulletin*.

Figure 13.3   Investment and merchandise imports (at current prices)

extending beyond the year in which the expenditure takes place (SARB Supplement, June 1991: 9). While the curves move in sympathy, not every good imported is of a capital nature, and not all capital goods are imported.

In the national accounts, investment is categorized by type of asset. The assets are residential building, non-residential building, construction and land improvement, transport equipment and machinery and other equipment. The last two categories are generally regarded as the most important sectors in terms of import demand (Kahn 1987: 239). Investment in *transport equipment* is measured as the purchase value of newly completed ships, aircraft, railway stock and motor vehicles as well as outlays for alterations or improvement to existing transport equipment. Investment in *machinery and other equipment* includes agricultural machinery, power-generating machinery, cranes and forklifts,

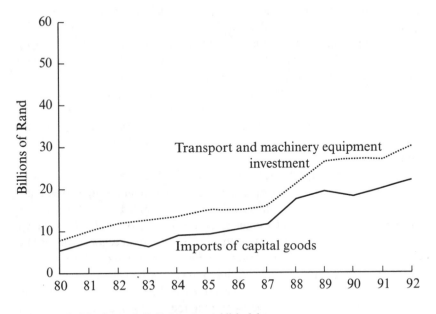

Sources: SARB, *Quarterly Bulletin* and unpublished data.

Figure 13.4   Imports of capital goods and investment in machinery and transport equipment (at current prices)

office machinery and furniture, computers and electrical equipment and instruments used in hotels and hospitals (SARB Supplement, June 1991: 11).

In South Africa, complex capital goods tend to be imported, and this tendency shows no sign of improvement in the period under review. The composition of imports in South Africa has shifted towards industries in which capital, skill and technology are requirements for viable domestic production (McCarthy 1988: 14). Figure 13.4 shows imports of capital goods and investment in transport equipment and machinery and other equipment. The values for investment in these two asset categories exceeds those of imports of capital goods, since not all investment requires imports. Over the period 1980–92, except for 1983, imports of capital goods represented about 70 per cent of the value of investment in transport equipment and machinery and other equipment. Although this percentage represents aggregate figures, the import ratio to domestic investment is confirmed upon examination of specific categories of import and investment. For example, if the fifth category of investment asset, machinery and other equipment (which includes electrical machinery), is compared to the import of machinery and electrical equipment (Categories 84 and 85 of the annual data of the Commissioner of Customs and Excise) then in 1992, imports made up just over 70 per cent of the total expenditure on investment. On average, expenditure on imports of machinery and transport equipment accounted for 64 per cent of investment expenditure on machinery and other equipment during the period 1980–92. In the input–output formulation of the multiplier (Kennedy and Thirlwall 1979), it can be shown that if the import coefficient of investment expenditure is sufficiently large, the multiplier effects of autonomous investment expenditure may be less than unity. The discussion of the import content of certain investment asset categories in South Africa suggests the application of the input–output formulation of the investment multiplier may be an interesting focus of future research.

South Africa displays the dependence on complex imported capital goods which is associated with small open economies. The relationship between the balance of payment and investment will now be examined.

The balance on the current account in South Africa from 1970–95 is shown in nominal terms in Figure 13.5. Movements on the current account can best be explained by dividing the series into two periods, pre- and post-1985. Prior to 1985, South Africa could generally afford to run a deficit on the current account. A persistent deficit on the current account can be addressed by obtaining financing or by macroeconomic adjustment in the economy, and, prior to 1985,

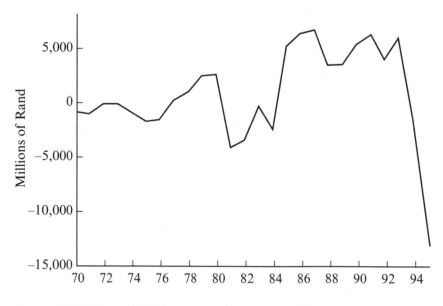

Source: SARB, *Quarterly Bulletin*.

Figure 13.5   Balance on the current account (at current prices)

inflows of foreign capital helped to finance a deficit on the current account. Financing a deficit on the current account allows the economy to postpone macroeconomic adjustment. Macroeconomic adjustment aimed at reducing a current account deficit may include tighter monetary policy, reduction of the budget deficit and exchange rate depreciation (Woodward 1992: 14). This last option is successful only if there is strong potential for substitution between imports and exports. In South Africa, the potential for substitution appears to be small, which is reflected in the low price elasticity of demand for imports (Kahn 1992: 83). This may account for the more frequent use of the alternative approach to reducing imports, expenditure-absorbing policy.

In the period preceding 1985, South Africa borrowed heavily abroad, its excellent debt record making it a sought-after borrower, and the provision of forward cover at attractive rates by the government, both serving to promote borrowing (Mohr et al. 1994: 137). During the early 1980s the nominal effective exchange rate tended to move in accordance with world prices of primary commodities, since gold and the mining sector were the major foreign exchange earners. The fall in the gold price in dollar terms in 1981 and 1983–84, was met by a fall in the nominal effective exchange rate (Kahn 1992: 87), so that gold in rand terms was kept relatively constant.

Although the depreciation in the exchange rate may have contributed to the support of the mining industry, it had a detrimental effect on South Africa's debt burden. During the period 1980–85, South Africa's foreign debt increased by about 50 per cent in dollar terms, and by about 500 per cent in rand terms (Van der Walt and De Wet 1993: 3). The refusal of the international banking community to roll-over debt in August 1985, resulted in the imposition of a debt moratorium by South Africa. The subsequent repayment agreements meant that with access to foreign finance greatly reduced, interest payments on the long-term debt had to be serviced by generating a surplus on the current account. In contrast with the years prior to 1985, capital outflows in 1985 amounted to 8 per cent of GDP (Kusi 1993: 255). The surplus on the current account was generated both by implementation of adjustment policy and by political uncertainty.

The policies which were put into place as a result of the capital outflow and balance of payments crisis include: the reintroduction of the dual exchange rate system to protect foreign exchange reserves; tariff protection on exports and surcharges on imports; the real depreciation of the rand and an increase in interest rates (1993: 256). Although the implementation of these policies is not in dispute, the current account had been in surplus since the first quarter of 1985, and there is a view that suggests that uncertainty in South Africa was so great that demand did not need further dampening (Mohr et al. 1994: 136).

Whether in response to policy implementation, or uncertainty, the decline in investment can be seen in Figure 13.6. Here, the decline in import as a percentage of GDE and investment as a percentage of GDP can be seen. Since the late 1970s investment appears to be on a downward trend which appears to have worsened since the second half of the 1980s. The decline in investment in 1977–78 could be attributed to the Soweto uprising in 1976, which did much to shake confidence at the time. During 1980–81, South Africa experienced a boom during which investment and imports of capital goods surged. However, events of 1984 eroded confidence once more, with political unrest in the Vaal Triangle and other areas culminating in the declaration of a partial state of emergency in July 1985.

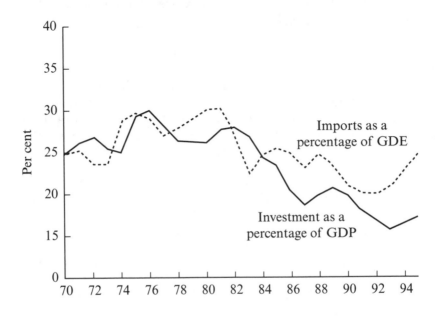

Source: SARB, *Quarterly Bulletin*.

Figure 13.6   Imports as a percentage of GDE and investment as a percentage of GDP (at current prices)

The political instability resulted in considerable lack of confidence. Although investment increased marginally in 1989, this did not reverse the downward trend. The increase in investment from the second quarter of 1994 may signal improved confidence in the light of the emergence of democracy in South Africa.

In Figure 13.7, investment as a percentage of GDP and the balance on the current account as a percentage of GDP are plotted. Post-1985, as investment declined, the balance of payments was in surplus. This suggests that investment was the adjustment variable which induced the surplus on the current account. The recovery of investment in 1994 is associated with a surge in imported capital

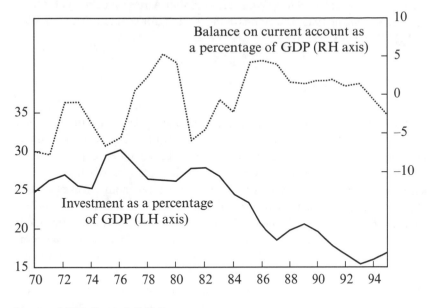

Source: SARB, *Quarterly Bulletin.*

Figure 13.7 Investment and the current account as a percentage of GDP (at current prices)

goods of some 70 per cent from 1993 to the end of 1994 (IDC: April 1995). This was accompanied by a current account deficit for the first time since 1985 and an inflow of long-term capital. It appears that the balance of payments cannot be ignored when analysing investment in South Africa.

The analysis above has attempted to show that South Africa is a small open economy, which imports the greater proportion of its capital goods. Importation of capital goods means that as investment increases, balance of payments problems may be encountered. In the absence of an inflow of foreign capital, adjustment to a deficit on the current account of the balance of payments requires that exports increase or imports decrease. In a country like South Africa, adjustment normally entails a reduction in imports, and since imports are largely capital goods, adjustment to the balance of payments takes place via a reduction in investment. Investment contains an endogenous element. This has implications for the long-term growth process: as investment is dampened, the equilibrium level of employment achieved is lower than the potential. The dampening of effective demand not only has implications for the income adjustment process, but also for the long-term growth rate, as the structure of capacity adjusts to investment in the long run (Park 1994: 45). The lowering of the achievable growth rate in South Africa since the balance of payments crisis in 1985, is a common theme (see, for example, Van der Walt and De Wet 1993: 11–20.

4   CONCLUSION

In small open economies, defined as such for their openness and their reliance on imported capital goods, investment does not stimulate the income adjustment process to the same extent as in the closed or consumption good importing country. When a country imports capital goods, the multiplicand of the multiplier stimulates the foreign sector rather than the domestic economy. This mean that although productive capacity may be enhanced, effective demand for this new capacity may not be forthcoming. In addition, importing investment goods stimulates imports relative to exports, and the balance of payments may come under pressure – both from the current and from the capital accounts. Adjustment to the balance of payments will involve a reduction in investment, dampening effective demand and income and employment. In a small open economy which imports capital goods, investment plays an endogenous, rather than an exogenous role.

NOTE

*   I should like to thank Chris Torr and Tony Thirlwall for their comments and suggestions on earlier drafts. The usual disclaimer applies. The financial assistance of the HSRC and the South African Network for Economic Research (SANER) is gratefully acknowledged.

REFERENCES

Bhaduri, A., A. Mukherji and R. Sengupta (1982), 'Problems of Long Term Growth: A Theoretical Analysis', in B. Jalan (ed.), *Problems and Policies in Small Economies*, London: Croom Helm: 49–68.

Casar, J. and J. Ros (1983), 'Trade and Capital Accumulation in a Process of Import Substitution', *Cambridge Journal of Economics*, 7: 257–67.

Coutts, K. and W. Godley (1992), 'Does Britain's Balance of Payments Matter any More?', in J. Michie (ed.), *The Economic Legacy*, London: Academic Press: 60–67.

Davidson, P. (1994), *Post Keynesian Macroeconomic Theory*, Aldershot: Edward Elgar.

Domar, E.S. (1946), 'Capital Expansion, Rate of Growth and Employment', *Econometrica*, 14: 137–47.

Dornbusch, R. and S. Fischer (1984), *Macroeconomics*, 2nd edn, Singapore: McGraw-Hill: 625–715.

Dow, S. (1986), 'Post Keynesian Monetary Theory for an Open Economy', *Journal of Post Keynesian Economics*, **9** (2): 237–57.

Galbraith, J.K. and W. Darity (1994), *Macroeconomics*, Boston: Houghton Mifflin.

Harberger, A.C. (1988), 'Policymaking and Economic Policy in Small Developing Countries', in R. Dornbusch and F.L. Helmers (eds), *The Open Economy*, New York: Oxford University Press: 249–63.

Industrial Development Corporation (IDC) (1995), *Manufacturing Trading Conditions*, April, Johannesburg: Industrial Development Corporation.

Jones, H. (1975), *An Introduction to Modern Theories of Economic Growth*, London: Thomas Nelson.

Kahn, S.B. (1987), 'Import Penetration and Import Demands in the South African Economy', *South African Journal of Economics*, **55** (3): 238–48.

Kahn, S.B. (1992), 'Foreign Exchange Policy, Capital Flight and Economic Growth', in I. Abedian and B. Standish (eds), *Economic Growth in South Africa*, Cape Town: Oxford University Press: pp. 74–98.

Kennedy, C. and A.P. Thirlwall (1979), 'The Input–Output Formulation of the Foreign Trade Multiplier', *Australian Economic Papers*, **18** (32): 173–80.

Keynes, J.M. (1936), *The General Theory of Employment, Interest and Money*, Cambridge: Cambridge University Press. Reprinted in 1973.

Kregel, J.A. (1976), 'Economic Methodology in the Face of Uncertainty: The Modelling Methods of Keynes and the Post-Keynesians', *Economic Journal*, **86**: 209–25.

Kusi, N.R. (1993), 'External Imbalance and Structural Adjustment: South Africa in the 1980s', *South African Journal of Economics*, **61** (4): 255–65.

Lipsey, R., P. Steiner and D. Purvis (1987), *Economics*, 8th edn, New York: Harper & Row: 481–513.

Lloyd, P.J. and R.M. Sundrum (1982), 'Characteristics of Small Economies', in B. Jalan (ed.), *Problems and Policies in Small Economies*, London: Croom Helm: 17–38.

McCarthy, C.L. (1988), 'Structural Development of South African Manufacturing', *South African Journal of Economics*, **56** (1): 1–23.

McCombie, J.S.L. (1993), 'Economic Growth, Trade Linkages and the Balance of Payments Constraint', *Journal of Post Keynesian Economics*, **15** (4): 471–505.

McConnell, C.R. (1987), *Economics*, 9th edn, Singapore: McGraw-Hill.

Mohr, P. (1993), 'South Africa's Economic Prospects: Can We Learn from Other Countries?', *Journal of Studies in Economics and Econometrics*, **17** (2): 21–31.

Mohr, P., M. Botha and P. Hawkins (1994), 'South Africa's Balance of Payments in the 1980s', *South African Journal of Economic History*, **9** (2): 127–44.

Mohr, P. and C. Rogers (1991), *Macroeconomics*, South African Adaptation of Dornbusch and Fischer (1984), *Macroeconomics*, 2nd edn, Johannesburg: Lexicon.

Nattrass, N. (1991), 'Rich Man, Poor Man … Redistribution Debates', *Indicator S.A.*, **8** (3): 29–32.

Park, M.-S. (1994), 'Keynes's Theory of Employment: Short Period Analysis in a Long Period Framework', *Contributions to Political Economy*, **13**: 45–68.

Pitchford, J.D. (1990), *Australia's Foreign Debt: Myths and Realities*, Sydney: Allen & Unwin.

Prachowny, M.F.J. (1973), 'The Effectiveness of Stabilization Policy in a Small Open Economy', *Weltwirtsschaftliches Archiv*, **109** (2): 213–31.

Prachowny, M.F.J. (1975), *Small Open Economies*, Lexington, MA: Lexington.

Prachowny, M.F.J. (1985), *Money in the Macroeconomy*, Cambridge: Cambridge University Press.

SA Reserve Bank (SARB), *Quarterly Bulletin*, Various.

SA. Reserve Bank (SARB) (1991), 'South Africa's National Accounts, 1946 to 1990', *Supplement to Quarterly Bulletin*, June.

Serven, L. (1995), 'Capital Goods Imports, the Real Exchange Rate and the Current Account', *Journal of International Economics*, **39**: 79–101.

Stiglitz, J.E. (1993), *Economics*, New York: Norton.

Stolper, W.F. (1964), 'The Multiplier if Imports are for Investment', in R.E. Caves, H. Johnson and P. Kenen (eds), *Trade, Growth and the Balance of Payments*, Chicago: Rand McNally: 126–39.

Streeten, P. (1993), 'The Special Problems of Small Countries', *World Development*, **21** (2): 197–202.

Swan, T.W. (1960), 'Economic Control in a Dependent Economy', *Economic Record*, **36**: 51–66.

Taylor, L. (1969), 'Development Patterns: A Simulation Study', *Quarterly Journal of Economics*, **83**: 220–41.

Thirlwall, A.P. (1979), 'The Balance of Payments Constraint as an Explanation of International Growth Rate Differences', *Banca Nazionale del Lavoro*, **32** (128): 45–53.

Van der Walt, J.S. and G.L. De Wet (1993), 'The Constraining Effect of Limited Foreign Capital Inflow on the Economic Growth of South Africa', *South African Journal of Economics*, **61** (1): 3–12.

Woodward, D. (1992), *Debt, Adjustment and Poverty in Developing Countries*, London: Pinter.

14. The relevance of the principles of Keynesian economics for the transition to capitalism in today's underdeveloped world

Hartmut Elsenhans

1 MICROECONOMIC EFFICIENCY THROUGH FORMALLY PRIVATE INVESTMENT PROCESSES AND MACROECONOMIC EFFICIENCY THROUGH THEIR SOCIAL CHARACTER AS WEAK POINT OF THE ARTICULATION BETWEEN MICRO AND MACRO IN CAPITALISM

In concentrating my interpretation on power relations favourable to labour in order to overcome the instability of the investment decision in a capitalist economy, I do not deny the importance of uncertainty and credit markets. Pessimistic expectations with low propensities to investment, in turn, have considerable importance for this very power relation because of their influence on the level of employment. I argue, however, that uncertainty may be reduced if power relations allow labour to command as much of the productive potential for consumption as to reduce surplus to the very amount necessary for investment. The ultimate source of lack of investment is the expectation of a future deficient aggregate demand. The more the economy tends to be pushed by labour to the level of full capacity utilization, the less there is potential surplus (the production of which requires improved expectations on the side of the capitalist) and the larger the pressure of final demand on available capacities. The link between investment and expectations regarding the development of costs is considered in my chapter as only of secondary importance, and this for two reasons. First, it is assumed that in a capitalist economy technical innovation, for the deployment of which financial resources are invested, will always reduce unit costs and hence contribute to productivity increases. The challenge for such a system is not a lack of productivity-raising innovations but a lack of demand, as it is assumed that there is unlimited technical progress due to competition. Second, it is assumed that in the case of a full-employment growth path, the real rate of net return on investment is higher than the necessary real rate of interest on monetary resources. This implies not only a positive but a minimum rate of technical innovation, which for practical reasons cannot be discussed here.

My argument therefore implies that capitalism depends and, by the way, has depended[1] on a power relation in favour of labour which allows labour to reduce surplus appropriation to those financial resources that are used effectively for net investment. Capitalists can appropriate only those financial resources as profit via the prices for their products on competitive markets without any political intervention which they use for investment spending. Such net investment has to correspond to the creation of capacities of production in line with the growth path of aggregate demand.

Such a formulation of the instability problem raises the question why labour should accept private property of the means of production if the smooth functioning of an economy based on private property of means of production requires a set of power relations which narrowly circumscribes the right of disposal of capital which business as the formal owner of capital enjoys. Labour here is required to be able to reduce the power of business without attempting to abolish private property, the basis of this power. There are at least two important reasons for labour to accept such a restraint. Labour's goal to increase consumption in relation to alienated work is compatible with decison making about investment by private business as this guarantees microeconomic efficiency. The alternative to private ownership of means of production would not be social control and socialization of the investment decision but statization, state's control with increasing inefficiency and lack of control, finally waste in the name of pretendedly high costs of the enlargement of existing productive capacity, exploitation by inefficiency.[2]

Although the private form of property is a guarantee for labour's capacity to act in an independent manner, it constitutes the weak link in any capitalist economy and political system. The investment decision is formally a private one, but social and political in character as it determines the maintenance and good functioning of a whole series of regulating mechanisms, some of them linked to multiplier effects. Private property in assets does not enter into conflict with the objectively social functions of private investment decisions only if the incentive system is kept favourable for investment, to the stabilization of which the system of formally private property rights does not necessarily contribute.

The neoclassical solution to the dilemma described centres on its theory of wage determination. Entrepreneurs are expected to increase their demand for labour as long as marginal product still exceeds the wage rate so that the entrepreneurs' bid for labour raises real wages automatically up to the level of marginal product. This theory is tautological for all situations in which there is no tendency to full employment.[3] If labour is a homogeneous commodity and if high-skilled labour can be considered as a special form of this homogeneous commodity which will be replaced by average-skilled labour in case of inappropriate cost relations between the two types of labour, then the amount of wages paid to workers constitutes the most important element of final demand for consumption goods and derived demand for investment goods. It is the wages themselves which determine the price which can be fetched for any additional product of an enterprise. So, a decrease in real wages due to lack of demand further decreases marginal productivity of labour.[4]

I interpret Keynes and his proposal for state or state-supported investment in the case of persisting unemployment as the lowest cost solution for empowering labour in order to bring the labour markets back to their normal functioning in the case of full employment. With this spending, the state does not pursue aims other than empowering labour. State-sponsored investment is not meant to increase productive capacity by itself. Especially, the state has not to intervene directly in the distribution of bargaining power between capital and labour, nor does it intervene in the direction of the process of growth. It contributes by its spending to recreating scarcity of labour which raises real wages in line with increases in productivity and this, in turn, leads to the growth process being relaunched in order to satisfy (new) mass needs.[5]

Such a limitation of the extent of state intervention implies that capitalist economies are endowed with certain structural traits, which are lacking in underdeveloped countries. We could define the set of these traits as constituting a benign situation of a market economy in which the following basic mechanisms operate. Labour is scarce. Because of its scarcity, it increases in cost with rising productivity and thus with increasing wages, final demand increases. This consequently triggers off additional employment-creating investment, which in turn creates additional demand for labour and increases productivity and so on.

This set of traits is essential not only for the economy but even more so for the political structures of a capitalist system. These traits are the basis of the existence of civil society with social actors which do not depend on a political process of appropriation of financial resources which would involve the support of the 'sultan', a sort of distributive patrimonial state. The described interaction between labour and business during the cycle finds its political correspondence in the existence of two classes in a capitalist society, which continuously empower each other: by proceeding to cost-reducing investments, business creates scarcity of labour and empowers it. Rising mass incomes create the additional outlets which make capacity-increasing net investment profitable and provide for net profits on the macroeconomic level. The Keynesian analysis implies not only that real investment may be below potential investment with resulting unemployment, but that due to this possibility a pluralist distribution of power in a capitalist system may be wrecked.

I therefore interpret the Keynesian proposal of state-sponsored investment as an attempt to limit state intervention by restoring the mechanism on which growth and power diffusion in a capitalist system are based, and this with the lowest possible profile of the non-market economy in order to preserve not only efficiency in the economic system, but also the autonomy of civil society to the greatest possible degree. It is only through this mechanism that business can be kept within its microeconomic limits without being entrusted with the responsibility for macroeconomic equilibria as the ruling class of a traditional tributary mode of production would claim. The denial of such a macroeconomic competence to business is a basic guarantee for other classes not being excluded from political participation. If business could add to the property rights in the means of production also the competences for the macroeconomic and consequently macropolitical orientation of society, then the process of negotiated determination of the options of society at the political levels would certainly be replaced by a patrimonial state which fixes consumption according to the needs for financing investment as defined by business.

Because of the formally private character of the investment decision and its influence on empowerment of labour via the level of aggregate demand, monetary policy and state or state-supported investment can certainly contribute to appropriate final demand and hence the power of labour. However, the larger the gap between actual demand and capacity-exhausting potential demand, the more difficult it is to bring the economy to full-employment levels of production and to maintain power diffusion. All other instruments of influencing the investment decision can, at least in the long run, be efficient only if mass demand is maintained at appropriate levels and to the extent that they contribute to this aim.

Keynes's theory of the responsibility for the level of investment is primarily a theory of the empowerment of labour which is necessary for maintaining capitalism, because in order to benefit from the privatization of losses through inappropriate use of surplus, the fundamentally social character of the investment decision is threatened by the absence of appropriate institutions which otherwise, and not through the labour market, could allow society to make its influence felt. Keynes therefore does not present a theory for the non-market economy and of waste through state officials. He was certainly aware of such dangers and was even opposed to a Leviathan. Waste in the wake of state or state-sponsored investment was, however, negligible compared to the waste of resources constituted by involuntarily forgone activity during available labour time. Referring to pyramid building,[6] he makes clear that he only expects an increase in income otherwise not produced. This position is perfectly compatible with the aim of maintaining efficiency, if it is assumed that such additional employment-creating investment restores the basic capitalist mechanism of growth.

2 KEYNES HIJACKED BY THE THEORY OF ECONOMIC MODERNIZATION

Two interpretations can be deduced from the previous argument about the relevance of Keynesian economics for underdeveloped economies. The usual interpretation insists on the fact that there are no underutilized capacities. My interpretation insists on the structurally determined impossibility of creating labour's bargaining power.

If there are no productive capacities which can be brought on stream through the creation of additional purchasing power, prices rise for the existing limited supply of goods.[7] The inelasticity of wage goods production holds down economic expansion.[8] Underdeveloped economies are considered as characterized by surplus labour which is unproductive in the short run and can only become productive with additional investment.[9] Such additional investment is, however, considered as not forthcoming without previous coordination as incomes created by one investor will not necessarily transform into sole demand only for his or her own products. In his seminal contribution, Rosenstein-Rodan[10] argues that a net profit for all investors will result only from parallel investment of other investors which all face uncertainty about the forthcoming parallel investment of their counterparts. Balanced and unbalanced growth are specifications of this general scenario: additional purchasing power created through investment can lead to increased demand for any particular investor only if the state assures all investors that the sum of additional income created will allow the profitable sale of the additional products put on the market by them. Investment and additional production have to be created *uno acto* if rationing through inflation and lack of profitability of particular enterprises are to be avoided, either by adapting the productive potential in various branches through planning (balanced growth[11]) or by voluntarily creating growth-inducing imbalances for other branches (unbalanced growth).[12]

Investment now assumes a role quite different from the one Keynes assigned: it is no longer meant to relaunch the growth process from the demand side, but to create a growth process from the supply side. The theory of economic modernization does away with the Keynesian restraint with respect to the role of the state and makes the state the principal coordinator of public and private investment. With this shift in relevance from the demand to the supply side, the rate of growth becomes a function of investment. From this a discussion about the choice of techniques originated which stressed the importance of reinvestible funds to the detriment of demand which ended up in the Rostowian analogy to Stalinist industrialization.[13] An ever-growing investment outlay is assumed to create jobs and incomes which trickle down to the mass of the population ultimately by way of creating labour scarcity and hence the foundations of a capitalist economy. The labour surplus models with their orientation to absorb labour by the growth process of the modern sector can be quoted as examples.[14] They expect increases of employment and income simply from the growth of the modern sector, whatever its orientation may be. The Mahanalobis[15] model of concentrating on the production of machine tools in order to produce machinery and so on seems to be the most consequential formulation of this approach.

Only with this new role of the state could the question emerge whether the state personnel would abide by the role of allocating resources for investment in the interest of the public good. The question was initially resolved by complementing the Weberian assumption of a culturally determined austerity of Calvinist businessmen by the assumption of a parallel behaviour of modern (that is, westernized) elites in non-market regulated sectors of societies of the Third World, which political modernization theory thought to be able to identify in the tie-wearing bureaucracies and the western-style clothed officer corps; the two institutions where most of the western-style educated climbers of the so-called new middle classes were finding employment.[16]

The contending view insists on the power relations possible in an underdeveloped economy. It highlights one condition implied in the Keynesian model which was rarely substantiated. This condition is that any labourer/worker is able to produce a marginal product equal to the wage rate which is necessary for maintaining appropriate aggregate demand. If there is an unlimited supply of unskilled labour because part of this labour at least cannot produce as much as it has to consume for its survival, any amount of non-productive spending will not clear the labour market, even in the case of inflation. This condition is incorporated into a model of underdeveloped economies which puts at its centre the argument that the principal (and in reality the only) characteristic of an underdeveloped economy is the existence of marginal labour which at the level of technical mastery achieved over 'nature' does not produce as much as it needs for subsistence.

In the closed economy, the condition can occur only in the case of a predominantly agricultural economy with a low level of economic productivity and a low level of mass consumption. Marginal product can be lower than marginal input only in branches of production where outputs are identical at least with a large part of the inputs. In a market with a high variety of goods, a low level of productivity in the production of some few goods leads to an increase in their prices. They will be produced if overall productivity reaches levels where they are in demand even at such a high cost. Spaceships are built because the productivity in wage goods is sufficient to allow additional demand for spaceships not because physical productivity in spaceship production is high. In addition to this, marginal product can be lower than average product in the long run only in branches of production where natural conditions are important for productivity. In all other cases, marginal productivity being lower than average productivity will be met by duplication of existing state-of-the-art plants. Only agriculture is concerned by both these conditions, at least as long as ecological limits do not make themselves felt also in the production of industrial wage goods.

The structure of an underdeveloped economy can hence be shown in Figure 14.1.[17] Because of the low level of economic development, the share of food in mass consumption is important in typical underdeveloped economies, namely about 50–60 per cent of household incomes. With increasing employment, marginal product in agriculture decreases, although it is still positive. The condition holds $Y_{agr} = f(L)$, where $0 < f' < 1$ and $f'' < 0$. Suppose that all unskilled labour receives incomes that cover just the cost of physical survival of the worker and his or her family (necessary to reproduce the labour force), which I call subsistence cost. The cost of labour is hence a linear function of the quantity of labour. Theoretical maximum employment in case of a non-capitalist economy is reached at the intersection of both curves at point B. In the case of a surplus maximizing land-owning class which employs a dependent working class or tenants, maximum employment is reached when marginal product is equal to the subsistence wage at point A. Any additional worker beyond the level of employment A adds less to production than his or her cost and hence reduces the available surplus of agriculture. I call this level of employment the threshold of marginality. As agricultural labour consumes not only food but also other products, there is in addition a mass-consumption-based level of employment in non-food activities. The sum of productive employment in agriculture and in non-agricultural wage goods production can be called basic employment.

At the threshold of marginality, there exists an economic surplus and one of unskilled labour. Further employment depends on the use of the surplus of agriculture by the landowners. If they eat it up totally, total employment does not exceed basic employment. If their numbers are low enough in relation to available surplus to develop new tastes beyond their food needs, they may use part of the surplus for luxuries and services. This increases total employment. There is no incentive for landowners to limit agricultural production below the threshold of marginality as they can use any surplus for services and luxuries, if necessary by retreating into the closed estate economy. State intervention may lead to a more efficient use of this surplus, as implied in the economic theory of modernization, but can increase the level of employment beyond the threshold of marginality only in the case of subsidizing labour in agricultural production in order to raise total agricultural production.

Economic theory of modernization saw in the state a major instrument of overcoming poverty which was considered to depend on investment. The investment decision is statized due to the absence of opportunities for profit-bearing investment and increasing investment is executed by the state. The absorption of labour is considered as dependent on the share of investment in

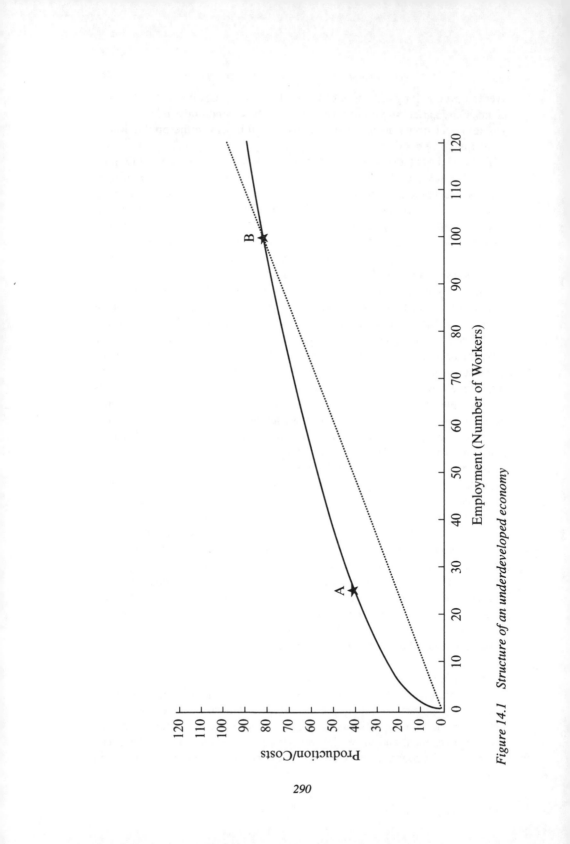

Figure 14.1   Structure of an underdeveloped economy

national income. There is control neither of the market nor of democratic institutions over the state. The absence of competition leads to inefficiency and waste. The low levels of mass consumption preclude the development of a local technology production and the operation of large series which improve capital productivity.[18] Both effects form the basis of high capital–output ratios which bring accumulation to exhaustion.

The interpretation of the underdevelopment trap as being based on a lack of empowerment of labour requires much less state interventionism, as it does not assume that there are no capitalist entrepreneurs in society. Without going into details, it seems quite clear that the actual experience of structural adjustment crises in the Third World show clearly that the so-called informal sector with its non-tie-wearing businessmen does, with some problems of adaptation, represent fairly well a flexible industrial sector, provided that the extension of incomes concentrates on mass demand. In order to allow it to grow and modernize, a much narrower but more precisely targeted form of state intervention is necessary, which should concentrate on the bottleneck of marginality, that is, on low productivity in agriculture. The transition to capitalism would then depend on a thriving agricultural sector.[19]

With the described shift, the economic variant of modernization theory neglected the fundamental Keynesian proposal which consisted of reinforcing the socialization of investment (and not its statization) and the appropriation of the investment decision via final demand of the mass of the population. The latter gains its empowerment through purchasing power. Instead, the state was reinforced. It was thought to become increasingly autonomous but in reality became increasingly the instrument of the appropriation of resources in the hands of a privileged minority.

Maintaining the political rationality of Keynes would, however, have meant only to step up the availability of wage goods and, supported by such an orientation of consumption goods production, a choice of techniques which favoured an early entry into capital goods production on the basis of low quality requirements and homogeneity of demand which both originate from a concentration of purchasing power in the hands of the poorer sections of society.

3 EMPOWERMENT OF LABOUR IN CONDITIONS OF MARGINALITY OF SUBSTANTIAL PARTS OF THE LABOUR FORCE

The stylized model of underdevelopment as determined by the coexistence of marginality of substantial parts of the labour force and economic surplus from agriculture is resistant against most forms of technical progress as well as against the introduction or reinforcement of competitive structures within the surplus appropriating class. Technical progress in luxury production has no effect whatsoever on employment, if it does not lead to income concentration within the surplus-appropriating class. Otherwise, this class will just use the same amount of labour either for better or for more luxury goods or services.

Technical progress in mass consumption goods production outside agriculture lowers the cost of labour and raises the level of marginality due to lower labour costs, but within rather narrow limits as employment in agriculture cannot exceed the level where marginal production in agriculture is equal to food consumption per household. In that case, non-food items in mass consumption are reduced to zero, either because labour is no longer allowed to consume non-food items or because these items become free goods. The effect evaporates all the more rapidly with non-food items having a lower share in mass consumption at the initial stage. The model is consistent with the argument that societies in temperate climatical zones with costly clothing and shelter are more prone to be industrialized than hot societies where subsistence depends only on enough food.

Technical progress in agriculture normally has – simultaneously but in different combinations – two effects with different implications. Technical progress in agriculture of already employed labour will increase the surplus but not necessarily employment in agriculture or related mass consumption goods production. This seems to have occurred in what is called the green revolution in some countries of the South. Only such technical innovation in agriculture which leads to a rise in the threshold of marginality will lead quasi-automatically to higher employment. The Keynesian objective of empowering labour in an underdeveloped marginality-ridden economy can only be achieved through 'labour-intensive' agricultural progress which raises the threshold of marginality, yet very often may have to combine with capital-intensive production of inputs and so on.

The model does not exclude that those in control of the surplus may use it also for measures which ultimately will lead to increases in productive potential. Unlike capitalists, members of a non-capitalist surplus-appropriating class are, however, not forced to do so by competition and the market mechanism, as they are always able to retreat into their estate economy, where they can have luxuries produced and services performed by workers they feed from the surplus they appropriate directly.

The emergence of capitalist entrepreneurs cannot be expected from the spontaneous tendencies of such a system. Because of low levels of mass consumption, there are only limited opportunities for using machinery in low-quality standardized products, the material counterpart of investment spending. Especially in rich economies with a high surplus, capitalist investors will not perceive investment opportunities of the same amount as can be financed through the available surplus even if the demand originating from the landowners provokes some investment. Hence there is no scope for capitalist entrepreneurs to deprive the non-capitalist landowners of their access to the surplus. The capitalists will be able to prevent the landowners from appropriating even substantial parts of the surplus only if because of their demand for labour the cost of labour rises and with this the surplus declines. As long as the landowners can appropriate important parts of the surplus, it is their demand which will orient industrial output. Capitalist entrepreneurs in industry will look to be on good terms with this market, for example, by becoming 'suppliers to the court'. Hence capitalists, where they may emerge from long-distance trade or local production of non-food items, will tend to integrate into the ruling class through the acquisition of land, positions of office and titles.

The only condition necessary for the landowners' appropriation of surplus is adequate 'supply' of people. It is, however, not only them who will favour demographic growth against the scarcity of hands. As the labour market is organized in a lottery-type manner each family tries to increase its chances of bringing at least one of its members into employment.[20]

An opening of such an economy to the world market may even lead to a reduction of employment if the surplus of agriculture is exported because the amount or the type of products which can be bought from export earnings is superior to those which can be produced locally. Elites may consider the surplus as qualitatively better in case of exports. The surplus is not diminished through these exports, as the workers employed in non-agricultural production are not themselves producing a surplus, but are fed out of the surplus of agriculture. Obviously, the foreign trade relations of such an economy conform to the vent-for-surplus model.

The proposed model is consistent with three well-established patterns of behaviour in underdeveloped economies, the 'rotating credit association', South Asian forms of labour protest and clientelism. In the rotating credit association, savings accumulated by its members are allotted to one among them (often on a random basis) for investment purposes with repayment not being guaranteed but admittedly dependent on later economic success. Those who save without being assured of interest receive the right to stand in the next selection round of allotment of credit. This is rational for them if and because they accept that the debtor cannot be certain of reaching increases in productivity even in the case of carefully selected projects, as is the case in marginality-ridden low productivity types of agriculture.[21] Strike as work stoppage is no efficient weapon in the case of overwhelming unskilled labour supply. He or she who does not add to surplus cannot impose any loss through his or her refusal to work. He or she who wants to prevent surplus production has to keep employed unskilled labour from working. Bengali '*hartal*' and Indian '*bandh*' consist in the occupation of any relevant means of transportation (roads, railway stations and so on). Labour which cannot achieve employment by offering better work and hence additional surplus in relation to competitors can still try to offer immaterial services, such as political support. The implied ties of patronage or clientelism are in demand in societies where those in control of the surplus can enhance their position within the surplus-appropriating class through political power. They operate within a politically determined power structure, where clients are counted as a potential source of violence against rivals.

4   ON SUPPORTING EMPOWERMENT OF LABOUR IN MARGINALITY-RIDDEN ECONOMIES

Assuming that a short-term rise in marginal product in agriculture as well as the development of productivity-raising technical competence in the rest of the economy are difficult to achieve without creating a pull effect via increasing market demand, the overcoming of marginality depends on redistribution associated with growth.[22] On the basis of the proposed model it can be shown that all successful development strategies, so-called alternative ones as well as the Washington Consensus of the World Bank and the IMF, consist in a reduction of surplus in favour of mass consumption which can allow the emergence of profit provided that the exchange rate is appropriate. They are forms of an empowerment of labour through access to subsistence income despite insufficient marginal productivity which guarantees labour's bargaining power on the labour market. An increase in that part of labour which is entitled to subsistence will contribute to impose an orientation of technical progress and investment to the better satisfaction of mass needs which in turn may lead to a rise of the threshold of marginality in agriculture. All such strategies are based on a redistribution of surplus to the marginal population on a permanent basis which confirms the expectations of entrepreneurs about the reliability of the enlargement of the demand for machine-produced products. This can be shown in discussing agrarian reform, the English poor laws, the creation of employment through an artificial industry, the activities of NGOs, but as well as a successful export-oriented strategy.

After an egalitarian redistribution of land, marginal labour time is incorporated into the small farm where owner-operators achieve an already high level of production with only a limited part of their labour time.[23] Because of scarcity of land, as assumed, this production is not sufficient to feed their families and to produce the surplus necessary for the acquisition of other necessities, so that additional labour time with low but positive additional results has to be mobilized on the farms (formerly the marginal labour time). This interpretation of an egalitarian agrarian reform conforms with the observed low labour productivity in the theory of the *latifundio-minifundio* complex. It implies the possibility of very low labour costs in industry. If labour productivity in non-rural activities is independent of personal characteristics of workers, farmers who are relatively inefficient in agriculture will find non-agricultural by-employment more rewarding than using their marginal labour time on their farm. Their individual rate of exchange between food and non-food items is lower than the one of more efficient farmers. As they still earn a greater part of their subsistence needs during their highly productive farm labour time they can offer their additional labour time at a low wage rate. The surplus from the highly productive labour time is used for subsidizing non-agricultural production.

The English poor laws[24] consisted in subsidies to the poor in exchange for their being farmed out to landlords who paid lower wages than the costs of subsistence. They imply the taxing away of part of the surplus produced by already productive labour and the use of this surplus by the parishes for covering the difference between the wages and the costs of subsistence of the poor. The 'rich' paid naturally for the poor – in contrast to the interpretation of Marx of these laws[25] – but only partly as rewards for the work performed, the other part being paid because of redistributive measures imposed by means of the non-market sector. Surplus is reduced because part of it is used for supporting labour which adds less to production than it consumes.

The same applies to employment programmes provided that subsidies trickle down to the poor. In dealing with the problems of Bangladesh, I have simulated the result of foreign aid being used only for an artificial 'industry' of stone-collecting in which the poor would be remunerated for a gathering activity by the aid-giving donors. The poor would be lifted above the poverty line and create a mass market which would induce farmers who are slightly better off to increase the marketable surplus with the ultimate result of also increasing the outlets for simple products of the small-scale sector.[26] Here, the surplus comes from an aid-giving agency which is ready to buy otherwise non-tradeable goods and which chooses to do so only because they constitute the proof of labour having been effectively employed. The advantage of this measure consists in lower costs of supervision as compared to other development measures which aim not only at income creation but also at capacity creation. The measure implies a real transfer of food from the donor corresponding to the amount of money transferred at least for the initial period.

This allows one to shed new light on the much-praised efficiency of NGOs.[27] Because of their size, NGOs cannot expect to channel surplus into capacity-creating investment, from a rent-generating branch of production to a low-productivity activity. They are also not superior to small entrepreneurs in choosing or creating efficient technologies. But they channel resources from external and internal donors to the poor for consumption and possibly create a new consciousness among the poor.

Such a reduction of the surplus to the benefit of consumption is also implied by the Washington Consensus as proposed in the programmes for structural adjustment. These programmes invariably suggest an increase in employment by means of devaluation of the national currency and hence low international prices for the local labour force. Devaluation has, however, limits as discussed in its secondary effects on prices and incomes. An economy which has a surplus of agriculture sufficient to feed all available marginal labour can bring this labour into productive employment via exports through devaluation, whatever the prices it fetches for such exports. A rise in the threshold of marginality is not necessary. Differences in real earnings between the advanced industrial economies and the marginality-ridden economy have no bearing on the possibility of additional exports but only on the possibility of the underdeveloped economy to bear devaluation, hence its capacity to produce a surplus of agriculture. The international price of labour in East and South East Asia was or still is now much lower than in actual Sub-Saharan Africa, but not the real wage. The reason is that the successful exporters in Asia did achieve early food self-sufficiency which allowed them to feed additional export workers at any rate of devaluation. The only condition which has to be fulfilled in the case of the availability of a local surplus of agriculture consists in preventing a rise in local food prices after devaluation. Export taxes and other regulations of food exports are well-known instruments even from historical experience of Western Europe. If there is food self-sufficiency, an economy can accept even negative marginal earnings in exports with increasing rates of devaluation in order to increase employment. Additional employment leads to increasing purchasing power in local currency of those who are employed. They buy the surplus of agriculture against foreign exchange earnings of a decreasing amount, so that the surplus available for the surplus-appropriating class in terms of imported goods decreases because of the decline of its purchasing power for imports, ultimately also because of rising local labour costs.[28]

In contrast to the economic theory of modernization, all solutions discussed do not expect a state-driven process of appropriation of surplus to be superior to a demand-driven one and concentrate not on the effect of directly increasing capacity through the utilization of available additional surplus for investment, but on the effect of mass consumption empowering labour and ultimately provoking such investment which will increase the availability of wage goods via demand. They limit the state to the establishment of structures where mass-consumption-oriented investment can be provoked by the market, hence where the control of market competition is maintained and waste in favour of those who have access to surplus is reduced. I consider this as the application of the principles of Keynesian state-sponsored spending on investment for the problem of transition to capitalism and of overcoming underdevelopment as it does not consist in an enhanced role of the state as the organizer of the process of accumulation but in the empowerment of labour through which a demand-driven process of accumulation can be launched.

State intervention for capacity creation can be reduced in this model to the area of agriculture. Here success will only be achieved if additional financial resources are combined with the available unskilled labour and hence, if it is able to mobilize that labour, by ultimately empowering it.

5   IMPLICATIONS OF THE PROPOSED INTERPRETATION FOR THE ACTUAL CRISES IN THE WORLD ECONOMY

Marginality, although not existing in capitalist developed economies, can be 'exported' to them through the processes which are actually dealt with under the label of globalization. With respect to the often claimed necessity of an alignment of real wages to low levels as they exist in underdeveloped economies, two remarks apply. First, the level of real wages in developed capitalist countries depends on productivity levels, and not on the terms of trade with underdeveloped countries, which can, however, add to prosperity. This argument is the more important as it implies that the alignment of First World wages to Third World wages will lead to a Keynesian underconsumptionist crisis and not to more employment.[29] Second, international prices of labour do not depend directly on real wages but on exchange rates as already mentioned in comparing Sub-Saharan Africa with East and South East Asia. If wages were too high for full employment in Germany, this country would have a balance-of-trade deficit, through which a stop to the ever-appreciating Deutschmark would bring the international price of German labour down. In fact, Germany has a balance-of-trade surplus despite high unemployment.[30]

For explaining unemployment despite real wages which are too low with respect to productivity increases in the last decade, three other processes have to be examined:[31] new possibilities of transforming already built-up comparative advantage for underdeveloped economies; achievement of comparative advantage in industry as against agriculture; and a new pattern of distribution of comparative advantage for underdeveloped economies.

The reasons why differences in productivity increases in the developed capitalist world which obviously have already emerged since the very beginning of the industrial revolution in the West have not led to competitiveness in manufacturing of industrially underdeveloped economies, which still lag behind, may be traced to the fact that some of these countries had acquired comparative advantage in raw material production where developed countries had to cope with declining increases in productivity because of the depletion of rich, low-cost deposits. But not all underdeveloped countries had the chance of becoming raw material exporters. At least those of them who were not rich in resources should have experienced new chances in manufacturing exports due to the fact that productivity increased more rapidly in some branches of the industrially leading countries than in others.

In order to transform comparative advantage into cost effectiveness for the country which is relatively less productive in all branches, devaluation of the currency is necessary. In order that the British customers realize Ricardo's advice and buy wine, where England's advance over Portugal is assumed to be less big than in textile production, the factors of production necessary in greater quantity for Portuguese wine in comparison to English wine have to be cheaper in Portugal as measured in international currency than in England. Portuguese labour's inability to migrate to England forces it to accept such a lower international price for its services. Comparative advantage is transformed into lower international prices through devaluation. This has very little to do with real wages: if wine does not enter mass consumption in England and if textiles are a part of mass consumption in Portugal, Portuguese real wages rise in the case of specialization with devaluation while English wages do not.

In discussing the Washington Consensus, limits to devaluation were shown: employment creation through unlimited devaluation becomes possible if the economy produces a surplus of agriculture large enough to feed additional export workers. As well, additional export workers can be fed, and in that case from imports, if in the developed capitalist countries productivity in agriculture increases more rapidly than in some industrial branches of production, because the terms of trade between these industries and agriculture would improve. With an unchanged level in productivity in the respective branch, an underdeveloped economy with comparative advantage here becomes able to buy more food on the world market for exports of this group of products than before agricultural productivity in the developed capitalist countries had improved, with no other changes in the underdeveloped economy. The rapid rise of agricultural productivity in the developed capitalist countries since the 1930s is well known.

Obviously, lower real wages in all activities of the industrial countries cannot preclude an enhanced capacity of transforming comparative advantage into cost advantages through devaluation on the basis of changing relative prices between agricultural and industrial products, or on the basis of an increase of agricultural surplus in the South. Only higher prices for exported food could limit these new opportunities for food-deficit countries, which, however, are not the main competitors on world markets for manufactures.

The same consequences result from the improvement in productivity in underdeveloped countries in industrial exports through technology transfers by multinational corporations as well as efforts deployed by governments.

As long as comparative advantage of the underdeveloped countries is concentrated in a small sector of production (for example, raw materials), the resulting improvement of the developed capitalist countries' terms of trade enlarges here the scope for price-neutral wage rises, as criticized since Lenin in the theory of the developed capitalist countries' labour aristocracy. The two new processes mentioned do not put an end to the improvement of the terms of trade of the leading countries through increasing specialization. The resulting scope for increasing mass incomes in developed capitalist countries can, however, no longer be realized by labour in the wage bargain due to more and more labour in the developed capitalist countries becoming too costly in international prices on the basis of exchange rate appreciations. Obviously, the balance-of-trade surpluses which maintain high exchange rates between developed capitalist countries and underdeveloped countries are the result of continuing high comparative advantage of the developed capitalist countries in a relevant sector of economic activities which earn enough on the world market to keep the exchange rate at high levels. The problem, however, is that these sectors are no longer large enough to provide full employment for all workers. The mass of German workers has become internationally uncompetitive because some German labour is so productive that the exchange rate remains at a level which is too high for the rest of the workforce. This is nothing other than 'Dutch disease'. This time it is based on high-technology manufacturing exports, now hitting capitalist developed countries in the same way as it has formerly hit underdeveloped raw-material exporters, who had also enjoyed a high comparative advantage in a very narrow segment of international production.

Such Dutch disease destroys the process of adjustment of prices to differences in the growth of productivity in the developed capitalist countries, on which cohesion of labour in these polities is based. Through this adjustment wages can increase in all activities in parallel with economy-wide average productivity, quite independently from the particular development of productivity in a particular branch, so that labour of a branch, with stagnant productivity (for example, barbers) can increase its wage rates without becoming marginal. If this process is blocked for part of the labour force because of international competitivity of labour from underdeveloped countries, the cohesion of the working class in developed capitalist countries has by necessity to be severed. Marginality has to appear because the economic value of an even constant marginal product of labour in low-productivity branches of the First World decreases because of lower prices of competitors in low-cost countries. The salaries of the workers in branches with below-average productivity increases can no longer be raised when the exchange rate is too high because of the productivity achieved in the high-technology branches of the economy and the resulting exchange rate.

Enhanced capacities of underdeveloped economies to transform comparative advantage into lower costs and Dutch disease in the developed capitalist countries due to high-technology sectors make marginal product in tradeables with low-productivity increases in the developed capitalist countries dependent on international prices of underdeveloped countries and ultimately on marginal product in the underdeveloped economies.

The maintenance of adequate demand in the developed capitalist countries is still possible but no longer primarily on the basis of higher wages according to average productivity increases but only through the expansion of employment in non-tradeable, often public goods through which labour becomes dependent on state spending and loses its autonomy and its cohesion, the importance of which for the capitalist economy and polity I have already mentioned.[32]

The threat to the maintenance of capitalist systems with autonomous civil societies and reduced state intervention does not come, however, from globalization but from the fact that through the above-mentioned processes non-capitalist societies with large pockets of marginality become internationally competitive on the basis of new opportunities to transform comparative advantage into absolute advantage, and this in an important sector of world production.

Two scenarios can be distinguished. In a benign case, devaluation in the backward economy can be pushed until full employment is reached with the result that rising productivity in wage goods production leads to a catching-up process with rising real wages, less trade dependency and expanding internal markets also in the South, as has occurred in the East Asian tiger economies. If, however, despite devaluation full employment cannot be reached, the devaluating economy remains trade dependent and transforms any increase in sectoral productivity into lower prices on the world market. It contributes to increasing world productive capacity without sharing in the necessary increase in world consumptive capacity so that productivity will outrun production.

Hence, in order to find a substitute to the mechanism for empowering labour in western industrial countries through state-sponsored spending, the various patterns of overcoming marginality in the underdeveloped world become essential.

The fundamental contribution of Keynes to my view has been his insisting on the necessity of empowerment of labour in order to guarantee that the privately organized investment process leads to full employment, which is the condition for economic and social equilibria within capitalist economies and societies. This empowerment requires new types of instruments in the case of underdevelopment, which, however, are not as complicated as the growth scenarios of the planning version of economic modernization theory want to make us believe. State intervention can concentrate on the support of labour-intensive techniques in agriculture that raise the threshold of marginality and redistributive measures which, for a transitional time, take the offensive character from existing marginality by keeping the marginals from disempowering already productively employed labour through employment programmes. They do not upset the welfare state, as demonstrated by Germany's employment companies after unification where up to 20 per cent of the initial industrial labour force have been employed unproductively. It is true that here the political issue was important enough that the politicians decided to keep mainstream economists from imposing their advice.

By reducing Keynes's contribution to a technical instrument of state spending, devoid of its meaning with respect to social structure – empowerment of labour in the interest of maintaining (welfare) capitalism – some of Keynes's followers have considerably weakened the reformist tendencies which could have drawn their intellectual inspiration from Keynes. They opened up the fora for the followers of planning, who considered investment no longer as a form of empowerment of labour, but as a sort of superior service for human advance, despite the fact that any investment naturally is an appropriation of surplus, which has to be produced by alienated labour. Keynes's solution tries to empower labour and at the same time to keep the necessary amount of surplus low by maintaining competition between private investors. His orthodox followers thought that this empowerment of labour is not necessary and accepted crises. His statist critics deemphasized the role of limiting the amount of surplus necessary for growth and, perhaps unintentionally, created the possibilities for exploitation by inefficiency.

NOTES

1. Elsenhans, Hartmut, 'Rising Mass Incomes as a Condition of Capitalist Growth: Implications for the World Economy', *International Organization*, **37** (1) (Winter 1983): 1–38. Elsenhans, Hartmut, 'Foundation of Development of the Capitalist World Economy', in Hartmut Elsenhans (ed.), *Equality and Development* (Dhaka: Center for Social Studies, 1992): 21–79.
2. Elsenhans, Hartmut, *Abhängiger Kapitalismus oder bürokratische Entwicklungsgesellschaft. Versuch über den Staat in der Dritten Welt* (Frankfurt am Main/New York: Campus, 1981); 90 fn 89. Engl. Elsenhans, Hartmut, *State, Class and Development* (NewDelhi/London/Columbia, Mo.: Radiant/Sangam/South Asia Books, 1996): 144 fn 89.
3. Irsch, Norbert, *Lohnbestimmungsmechanismen bei restringierten Substitutionsbeziehungen. Kritische Analyse grenzproduktivitätstheoretischer Verteilungsaussagen* (*Mechanisms of Wage Determination with Restricted Relations of Substitution. Critical Analysis of Arguments on Distribution Based on Marginal Productivity Theory*) (Aachen: Rheinisch-Westfälische Hochschule Aachen, 1979): 46f.
4. Even a neoclassical author has therefore accepted that a decline in business activity may lead to a secondary crisis on the basis of a demand-induced decline in productivity of labour, compare Röpke, Wilhelm: *Crises and Cycles* (London/Edinburgh/Glasgow: William Hodge, 1936): 119.
5. On this and the following: Elsenhans, Hartmut: 'Economie sous-développée et société civile: Surcharge du système politique et possibilités de pluralisme politique' ('Underdeveloped Economy and Civil Society: Overburdening of the Political System and Chances of Political Pluralism'), in CERES (ed.), *Actes du Colloque: Pluralisme social, pluralisme politique et démocratie* (*Acts of the Colloquy on Social and Political Pluralism and Democracy*). *Cahier du CERES, Série Sociologie No. 19* (Tunis: Université de Tunis, Centre d'Etudes et de Recherches Economiques et Sociales, 1991): 31–42.

6. Keynes, John Maynard, *The General Theory of Employment, Interest and Money. The Collected Writings of John Maynard Keynes* (Cambridge University Press: Macmillan, 1973): 220.
7. Robinson, Joan Violet, *Aspects of Development and Underdevelopment* (Cambridge: Cambridge University Press, 1979): 32.
8. Vakil, C.N.and P.R. Brahmananda, *Planning for an Expanding Economy: Accumulation, Employment and Technical Progress in Underdeveloped Countries* (Bombay: Vera, 1956): 219.
9. Ardant, Gabriel, 'Financial Policy and Economic Infrastructure of Modern States and Nations', in Charles Tilly (ed.), *The Formation of National States in Western Europe* (Princeton, NJ: Princeton University Press, 1975): 239. Raup, Philip M., 'Land Reform and Agricultural Development', in: Herman M. Southworth and Bruce F. Johnston (eds), *Agricultural Development and Economic Growth* (Ithaca, NY: Cornell University Press, 1967): 275.
10. Rosenstein-Rodan, P.N., 'Problems of Industrialization of Eastern and South Eastern Europe', *Economic Journal*, **53** (210) (June–September 1943): 202–11.
11. Nurkse, Ragnar, *Problems of Capital Formation in Underdeveloped Countries* (New York: Oxford University Press, 1953).
12. Hirschman, Albert O., *The Strategy of Economic Development* (New Haven, Conn.: Yale University Press, 1958).
13. Carré, Olivier, *L'utopie islamique dans l'Orient arabe (The Islamic Utopia in the Arab East)* (Paris: Presse de la Fondation Nationales des Sciences Politiques, 1991): 85.
14. Fei, John C.H. and Gustav Ranis, *Development of a Labor Surplus Economy. Theory and Policy* (Homewood, Ill.: Irwin, 1964): 27ff. Lewis, William Arthur, 'Economic Development with Unlimited Supply of Labour', *Manchester School of Economic and Social Studies*, **22** (4) (May 1954): 139–91.
15. Mahalanobis, P.C., 'Some Observations on the Process of Growth of National Income', *Sankhya*, **12** (4) (1953): 307–12.
16. Halpern, Manfred, 'Egypt and the New Middle Class: Reaffirmations and New Explorations', in *Comparative Studies in Society and History*, **11** (1) (January 1969): 97–108.
17. The model is presented in Elsenhans, Hartmut, 'Rent, State and the Market: The Political Economy of the Transition to Self-sustained Capitalism', *Pakistan Development Review*, **33** (4) (December 1994): 393–428.
18. Young, Allyn, 'Increasing Returns of and Economic Progress', *Economic Journal*, **38** (1928): 533.
19. Adelman, Irma, 'Beyond Export-led Growth', *World Development*, **12** (9) (September 1984): 937–49. Mathur, Ashok, 'The Interface of Agriculture and Industrial Growth in the Development Process: Some Facts of the Indian Experience', *Development and Change*, **21** (2) (April 1990): 276. Gray, Patricia and Hans W. Singer, 'Trade Policy and Growth of Developing Countries: Some New Data', *World Development*, **16** (3) (March 1988): 403. Hwa, Erh-Cheng, 'The Contribution of Agriculture to Economic Growth: Some Empirical Evidence', *World Development*, **16** (11) (November 1988): 1337. Oshima, Harry T., 'Labour-Force Explosion and the Labour Intensive Sector in Asian Growth', *Economic Development and Cultural Change*, **19** (2) (January 1971): 161–83.
20. Number of jobs being lower than the number of average skilled workers who come up with the skill requirements, compare Elsenhans, Hartmut, 'Die Rolle internationaler Entwicklungszusammenarbeit unter veränderten wirtschaftlichen und gesellschaftsstrukturellen Rahmenbedingungen' ('The Role of International Development Cooperation under New Social Environment and Economic Conditions'), in Dietrich Barsch and Heinz Karrasch (eds), *Die Dritte Welt im Rahmen weltpolitischer und weltwirtschaftlicher Neuordnung (The Third World in a New Political and Economic Order)* (Stuttgart: Franz Steiner, 1995): 140–44.
21. This also applies to non-agricultural investment: if markets do not expand net profit, in the model, does not increase. Positive rates of profit can only be achieved through high rates of technical progress of particular firms in comparison to other firms.

22. This is consistent with the observation that distributional patterns matter for growth, compare Adelman, Irma and Cynthia Taft Morris, 'Patterns of Industrialization in the 19th and Early 20th Century', *Research in Economic History*, **5** (1980): 35.

23. Elsenhans, Hartmut, 'Agrarverfassung, Akkumulationsprozeß, Demokratisierung' ('Agrarian Structure, Process of Accumulation, Democratization'), in Hartmut Elsenhans (ed.), *Agrarreform in der Dritten Welt (Agrarian Reform in the Third World)* (Frankfurt-on-Main/ New York: Campus, 1979): 550–62.

24. Elsenhans, Hartmut, 'Englisches Poor Law und egalitäre Agrarreform in der Dritten Welt. Einige Aspekte der Theorie, daß Wachstum historisch die Erweiterung des Massenmarktes erforderte und heute die Erweiterung der Massenmarktes erfordert', *Verfassung und Recht in Übersee*, **13** (4) (April 1980): 283–98. Engl. translation Elsenhans, Hartmut, 'English Poor Law and Egalitarian Agrarian Reform in the Third World', in Hartmut Elsenhans, *Equality and Development* (Dhaka: Center for Social Studies, 1992): 130–52.

25. Marx, Karl: *The Capital. A Critique of Political Economy*, Vol. 1 (Moscow: Progress Publishers, 1954), 687–88.

26. Elsenhans, Hartmut, 'Problems Central to Economic Policy Deregulation in Bangladesh', *Internationales Asienforum*, **22** (3–4) (November 1991): 281–4.

27. Elsenhans, Hartmut, 'Marginality, Rent and Non-Governmental Organizations', *Indian Journal of Public Administration*, **41** (2) (April–July 1995): 140–58. Elsenhans, Hartmut, 'Non-Governmental Organisations, Marginality and Underdevelopment, and the Political Economy of Civil Society', in K.S. Gopal and Peter J. Bumke (eds), *Foreign Funding in Andhra Pradesh* (Hyderabad: Centre for Environmental Concerns, 1996): 144–6.

28. Here is an interesting aspect of the model: it implies that the local surplus appropriating class is able to defend its income position as long as it refrains from consuming imported luxuries. This would constitute a basis for explaining initial violence in the case of integration into the international division of labour.

29. Elsenhans, Hartmut, 'Absorbing Global Surplus Labor', *Annals of the American Academy for Political and Social Science*, **492** (July 1987): 124–35. Elsenhans, Hartmut, 'Social Consequences of the NIEO. Structural Change in the Periphery as Precondition for Continual Reforms in the Centre', in Egbert Jahn and Yoshikazu Sakamoto (eds), *Elements of World Instability: Armaments, Communication, Food. International Division of Labour. Proceedings of the International Peace Research Association. Eighth General Conference* (Frankfurt-on-Main/New York: Campus, 1981): 86–95.

30. Compare the same position in a business-related newspaper: Mundorf, Hans, 'Die realen Nettolöhne sind nicht zu hoch' ('Real Net Wages are Not Too High'), in *Handelsblatt* 29 August 1995: 2; *Handelsblatt* 29/30 December 1995: 11; 11 August 1994: 2; 3 August 1994: 2; 5 June 1993: 13. In the meantime a real controversy has developed within German business, compare *Handelsblatt* 25 July 1996: 6, 11; 8 July 1996: 1, 6; Mundorf, Hans, 'Der technische Fortschritt läßt sich durch Lohnsenkungen nicht aufhalten' ('Technical Progress Cannot be Stopped by Lower Wages'), in: *Handelsblatt* 19/20 July 1996. Van Suntum, Ulrich, 'Die Wechselkurse sind keine Entschuldigung für die Lohnpolitik' ('Exchange Rates are No Excuse for the Wage Policy'), in *Handelsblatt* 4 July 1996: 2.

31. About the following in more detail: Elsenhans, Hartmut, 'Gegen das Gespenst der Globalisierung' [Debunking the Spectre of Globalization], in Werner Fricke (ed.), *Jahrbuch Arbeit und Technik* (Bonn: Dietz, 1996): 25–36.

32. Compare in more detail: Elsenhans, Hartmut, 'The Logic of Profit and the Logic of Rent', *Voice of Peace and Integration*, **1** (1) (October 1992): 36–9.

15. Globalization and international competitiveness

William Milberg*

1 INTRODUCTION

The principle of comparative advantage has made a comeback in the 1990s. Pushed to the side in the 1980s by the 'New International Economics' which rooted trade in imperfect competition, scale economies and strategic behaviour by firms and states, the principle of comparative advantage has returned to the centre of the debate in economic policy. The leading New International Economics theorist, Paul Krugman, has become the main proponent of this back-to-comparative-advantage-basics movement. Krugman writes:

> In the last decade of the 20th century, the essential things to teach students are still the insights of Hume and Ricardo. That is, we need to teach them that trade deficits are self-correcting and that the benefits of trade do not depend on a country having an absolute advantage over its rivals. If we can teach undergrads to wince when they hear someone talk about 'competiveness,' we will have done our nation a great service. (Krugman 1993: 26)

In this chapter I argue that the increased internationalization of production and finance since the 1960s ('globalization', for lack of a better word) has altered the nature and determinants of international trade. In particular, the two prongs of globalization, the increased international mobility of portfolio capital and the rise in foreign direct investment, and their associated systemic deflationary bias, have reduced significantly the relevance of the principle of comparative advantage in the determination of trade flows. Comparing the conditions in the industrialized countries in the period since 1980 with those in the period 1960–80, we find that in the recent period these countries have experienced higher rates of unemployment and excess capacity, greater exchange rate disequilibria, and large and more persistent current account imbalances. The evidence indicates that, contrary to the dictates of the principle of comparative advantage, countries can be 'undersold all around' for considerable periods of time. If the theory of international trade is to adequately take into consideration these changed conditions, it must bring the firm, its industrial relations and its organization of technological change to the centre of the analysis.

2 GLOBALIZATION: TODAY VERSUS 1913

The degree of globalization today is not much greater, and in a number of important ways less, than in 1913. This is most starkly seen in the figures on foreign direct investment. The foreign-owned share of the world's capital stock has risen steadily since 1960, but attained its 1913 level only in 1993 (Table 15.1). And the degree of trade openness in the world economy surpassed its 1913 level only in the late 1970s (Table 15.2).

Table 15.1   Foreign direct investment, relation to trade and total investment

	1913	1960	1975	1980	1985	1993
World FDI outflows						
as % of world output	—	0.3	0.3	0.4	0.4	—
as % of world gross fixed capital formation	—	1.1	1.4	1.8	1.8	4.3
FDI stock ($ billions)	—	68	282	514	679	2,135
FDI outward stock as % of world output	9.0	4.4	4.5	4.8	6.4	9.2

Sources: Kozul-Wright (1994) and United Nations (1995).

Table 15.2   Merchandise exports as a percentage of GDP

	1870	1913	1950	1973	1985	1993
World	5.1	11.9	7.1	11.7	14.5	17.1
US	5.4	6.4	3.8	5.2	5.2	7.0

Sources: Krugman (1995), Bairoch and Kozul-Wright (1996) and ERP (1996).

3 GLOBALIZATION: TODAY VERSUS 1960

The comparison with 1913 is interesting, and provides an important warning to those who claim the current degree of globalization is unprecedented in world history.[1] But for the purposes of this chapter, the more important comparison is with the 'golden age' of capitalism, that is, the period 1945–73. The degree of globalization today is considerably greater than it was in 1950, 1960 or 1970. This can be seen in the figures on trade openness (Table 15.2), foreign direct investment (Table 15.1) and especially in gross portfolio capital movements (Table 15.3) and international banking (Table 15.4). While the figures give us little indication of whether or not the increase in globalization is slowing, it clearly indicates an upward overall trend.

Table 15.3 Gross capital inflows in the industrial and developing countries (annual averages in $billion)

	1975–1979	1980–1984	1985–1989
Industrial countries			
Portfolio	99.1	175.7	463.3
FDI	21.0	36.9	96.2
Developing countries			
Portfolio	52.1	105.5	110.0
FDI	6.6	16.4	15.5

Source: Kregel (1994: Table 2).

Table 15.4 International banking in relation to output, trade and investment

	1964	1972	1980	1985	1991
As a percentage of world trade					
Net international bank loans	7.5	31.5	42.6	80.4	104.6
Gross size of international banking market	12.4	53.7	86.3	169.7	215.6
As a percentage of world gross fixed investment					
Net international bank loans	6.2	25.6	51.1	103.7	131.4
Gross size of international banking market	10.3	43.7	103.6	219.2	270.9

Source: Akyuz (1994: Table 3.3).

Along with globalization, the period since 1980 is also characterized by higher interest rates (Figure 15.1) and unemployment rates (Table 15.5), and lower rates of economic growth than the golden age.[2] Globalization and slow growth are of course linked. One view (UNCTAD1995) is that the surge in international financial flows that has resulted from financial liberalization has created unprecedented volatility in financial asset and foreign currency prices

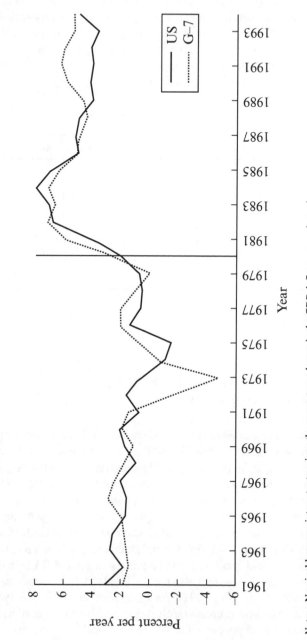

Note: Nominal long-run interest rate minus the percentage change in the GDP deflator at market prices.

Sources: OECD (1995), and author's calculations.

Figure 15.1 Long-term real interest rates, 1961–1994

which has raised liquidity preference. The result is greater volatility around a rising trend in interest rates. Eatwell (1996) argues that the key link between the globalization of finance and poor economic performance is the result of the discipline that liberalized financial markets have imposed on policy makers, who see international financial market 'credibility' to be the foremost policy goal. In either case, globalization of finance is seen as imposing a deflationary bias on the macroeconomy, precisely the opposite result to that predicted by economists who equate market liberalization with efficiency gain.

Table 15.5   Rate of unemployment (annual average in per cent)

	1970–1980	1981–1994
Canada	5.9	9.8
France	3.4	9.9
Germany	1.7	7.5
Italy	5.9	10.8
Japan	1.5	2.5
United Kingdom	2.8	9.1
United States	5.6	6.9

Source: OECD (1995).

4   GLOBALIZATION AND THE NATURE OF INTERNATIONAL TRADE

Whether or not the rising globalization of production and finance over the past 25 years constitutes a dramatically new historical epoch is a question I shall leave to historians. Here I argue simply that globalization has been associated with significant changes in the nature and determinants of international trade. While most international trade continues to be between industrialized countries (the exception being the dramatic rise in world export market share by Asian and Latin American NIEs) that trade has been characterized by a steady rise in intraindustry trade (Rayment 1983; Balassa and Bauwens 1987), trade in high-tech goods (Table 15.6) and goods requiring a greater amount of R&D in their production, as well as in services that also require highly skilled human capital inputs (Thurow 1995; Dosi et al. 1991). As FDI flows surged in the 1980s, intrafirm trade has become a consistently large portion of overall trade, accounting for more than 25 per cent of Japanese trade, and well over one-third of US trade (Table 15.7). Trade in intermediate goods has also risen, as transnational corporations increasingly use international outsourcing (Table 15.8).

Table 15.6   High-technology exports as a share of total manufactures exports, selected countries, 1970–1986 (percentages)

Year	All countries	France	Germany	Japan	United Kingdom	United States	Other	Europe
1970	16	14	16	20	17	26	11	14
1975	16	14	15	18	19	25	11	14
1980	17	14	16	24	21	27	11	15
1982	19	18	18	26	24	31	12	16
1984	21	18	18	32	26	34	12	16
1985	22	19	18	32	27	36	13	17
1986	22	19	18	33	28	37	14	18

Note: High-technology products are those defined by the OECD as 'high-technology intensive products'.

Source: Tyson (1992).

Table 15.7   Intra-firm trade, Japan and United States, selected years ($ billion)

	Japan			United States		
	1983	1989	1992	1982	1989	1992
Intrafirm exports	32.8	65.9	89.1	72.1	130.1	163.9
Of which						
Parent firms	31.4	62.9	85.6	47.1	89.4	106
Foreign affiliates	1.4	3.0	3.5	25.0	40.7	57.9
Intrafirm imports	17.2	29.4	29.3	91.2	204.3	228.2
Of which						
To parent firms	5.0	19.4	15.5	39.2	74.4	93.9
To foreign affiliates	12.2	10.0	13.8	51.9	129.9	134.3
Addenda						
Share of intrafirm exports in country exports (%)	22.5	24.5	26.9	34.2	36.0	37.2
Share of intrafirm imports in country imports (%)	15.1	15.3	14.8	36.8	42.8	42.5

Source: United Nations (1995): 194.

Table 15.8   Ratio of imported to domestic inputs, selected countries (percentages)

	Early 1970s	Mid/late 1970s	Mid-1980s
France	21	25	38
Germany	n.a.	21	34
United Kingdom	26	32	37
Canada	34	37	50
United States	7	8	13
Japan	5	6	7

Source: United Nations (1994).

5   THEORETICAL ROBUSTNESS OF THE THEORY OF COMPARATIVE ADVANTAGE

When we speak of the 'determinants of international trade', we are implying a positive (as opposed to normative) theory of trade. For example, the direction of trade in the Heckscher–Ohlin model is determined by relative factor endowments. In the Ricardian model, relative productivities determine the direction of trade. These theories constitute two versions of the theory of comparative advantage. In either version, the conditions required for comparative advantage to determine the commodity composition and direction of international trade include (a) full employment of capital and labour; (b) no international capital mobility; (c) full and costless factor mobility domestically; (d) trade in final goods only; (e) a price adjustment mechanism that converts differential comparative costs into differences in absolute money costs.[3]

While the emphasis in this chapter is on the empirical relevance of the assumptions of the theory of comparative advantage, it is worth noting that there exists a considerable body of theoretical literature exploring the implications for the theory of violations of its assumptions. The question of international factor mobility has received the most attention. Jones (1980), Caves (1982) and Brewer (1985) show that the introduction of an internationally mobile factor of production reduces the relevance of comparative advantage in the determination of trade patterns. With free capital mobility, a good will be produced only where it is most profitable, that is, where unit labour costs are lowest. Thus, in a two-country, two-good model, if the home country has an absolute advantage in both goods (that is, if unit costs are lower in the production of both goods), the home country will attract foreign capital, reducing foreign production and employment to zero in equilibrium.[4] Caves (1982: 55) describes such a situation, worth quoting at length:

> So far we have assumed implicitly that the presence of internationally mobile capital (through the agency of MNEs) leaves the basic pattern of comparative advantage unchanged. That is, Home exports food, Foreign exports clothing, and this pattern persists no matter how capital is reallocated internationally by MNEs. But that assumption could be false! Let us change the model slightly to bring out the reasoning, by making sector-specific capital a necessary input to food production, along with labor, whereas clothing production requires only labor. Workers do not move internationally, but capital moves freely to wherever it can earn the larger rentals. Now, David Ricardo would have said that the question which country exports clothing and which exports food depends only on comparative labor productivity. That factor still weighs in, but also relevant is the absolute advantage that mobile capital has for producing food in the two countries. Home labor may be relatively more efficient in textile production than in food, and yet the food productivity of capital in Home may be so high that all or most capital locates in Home, coopting enough of Home's labor supply to make food Home's export good. In general, the more mobile are factors of production, the less does comparative advantage have to do with patterns of production. If all factors are more productive in the United States than in Iceland and nothing impeded their international mobility, all economic activity would be located in the United States.

Jones (1980: 258) makes a similar point:

> Although each nation can, by the law of comparative advantage, find something to produce, it may end up empty-handed in its pursuit of industries requiring footloose factors. Once trade theorists pay proper attention to the significance of these internationally mobile productive factors, the doctrine of comparative advantage must find room as well for the doctrine of 'relative attractiveness' where it is not necessarily the technical requirements of one industry versus another that loom important, it is the overall appraisal of one country versus another as a safe, comfortable, and rewarding location for residence of footloose factors.

Deardorff (1979) shows that the presence of trade in intermediate goods also renders comparative advantage invalid.

Another line of theoretical critique of the theory of comparative advantage focuses on its implied adjustment mechanism – be it Hume's price–specie-flow mechanism or its modern equivalent in the form of exchange rate adjustment – whereby a case of one country's absolute disadvantage in all sectors is transformed in response to its temporary trade deficit, so that it is able to export to the point where trade is balanced. The country with lower (higher) prices experiences an inflow (outflow) of money and a rise (fall) in its price level, corresponding to a rise (fall) in the price in all sectors. These relative price changes occur until the high-cost country has a lower money price for one or more goods and can export sufficient value to balance its trade account. This monetary adjustment mechanism is perhaps the most important and most commonly ignored part of the theory. It is this adjustment process that allows all countries, regardless of low productivity or high wages, to participate with balanced trade in the international division of labour. Darity (1987) shows that the presence of increasing returns in the production of specie invalidates the Humean mechanism. He concludes:

> David Hume's price–specie-flow mechanism does not provide an unequivocal refutation of mercantilist fears over specie loss through international trade. On the contrary, Hume's projected outcome rests heavily on the way specie is conceived of as entering or being withdrawn from the world economy. Even when the most mundane assumptions are made – competitive mining under conditions of increasing costs – there still are parameterizations of the model that rule out Hume's conclusions. Moreover, a host of less mundane assumptions – especially decreasing costs in mining – magnify the difficulties associated with the attainment of the Hume equilibrium.
>
> If the world's specie supply was fixed and invariant Hume's results become more reasonable. But with a cumulative process at play leading to augmentation or reduction in global specie the mercantilist concerns retain a sense and logic that cannot be dismissed merely by invocation of the price–specie-flow mechanism.

Shaikh (1980) argues that the price–specie-flow mechanism fails to operate when there is less than full employment. In this case, trade imbalances lead to interest rate changes, not price adjustments.[5] The result is, once again, persistent trade imbalances.

6　RELEVANCE OF RICARDO, IRRELEVANCE OF COMPARATIVE ADVANTAGE

Ricardo's famous example about England and Portugal is still relevant, since even today, high-productivity countries tend to have high productivity in many sectors. Table 15.9 shows the Pearson and Spearman correlation coefficients between aggregate manufacturing productivity across countries and the productivity across countries in each of 18 manufacturing sectors for the year 1994. There is a high and generally statistically significant correlation between the ordering of countries by aggregate manufacturing and in each sector, indicating that countries with relatively high overall productivity have relatively high productivity across a wide variety of sectors. These correlations are perhaps not surprising, given the support for Verdoorn's Law linking manufacturing productivity growth to overall economic growth already in the 1970s (Cripps and Tarling 1975). Logically, different aggregate productivity growth rates across countries eventually lead to significantly different productivity levels. The results in Table 15.9 are simply the outcome of an extended cumulative process of productivity growth.

Table 15.9   Correlation between aggregate and sectoral productivity for G–7
             countries, 1993

Industries	Pearson	Spearman
Food, beverages and tobacco	0.8113*	0.5714
Textiles, apparel and leather	0.7784*	0.4286
Wood products and furniture	0.8923**	0.8929**
Paper, paper products and printing	0.9037**	0.7500
Chemicals and drugs	0.9569**	0.7500
Petroleum refineries and products	–0.3257	–0.2857
Rubber and plastic products	0.7981*	0.6071
Non-metallic mineral products	0.9207**	0.8571*
Iron and steel	0.9175**	0.8929**
Non-ferrous metals	0.4879	0.7500
Metal products	0.9479**	0.8929**
Electrical equipment and machinery	0.9833**	0.9286**
Shipbuilding and repairing	0.2657	0.5714
Motor vehicles	0.8500*	0.7857*
Aircraft	0.9575**	0.7857*
Other transport equipment	0.5203	0.8286*
Professional goods	0.8876*	0.2571
Other manufacturing	0.4369	0.4643
Average	0.7217	0.6516

Notes: Productivity is value added per unit of output in 1985 US dollars converted with actual exchange rates.
* and ** indicate significance at the 5 and 1 per cent level, respectively, using two-tailed tests.

Sources: OECD STAN Database and author's calculations.

But if Ricardo's Chapter 7 example is relevant, his trade theory is not. The assumptions of the theory of comparative advantage have less empirical validity today than they did 25 years ago, partly due to the globalization of production and finance that has occurred over that period. As a result, the actual pattern of international trade does not reflect the complementary international division of labour indicated by the theory of comparative advantage. And trade balances have become increasingly and persistently out of balance.

The recent era of globalization has been characterized by higher rates of unemployment and lower rates of capacity utilization than the earlier part of the post-war period (Table 15.5). Gross international capital flows have surged in the past 15 years for both direct and portfolio investment (Table 15.3). Trade in intermediate goods has also risen dramatically since the 1970s (Table 15.8).

Moreover, neither the price adjustment process, nor its expected outcome of balanced trade, has been observed. Exchange rate changes have been dominated by capital flows, not trade imbalances (Harvey 1995). Thus exchange rates have continued to deviate considerably from levels required for sustainable current account imbalances. Empirical assessment of this claim requires estimating an equilibrium real effective exchange rate. Williamson's (1994) 'fundamental equilibrium exchange rate' takes into consideration current account sustainability, but has not been estimated for more than a few discrete points in time. Blecker (1995) compares the actual value of the real, effective exchange rate of the dollar with its extrapolated trend for the 1970s (see Figure 15.2). Blecker associates this trend with the secular decline in competitiveness of US industry. The trend would thus indicate the real dollar depreciation necessary to keep the current account at its sustainable level of the 1970s. It is clear from Figure 15.2 that the deviations from this trend exploded in the 1980s as the current account deficit ballooned, then receded until the late 1980s when the deviations expanded again. I performed a similar exercise, comparing deviations of the actual exchange rates *vis-à-vis* the dollar with the purchasing power parity exchange rate. The results are much less dramatic than those of Figure 15.2. The average of annual deviations for the period 1980–93 was essentially unchanged from the level for the period 1973–79.

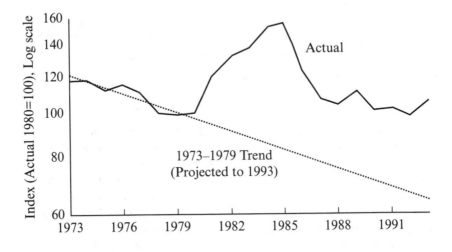

Figure 15.2   Real value of the US dollar, actual 1979–1993 versus trend for 1973–1979

Table 15.10   Deviation of actual dollar exchange rates from purchasing power parity, G–7 countries (annual average in percentages)

	A 1973–1979	B 1980–1993	A/B
Canada	16.44	6.30	2.61
France	11.45	15.73	0.73
Germany	22.77	19.59	1.16
Italy	20.79	16.48	1.26
Japan	10.62	29.93	0.35
Great Britain	19.04	12.30	1.55
Average	16.85	16.72	1.01

Source: OECD (1995) and author's calculations.

Current account imbalances of the G–7 have been larger on average in the past 15 years than in the period 1960–80 (Table 15.11). Such imbalances have also been more persistent in the more recent period. Table 15.12 (columns 3 and 4) shows the number of consecutive years that the current account balance was of a given sign. In the more recent period, such imbalances – both surpluses and deficits – have lasted longer than in the earlier period.

In addition to the problem of exchange rate 'misalignment', the growing role of non-price competition (for example, over technological change) and 'pricing to market' (limited exchange rate pass-through) has further reduced the effectiveness of the Hume mechanism in balancing trade. Exchange rate imbalances can have cumulative effects, especially for firms in industries in which innovation is important and cash flow constrains innovative effort (Gray and Milberg 1992; Gray 1995).

While considerably more empirical work must be done, a first glance indicates that the complementary international division of labour implied by the principle of comparative advantage is not an accurate description of trade among industrialized countries. Countries with high aggregate world export market share have a high world export market share across most manufacturing sectors. Table 15.13 gives the relative export market shares of the G–7 countries. These countries account for about 75 per cent of total OECD exports. We would expect, according to the principle of comparative advantage, a diverse specialization pattern across countries, each country's export strength in its area of comparative advantage. Instead, the variation (as measured by the dispersion) of export market shares within a country across industries was less on average than the variation in export market shares within an industry across the seven countries. This

Keynes and economic development

indicates that countries have high or low export market shares across manufacturing sectors.[6]

Table 15.11   Current account balance as percentage of GDP (annual average in percentages)

	1970–1980	1981–1994
Canada	−0.93	−2.47
France	0.06	−0.37
Germany	0.69	1.58
Italy	−0.19	−0.77
Japan	0.59	2.46
United Kingdom	−0.20	−0.81
United States	0.09	−1.83

Source: OECD (1995).

Table 15.12   Cumulative current account balances

	Cumulative current account balance ($ million)		Consecutive years with the same sign (no. of years)		Cumulative trade balance as percentage of end-period exports (%)	
	1970–80	1981–94	1970–80	1981–94	1970–80	1981–94
Australia	−20,668	−144,372	7*	14*	−95.8	−288.2
Belgium	−4,088	45,666	6	10*	−7.2	39.1
Canada	−22,115	−176,517	6	12*	−32.8	−107.9
France[2]	4,400	−30,712	2	5	4.1	−13.8
Germany[1]	20,303	197,307	8	9	10.6	46.0
Italy	−6,652	−82,380	3	6	−8.5	−43.5
Japan	20,511	913,042	3	14*	16.2	237.7
Netherlands	4,089	85,672	6	14*	6.1	65.9
United Kingdom	−2,245	−127,399	5	9*	−2.0	−61.6
United States[2]	3,823	−1,238,154	4	13*	1.7	−246.4
Asian NIEs[1,3]	−10,530	415,091.5	3	12*	−14.3	47.5

Notes
*   Asterisk indicates the series of consecutive surpluses or deficits includes end-year.
[1]   Series begins in 1971.
[2]   Series begins in 1973.
[3]   Asian NIEs are South Korea, Hong Kong, Singapore and Taiwan.

Source: OECD (1995).

Table 15.13 Export market shares for G–7 countries, 1993 (exports as a percentage of total exports of 20 OECD countries)

22 Industries	Canada	France	Germany	Italy	Japan	UK	US	G–7 Total	Dispersion	Variance
Total manufacturing	5.07	8.60	16.26	7.36	15.94	7.17	17.41	77.80	0.43	23.11
Food, beverages and tobacco	3.75	14.04	11.37	5.63	1.14	7.02	16.56	59.51	0.61	27.30
Textiles, apparel and leather	1.17	9.56	14.99	23.14	5.52	6.18	10.46	71.02	0.66	44.36
Wood products and furniture	22.54	5.29	10.10	12.52	1.01	1.87	14.43	67.77	0.73	50.26
Paper, paper products and printing	14.93	7.09	13.52	4.36	2.98	6.35	16.80	66.02	0.54	26.23
Chemicals excluding drugs	3.23	10.80	19.16	4.58	10.85	9.05	18.56	76.22	0.53	32.74
Drugs and medicines	0.93	13.22	18.27	6.69	3.87	13.96	14.75	71.70	0.58	35.35
Petroleum refineries and products	6.04	5.93	8.05	6.99	4.43	12.33	13.39	57.15	0.39	9.93
Rubber and plastic products	4.65	11.83	18.09	9.36	11.21	6.68	13.95	75.77	0.38	17.30
Non-metallic mineral products	2.49	10.72	15.42	17.51	11.04	5.66	9.50	72.34	0.47	23.17
Iron and steel	3.49	10.44	16.52	8.33	20.01	6.55	5.10	70.45	0.56	32.00
Non-ferrous metals	14.05	7.82	15.88	3.78	6.39	6.89	12.14	66.96	0.43	17.19
Metal products	3.57	8.71	20.67	13.01	10.53	5.81	13.70	76.00	0.48	27.47
Non-electrical machinery	2.26	6.04	22.12	10.68	18.38	6.76	18.74	84.99	0.58	49.69
Office and computing equipment	2.83	5.42	8.42	4.12	28.13	11.81	26.91	87.63	0.79	97.59
Electrical machines excluding commercial equipment	1.72	8.89	19.71	7.49	22.29	5.91	17.85	83.85	0.61	53.17
Radio, TV and communications equipment	2.96	5.25	10.13	2.78	34.46	7.87	22.59	86.04	0.90	121.29
Shipbuilding and repairing	0.66	4.05	10.38	3.90	45.82	1.80	5.47	72.08	1.44	218.58
Motor vehicles	10.68	7.58	19.38	3.56	25.13	4.33	13.72	84.39	0.61	54.46
Aircraft	4.98	15.09	11.68	2.77	0.99	11.38	45.37	92.27	1.06	195.63
Other transport equipment	6.19	6.22	12.54	10.92	40.17	2.67	8.43	87.14	0.94	137.22
Professional goods	1.54	6.47	17.24	3.96	24.85	8.10	24.06	86.21	0.72	79.58
Other manufacturing	1.32	6.51	10.03	14.85	12.64	10.21	12.29	67.85	0.43	17.53

Table 15.13 continued

22 Industries	Canada	France	Germany	Italy	Japan	UK	US	G–7 Total Dispersion Variance
Dispersion	1.02	0.36	0.28	0.64	0.83	0.44	0.52	
Variance	29.07	9.19	17.54	27.40	164.48	9.98	69.20	
A: Average cross-industry dispersion (7)	0.583							
B: Average cross-industry dispersion (22)	0.657							
A/B	0.887							
C: Average cross-industry variance (7)	46.695							
D: Average cross-industry variance (22)	62.184							
C/D	0.751							

Note: Export data in current prices converted to US dollars using actual exchange rates.

Source: OECD Stan Database.

A number of recent papers question the empirical relevance of the theory's assumptions. Thurow (1995) focuses on the assumptions of full employment and costless factor mobility domestically. Shaikh (1996) emphasizes the automatic adjustment mechanism (especially through real exchange rate changes) and its implications for balanced trade. Prasch (1996) considers the assumptions of no externalities, full and costless factor mobility within a country, full employment of labour and capital, balanced trade, no international factor mobility and fixed technology. Of all these studies, however, only Thurow emphasizes the increased irrelevance of the theory due to changed global economic conditions. He sums up the situation succinctly:

> Historically, one could always quarrel with the assumptions of no unemployment and zero transition costs (and some economists have), but yesterday's perhaps unrealistic assumptions have become today's counterfactual assumptions. ... In short, if natural resources have ceased to dominate economic activity in a world of brainpower industries, if factor proportions have dissolved in a world of global capital markets and worldwide logistics, if high and persistent unemployment is a worldwide fact of life, and if transition costs are very large, the real world is far removed from the standard theory of comparative advantage. (Thurow 1995: 215, 217)

7   CONCLUSION

The rejection of comparative advantage implies the need for a new theory of international competition. Firms seek profits and growth by creating an advantage over rivals, be it through innovation, foreign direct investment, international outsourcing, interfirm cooperation or state subsidies. A firm's export market share will depend on the pattern of these advantages in a given sector. Trade for a given nation will not automatically be balanced, and persistent imbalances will have real and cumulative effects.[7]

Professor Krugman (1994) has characterized the concern with 'international competitiveness' as a 'dangerous obsession', since 'there are stong equilibrating forces that normally ensure that any country remains able to sell a range of goods in world markets, and to balance its trade on average over the long run, even if its productivity, technology, and product quality are inferior to those of other nations' (Krugman 1991: 814). Fifty years ago Keynes warned economists about another obsession – economists' dismissal of policy makers' concern with trade imbalances. Keynes (1936: 339) wrote:

> the weight of my criticism is directed against the inadequacy of the theoretical foundations of the laissez-faire doctrine upon which I was brought up and which for many years I taught; – against the notion that the rate of interest and the level of investment are self-adjusting at the optimum level, so that preoccupation with the balance of trade is a waste of time. For we, the faculty of economists, prove to have

been guilty of presumptuous error in treating as a puerile obsession what for centuries has been a prime object of practical statecraft.

In today's globalized economy, international economists would benefit from a serious consideration of Keynes's words. At a minimum, international economists should be more modest in their insistence on the primacy of a theory whose validity is increasingly questionable due to historical change.

NOTES

*   I am grateful to David Kucera and Heather Boushey for valuable research assistance.
1.   Gordon (1988) presents the most comprehensive case that the rate of globalization in the post-Second World War era was less than that in the pre-First World War era.
2.   For this reason, Nell (1996) designates the more recent period the 'iron age'.
3.   See Milberg (1994) for a more detailed discussion of these conditions.
4.   Brewer's example also assumes fixed real wages. Caves's discussion is in the context of a specific-factor model of trade.
5.   In Milberg (1996) I argue that this position can also be found in the works of both Keynes and Marx.
6.   In another simple test of comparative advantage in a multicountry, multicommodity context, I estimated the Jones (1961) algorithm using input–output data for a group of five OECD countries. A simple absolute advantage algorithm more closely predicted the actual trade pattern than the Jones algorithm for comparative advantage. See Milberg (1994).
7.   There has been a recent flurry of interest in the relevance of Thirlwall's (1979) concept of balance of payments constrained growth for US growth prospects. See Godley and Milberg (1994), Blecker (1995) and Howes (1996).

REFERENCES

Akyuz, Y. (1994), 'Taming International Finance', in J. Michie and J. Grieve-Smith (eds), *Managing the Global Economy*, Oxford: Oxford University Press: pp. 55–92.

Bairoch, P. and R. Kozul-Wright (1996), 'Globalization Myths: Some Historical Reflections on Integration, Industrialization and Growth in the World Economy', *UNCTAD Discussion Paper*, No. 13, March.

Balassa, B. and L. Bauwens (1987), 'Intra-Industry Specialisation in a Multi-Country and Multi-Industry Framework', *The Economic Journal*, **97**, December: 923–39.

Blecker (1995), 'The Trade Deficit and U.S. Competitiveness', in R. Blecker (ed.), *U.S. Trade Policy and Global Growth*, Armonk: M.E. Sharpe and the Economic Policy Institute: pp. 179–214.

Brewer, A. (1985), 'Trade With Fixed Real Wages and Mobile Capital', *Journal of International Economics*, **18**: 177–86.

Caves, R. (1982), *Multinational Enterprise and Economic Analysis*, Cambridge: Cambridge University Press.

Cripps, F. and R. Tarling (1975), 'Cumulative Causation in the Growth of Manufacturing Industry', mimeo, Department of Applied Economics, Cambridge University.

Darity, W.A. (1987), 'The Hume Process, Laws of Returns, and the Anglo-Portuguese Trade', *Southern Economic Journal*.

Deardorff, A. (1979), 'Weak Links in the Chain of Comparative Advantage', *Journal of International Economics*, **9**: 197–209.

Dosi, G., K. Pavitt and L. Soete (1991), *The Economics of Technical Change and International Trade*, New York: New York University Press.

Eatwell, J. (1996), 'International Financial Liberalization: An Assessment', mimeo, New York: UNDP.

Economic Report of the President (ERP) (1996), Washington, DC: US GPO.

Godley, W. and W. Milberg (1994), 'The U.S. Trade Deficit: Weak Link in the Recovery?', *Challenge Magazine*, June: 40–47.

Gordon, D. (1988), 'The Global Economy: New Edifice or Crumbling Foundations?', *New Left Review*, No. 168, March/April: 24–64.

Gray, H.P. (1995), 'Dangers in the Assumption of Balanced Trade', mimeo, Rutgers University.

Gray, H.P. and W. Milberg (1992), 'International Competitiveness and Policy in Dynamic Industries', *Banca Nazionale del Lavoro Quarterly Review*, (180), March: 59–80

Harvey, J. (1995), 'The International Monetary System and Exchange Rate Determination: 1945 to the Present', *Journal of Economic Issues*, **XXIX** (2), June.

Howes, C. (1995), 'Long Term Economic Strategy and Employment Growth in the US: An Analysis of Clinton's Economic Policies', *Contributions to Political Economy*, **14**: 1–32.

Howes, C. (1996), 'U.S. Competitiveness and U.S. Growth: A Critique of Clinton's Economic Policy', *Contributions to Political Economy*, **14**: 1–32.

Jones, R. (1961), 'Comparative Advantage and the Theory of Tariffs: A Multi-country, Multi-commodity Model', *Review of Economic Studies*, June, **28**: 161–75.

Jones, R. (1980), 'Comparative and Absolute Advantage', *Schweizerische Zeitschrift für Volkswirtschaft und Statistik*, September: 235–60.

Keynes, J.M. (1986:1936), *The General Theory of Employment, Interest and Money*, London: Macmillan.

Kozul-Wright, R. (1994), 'Transnational Corporations and the Nation State', in J. Michie and J. Grieve-Smith (eds), *Managing the Global Economy*, Oxford: Oxford University Press: pp. 135–71.

Kregel, J. (1994), 'Capital Flows: Globalization of Production and Financing Development', *UNCTAD Review*: 23–38.

Krugman, P. (1991), 'Myths and Realities of U.S. Competitiveness', *Science Magazine*, November: 811–5.

Krugman, P. (1993), 'What Do Undergrads Need to Know About Trade?', *American Economic Review*, **83** (2), May: 23–6.

Krugman, P. (1994), 'Competitiveness: A Dangerous Obsession', *Foreign Affairs*, March/April: 28–44.

Krugman, P. (1995), 'Growth in World Trade: Causes and Consequences', *Brookings Papers on Economic Activity*, **1**: 327–77.

Milberg, W. (1994), 'Is Absolute Advantage Passé? Towards a Post Keynesian/Marxian Theory of International Trade', in M. Glick (ed.), *Competition, Technology and Money: Classical and Post Keynesian Perspectives*, Aldershot: Edward Elgar: pp. 219–36.

Milberg, W. (1996), 'Say's Law in the Open Economy: Keynes's Rejection of the Theory of Comparative Advantage', mimeo, New School for Social Research.

Nell, E. (1996), 'Two Phases of post-War Growth', in J. Eatwell (ed.), *Global Unemployment: Loss of Jobs in the '90s*, Armonk: M.E. Sharpe: pp. 109–36.

OECD (1995), *Economic Outlook*, No. 58.

Prasch, R. (1996), 'Reassessing the Theory of Comparative Advantage', *Review of Political Economy*, **8** (1): 37–55.

Rayment, P. (1983), 'Intra-"Industry" Specialization and the Foreign Trade of Industrial Countries', in S. Frowen (ed.), *Controlling Industrial Economies: Essays in Honour of Christopher Thomas Saunders*, London: Macmillan.

Shaikh (1980), 'On the Laws of International Exchange', in E. Nell (ed.), *Growth, Profits and Property: Essays in the Revival of Political Economy*, Cambridge: Cambridge University Press: pp. 204–36.

Shaikh (1996), 'Free Trade, Unemployment and Economic Policy', in J. Eatwell (ed.), *Global Unemployment: Loss of Jobs in the '90s*, Armonk: M.E. Sharpe: pp. 59–78.

Thirlwall, A. (1979), 'The Balance of Payments Constraint as an Explanation of International Growth Rate Differences', *Banca Nazionale del Lavoro Quarterly Review*, **32** (128): 45–53.

Thurow, L. (1995), 'Comparative Advantage, Factor-Price Equalization, Industrial Strategies, and Trade Tactics', Chapter 11 in C. Whalen (ed.), *Political Economy for the 21st Century*, Armonk: M.E. Sharpe.

Tyson, L. (1992), *Who's Bashing Whom: Trade Conflict in High-Technology Industries*, Washington: Institute for International Economics.

UNCTAD (1995), *Trade and Development Report*, Geneva: United Nations.

United Nations (1994), *World Investment Report*, Geneva: United Nations.

United Nations (1995), *World Investment Report*, Geneva: United Nations.

Williamson, J. (1994), 'Estimates of FEERs' in John Williamson (ed.), *Estimating Equilibrium Exchange Rates*, Washington: Institute for International Economics.

PART IV

Income Distribution

16. Changes in income distributions and poverty rates in Central European transitional economies

Christopher J. Niggle[*]

The outstanding faults of the economic society in which we live are its failure to provide for full employment and its arbitrary and inequitable distribution of income. (John Maynard Keynes, Chapter 24, 'Concluding Notes on the Social Philosophy towards which the General Theory might lead', *The General Theory of Employment, Interest and Money*, London: Macmillan: 372)

1 INTRODUCTION

The former centrally planned socialist economies of Central Europe are in transitions to market capitalist economies. Economic theory and the historical experiences of countries which have previously gone through similar transitions would lead us to expect increases in the degree of inequality in the distributions of both earnings and incomes in those societies, declines in average levels of real wages, and increases in poverty, at least in the early phases of the transitions (see Polanyi (1944) and Marx (1967) for early discussions of the transition to capitalist economies).[1]

If these effects were to be important they might weaken the political consensus favouring the transitions enough to end or distort their paths, as well as causing misery for those adversely affected (consider the political debates preceding the 1996 elections in Russia and the election of former communist parties in several transitional countries). The recent attempts to estimate distributional changes discussed in this chapter report significant but probably tolerable increases in inequality and poverty in most of the transitional economies over the first five years of the process, but with significant variation in the degree of these changes; real wages, real GDP, and employment declined in all of these economies during the early transition period (see Table 16.1 for macroeconomic performance).

The purposes of this chapter are to set the stage for further investigation of these phenomena by surveying, evaluating and comparing recent studies and discussing the methodological problems entailed in such work. Although

Table 16.1   Macroeconomic performance

Variable	Czech Republic	Slovakia	Hungary	Poland	Russia
Annual growth in real GDP					
1990	−1.2	−2.5	−4.0	−11.6	—
1991	−14.2	−11.2	−10.7	−7.0	—
1992	−6.4	−7.0	−4.5	+2.6	—
1993	−0.9	−4.1	−0.9	+3.8	—
1994	+2.6	+4.8	+2.0	+5.0	—
1995	+5.0		+1.5	+7.0	−4.0
Real GDP per capita in 1992 US dollars					
	$7,700	$6,450	$6,260	$5,010	—
Annual price inflation (CPI)					
1989	1.4	1.3	17.1	251.1	—
1990	9.7	10.4	28.9	585.8	—
1991	56.6	61.2	35.0	70.3	—
1992	11.1	10.0	23.0	43.0	—
1993	20.8	23.2	22.5	35.3	—
1994	10.0	13.4	18.8	29.5	—
1995	8.5	—	24.4	20.5	68.3
Annual growth in real wages					
1989	0.8	1.4	0.8	11.6	—
1990	−5.5	−6.1	−0.2	−27.4	—
1991	−26.3	−25.2	−3.7	0.2	—
1992	10.3	8.7	1.7	−2.9	—
1993	3.6	−4.3	−0.4	−1.1	—
Growth 1989–93	−19.1	−25.5	−1.9	−22.0	—
1994	6.5	2.6	5.0	1.9	—
Unemployment					
1991	2.6	11.8	8.5	12.3	—
1992	2.6	10.4	12.3	13.6	—
1993	3.5	14.4	12.1	16.4	—
1994	3.2	14.8	10.4	16.0	—

Sources: Torrey et al. (1996) and Vecernik (1995); *The Economist*, June 1995; ultimate sources:
Employment Observatory, Central and Eastern Europe No. 6, European Commission, October 1994;
World Bank 1994; IMF, *World Economic Outlook*, 1994.

poverty and the level of real wages are also discussed, the primary focus of the chapter is distributional changes. Another related line of inquiry is how the cultural, historical and institutional context within which these transitions are taking place influences the distributional changes; much of the variance in distributional changes appears due to such factors, and especially to the characteristics of transfer systems and the countries' pretransition histories. The next section of the chapter presents the reasoning behind the assumption that inequality would be likely to increase; Section 3 briefly discusses methodological problems; Section 4 reports and analyses empirical work; and the last section sets out some suggestions for future research.

2   TRANSITIONAL CHANGES IN INCOME DISTRIBUTION

The economic concept 'income' represents a flow of purchasing power or its . non-monetary equivalent accruing to an economic unit over a period of time: it measures the unit's ability to access and control economic resources. It is useful to distinguish among several types of income: between market and non-market income, and between money and non-money income. The first pair distinguish sources of income; the second distinguish forms of income.

Market income represents the payments made to owners of the factors of production or economic resources in exchange for the services of these resources, and is often termed factor income. Market income is broken down into income from labour ('earnings' – wages, salaries and other forms of compensation) and income from property ('unearned income' – interest, rent, profits and capital gains). Most market income is in money form ('cash'), but some market income may appear in non-cash form (meals in the cafeteria, subsidized housing, a company car, holidays, membership in a club, educational benefits provided by employers). Conceptually, market income means income which flows from participation in the market economy.

Non-market income consists of transfer payments (for example, cash payments such as social insurance and intrafamily gifts, and non-cash income such as food stamps), the imputed value of non-market economic activity (farm family consumption of food raised by themselves or the value of rental services provided by owned homes), and the value of non-market access to goods and services (party official or administrator access to certain privileges not a function of economic role).

Non-market income does not result from participation in the market economy (at least not directly or immediately during the accounting period; pension payments – a form of transfer – often are predicated upon past market activity).

A review of this elementary taxonomic conceptualization is useful for our purposes, because income in the 'Socialist Economies in Transition' or 'SEITs' was and often still is a complex mixture of all these forms of income, probably to a greater extent than in mature capitalist economies (Atkinson and Micklewright 1992 and Vecernik 1995).

An economic unit's income is the sum of its market and non-market income flows, which are received in both cash and non-cash forms; the economic unit's wellbeing is then a function of its ability to earn market income and connect to non-market sources of income, given the institutional set within which it operates. As a SEIT goes through the process of transformation into a market economy, profound changes occur in the manner in which income is generated and distributed. First, significant property income begins to appear in the forms of profit, interest, rents and capital gains, and this income flows to individual non-governmental units which own the private property. To the extent that private property is unequally distributed, income inequality should be enhanced by the process.

Second, labour markets are transformed or, in their specific capitalist form in which labour services are more-or-less freely sold at competitive prices, are created where they had not previously existed. In such markets, if the supply of labour exceeds demand, wages normally fall. And an excess supply of labour is to be expected in these economies since the transitional process in most cases eliminates the workers' guarantee of employment (a form of property for them in the socialist economy) and allows the enterprises (whether state, cooperative or private) to disemploy redundant workers. Most state enterprises employed (or underemployed) many redundant state workers before the transition. Thus the transformation of labour markets works towards altering the distribution of market income by reducing wages (at least for some workers) and ending labour income payments for those unemployed.

But the transition also creates employment opportunities: new enterprises emerge, different occupations appear and different skills are required as entrepreneurs, workers and firms seek rents, the economies are opened to trade with non-socialist countries, and the economies begin to transform themselves structurally to adapt to these processes. The structures of the economies change and the relative rewards to different labour services are altered; in particular, the return to investment in human capital is likely to increase relative to the returns to seniority, age and 'proletarian-ness' of an occupation, all of which were rewarded with high wages in most socialist economies. Manual workers such as miners were often paid more than mental workers such as teachers and bankers; and wages in preferred industries such as construction and manufacturing were higher than in services (Vecernik (1995) refers to the replacement of 'demographic' determinants of wage differentials by 'market' factors). A priori the net effects of these processes on the distribution of labour earnings is open;

the relative earnings of individuals could be changed (some winners, some losers) without significant effect on the contours of the overall aggregate distributions.

Third, the complex set of transfer systems (for example, pensions), non-market subsidies from enterprises (meals, holidays, housing, education), and state provision of public consumption (health services) and investment (education) goods and services characteristic of the socialist economies has been dismantled, allowed to deteriorate, or at least significantly transformed in these societies, while new systems have been or are being put into place. Again, the net effect of these changes on distribution is unclear a priori.

Fourth, macroeconomic stabilization policies required by external constraints (such as IMF conditions) and domestic politics affect income distribution. Most often, these include tight fiscal and monetary (credit) policies designed to reduce inflationary pressure, impose hard budget or finance constraints on state enterprises, and stabilize foreign exchange values. These would be expected to have their most important effects on inequality through their influence over the labour market (increasing unemployment, at least temporarily), but these policies also affect incomes flowing through transfer systems as fiscal constraints may not allow them to be funded at the same levels of real benefits. In some cases, the transfer systems may affect the distribution of property income as well.

Fifth, all of these transitional economies have gone through periods of deep recession and price inflation (and several through periods of hyperinflation) which should alter the distribution of income between labour and capital as well as across wage earners and households. Table 16.1 reports macroeconomic data for the SEITs under investigation; all of the SEITs in Central Europe appear to be experiencing growth in GDP, real wages, industrial production and employment since the mid-1990s, although rather high inflation persists in several of the countries.

3 METHODOLOGICAL ISSUES

Attempting to measure changes in the degree of inequality of income distributions requires choosing the income concept to be studied (labour income, market income, total cash income, total cash and non-cash income, pre-tax, pre-transfer or disposable income) as well as the economic unit of analysis (individual, household or family). Each of the various measures of inequality most frequently used to measure degrees of inequality such as Atkinson, Gini and Thiel coefficients, variance, coefficient of variation, or ratios of deciles within distributions have advantages and disadvantages; the Gini coefficient is the primary measure of inequality in most of the studies reported here.[2]

All of these issues should be considered with an eye to the purpose of the study; for example, researchers concerned with changes in income inequality and their effect on relative poverty, usually choose to focus on the disposable cash income of household units defined as groups of individuals living together who purchase some commodity groups jointly, and pick a particular set of weights to assign to non-adult household members to define an 'equivalence scale' of adjusted household income. The weights attempt to compensate for the effects of economies of scale in consumption; estimates of inequality and poverty are quite sensitive to the chosen weights.[3]

If one were primarily concerned with the probable effects of distributional changes on political opposition one might look to the distribution of income across classes of individuals with political identities; for example, to the particular effects on the middle-aged and elderly versus other demographic groups, to the relative status of rural versus urban populations, or to the ratio of property to non-property income. And data availability, reliability and correspondence to conceptual measure must be evaluated. Researchers in Central Europe most often express concerns with data availability and reliability, and with methods of estimating distribution characteristics before the transitions (in particular, how to evaluate non-market income). See Atkinson and Micklewright (1992), Gorecki (1994), Hauser (1994), Forster and Toth (1994), Vecernik (1994a, 1995), and Torrey et al. (1996) for discussions of these issues. Most work known to this writer and discussed in the next section has focused on estimates of cash market income or disposable income (after tax, after transfer) of households and wage earners because of their availability and relative reliability, and some (Vecernik 1994a) have limited themselves to earnings from labour for the same reasons, but also because property income and income of the self-employed is thought to be seriously underreported or estimates unavailable.

4   INCOME DISTRIBUTION AND POVERTY

The estimates of income distribution and poverty rate changes in the Czech and Slovak Republics, Germany, Hungary, Poland and Russia discussed in this chapter are mainly taken from LIS working papers and from lectures presented to the Luxembourg Income Study's Summer Workshop held in Walferdange, LX in July 1994. The LIS project objectives include gathering economic and institutional data collected by countries, standardizing these data sets as much as possible ('LISification'), and making the data available to social science researchers on site in Luxembourg or remotely.[4]

A consistent pattern emerges from the data and analyses reported in these studies.

1. Income distributions as measured by official statistics were fairly equal by western standards before the transitional processes began, with some

significant differences across the countries. However several authors (see Vecernik 1994a) consider the non-market incomes of social elites in the socialist societies to have been very high, so that inequality was probably greater than reflected in the official data.

2. A significant increase in inequality occurred in most of these countries within a brief period after the transition began, although the ranking of degrees of inequality across the countries remained roughly stable through the first five years of transition, and inequality still remains somewhat below levels in most western countries.

3. Poverty also increased in most of the transitional countries, although still remaining within the low range of most Western European nations by most measures (see Table 16.2, Deleek and Van den Bosch (1992), and Ramprakash (1994) for comparative measures of Western European poverty rates). Some researchers such as Vecernik (1994b) and Fabian (1994) think that poverty may have been underestimated during the socialist era.

4. The degree of inequality and its incidence is importantly influenced by institutional factors such as the design of transfer systems and patterns of housing ownership and occupation, demographic factors, cultural attitudes towards gender and other forms of discrimination, and the earnings patterns which had evolved in the various socialist states before the transitions.

Most of the authors consider that their data probably underestimate both the degree of income inequality and its increase largely due to the unavailability or unreliability of data reflecting property income post-transition and both self-employed and informal economy income in both periods. One study (Torrey et al. 1996) attempts to estimate the effect of the 'second economy' on both income distribution and poverty in Hungary; they provisionally conclude that including the second economy reduces poverty somewhat without significantly altering the degree of inequality since most second-economy income goes to the top and bottom quintiles.

In a very interesting paper, Jiri Vecernik (1994a) reports his estimates of characteristics of wage-earner income for both the Czech and Slovak Republics before (1984 data) and after the transition began (1992 data). In addition to estimating Gini coefficients for these distributions he estimates returns to education, coefficients for gender, and coefficients for industry branch across skills. And he provides a valuable table of comparative earnings distributions in percentages of median income for Poland, Hungary, Germany (East and West), as well as for the Czech and Slovak Republics. The Czech and Slovak data come from firm and household surveys; Vecernik observes that small firms are less likely to be sampled than are larger ones and he reminds the reader that self-employment income, which is probably an important form of labour income, is not included.

Table 16.2   Measures of inequality and poverty in OECD and transition economies

Country	Year for Gini coefficient	Gini coefficient	Year for poverty estimate	Poverty rate estimates
OECD countries				
Finland	1991	0.223		
Austria	1982	0.228		
Sweden	1992	0.229		
Belgium	1992	0.230	1985	6.3
Norway	1991	0.233		
Luxembourg	1985	0.238		
Germany (West)	1984	0.250	1985	10.3
Netherlands	1991	0.254	1985	6.9
Italy	1991	0.255		
Denmark	1987	0.257	1985	8.0
Canada	1991	0.286		
France	1984	0.296	1985	18.0
Spain	1990	0.308	1985	20.3
Australia	1989	0.301		
United Kingdom	1986	0.304	1985	14.1
Switzerland	1982	0.323		
Ireland	1987	0.330	1985	18.5
United States	1991	0.343		
Transition countries				
Czech Republic	1992	0.210	1992	6.9
Slovak Republic	1992	0.173		
Germany (East)	1993	0.216	1993	7.3
Hungary	1991	0.295	1992	7.8
Poland	1992	0.243	1992	6.3
Russia	1992	0.437	1992	17.5

Note: Poverty defined as income less than 50% of median income (both data adjusted equivalent household income).

Sources: The Gini coefficients for all countries but East Germany are from Torrey et al. (1996); East Germany from Hauser et al. (1994). The poverty estimates for the OECD countries are from Deleek and Van den Bosch (1992); the poverty estimates for the transition countries are from Torrey, Smeeding and Bailey (1996), except for East Germany which is from Hauser et al. (1994) and Russia, which is from Popova (1996). The three sets of poverty estimates use slightly different weights to estimate adjusted equivalent income for households; they define poverty as adjusted income less than or equal to 50 per cent of the median income.

For the Czech Republic, the Gini coefficient for the labour earnings distribution increased from 0.199 to 0.263 from 1984 to 1992; the coefficient of variation increased from 0.363 to 0.652 over the same period. For the Slovak Republic, the Gini went from 0.194 to 0.238 and the coefficient of variation from 0.360 to 0.707. The ratio of the income of the 90th percentile of the Czech distribution to that of the 10th was 2.43 in 1984 and 2.91 in 1992; for the Slovak Republic the ratio went from 2.38 to 2.42. For comparison, the same ratio was 4.57 for the United States, 2.77 for West Germany, 2.29 for East Germany, 3.49 for Austria and 3.64 for Hungary in 1991 or 1992 (various sources, reported in Vecernik's Table 8).

Earnings inequality increased in both the Czech and Slovak Republics, although more so in the Czech Republic. Vecernik explains the Czech–Slovak differential as due to the preponderance of heavy state industry with a compressed wage scale in the Slovak Republic before the transition and its independence, and to the Czech Republic's more rapid movement towards a market economy. Note that his data also show the Czech and Slovak distributions as still much less unequal than those of the western economies, and less unequal than some of the other Central European economies, notably Hungary (in which the 90/10 ratio went from 2.56 in 1984 to 3.64 in 1991). In another paper Vecernik (1994b) presents estimates of poverty and real wages for the Czech Republic. Real wages fell by 30 per cent in the 1989–91 period but increased by about 15 per cent in 1992–93 and appeared to be increasing throughout 1994 (1994b: Table 2). Using four measures of poverty (including the EU Community Standard of 50 per cent of median income adjusted for family size and composition) his research found no significant increase in poverty. Vecernik credits this success in the face of falling real wages and increasing unemployment (until 1994) to the successful implementation of the Czech Social Security System (1994b: 13).

Vecernik (1995) provides estimates for adjusted equivalent household income distributions in the Czech Republic and Slovakia. The Gini coefficient for the Czech Republic increased from 0.29 in 1988 to 0.32 in 1992; the Gini coefficient for Slovakia decreased from 0.29 to 0.28 over the same period. Vecernik reports no significant increase in poverty as measured by the OECD 50 per cent of average income for either country, but reports that opinion surveys report increases in subjective poverty rates.

Richard Hauser (1994) and Hauser et al. (1994) present data on both income distribution and poverty for Germany. They calculate Gini and Atkinson coefficients for the distribution of household equivalent income (before tax, after transfers with some imputations, adjusted for family size; a comprehensive measure) in both the eastern and western states of Germany. The Ginis for Eastern Germany went from 0.185 in 1990 to 0.216 in 1993; for Western Germany from 0.267 to 0.274 in 1993 (a recession year for West Germany). Atkinson coefficients in which household income is adjusted for size and composition and a weight is assigned for sensitivity to changes in income differences among low incomes, went from 0.55 to 0.78 in the East; the Atkinson increased from 0.114 to 0.119 in the West in the same time period suggesting a significant increase in inequality on the lower end of the distribution in East Germany. West Germany's income distribution is still significantly more unequal than in the eastern states; but inequality in the East has increased significantly. For purposes of comparison with Vecernik's data, note that Hauser uses a much more comprehensive measure of income than the Czech earnings distribution; a priori we might expect this to be a more unequal distribution given that it includes at least some property income. The transfer components obviously reduce the inequality. Hauser (1994) and Hauser et al. (1994), also present estimates of poverty in Germany. According to the EU Community Standard (poverty defined as a weighted household income less than 50 per cent of median), 3.4 per cent of the East German households were poor in 1990 and 7.3 per cent were poor in 1993 – a significant increase. However, this is a relative measure of poverty and the standard of living in the East also increased during this period (median household income in the East was 46 per cent of that in the West in 1990 and 72 per cent in 1993) primarily due to the generous transfer system put into place after the consolidation of the two Germanies.

Michael Forster and Istvan Gyorgy Toth (1994) use four concepts of poverty (relative and absolute measures, adjusted for income sources and family composition) and also estimate the intensity of poverty (how far below poverty lines the poor are) in their comprehensive study of poverty in Hungary. They argue that for a society in transition the most relevant poverty index is an absolute index such as their subsistence level line. By all measures poverty had increased substantially in Hungary in the 1989–93 period after declining in the early to late 1980s (about 25 per cent of Hungarian household incomes fell below the subsistence level in 1992–93, up from about 15 per cent in 1991-92; about 7 per cent of household income was below 50 per cent of the median after-transfer income). Forster and Toth do not report changes in income distribution, but we can look to Vecernik and Torrey, Smeeding and Bailey (below) for estimates for Hungary.

Zoltan Fabian (1994) surveys pretransitional studies of poverty in Hungary and argues that they probably were correct in their characterization of poverty as declining in the socialist era, but that they probably seriously underestimated poverty for methodological and political reasons (which were interactive).

Brunon Gorecki (1994) reports on household income and poverty in Poland. Gini coefficients for household income after transfers went from 0.2348 in 1987 to 0.2753 in 1992. Twenty per cent of families had incomes less than 50 per cent of median income in 1987; 33.6 per cent had incomes less than 50 per cent of the median in 1992. Gorecki reports the data for five different poverty measures (some relative, some absolute with different weights for family size and composition) and observes that three of the five show significant increases, while one shows a slight decline and another no significant change; his evaluation is that poverty probably increased significantly over this period. He also observes that the incidence of poverty is increasiɩ.gly on the children of worker or farm families (there are relatively few single-parent families in Poland) and is heavily rural (87 per cent of the poor are in small towns or villages). Pension system reform has reduced poverty among the elderly and urban workers (workers have been allowed to retire quite young as a response to structural unemployment in heavy industry).

Torrey et al. (1996) provide a very useful survey and analysis of estimates of income distribution characteristics and poverty rates for the Czech Republic, Slovakia, Poland and Hungary (they also provide some data for Russia) over the first five years of the transition; their sources include papers presented to LIS workshops in 1995, including more recent studies by some of the authors discussed above. They begin by observing that although real GDP and real wages fell during the early transition, this process appears to have been reversed recently; and they observe that income inequality and poverty rates increased only modestly during this period.

Gini coefficients for adjusted equivalent household disposable income (persons) increased from 0.192 (1988) to 0.210 (1992) for the Czech Republic; from 0.237 (1988) to 0.295 (1992) for Hungary; from 0.217 (1987) to 0.243 (1992) for Poland; the Gini for Slovakia was 0.173 in 1992, while the overall Gini for Czechoslovakia had been 0.158 in 1988. Inequality in Poland and Hungary is higher than in either the Czech or Slovak Republics; inequality in Poland and Hungary approximates that in Australia, France and Canada, while inequality in the former Czechoslovakia approximates the levels in Scandinavia (see Table 16.2 for Gini coefficients for OECD countries). Only Russia has a Gini coefficient measure of inequality (0.437, greater than for the United States) above the normal range for western countries. The increases in inequality for individuals exceed those for households; child poverty rates appear not to have increased; pensioners appear better off relatively after the transition in all countries but Hungary; single-parent families and women are relatively a bit worse off than before the transition; and urban populations are relatively better off than rural populations. Households in the middle three quintiles lost income relative to populations on the top of distributions in most of the countries.

Torrey et al. (1996) report that poverty rates measured by the percentage of persons living in households with incomes below 50 per cent of the adjusted equivalent disposable household income increased from 3.1 (1988) to 6.9 per cent (1992) in the Czech Republic; from 3.5 (1988) to 5.7 per cent (1991) in Czechoslovakia; from 3.6 (1987) to 7.8 per cent (1992) for Hungary; poverty increased by this measure from 4.3 (1987) to 6.3 per cent (1992) in Poland.

Summarizing the analysis of the various studies they survey, they conclude that the relatively small increases in inequality and poverty are largely due to the transfer systems put in place or modified during the transitions, and also to the importance of family and social networks which have provided for intra- and interfamily transfers outside of the state. They also argue that the secondary or 'shadow' economy has been helpful in reducing inequality and poverty. Additional evidence that the transition's negative effects on poverty have been relatively small is the reported increase in household ownership of consumer durables, which occurred in all of the countries studied.

Studies by Popova (1996) and Szulc (1996) support Torrens et al.'s argument that the transfer systems put into place in the Central European transitional economies have been important in cushioning the increases in poverty and inequality which have occurred in these economies. Popova observes that this is in sharp contrast to the experience in Russia, where poverty increased from 13.5 (1989) to 17.5 per cent (1992; poverty defined as equivalent income less than 50 per cent of median adjusted income) while inequality as measured by a Gini coefficient for equivalent household income increased 27.8 to 45.3. Popova reports that the share of household income coming from government transfers in Russia is only 19.2 per cent (1992) while it is 29 per cent in Poland, for example.

Marc Rubin (1996) presents the results of a counterfactual simulation for the economies of both Hungary and Poland; he estimates that without their transfer systems, poverty rates would be five to six times the current levels (about 45 per cent instead of 8 per cent).

5   SUMMARY AND CONCLUSIONS

A review of recent research shows an apparent increase in inequality in income distribution and poverty in four or five of the Central European economies in transition, although currently these parameters do not much differ from those in Western Europe (absolute levels of income are of course lower). The estimates available probably underestimate the degree of inequality and its increase, and may also underestimate poverty in the absolute sense. We observe some significant differences in the degree of inequality, in the increase in inequality, and in poverty rates across these countries which appear to be largely due to their willingness and ability to put into place social insurance systems which mitigate the consequences of the creation of market capitalist economies – a second 'primitive accumulation of capital' in Marx's evocative phrase. The Germans, Czechs and Slovaks appear to have protected those adversely affected by the transitional process a bit more than have the Hungarians and Poles, although we must remind ourselves that the Czechs have a more productive economy than the Hungarians and Poles (Table 16.1), allowing them to afford more generous transfer systems. And of course Germany is a special case in which the wealthy West was able (and to its credit willing) to directly assist the East by assimilation.

One inference is that countries going through such transformations need not experience large increases in inequality and poverty, given the political will to create adequate transfer systems and safety nets and the wealth to afford them. In all the countries surveyed, the distributional changes by themselves do not appear large enough to significantly alienate the population from the transition process, although some studies have detected an increased dissatisfaction with the perceived changes (Vecernik 1995). The stability or improvement in these indices of social welfare are dependent upon the continued growth of the economies of Central Europe. An interesting and useful research line suggested by this work would be a detailed comparative institutional study of the various transfer and regulatory systems in these countries with an eye to learning which systems seem most efficient in reducing inequality and poverty in the context of transitions.

NOTES

*   This chapter relies heavily upon presented papers, lectures and conversations with faculty, staff and participants at the Luxembourg Income Study's Summer Workshops held in Walferdange and Differdange, LX in July of 1994 and 1996, as well as upon the published papers cited. Subsequent conversations with Jiri Vecernik of the Institute of Sociology of the Czech Academy of Science, Zoltan Fabian of TARKI Research Institute in Budapest, Professor Katalin Szabo of the Budapest University of Economics, and Marc Rubin of the US Census Bureau were also very helpful as were comments on the paper by participants in the Post Keynesian Workshop in Tennessee, including James Galbraith, Paul Davidson and Gary Dymski; thanks to all.

1.   Although it is uncertain that all of the 'socialist economies in transition' or 'SEITs' will be transformed into capitalist economies, this chapter proceeds from the assumption that the recent history of the Central European countries can be interpreted as the result of intentional action by their dominant political elements to create a 'social democratic' or 'social market economy' version of a capitalist economic system.

2.   Most of the studies reported rely primarily upon the Gini coefficient to estimate degrees of inequality. Gini coefficients reflect the area under a line of complete equality on a graph showing the percentage of total income received by percentages of the population rank-ordered from lowest to highest incomes; the Lorenz curve falls below the curve of complete equality – a 45 degree line – reflecting the degree of inequality and the Gini is the ratio of the area below the 45 degree line and the Lorenz curve to the total area. For complete equality, the Gini = zero; for complete inequality, the Gini = one. Twice the Gini coefficient is equal to the expected absolute difference in incomes, relative to the mean, between any two persons drawn at random from the population.

      Although the most commonly used measure of inequality, the Gini has several weaknesses; another measure commonly used is the Atkinson coefficient, in which a subjective value is assigned to the degree of inequality aversion to detect changes in distribution affecting units on the lower tails of distributions. See Atkinson (1970) and Jenkins (1991) for interesting discussions of the advantages and disadvantages of various inequality measures.

3. Equivalence scales are applied to measures of household income to compensate for the effects of economies of scale in consumption (family members sharing housing) and the differential needs of individuals of different age (children may need less food than working adults). The equivalence scale used in most of these studies is either the OECD declining scale, in which the first adult is given a value of 1.0, the second adult 0.66, and each child 0.33 or the LIS scales in which each individual has a value of 0.5 or 0.66 (some LIS studies use a weight of the square root of family size). Equivalent or adjusted income EI is then equal to household income Ihh divided by family size S, in which a weight E is given to the family size to capture economies of scale in consumption; E may be an exponent applied to S ($EI = Ihh/S^E$) or a coefficient.

Measures of inequality and poverty for households are quite sensitive to the weights given to family size; large families appear poorer if $E = 1$ as in a simple per capita measure of household income. Coulter et al. (1992) discuss equivalence scales and the sensitivity of measures of poverty and inequality to various weights.

An alternative approach to poverty measurement defines a minimum level of consumption expenditures and then surveys a sample of the population to estimate its actual expenditures; expenditure levels below the minimum are assumed to have been constrained by income. Expenditure-based poverty measures may be more accurate; surveyed expenditures often exceed survey estimates of income, implying under-reporting of income (see Ramprakash 1994).

4. The principal sources of the data used in these studies are the household surveys conducted by the central statistical offices of the countries, which date back to the 1950s. Random samples of households are interviewed with standardized questionnaires which ask detailed questions about household finances (income levels, sources of income and expenditure patterns), composition and economic activity. Garner et al. (1991) present detailed descriptions of the surveys; Torrey et al. (1996) describe and compare several surveys; De Tombeur, Ladewig and O'Connor (1994) provide an excellent introduction to the LIS project and method of standardization of datasets. Vecernik (1995) reports additional data bases.

REFERENCES

Atkinson, A.B. (1970), 'On the Measurement of Inequality', *Journal of Economic Theory*, **2**: 244–63.

Atkinson, A.B. and J. Micklewright (1992), *The Economic Transformation of Eastern Europe and the Distribution of Income*, London, Cambridge University Press.

Coulter, Fiona, Frank A. Cowell and Stephen P. Jenkins (1992), 'Equivalence Scale Relativities and the Extent of Inequality and Poverty', *Economic Journal*, **102**, September: 1067–82.

Deleek, Herman and Karel Van den Bosch (1992), 'Poverty and Adequacy of Social Security in Europe: A Comparative Analysis', *Journal of European Social Policy*, **2** (2): 107–20.

De Tombeur, Caroline, Nicole Ladewig and Inge O'Connor (1994), 'LIS Information Guide', LIS Working Paper No. 7, Maxwell School, Syracuse University.

Fabian, Zoltan (1994), 'Review of the Social Science Research into Poverty in Hungary', Manuscript, Tarki: Social Science Research Informatics Centre, Budapest.

Forster, Michael and Istvan Gyorgy Toth (1994), 'Income Poverty and Household Income Composition in Hungary', Manuscript, Tarki: Social Science Research Centre, Budapest and LIS, Walferdange, LX.

Garner, T., W. Okrasa, T. Smeeding and B. Torrey (1991), *Economic Statistics for Economies in Transition: Eastern Europe in the 1990s*, Washington, DC: Bureau of Labor Statistics.

Gorecki, Brunon (1994), 'Recent Developments in Income Distribution and Social Policy in Poland', Paper presented to the Luxembourg Income Study Summer Workshop, Walferdange, LX.

Hauser, Richard (1994), 'Recent Developments in Incomes in the Eastern Lands of Germany', Paper presented to the Luxembourg Income Study Workshop, Walferdange, LX.

Hauser, R., J. Frick, K. Mueller and G.G. Wagner (1994), 'Inequality in Income: A Comparison of East and West Germans before Reunification and during Transition', *Journal of European Social Policy*, **4** (4): 277–95.

International Monetary Fund (1994), *World Economic Outlook*, Washington, DC: IMF.

Jenkins, Stephen (1991), 'The Measurement of Income Inequality', in Lars Osberg (ed.), *Economic Inequality and Poverty: International Perspectives*, Armonk and London: M.E. Sharpe: pp. 110–33.

Marx, Karl (1967), *Capital*, Vol. I, 'The So-Called Primitive Accumulation of Capital', New York: International

Niggle, Christopher J. (1994), 'Impressions of Central European Economic Conditions', Manuscript.

Polanyi, Karl (1967) (first published in 1944), *The Great Transformation: The Political and Economic Origins of Our Time*, Boston: Beacon Press.

Popova, Marina (1996), 'Income Inequality and Poverty of Economies in Transition', Working Paper No. 144 (July), Luxembourg Income Study; Maxwell School, Syracuse University.

Ramprakash, Deo (1994), 'Poverty in the Countries of the European Union: A Synthesis of Eurostat's Statistical Research on Poverty', *Journal of European Social Policy*, **4** (2): 117–28.

Rubin, Marc (1996), 'Poverty, Labor Force Status and the Social Safety Net in Eastern Europe', Working Paper No. 141, May, Luxembourg Income Study; Maxwell School, Syracuse University.

Szabo, Katalin (1994), 'From Privatization to Marketization: Schizophrenic Actors in the Transitory Economies', Manuscript, Budapest University of Economic Sciences.

Szulc, Adam (1996), 'Economic Transition and Poverty: The Case of the Vysehrad Countries', Working Paper No. 138, March, Luxembourg Income Study; Maxwell School, Syracuse University.

Torrey, Barbara Boyle, Timothy Smeeding and Debra Bailey (1996), 'Rowing Between Scylla and Charybdis: Income Transitions in Central European Households', Working Paper No. 132, Luxembourg Income Study; Maxwell School, Syracuse University.

Vecernik, Jiri (1994a), 'Changing Earnings Inequality Under the Economic Transformation: The Czech and Slovak Republics, 1984–1992', Paper presented to the Luxembourg Income Study Summer Workshop, Walferdange, LX, and manuscript, Institute of Sociology, Academy of Sciences, Prague.

Vecernik, Jiri (1994b), 'Changes in the Rate and Types of Poverty: The Czech and Slovak Republics 1990–1993', Manuscript, Institute of Sociology, Academy of Sciences, Prague.

Vecernik, Jiri (1995), 'Incomes in East-Central Europe: Distributions, Patterns and Perceptions', Working Paper No. 129, Luxembourg Income Study; Maxwell School, Syracuse University.

Index